"Loguidice and Barton prove that excellent research and technical accuracy can make for delightfully easy and fun reading. *Vintage Games* takes us through gaming's evolution one exemplary game at a time. Charting the history of dance and music games with the first *Dance Dance Revolution;* Roberta Williams' game design work as it leads up to *King's Quest* and *King's Quest's* place within the history of adventure gaming and even within Sierra's game guide market; and the place of many other games as articulated within the overall gaming history."

"While some of these titles won't seem old enough to be 'vintage' to seasoned players, these games are like good wine—their vintage is one of quality as it relates to a particular place in history. Not only are the games featured in *Vintage Games* historically important for the qualities they possess, so too is writing like that by Loguidice and Barton. The pair has written extensively on games and gaming history, most notably for Armchair Arcade, and their writing time and again shows that quality writing crosses normal boundaries, engaging scholars, fans, and even casual readers."

—Laurie N. Taylor, Digital Library Center, University of Florida

"I've seen dozens of video gaming books over the years, but rarely do you find one that is almost as fun to read as the games they talk about. Historically accurate, written with an obvious passion that never leaves the reader feeling left out or belittled. A must-read for anyone even remotely interested in video gaming history—from the hardcore to the casual, this is a book that anyone that has ever held a joystick would enjoy. *Vintage Games* is highly recommended to my listeners."

—Shane R. Monroe, Host of RetroGaming Radio/Monroeworld.com

"While calling games from the last two decades of the twentieth century 'vintage' might not sit well with thirty-something gamers, in so doing Barton and Loguidice remind us (through superb detail and smart, conversational prose) of the enormously rich history that games have already enjoyed and the rapidity with which they have reached the very core of popular culture. Barton and Loguidice will please scholars with their comprehensive research and excellent detail, but *Vintage Games* doesn't feel 'researched': the authors' love of the games is also clearly apparent. And that makes for a thoroughly enjoyable read. The book is smart and fun—much like the games it addresses."

—Dr. Matthew S. S. Johnson, Southern Illinois University Edwardsville

"They say you can't go back again, but reading *Vintage Games* comes close. Open the book, and I'm back in the video arcades of my youth. Turn the page, and I'm in college again, discovering the secret joys of the early PC games. Turn the page again, and I'm back in my living room, playing *Mario* with my young kids. But *Vintage Games* is more than just a trip down memory lane, because the authors analyze each game in ways that bring fresh insights to those nostalgic memories."

—Steve Meretzky, Veteran Game Designer

"An interesting and insightful trip down a gamer's memory lane, focusing on titles that have become benchmarks in videogame history."

—Didi Cardoso, Managing Editor, Grrlgamer.com

"The videogame industry has a poor track record when it comes to preserving its history. Fortunately, scholars and enthusiasts have stepped in to fill the void, and *Vintage Games* is an essential contribution to this effort. Loguidice and Barton are to be commended for documenting the history of gaming's greatest landmarks."

—Michael Abbott, The Brainy Gamer Blog and Podcast and
Professor of Theater and Film Studies, Wabash College

VINTAGE GAMES

An Insider Look at the History of *Grand Theft Auto,* *Super Mario,* and the Most Influential Games of All Time

BILL LOGUIDICE
MATT BARTON

Routledge
Taylor & Francis Group

New York London

First published 2009 by Focal Press

Published in the UK by Routledge

711 Third Avenue, New York, NY 10017, USA
2 Park Square, Milton Park, Abingdon, Oxon OX14 4RN

First issued in hardback 2017

Routledge is an imprint of the Taylor & Francis Group, an informa business

Library of Congress Cataloging-in-Publication Data
Loguidice, Bill.
  Vintage games : an insider look at the history of Grand Theft Auto, Super Mario, and the most
influential games of all time / Bill Loguidice, Matt Barton.
    p. cm.
  Includes index.
  ISBN 978-0-240-81146-8 (pbk. : alk. paper) 1. Video games—History. I. Barton, Matt. II. Title.
  GV1469.3.L64 2009
  794.8—dc22
                        2008048031

British Library Cataloguing-in-Publication Data
A catalogue record for this book is available from the British Library.

ISBN 13: 978-0-240-81146-8 (pbk)
ISBN 13: 978-1-138-42851-5 (hbk)

Typeset by diacriTech, Chennai, India

CONTENTS

BONUS ONLINE CHAPTERS

Available at www.armchairarcade.com/vintagegames along with over 100 additional screenshots and images!

Defender (1980): The Joys of Difficult Games

Elite (1984): Space, the Endless Frontier

Pinball Construction Set (1982): Launching Millions of Creative Possibilities

Pong (1972): Avoid Missing Game to Start Industry

Robotron: 2084 (1982): Running Away while Defending Humanoids

Rogue (1980): Have @ You, You Deadly Z's

Spacewar! (1962): The Best Waste of Time in the History of the Universe

Star Raiders (1979): The New Hope

Tony Hawk's Pro Skater (1999): Videogame Ollies, Grabs and Grinds

Preface

This book is about vintage games—or, more specifically, the vintage games that have had the most potent in uences on both the videogame industry and the culture that supports it. These are the paradigm shifters; the games that made a difference.

The word *vintage* has its origins in the wine industry, where it usually denotes wine produced during a special year—a year in which the grapes were particularly delightful. Your humble authors, both lifelong and dedicated gamers and enthusiasts, beg your indulgence: let us be your connoisseurs, your guides on a wondrous tour through the history of some of the finest games ever made. And if during your journey through these pages, you desire a sip of *Chateau Haut-Brion Pessac-Lognan* (v. 1982), we promise not to stop you. It was a good year.

Before we embark, however, you might want to know how we selected your destinations. How did we decide which games were truly the "most in uential"?

When we were first asked to write this book, we were skeptical, particularly because we've become disenfranchised with the "best ever" lists that saturate the Internet. Major gaming websites never tire of trotting out some "top ten" this or that—yet despite so many varied attempts, not one has gotten it right. The latest over-hyped movie crossover is as likely to appear on these lists as *Pac-Man* and *Pole Position*. About the only thing these lists are good for is stirring up controversy on blogs and community sites: "What—they didn't mention *Tunnels of Doom*? And where the heck is *Ultima*?" As is always the case, the true criteria of such lists is the whims and personal experiences of their creators. If you grew up with a TI-99/4a in the house, of course you think *Tunnels of Doom* is a great game, and we agree, but it's only mentioned here. *Ultima* is Chapter 23.

What really, then, constitutes a great game? Does it mean "a bestseller"? If so, this list would look quite different, with far more modern and far fewer vintage titles. Why? Because there are millions more gamers now than ever before, and the industry continues to expand. Even the most wretched sequel of a sequel may sell more copies than several of the games discussed in this book. Meanwhile, several of the games we discuss in this book weren't sold at all—or at least were initially distributed for free: *Rogue*, *Spacewar!*, *Tetris*, and *Zork* all fit this description.

If not sales, perhaps "innovation" is the key to separating the vintage from the vinegar. If a game does something first, doesn't that make it more in uential than the later games that did it better? Alas, if this were so, the outline of our book would look like a Gordian Knot. As we'll see, videogames have not followed a nice, neat linear evolution, and even the most original-seeming game had plenty of predecessors and in uences, whether it was an earlier game or some other cultural phenomenon.

Even if we could prove, beyond all doubt, that a game had done something first—though important, that fact doesn't necessarily mean it was in uential. *Spacewar!* wasn't the first videogame; it was preceded by at least two earlier and all but forgotten projects, *OXO* and *Tennis for Two*. Does that make *Spacewar!* less in uential? Certainly not. The game developers who would make such a difference in the 1970s and 1980s probably had never heard of *OXO* or *Tennis for Two*, but many of them played *Spacewar!*. In short, innovation alone doesn't suffice to make a game in uential; it also requires exposure and recognition. Why dote on an old clunker like Vectorbeam's *Warrior* (1979) when it's obvious to everyone that Capcom's *Street Fighter II* (1991) is the fighting game that defined (and continues to define) the fighting genre?

Neither is novelty a reliable sounding board. If we shared this view, we'd be talking primarily about titles like Atari's *Tempest* (1981; Arcade), Namco's *Dig Dug* (1982; Arcade), Datasoft's *Mancopter* (1984; Commodore 64), or Nintendo's *Kirby: Canvas Curse* (2005; Nintendo DS), each examples of brilliant games with unique features. Are these great games? Sure. Did they inspire hundreds—if not thousands—of clones and derivatives? No.

The games chosen in this book represent every significant genre. Readers who are disappointed to find that their favorite game didn't receive its own chapter might still find it referenced and described in the context of a game that did. We make no claims, however, to offering anything like a comprehensive listing of all videogames, which would be about as much fun as reading a dictionary. The book's main focus is to provide a concise yet detailed overview of an in uential game, its antecedents, and its predecessors. We might also warn readers that we have not let our recognition of these games restrain our criticism of their weaknesses.

Who is this book for? Clearly, it's for anyone with a passion for videogaming, but most particularly those who enjoy learning the history of their favorite pastime. It's also sure to be useful for both experienced and aspiring game designers. There is probably no better way to learn the 50+-year history of videogames than to read about (and hopefully play) the greatest and most in uential games of all time. Such experience benefits both designers and players, who may be surprised at the depth and diversity of our gaming heritage. Designers should know what's been done before, what's worked, and what hasn't worked. These pages offer an endless source of inspiration for a developer longing to create the next great game. As a player, it's important to have a respect for the past, not just callously dismissing everything before the current generation as obsolete. Besides leaving the gamer woefully ignorant and even naive, such an attitude leads to the boring sameness we currently find so much of in the industry. Read this book, and let us know if you still think every new game has to be a sequel of a sequel. If nothing else, this book should raise your expectations about what developers are truly capable of producing.

Does the world really need another compilation of the best games ever—even if it is, for the sake of argument, one hell of a fine read? Because our experiences and palates are so very distinct, what does "best" or "greatest" really mean anyway? There are few objective criteria that we can bring to bear on the matter. What we can bring, though, is our own extensive experience playing, studying, writing about, and discussing thousands upon thousands of games from all eras and all platforms. Whether we're talking arcades, consoles, computers, handhelds, or mainframes—if it's a game, we've probably played it. If we say a game is great, it is not because it is great compared to the games of the previous few years, or even the past few decades, but because it is great, period. Plus, we really like these games.

We decided to take this project on as a challenge—a challenge not only to pick a truly representative list of the greatest and most in uential games of *all* time—not just from the period when *we* first started playing games—but to truly add something useful to the often-haphazard videogame literature out there. These may not have been the bestselling or even most memorable games, but each of these carefully chosen titles in their own special way changed videogames forever. In addition to discussing the games themselves, we'll also direct your attention to other critically important titles that either in uenced or were in uenced by them. If you find yourself convinced by this book to seek out the many forgotten gems of game history, drop us a postcard (or at least an email!) at Armchair Arcade.

Now sit back and let the videogames begin!

Acknowledgments

Bill Loguidice

I'd like to thank literary agent Matt Wagner, Focal Press representatives Chris Simpson and Anaïs Wheeler, and technical editor Alexandra (Alyx) Hall, for all of their help before and during production of this book. Of course, I can't forget my co-author and friend, Matt Barton, whose talent and drive help to keep me on my toes. There's no one I'd trust to partner with on challenges like this book more. I'd also like to thank fellow Armchair Arcade editor Mark Vergeer for providing comments and supplying us with the invader images for our cover, and a whole range of our members and friends for their input during the writing of this book, including "Rowdy Rob," "Calibrator," "yakumo9275" (Stu), "CkRtech," "steve," and "davyK." The discussions with you guys were a big help! Finally, I'd like to thank my family for being there for me through all the trials and tribulations, especially my wife Christina, who was a huge help with the book, particularly with the *Super Mario Bros.* and *Tony Hawk's Pro Skater* chapters, and my daughters, Amelie and Olivia. I love you all more than anything!

Matt Barton

I'd like to thank everyone at Armchair Arcade for their support and assistance during this project. I also appreciate Simon Carless and Christian Nutt of Gamasutra for recommending our great reviewer, Alyx, who has been a great help. I'm also indebted to my colleagues Patty Remmell and Dennis Jerz, who helped with *The Sims* and *Zork* chapters, respectively. Of course, no one has done more to make this project than my long-time collaborator and friend Bill Loguidice. It seems like only yesterday when Bill and I were writing those lengthy posts on the forums of RetroGaming Radio!

ALONE IN THE DARK (1992):
THE POLYGONS OF FEAR

When most people think of survival horror, they think of Capcom's *Resident Evil* series, which debuted in 1996 and sold nearly 35 million copies in just over 10 years.[1] However, the conventions of Capcom's survival horror games, as well as others like *Silent Hill* (Konami, starting 1999), owe much of their success to Infogrames' *Alone in the Dark*, a PC game released in 1992.

Part of the opening cut scene from *Alone in the Dark*, showing female protagonist Emily Hartwood approaching the mysterious Derceto mansion.

Alone in the Dark, designed principally by Frederick Raynal and Franck de Girolami, is an early blend of 2D and 3D technology; specifically, of software-based 3D polygons for characters and items, and prerendered 2D images for backgrounds. This hybrid engine allowed characters and items to be rendered (redrawn)

---

[1]March 4, 2008, Capcom Co. Ltd., press release.

on the fly and free to move to and from any position, whereas the environments or rooms could be shown only from a certain fixed camera angle that was dependent upon the player character's location. The technique allowed for dramatic, predetermined camera angles, but also meant that the player didn't always have a clear view of the action. Arguably, this feature made the engine work well for horror, as such camera angles are a quintessential aspect of most horror films—you know something is around the corner, but can't make it out until it is too late.

Although the 3D graphics of *Alone in the Dark* were crude and blocky by today's standards, with flat-shaded rather than textured polygons, they were remarkable for their time. Combined with superb atmospheric sound effects and a rich soundtrack, the overall presentation created a potent feeling sense of horror.

Because this was an early software-based 3D engine, it does not move as quickly as gamers might expect. However, the development team was able to turn this potential liability to their advantage—the slowness of some of the in-game actions heightens the sense of panic when the character is about to be attacked; direct or impending attack: it's like the nightmare in which you can't run fast enough to get away from the monster. In fact, the designers took this one step further by slowing down the player character even further when hurt, a realistic touch that few other games share.

Of course, *Alone in the Dark* was certainly not the first graphic action adventure or even the first horror-themed adventure. As far back as Atari's 1981 *Haunted House* for the Atari 2600 Video Computer System (VCS), action, adventure, and horror were logical combinations.

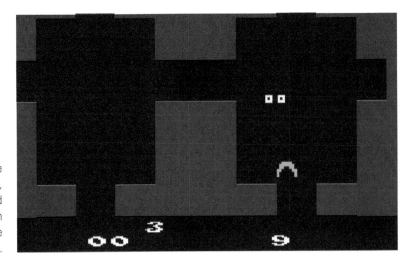

If *Haunted House* looks a lot like Atari's classic *Adventure* (1979), it's no coincidence—it's based on the same engine. Shown are the eyes that represent the protagonist and a bat.

In *Haunted House*, the player's avatar is a pair of eyes oating about a darkened mansion. The player's goal is to find the pieces of a magic urn and escape, all the while avoiding tarantulas, bats, and a ghost. Clever use of simple sound effects for actions like walking up and down stairs, wind blowing, and doors shutting help set the mood, and the visuals are blocky but still easy to identify. Although the programming effort that went into *Haunted House* was masterful, the VCS just wasn't powerful enough to set a truly horrific mood.

Other attempts at horror videogames on the VCS would follow, like Wizard Video's *Halloween* (1983), based on the popular 1978 slasher film. The player assumes the role of a babysitter in a two-story house, and scores points by escorting children to safe rooms or stabbing the killer with a kitchen knife. Michael Myers, the famous antagonist from the film, is also the killer in the game, and pursues the player in his iconically slow but relentless manner. Again, although the visuals and sound were pretty much what was expected on the platform at the time, the system's capabilities limited how terrifying the game could actually be. Other than the tension sparked by Michael Myers' appearances, there was little to genuinely frighten the player.

Other platforms, like Mattel's Intellivision, also witnessed pioneering attempts at what would become the survival horror genre. Imagic's 1982 *Dracula* puts a slight twist on the standard formula by casting the player as the titular vampire. The vampire has the ability to transform into a bat and must stalk and bite a certain number of victims and return to his resting place before sunrise. Antagonists include wolves, vultures, and stake-throwing constables. Although the Intellivision had greater technical capabilities than the VCS and *Dracula*'s presentation was fairly well done for the time, there was also nothing particularly scary about the game other than the system's controllers.

Even the arcade had its fair share of horror-themed games, like the gory and sadistic light gun shooter from Exidy, *Chiller* (1986), which tasked the player with shooting everything on screen, including humans chained and tortured in a dungeon. With more realistic graphics and sound, the game might have actually achieved more than mere revulsion.

The closest that the arcade came to something like survival horror was the visually rich *Splatterhouse* (1988), a side scrolling beat 'em up from Namco. The game casts the player as Rick, who must rescue his girlfriend held captive in yet another apparently abandoned, creepy, demonic mansion. Luckily for the player, an evil hockey-like mask attaches itself to Rick's face and gives him super strength, with which he battles the ghouls and demons throughout the house. Despite having many home translations and sequels, including a 2009 home console remake from Namco Bandai Games for the Microsoft Xbox 360 and Sony PlayStation 3, the *Splatterhouse* series remains firmly in the horror action category, with little apparent in uence on or from other horror-themed games.

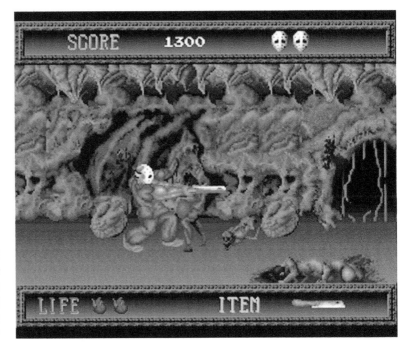

The only obvious way *Splatterhouse* relates to *Alone in the Dark* is that the in-game mansion is supposedly that of Dr. Herbert West, H. P. Lovecraft's "Reanimator."

There is little to indicate that any of these earlier games or the myriad other titles that failed to deliver videogame scares for predominantly technical reasons, like Avalon Hill's *Maxwell Manor* (1984; Apple II, Atari 8-bit, Commodore 64) or LJN's *Friday the 13th* (1988, Nintendo Entertainment System), had any in uence on *Alone in the Dark*'s design. Instead, American author and horror icon, Howard Phillips Lovecraft (1890–1937), better known as H. P. Lovecraft, with his famed Cthulhu Mythos, was the credited inspiration for the final product, right down to the tagline: "A Virtual Adventure Game Inspired by the Work of H. P. Lovecraft" on the front of the box. However, Raynal was also inspired by zombie movies. In an August 3, 2006, *Adventure Europe* interview, Raynal stated, "Romero's *Zombie* can be considered as my first inspiration. Since that movie, I [have] wanted to make a game where you need to fight against zombies, add to this the atmosphere from a lot of horror movies, which I found very entertaining, especially those where you are alone against the environment and your only goal is to survive. … So Cthulhu wasn't the main in uence, but as I wanted the player to read texts to find clues, we used Cthulhu for its atmosphere and to add a few monsters."[2]

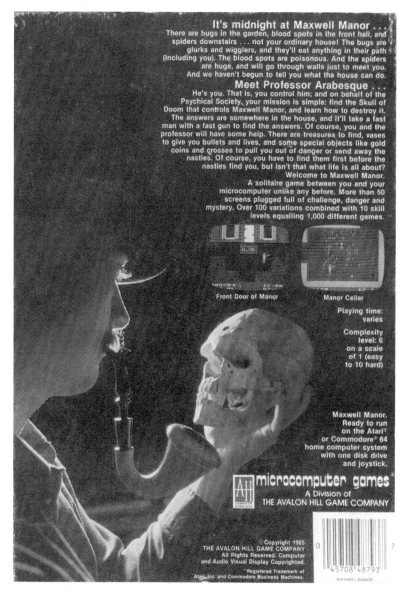

The back of the box for *Maxwell Manor*. Creepy mansions and haunted houses have been videogame staples for the 35+-year history of mainstream videogames.

However, this does not mean that there were no games that in uenced *Alone in the Dark*'s development. In fact, in that same *Adventure Europe* interview, Raynal states that it was his own work on porting Christophe de Dinechin's little-known but

[2]http://www.adventure-eu.com/index.php?option=com_content&task=view&id=207&Itemid=29.

groundbreaking *Alpha Waves* (1990, Atari ST) to the PC that was one of the game's biggest in uences.

Alpha Waves, one of the first 3D home videogames, was a surprisingly robust software-driven, polygon-based platform jumping and exploration title that featured simple shapes and multiobject interactions. A quick glance at the game in motion is enough to see how in uential it was on the implementation and design of *Alone in the Dark*. As Raynal described:

> When I was making the PC conversion of *Alpha Waves*, a very primitive 3D game, I had the feeling that it was time for 3D to offer something new to gameplay; I was convinced that it was possible to create a new animation system for human characters (angles interpolation in real time), then everything became obvious in less than three seconds, a man in a house, zombies, my old dream at least possible? But I knew that it was not possible at this time to have realistic 3D backgrounds needed to give the player the feeling that he is trapped in a real haunted manor. So I came out with the idea of 3D bitmapped backgrounds. In the beginning, I thought I could use digitalized photos of a real manor but hand drawn pictures came out to be better for characters' integration and ambiance. Then I had to program all those 3D tools to make it happen as nothing existed for real time 3D at this time.

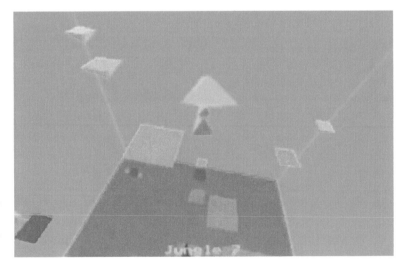

Screenshot from *Alpha Waves*, which was a major influence for Frederick Raynal in the implementation of *Alone in the Dark*. The triangular blue object casting a black shadow is the player, and the floating orange objects are the platforms. Similar jumping-centric 3D platforming elements would appear again in other 3D games like *Jumping Flash!* (SCE, 1995; Sony PlayStation) and *Montezuma's Return* (WizardWorks, 1998; PC).

Alone in the Dark is set in 1925. The action takes place in Derceto, a Louisiana mansion owned by the late Jeremy Hartwood, who apparently committed suicide after being haunted by a strange presence. Before passing, Hartwood translated many of the ancient manuscripts found within the house. The player must investigate the mansion, and has a choice of two avatars: a mustachioed private detective, Edward Carnby, who was sent to find a piano for an antique dealer, or Jeremy's niece, Emily Hartwood, who wants to find the piano for a possible hidden clue to her uncle's suicide. The choice makes little difference to the story, but does affect the look of the player's character.

As the game loads, a rendered Infogrames armadillo mascot spins, followed by the image of a book that is turned to reveal credits. After answering a copy protection question from the manual, the player is asked to choose either Emily on the left, or Edward on the right, where a picture of the chosen character alongside some introductory text is then displayed while ominous music plays. Once the introductory text is finished, the scene shifts via an in-engine cut scene to the player's character being driven in a jalopy, speeding up a dirt road leading to the mansion. This sequence gives an initial sense of the game's third-person perspective presentation, with a rendered car and passengers in richly prerendered environments that change perspective at key points. Once the character gets out at the front gate he or she starts to walk the rest of the way to the mansion, demonstrating the nice walking animation; movement point interpolation is a key feature of the game engine. The camera angle changes again, this time to the perspective of the eyes of a mysterious creature looking down at the character from a window, with only its hands showing, as the car drives off.

Once the character enters the mansion, the front doors quickly close, offering no escape for the startled character, who now has no choice but to continue on. The player takes control of the avatar's actions only after he or she reaches the attic, ratcheting up the tension and giving the player a small tour of the mansion on the way. The sequences also introduces the abrupt changes in camera angle as the character steps into certain predetermined points.

Although the animation is excellent (if somewhat deliberate) and the environments are well drawn, the characters are noticeably blocky (and in the case of Emily, "pointy"), consisting of a minimal number of flat-shaded polygons. Nevertheless, with clever use of color and clear distinctions between body parts and clothing, the characters are at least identifiable and work well within the game's carefully orchestrated art direction.

Once the character reaches the attic, players learn (often after a few restarts) that they must figure out how to block the trap door and the window so monsters can't make their way in, demonstrating the game's special mix of action and puzzle solving right away. By pushing a large chest over the trap door and an armoire in front of the window, the character is then free to explore the attic.

Soon enough, the player finds items in the armoire (blanket), piano (letter), chest (shotgun), and bookshelf (book). As this exploration takes place, a monster breaks the window's glass, but can't get past the armoire, while another monster tries to push up the trap door in the oor, but can't move the chest. After finding and taking an oil lamp on the table, the character can safely direct the character to an exit out a side door and down the stairs. The goal is to search for further clues about the mansion's deadly occupants and ultimately find a way out.

In this screenshot, Emily successfully covered the trap door, but failed to block the window, allowing the toothy creature to burst through.

The atmosphere is retained throughout the rest of the game with creaky doors, weakened oors, and the sudden appearance of monsters who the character may not be equipped to fight and trying to stay one step ahead of the monsters—which the character isn't always equipped to fight. This is a mix that few games before or since, including the game's sequels, have been able to get quite right.

All player commands are executed from the keyboard, with the up and down arrow keys moving the avatar, and the left and right arrow keys changing direction. By tapping twice then holding the up arrow key, the player can make the avatar run (one of a handful of animation sequences in the game that doesn't look quite right). Running is a very imprecise affair and can heighten the sense of panic when trying to move the character away from danger.

Pressing the "I" or Enter/Return keys brings up the options screen, which lists inventory items, character portrait, and any active items, and possible actions. Fight, Open/Search, Shut, and Push are always available, and Jump (Hop, Jump, or Leap) is possible in certain situations. Further, certain items allow for additional commands, like Reload, Eat, Drop, and Throw. When one of the actions is selected, the player is returned to the game to carry them out. For combat, the player can engage in hand-to-hand fighting consisting of punches and kicks, or use cutting or thrusting weapons and firearms.

In this screenshot, Edward has successfully made it down from the attic and avoided falling through the rotten floor just outside this room. After finding nothing in the armoire, he is attacked by a shuffling zombie.

In 1993, a CD-ROM version was released for the PC that included voiceovers for the in-game text and an enhanced soundtrack, as well as a small bonus game, *Jack in the Dark*, billed as an interactive Christmas adventure, but set during Halloween, somewhat like the animated Tim Burton film from the same year, *The Nightmare Before Christmas*. The player takes the role of a young child, Grace Saunders, who enters a toy store after dark and gets locked in. She finds that the toys are alive. Her ultimate goal is to save Santa Claus from an evil jack-in-the-box. With an emphasis on puzzle solving over combat, the game is a decidedly different experience from *Alone in the Dark*, though it obviously utilizes the same engine as that game and two of its sequels. *Jack in the Dark* was also made available by itself on a single 3.5 disk and on the CD-ROM version of *Alone in the Dark 2*, where is served introduction to that game's main nemesis.

Alone in the Dark was ported to the 3DO and Apple Macintosh in 1994, with the former port making use of the standard gamepad instead of keyboard controls. *Alone in the Dark 2* was released in 1994 for the PC, 1995 for the 3DO, and 1996 for the Apple Macintosh, Sega Saturn, and Sony PlayStation, with improved visuals for the latter two platforms. Unfortunately for fans of the previous games, Raynal was no longer involved with the series. As he described in the *Adventure Europe* interview:

I didn't decide to leave the license, but Infogrames itself, because of many disagreements with them. At this time, games were completely handled by the creator who usually was also the main programmer so I never wrote anything about game mechanics and ambiance secrets. I think they didn't understand what I did, the engine was brand new and helped the success of the game, but a game is not an engine or a movie, it's a whole system where situations and gameplay are the first things to think about. There are complex links between technology, gameplay, and story, all of them always sending the ball back to each other, a game is good when the players feel this synergy.

Alone in the Dark 2 takes place at Christmas in the year 1924, where Edward Carnby (now known as the "Supernatural Private Eye") and his partner Ted Stryker are investigating the kidnapping of Grace Saunders, leading them to another mansion, "Hell's Kitchen," the home of infamous gangsters. Edward learns that Ted has disappeared in the mansion and investigates, but finds his partner murdered. Edward discovers that the mobsters are merely the corporeal forms of ghost pirates, and he must make his way through the house and eventually onto a hidden pirate ship to find a way to save Grace.

A sequence of four images from *Alone in the Dark 2*, showing from the top, left to right, an early unarmed encounter with a zombie gangster. To the chagrin of fans of the first game, the sequel was often more focused on combat than puzzle-solving exploration.

Beyond limiting the player to the initial choice of the one protagonist, the biggest differences between this sequel and the original is the downplaying of the horror theme and the emphasis on action. Interestingly, the player is occasionally asked to take the role of Grace, who—as in *Jack in the Dark*—is unable to fight, so she must sneak around and avoid direct confrontations with the gangsters, instead setting traps to defeat them. This feature brought a brief, but welcome change of pace for fans of the style of the original game.

Alone in the Dark 3 was released in 1995 for the PC, with a port to the Apple Macintosh following a year later. In the final game in the series that uses the original game engine, Edward Carnby is asked to investigate the disappearance of a film crew, one member of which is Emily Hartwood of the original game. Though the setting was different—this time a western ghost town called Slaughter Gulch, located in the Mojave Desert—the game's developers decided to go back to the original game's formula of more balanced action and puzzle elements.

Alone in the Dark 3 also makes a further concession to the sometimes overly challenging action sequences by allowing the player to adjust the difficulty of combat. Welcome changes from previous games are unlimited save game slots, which allow for more player experimentation, and an onscreen map that shows Edward's exact location. The map eliminates much of the frustration from the game's dramatic but sometimes disorienting camera angles, making it easier for the player to make progress in the large gameworld.

A collection of four scenes from *Alone in the Dark 3*, sequenced from the top, left to right. The third game was the last title in the series to use the by then creaky game engine, but it nevertheless delighted many fans of the original by placing less emphasis on combat.

Because the next entry in the series was not released until 2001, the time was ripe for many other games to take on the survival horror challenge. These included Acclaim's time-limited *D* (1995; 3DO, PC, Sega Saturn, Sony PlayStation); Capcom's B-movie homage, *Resident Evil* (known as *Biohazard* in Japan; 1996, Sony PlayStation), Konami's fog-laden and sound-centered *Silent Hill* (1999, Sony PlayStation), and Tecmo's *Fatal Frame* (known as *Project Zero* in Europe and Australia, and *Zero* in Japan; 2001, Microsoft Xbox, Sony PlayStation 2), which has the player battling ghosts by sealing their spirit in film. Of these, *Resident Evil* is the best known and has spanned the most sequels and series offshoots, though the others, with the exception of *D* and *D2* (2000, Sega Dreamcast), have also been critical and commercial successes.

Though said to be thematically inspired by Capcom's Japanonly Nintendo Famicom role-playing game, *Sweet Home* (1989, itself based on a movie), including the mansion setting, puzzles, and loading screen when opening doors, *Resident Evil* is in many ways a reimagining of the original *Alone in the Dark*. For instance, the player has a choice between two characters—one male, one female, each with a different backstory, the backgrounds are pre-rendered and the camera angles fixed, and character and creature movements are deliberate, with somewhat sluggish control. Further, many of the same surprises take place, such as monsters bursting through windows and startling the player. Naturally, in the span of four years, the visuals are significantly better and there are now numerous cheesy cut scenes to advance the story, with awkwardly translated and badly voiced dialog, including the infamous line, "Jill, here's a lockpick. It might be handy if you, the master of unlocking, take it with you."

In an attempt to cash in on the success of the *Resident Evil* series, Infogrames released the fourth game in the *Alone in the Dark* series in 2001 for the Nintendo Game Boy Color, PC, Sega Dreamcast, and Sony PlayStation. In *Alone in the Dark: The New Nightmare*, Edward Carnby is reimagined in a different timeline (the year is 2001), and as a darker and more sarcastic character exploring Shadow Island. The player can also choose to play as anthropologist Aline Cedrac. Though borrowing liberally from the control scheme and settings of the early *Resident Evil* games, *The New Nightmare* introduces more dynamic lighting effects that are worked into the game's mechanics (the creatures in the game are sensitive to light) and features two different styles of gameplay, much like playing as either Edward or Grace offered in *Alone in the Dark 2*. This time, playing as Edward presents a more action-oriented game, and playing as Aline offers a more puzzled-oriented experience. Despite some promising features, reviews were mixed and sales relatively tepid in a genre dominated and likely biased by higher-profile series.

Like the other genre staples, *Resident Evil* and *Silent Hill*, *Alone in the Dark* received a movie adaptation in 2005, very loosely based on *The New Nightmare*. Unfortunately, as bad as movies based on videogames can be, the *Alone in the Dark* movie was even worse than most of these, directed incompetently by the infamous Uwe Boll, who seemingly found most of the survival horror aspects of the game unimportant for inclusion in the film. As film critic Mark Ramsey quipped, "*Alone in the Dark* is certainly what you'll be if you're in the theater for *this* movie."[3]

Despite being saddled with the legacy of what is considered one of the worst movies of all time, Atari, which holding company Infogrames had a majority stake in before assuming the name, still released a new entry in the series. Under the now-overused title of *Alone in the Dark*, the game was released in 2008 for the Nintendo Wii, Microsoft Xbox 360, Sony PlayStation 2, and Sony PlayStation 3. Completing Edward Carnby's transformation from an unusual 1920s private detective to a rather generic leather-coat-wearing, five-o'clock-shadow-having Keanu Reeves lookalike, the game tasks the player with investigating rumors, allegations, and suspicions of clandestine activity in the tunnels below Central Park in New York City.

The 2008 version of *Alone in the Dark* adds a few intriguing elements to the classic formula, including driving cars, an option for first-person perspective (something present in light-gun-based *Resident Evil* games), and a highly publicized fire modeling element. The fire simulation boldly attempts to mimic the real thing, and can be used for taking out enemies and burning or melting objects in the environment. Unfortunately, some of the other newer elements—like fetch quests and extensive backtracking—don't work quite as well and drag down what could have been a tighter and more impactful gaming experience. Critical reception was mixed at best, with major criticisms being its glitchy gameplay and confusing controls. However, with sufficient sales, unlike *The New Nightmare*, the game should provide a strong foundation for additional sequels that might address some of the game's failings and help to deservedly restore the *Alone in the Dark* name to something more than a *Resident Evil* pretender in the eyes of many modern gamers.

---

[3]http://www.moviejuice.com/2005/alone.

2

CASTLE WOLFENSTEIN (1981): ACHTUNG! STEALTH GAMING STEPS OUT OF THE SHADOWS

Silas Warner's *Castle Wolfenstein*, published by Muse in 1981 for the Apple II (later ported to Atari 8-bit, Commodore 64, and PC) laid the foundation and set the standard for all other games of stealth. Set during World War II, *Castle Wolfenstein* puts the player in the boots of an Allied prisoner. The prisoner's mission is not only to escape the heavily guarded dungeon in which he is imprisoned, but also to steal Nazi war plans hidden elsewhere in the castle. This exciting setting creates the perfect environment for the game's emphasis on stealth. Years before games like Konami's *Metal Gear* (1987, MSX2; and later in a modified form for other platforms), *Castle Wolfenstein* and its 1984 sequel, *Beyond Castle Wolfenstein* (Apple II, Atari 8-bit, Commodore 64, PC), demonstrated that cleverly avoiding enemies can be just as fun as blowing them to bits.

One of the first things new players notice about *Castle Wolfenstein* is the depth and variety of its control options. On the Apple II version, there are options for the keyboard, paddles, or two-button joystick. However, only the keyboard option provides access to all commands; the space bar is used for searching and unlocking, the "T" key is used to throw a grenade, the "U" key is used to utilize a chest's contents, and the "Return" key is used to list the character's inventory. Control is based on separate and very deliberate movement and aiming, though simultaneous movement and independent aiming can be difficult or even impossible depending on the configuration.[1] Atari 8-bit owners can play with the keyboard alone or in conjunction with one or two single-button joysticks;[2] the

---

[1]See bonus chapter, *"Robotron: 2084* (1982): Running Away While Defending Humanoids," for games that offer smooth independent, simultaneous movement and aiming.

[2]When using two joysticks on the Atari 8-bit version, the first joystick's fire button throws grenades, and the second fires the gun.

Pictured on top of an Apple IIe with black paddles is the packaging for a later release of *Castle Wolfenstein* for the Apple II, with its iconic cover art and award note for *Electronic Games* magazine's 1983 Certificate of Merit for Outstanding Achievement. The inside back of the manual listing Muse's software catalog touts the game as "The #1 Best Selling Game in America!."

Commodore 64 and PC allow for a keyboard or a single joystick (one button on the former system, two on the latter). Needless to say, the variety of control options not only indicate the game's depth, but allow for different styles of play, including the participation of a second player.

Besides control options, the only other major differences between the versions are the visuals, and even those only vary cosmetically in color and detail. In each case, *Castle Wolfenstein* sports an unusual perspective. Each room is displayed from an overhead view, but the characters and objects are displayed from the side. Though the animation is jerky, the modified perspective and simple visuals set against a black background work well. It's easy to identify everything and know exactly where you are, an example that many modern 3D first- and third-person perspective games have failed to follow. In addition, regardless of what is happening, everything takes place on the current room screen, including informational text. The player is never taken away from the action.

Each room in the castle either has a doorway leading to another room or a stairway leading to another level. Other room elements are various combinations of interior doors, guards, and chests. Chests can be searched for useful items such as keys, and not-so-useful items, such as Eva Braun's diary,[3] which have zero

---

[3]The companion of Adolf Hitler. With the war obviously lost, she committed suicide alongside the German Fuhrer roughly 24 hours after their marriage.

impact on gameplay. Food items are typically in the not-so-useful, zero-impact category, save for alcoholic beverages, which if chugged will temporarily impair player control until the drunken stupor wears off.

Searching a chest in *Castle Wolfenstein.*

Guards can be searched (like chests), either when held up at gunpoint or when dead. Unlike a chest, which can take some time to unlock and search, searching a guard produces nearly instant results. Items are automatically transferred to the player's inventory if they are needed or exceed present supply, but the maximum is 10 bullets, three grenades, keys, a bulletproof vest, a uniform, and the war plans for Operation Rheingold.

When the prisoner is spotted by a guard from a distance, the guard will shout German-language commands like "Achtung!" ("Attention!") or "Halt!" ("Stop!"). If the prisoner stops, the guard will typically approach and touch (capture) him, effectively ending the game. If the prisoner ees, the guard will open fire. If the guard succeeds in killing the prisoner (which, realistically, occurs after only a few shots), the game also ends immediately.

The player can hold up a guard by surprising him with a drawn gun. Unfortunately, in one of a small handful of unfortunate design decisions, once held up and searched, guards cannot be disabled. The player must either quickly ee or just kill the guard anyway—assuming he has enough bullets. Indeed, bullet management is the key to the game. Ammunition tends to be sparsely available, and a clip can't be replenished, merely replaced with one containing more bullets. Players intending to "run and gun" their way through the game will have no chance; the only way to succeed is to methodically go from room to room, avoiding guards whenever possible. Players must carefully observe the guards' patrol patterns and walk by them when their backs are turned. Of course, guards within earshot will hear bullets and shouts, also alerting them to the player's presence and location. Interestingly, sometimes the very act of where the player kills a guard must be carefully considered; even if other guards don't hear anything, when they come across a fallen comrade, they will know something is amiss and be on alert.

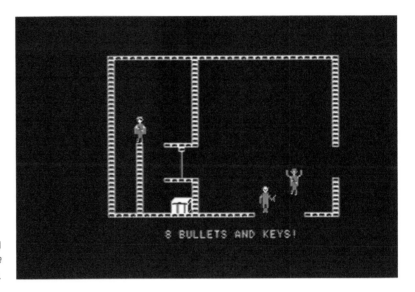

The end result of searching a held-up guard in *Castle Wolfenstein*.

Although guns are sometimes necessary to open locked doors (if there is no key or a guard doesn't open it first), chests can also be shot one or more times to speed up the time-consuming automatic unlock and search process. Unfortunately, chests sometimes contain explosives, which blow up if shot, immediately killing the player. In short, patience is less a virtue than a requirement.

SS stormtroopers can't be fooled as easily or intimidated like normal guards. They wear bulletproof vests, thus requiring a large number of bullets or a grenade to take them down. Grenades have a large zone of destruction and must be used with great care. Destructible environments are something that today's games are still struggling to fully implement, but *Castle Wolfenstein* offered a form of it over a quarter century ago. Though calling *Castle Wolfenstein*'s environments destructible is an exaggeration, the grenade could be used to damage interior walls, adding another layer of strategy to the already nuanced gameplay. For instance, the player could blow up a wall and kill a guard behind it, or create a hole with which to shoot through. Although certainly no *Crusader: No Remorse* (Origin, 1995; PC, Sega Saturn, Sony

PlayStation) in terms of destructible, interactive environments,[4] Warner's strategic design considerations never fail to impress.

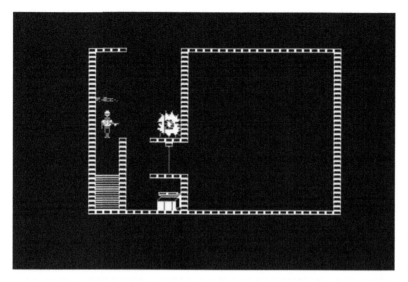

Here, the player has procured a bulletproof vest and lobbed a grenade at the wall, which will remove two of the rectangular bricks to the lower right of the explosion. Grenades in *Castle Wolfenstein* can easily accidentally kill the player, but are highly effective when used correctly.

Audio is perhaps *Castle Wolfenstein*'s most iconic element. Although there's no music and only sparse sound effects for walking and gunshots, where the game really shines is in its use of speech synthesis. Computers with poor sound capabilities like the Apple II and PC, which typically produced beeps and clicks on their tiny internal speakers, were nevertheless coaxed to generate recognizable speech in the form of eight German phrases and a scream. For fans of the game, hearing any of these clipped phrases brings an immediate nostalgia-tinged smile to their faces.

What can get lost in the haze of nostalgia beyond long load times is each room's inanimate objects, including the walls—or, more specifically, what happens when the player accidentally walks into one of them. The result is the player being momentarily subjected to a screeching, alarm-like sound effect, ashing screen, lack of control, and the character's return to an unarmed stance. Interestingly, as one of the game's most annoying features, there is no explanation for this in the game's manual. The only possible reasons from a design standpoint would be to force the player to play the game in a more methodical manner and make a quick escape from a dangerous situation even less certain. Of course, a comparison to Warner's unstated inspiration, *Berzerk*

---

[4]Though the *Crusader* series had other similarities to *Castle Wolfenstein* and its sequel, like the ability to loot intact dead bodies, working alarms, and enemies who made use of the environment, Origin's game was heavily biased toward frantic weapons-based combat and over-the-top deaths.

(Stern Electronics, 1980; Arcade, Atari 5200, Atari VCS 2600, GCE Vectrex), sheds further light on this and other features and design elements of *Castle Wolfenstein*.

Berzerk casts the player as a humanoid trying to escape individual rooms filled with robots before the indestructible Evil Otto appears. Armed with only a laser gun, the humanoid must avoid being killed by a robot's touch, shot, or explosion, as well as contact with the electrified walls. With its clever and early use of speech synthesis ("The humanoid must not escape"), modified perspective, single-screen encounters, enemies interacting with each other and the environment, and the requirement to sometimes escape a room without dispatching all enemies, *Berzerk* is the undeniable progenitor of *Castle Wolfenstein*.[5] However, while many games like Datamost's *Thief* (1981; Apple II, Panasonic JR-200U) were essentially shameless *Berzerk* clones, right down to mimicking Evil Otto's timed appearance that kept arcade players from dawdling, *Castle Wolfenstein* did something special with the base concepts, turning a pure action game into something much more thoughtful and slower paced.

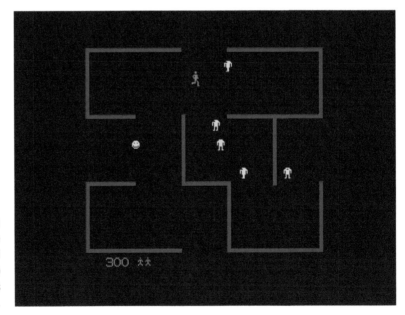

Screenshot from the arcade version of *Berzerk*. The indestructible Evil Otto (the round smiley face) has come out to attack because the player has lingered too long in the room.

Castle Wolfenstein's 1984 sequel, *Beyond Castle Wolfenstein*, released for the same platforms, kept most of the best play mechanics of the first game, while dramatically upping the

---

[5]Though *Berzerk*'s direct sequel, *Frenzy* (1982; Arcade, Coleco ColecoVision, Sinclair ZX Spectrum), featured slightly more sophisticated play elements and shootable walls, it's unlikely that *Castle Wolfenstein* had much, if any, in uence on its development.

in-game possibilities. As the escape specialist from the first game, the underground resistance movement has arranged to sneak you from a courtyard into Adolf Hitler's underground Berlin bunker with a gun, 10 bullets, 100 German Marks (money) and at least one pass to show the guards. Upon entry into the bunker, it's up to the player to find a briefcase containing a bomb, locate Hitler's private conference room, and plant the bomb. Once the briefcase is in place and the timer set, the hero must make it back to the courtyard before the explosion.

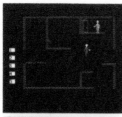

You're practically a secret weapon since you escaped torture in Castle Wolfenstein.™ Nobody gets past Nazi guards better than you. That's why your commanders have a favor to ask: deliver a "package" to the Fuehrer. The Underground has smuggled a bomb into a closet inside the Fuehrer's Berlin Bunker. Now it's up to you to move it to a secret conference room, set the timer . . . and escape. And that won't be easy. The bunker is crawling with elite stormtroopers. Any one of them will trip the alarm at the least suspicion of trouble. But you're not worried. You're ready for whatever it takes to win this war. You're ready to go Beyond Castle Wolfenstein.™

The Features

Beyond Castle Wolfenstein™ is the **sequel** to one of America's all-time best-selling **action adventure** games; **suspense, drama** and **tension** mount as the game demands **quick manual response** and even **quicker decision-making.**

The ingenuity that created Castle Wolfenstein™ is alive and well—and now more ingenious than ever.

MUSE
SOFTWARE

347 N. CHARLES STREET   BALTIMORE, MD. 21201   (301) 659-7212

Box and manual back for *Beyond Castle Wolfenstein.*

Sneaking past the guards is a bit more complicated this time, and involves passes. When a guard demands a pass, the player will have to show the proper pass or be asked again. The player can either try again with a different pass or attempt to bribe the guard with money. Besides the standard patrolling guards, there are guards seated at desks. These guards can also be bribed this time for information.

A guard asks the player for the correct pass in *Beyond Castle Wolfenstein*. Shown to the left, the player has passes 1, 4 and 5.

As usual, shooting guards must be done as covertly as possible, though now alarms add additional challenge. Not only will a guard pursue you if he thinks something suspicious is going on, he will also attempt to set off an alarm, which alerts the whole bunker to your presence. The alarm can only be disabled by finding and using a toolkit.

In a further nod to stealth over brute force, the grenades from the previous game have been replaced with a dagger, which can be used to silently kill guards. The player's character also has the ability to drag dead bodies to a less conspicuous location within a room. With additional emphasis on uniformed disguise, there are also new commands for holstering a weapon, helping to further mitigate the guard's suspicions.

There are no chests in the bunker—only closets. Instead of an automatic timed search, the player must crack a three-digit code, listening closely for when each of the lock's tumblers is triggered. If an incorrect number in any of the three slots is entered, the player must try again. Closets contain the usual assortment of items, as well as the occasional first aid kit, allowing the character to tend to injuries, which have a noticeable effect on his ability to maneuver.

In just about every way, *Beyond Castle Wolfenstein* is a sequel done right. Gameplay is more stealth-based, ambitious, and challenging; even accidentally walking into objects causes only a

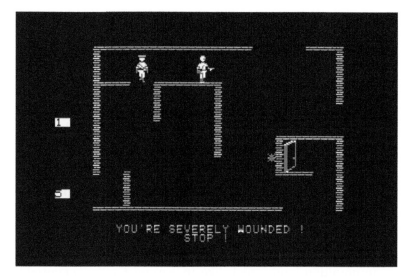

YOU'RE SEVERELY WOUNDED !
STOP !

In a very interesting design decision that actually works in making the gameplay notably different from the original, grenades have been replaced with a knife in *Beyond Castle Wolfenstein*, allowing for silent kills. Unfortunately for the player (gun drawn) in the screenshot, the alarm has already been set off from a failed gunfight in the prior room and he is severely wounded, making him an easy target for the oncoming guard.

slight pause this time around. It gives fans of the first game more of what they loved, but is a refreshingly distinct experience. It set an even higher bar for in-game interactivity.

Although there would be no other *Wolfenstein* games from either Warner or Muse, there were games from countless other sources that took some of the elements of the original two games much further. These include *Impossible Mission* (Epyx, 1984; Commodore 64, Nintendo DS, Sega Master System, and others), a side-perspective action adventure that casts the player as an athletic, acrobatic, and unarmed secret agent who needs to search through danger-filled rooms for puzzle pieces to ultimately bring down the diabolical Professor Elvin Atombender;[6] *D/Generation* (Mindscape, 1991; Atari ST, Commodore Amiga CD32, and others), where, from an isometric perspective, the player is tasked with getting through puzzle-heavy booby-trapped rooms in a high rise building; and *Relentless: Twinsen's Adventure* (Activision, 1994; PC, Sony PlayStation),[7] which is played from a 3D isometric perspective, with the player putting the main character into one of four different modes of behavior, including "Discreet," which includes quietly tip-toeing and the ability to hide.

Of course the most famous of these latter-day *Wolfenstein*-inspired games is the aforementioned *Metal Gear*, marking the first appearance of "Solid Snake," a now legendary videogame

---

[6]Like *Castle Wolfenstein* before it, *Impossible Mission* was famous for its speech synthesis, which included the game opening, "Another visitor. Stay awhile ... stay forever!"

[7]Released as *Little Big Adventure* through Electronic Arts in Europe, this underrated title was Frederick Raynal's next game after *Alone in the Dark*, which is discussed in Chapter 1, "*Alone in the Dark* (1992): The Polygons of Fear."

character used in countless games right up to 2008's *Metal Gear Solid 4: Guns of the Patriots* (Konami; Sony PlayStation 3). Each successive game in the series typically ramped up the original *Metal Gear*'s complexity and ambition levels and built further on the previous entry, right through its initial overhaul from a slanted overhead 2D perspective to state-of-the-art third-person 3D.

Metal Gear casts the player as special forces operative Solid Snake, who must infiltrate a fortified compound to ultimately destroy the titular machine, a bipedal walking tank capable of launching nuclear missiles from anywhere in the world. The player must carefully avoid visual contact and direct confrontation with patrolling guards. If Solid Snake is spotted, he must hide in a manner specific to the type of alert the guards are on. Initially unarmed, Solid Snake eventually becomes well equipped with a wide range of weaponry, which can also be used to clear obstacles. Punching guards can sometimes yield rations or ammunition, and, much like in *Beyond Castle Wolfenstein*, specific key cards are sometimes needed to gain access to additional areas.

In what amounted to nothing less than a lovingly crafted and well-executed tribute to *Castle Wolfenstein*, id Software released *Wolfenstein 3D* in 1992 (3DO, Apple Macintosh, PC, and others).[8] Though it's discussed in Chapter 6, "*Doom* (1993): The First Person Shooter Takes Control," for its in uence on *Doom*, it's important to note here that *Wolfenstein 3D* took all of the iconic elements from *Castle Wolfenstein* and its sequel, like the castle setting, the guards, and the clever use of speech synthesis, and turned it all into a silky-smooth and approachable single-player first-person shooter. Though there is some possibility for sneaking up on guards, the majority of stealth and slower-paced elements were removed in lieu of quick action, which favored the game engine and interface. Starting with 2001's *Return to Castle Wolfenstein* (Apple Macintosh, Microsoft Xbox, PC, and others), *Wolfenstein 3D* has received a semiregular stream of sequels, though the large jump in technology and player expectations have made them only marginally recognizable to fans of the original.

Castle Wolfenstein's legacy can't be overestimated, particularly in regard to its integration of basic stealth elements into its gamplay. Today, of course, there are countless games with some type of stealth-based elements in them, ranging from games that make stealth an integral part of their gameplay, like the critically acclaimed series-spawning action adventures, *Thief: The Dark Project* (Looking Glass Studios, 1998; PC), *Hitman: Codename 47* (Eidos, 2000; PC), and *Beyond Good and Evil* (Ubisoft, 2003;

---

[8]*Wolfenstein 3D* is the reason some refer to the original *Castle Wolfenstein* as "Wolfenstein 2D" today.

Back of the box for the Atari Jaguar version of *Wolfenstein 3D*, a game that focused more on action and aspects of the Nazi regime's infamous human experiments than its progenitors.

Microsoft Xbox, Nintendo GameCube, PC, Sony PlayStation 2), to games that include them as a small part of their total gameplay scope, like first-person shooter *The Operative: No One Lives Forever* (Fox Interactive, 2000; PC, Sony PlayStation 2), action adventure *The Legend of Zelda: The Wind Waker* (Nintendo, 2002; Nintendo GameCube), and the licensed *Kung Fu Panda* (2008, Activision; PC, Sony PlayStation 3, and others). It is a testament to Warner's genius that his brilliant gameplay designs, introduced so early in videogame history, are still inspiring developers and thrilling gamers to this day.

The dreaded castle Wolfenstein awaits you...

It is the height of WWII. Germany has conquered most of Europe, and Britain is suffering under constant siege by air. The dark shadow of fascism looms heavy over the free people of the world. You are Sgt. Kozwowski of the Polish Special Forces. Captured as part of a resistance cell opposing the German and Russian occupation of Poland, you are transported to the dreaded castle Wolfenstein just over the border in Germany for interrogation and execution, or possibly worse. Escape is your first priority, but as a member of the resistance you won't pass up this opportunity to hurt the German war machine and avenge the people of Poland. Good-luck soldier, the free world holds you in its prayers!

Eight different levels crawling with Nazis and their mad scientist progeny!

Wolfenstein

Will you be able to escape? Not if the SS guards have anything to do with it!

Kill or avoid the enemies and grab the item in each room to craft your escape!

Packrat Video Games www.packratvg.com © 2004 Robert Mundschau, Scott Dayton, Dave Dries, and Packrat Video Games

Beyond id's own contributions to the *Wolfenstein* legacy, fans of the series have also kept the torch burning, such as with 2004's homebrew cartridge *Wolfenstein VCS* for the Atari 2600 Video Computer System, box back shown, and its enhanced sequel, *Wolfenstein VCS: The Next Mission* (2006). Both of the homebrew games are based on code from the Atari 2600 version of Exidy's 1981 arcade game, *Venture* (Coleco, 1982), a fantasy-themed action adventure that shares similarities with both *Berzerk* and *Castle Wolfenstein*.

3

DANCE DANCE REVOLUTION (1998): THE PLAYER BECOMES THE STAR

At first glance, *Dance Dance Revolution* (Konami, 1998;[1] Arcade; other platforms and games in the series later), or *DDR*,[2] is a glorified game of "Simon Says."[3] After all, to play *DDR*, the gamer simply steps on one of four arrows positioned up, down, left, and right on a platform, trying to match a corresponding scrolling arrow when it reaches a specific point at the top of the screen (when the game "says"). If the player successfully steps on the right arrow at the right time, the player's score and status increases; if not, the player's status decreases (the game didn't "say"). This is of course set to any one of a number of original and licensed dance songs with a wacky disembodied DJ voice shouting encouragement like, "Yeah! Do it!" and "You're a dance animal!," and some not-so-positive comments like, "Did you have breakfast today?" and "Are your legs okay?," relative to your performance.

To understand what makes *DDR* truly a revolution, we need to first reflect on the gamer stereotype. It seems almost any time a "gamer" is represented in a film or television show, we see a pale, overweight teenager with awkward movements and stilted speech.

---

[1] From Konami's Bemani music videogame division, which (besides the title game) has produced many other popular performance games, including those that use faux DJ mixing boards and musical instruments. Many games in the Bemani series have been released only in Japan.

[2] Some territories and later entries in the series used the name *Dancing Stage* instead of *Dance Dance Revolution*, making the abbreviation *DS*.

[3] Or Milton Bradley's Ralph Baer–designed electronic handheld *Simon* game (1978), with its four large iconic colored buttons arranged in a circular formation. *Simon* would play a tone as each one of the colored buttons were lit. The player was required to repeat the colored lighting/sound sequence by pressing the corresponding buttons. *Simon* succeeded where the game that inspired it, Atari's arcade *Touch Me* (1974), failed, by focusing on color and pleasing sounds—in other words, providing a good interactive experience to go along with the core gameplay. This was a lesson obviously not lost on the designers of *DDR*.

A sequence of two screenshots from the Sony PlayStation version of *Dance Dance Revolution*, describing the simple gameplay.

Further, the mass media seems obsessed with vilifying the games industry for society's woes, blaming them for—among other things—the alleged crisis in adolescent and teenage obesity. Even avid gamers often deride their own favorite hobby, lamenting that they wasted so much time playing games when they should have been playing sports or enjoying the outdoors. As Dani Bunten Berry, developer of *M.U.L.E.* and *Cytron Masters* once put it, "No one ever said on their deathbed, 'Gee, I wish I had spent more time alone with my computer.'"[4] Part of the problem may be that, unlike most sports, watching someone play a videogame is seldom a rewarding activity for spectators, today's professional gaming leagues notwithstanding.[5] In short, even if all sorts of wonderful things are happening onscreen, the gamer seems to be doing little more than clicking buttons from a comfy seat. Few games offer opportunities for impressive physical performances.

The brilliance of *DDR* lies precisely in providing such opportunities. A dedicated fan of *DDR* will often develop the physical prowess necessary not only to achieve high scores in the game, but to impress spectators passing by the machine. Because players are penalized only for not hitting correct dance steps and can add in their own, many *DDR* aficionados create intricate flourishes and routines that are intended more for fun and the audience's delight than for winning the game.[6] In an interview with the authors, Ryan Cravens, Marketing Manager for arcade game and amusements

---

[4]See http://www.anticlockwise.com/dani/personal/biz/index.html for this and other Bunten quotations, and Chapter 6, "*Dune II: The Building of a Dynasty* (1992): Strategy in Real Time," for more on *Cytron Masters*.

[5]It can be argued that outside of certain countries like South Korea, professional gaming leagues are geared more to masses of competitors rather than masses of spectators.

[6]Episode 103 from Season 5 of the TV show *Malcolm in the Middle*, entitled "Dewey's Special Class," features the characters of Hal and Craig playing a fictional *DDR* clone called *Jump Jump Dance Party*. The half-hour comedy effectively spoofed the often over-the-top theatrics and choreographed antics that can result when the best players take to a *DDR* platform, even earning the show an Emmy Award nomination for outstanding choreography. A similar scenario would play out in a memorable scene from the otherwise forgettable comedy movie about a videogame tester, *Grandma's Boy* (2006).

distributor Betson Enterprises, draws a performance parallel to another phenomena—karaoke—stating, "Both came out of Japan, are music-related, and are all a more complicated version of the 'follow the bouncing ball' sing-a-longs from 1950s television."

A scene from an episode of sitcom *Malcolm in the Middle*, entitled "Dewey's Special Class," featuring fictional *DDR* clone *Jump Jump Dance Party*, complete with over-the-top theatrics.

In a way, *Dragon's Lair* (Cinematronics, 1983; Arcade; dozens of home ports later), one of the first laserdisc videogames, was all about performance as well. It certainly wasn't the compelling gameplay, which—like *DDR* well after it—consisted of moving up, down, left, or right at precisely the right time.[7] Whereas *Dragon's Lair*'s hook is in its animated film-quality visuals by former Disney animator Don Bluth, *DDR* draws the player in by physically involving them in the game, in fact paying little mind to its graphics.

Dragon's Lair was all about the novelty of its video quality, a fact punctuated by many arcade operators setting up additional video displays so the audience could view the play sessions.[8] Unfortunately for future games using similar technology, it was difficult for designers to invent ways for players to interact with canned video footage in an entertaining manner.[9] Thus, once the novelty of simplistic interactions with high-quality video wore off and profoundly interactive real-time graphics continued to

[7]*Dragon's Lair* did have an additional "direction" as an option, an action button for use of the sword, but, like the four-way joystick, it could be used only when a specific spot in certain video scenes required it.

[8]Author Loguidice confirms this from one of his summer visits to the arcades on the boardwalk at the Jersey Shore, where arcade operators would have additional *Dragon's Lair* displays not only around the machine, but also occasionally facing outside to attract passersby. *Dragon's Lair* was also one of the first games for which arcade operators charged 50 cents versus the usual 25 cents!

[9]Later video-based games, like Sega's *Tomcat Alley* (1994; PC, Sega CD) and Hudson Soft's fighting game for the Japanese market, *Battle Heat* (1994; NEC PC-FX), did eventually offer near-real-time interaction, but the interaction still fell short of games with traditional computer-generated visuals.

improve in quality, games that took inspiration from *Dragon's Lair* fell out of favor. It was therefore only with a performance hook that what amounted to little more than *Touch Me's* gameplay could be so influential.

Besides the common but unconscious habit of moving one's body in the direction one moves the controller, games that demanded more from the player than finger tapping have been, until recently, few and far between. Early products worth mentioning include *Video Jogger* and *Video Reflex* (Exus, 1983; Atari 2600 Video Computer System), a two-cartridge bundle with the Foot Craz controller; Nintendo's *World Class Track Meet* (1988, Nintendo Entertainment System), bundled with the Power Pad;[10] and Sega's Activator (1994), a controller designed primarily for use with fighting games like *Eternal Champions* (Sega, 1993; Sega Genesis).

The Foot Craz is a floor mat controller used in a similar manner as modern dance pads, save for its purely horizontal layout, which registers one of four directions on each of its colored stepping circles. A green circle, which acts like a standard Atari joystick's fire button, sits above the row of other circles. Besides achieving only a limited release before "The Great Videogame Crash of 1984"[11] and spotty responsiveness, the cartridges that accompanied the Foot Craz were mundane. *Video Jogger* required the player to run

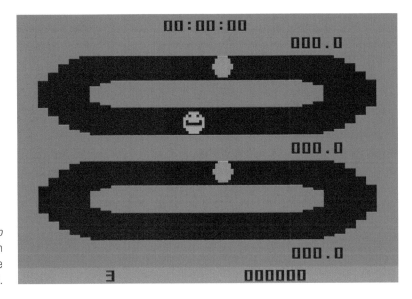

Screenshot from Exus' *Video Jogger*, designed for use with the Foot Craz controller on the Atari 2600.

[10]*World Class Track Meet* was originally *Stadium Events*, and the Power Pad was originally Family Fun Fitness, both released by Bandai before Nintendo bought out all rights. Naturally, today the Bandai versions are highly collectible.

[11]The iconic name given to a period of massive financial losses, stock liquidations, and generally bad times for the videogame industry at large in the United States.

in place, and *Video Reflex* tasked the player with stepping on the matching color or colors when a bug appeared. Although Exus should be praised for their innovative hardware ideas, it would take others to make equally compelling software for them.

Nintendo's Power Pad is a floor-mat controller taken to the extreme, with 12 numbered circles laid out in a 4×3 grid, with the circles on the left half in blue and on the right half in red. On the flip side of the large mat are eight unnumbered blue and red colored circles in a plus pattern. Though the 12-circle side of the pad allowed for two (careful) simultaneous players and 11 different total cartridges were released worldwide, with themes ranging from sports to aerobics to chasing and apprehending criminals, the now-obvious killer app of a dance game was not considered (perhaps because of the system's modest sound capabilities). Though faring better than many of the Nintendo Entertainment System's wacky add-ons in terms of support and general interest, the Power Pad failed to maintain momentum or further development beyond the lifespan of its release system.[12]

One side of Nintendo's oversized Power Pad for the NES, shown with the *Street Cop, Athletic World, Dance Aerobics, Super Team Games,* and *Short Order/ Eggsplode!* cartridges.

[12]Cravens adds, "You cannot take the Power Pad out of the equation as far as losing weight. As a child, I found it hard to play the game and eat Oreo cookies at the same time, so I had to lose a pound or three, playing with it ... but *DDR* is the poster child for the 'Active Gaming' initiative."

Sega's Activator, on the other hand, was undeniably exciting and groundbreaking in theory, but poor in execution. The Activator is a hollow, octagonal platform that registers an action in one of eight directions via infrared sensors. After stepping within the octagon, the player is asked to either punch or kick in one of the eight directions to perform an onscreen move. Unfortunately, the infrared sensors were easily distorted by common room elements like lights, and there were never any games designed specifically for the device. As such, performing the complex moves of standard fighting games of the day, like *Mortal Kombat* (Acclaim, 1993), requiring both precision and multiple keypresses (which are sometimes difficult to pull off even on a standard controller) to be matched by the player's physical contortions, quickly made even the most dedicated player give up. It's by keeping the technological ambition level reined in and a game designed specifically for the platform that *DDR* provides a sharp contrast to the Activator's failings.

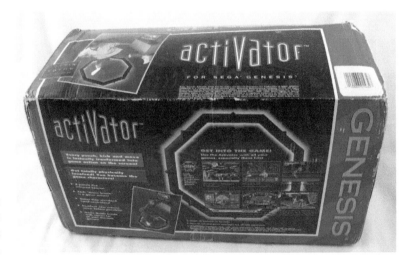

Box shot of Sega's Activator, a product that sounded great on paper, but disappointed in its actual execution.

With the passing of the fighting game craze by the latter part of the 1990s,[13] increased operating costs and further interest waning in the United States in light of ever-more-powerful consoles, arcades began to morph into something akin to mini amusement parks. Arcades began to showcase games that featured specialized hardware, environmental cabinets, and multiplayer competitive setups that were not easy to replicate at home. These games included *Top Skater* (Sega, 1997), in which the player performs tricks and other activities on a realistic skateboard

[13]See Chapter 17, "*Street Fighter II* (1991): Would You Like the Combo?" for more information.

platform; *Airline Pilots* (Sega, 1999), in which the player was tasked to fly a commercial Boeing 777 aircraft, complete with realistic controls and three-screen cockpit; *Beach Head 2000* (Global VR, 2000), a shooting game played using an immersive turret controller; *Arctic Thunder* (Midway, 2001), where one or more players sat on faux snowmobiles and competed in a high-speed, jump-filled race; and of course, *DDR*, with the arcade version's metal light-up dance pads and oversized speakers.[14]

After *DDR*'s success in arcades around the world, it was only natural for Konami to try to bring the experience home. Though Japan received home translations of *DDR* and other games in the Bemani series well before other territories, it was with the wide 2001 release of *Dance Dance Revolution* for the Sony PlayStation (PS1) that *DDR*'s legend began to grow, opening up the game to a whole new generation of players who may have never set foot in an arcade or been intimidated by the idea of being the center of public attention. As a March 2001 review from *GamePro* magazine put it, "*Dance Dance Revolution* [for the PS1] offers all the fun of the arcade and none of the humiliation." Further, as Cravens adds, "Players use the arcade version as a stage to show off the moves that they have been practicing at home on the console versions."

Screenshot for Epyx's *Breakdance* on the Commodore 64, which featured a crude audiovisual presentation and rudimentary "Simon Says"–style gameplay throughout its various play modes.

Although *DDR* could be played using just a standard controller without the soft, plastic, foldable dance pad, it was with this add-on, available either bundled with versions of the game or sold

---

[14]Similar to *Dragon's Lair* before it, arcade operators would often set up *DDR* machines in conspicuous locations for maximum audience impact.

Back of the box for the first U.S. home release of Konami's *Dance Dance Revolution* series for the Sony PlayStation.

separately,[15] that the game transcended other attempts at similar play styles and themes. These included Epyx's *Breakdance* (1984; Commodore 64), which made players remember and repeat the breaking moves of their opponent using a joystick; SCEI's surreal *PaRappa the Rapper* (1996; PS1), in which players direct a rapping dog by pressing controller buttons in the correct sequence and timing; and Eidos' *Mad Maestro* (2002; Sony PlayStation 2), which had players conduct an orchestra by tapping buttons on the controller[16] with varying degrees of pressure.[17] Though some of the other games in the genre were popular in their own right, their popularity never rose to the degree of *DDR*, which had the advantage of its specialized controller. To be fair, a dance pad, like any other controller that outputs standard signals, can be used to control other types of games—but it's ideally suited to *DDR*-like experiences.[18]

---

[15]Third parties would soon get in on the act, releasing their own pads with varying degrees of quality and innovation, including hard platforms; though, as Cravens states, "The arcade version of DDR will always be a much stronger version of the game, simply because the dance pad is superior to anything any company has developed [for the home]."

[16]The Japanese release supported a baton peripheral.

[17]Though plenty of other systems, including the PC and units from Microsoft and Nintendo, received many of the same games, it's Sony's PlayStation series of consoles where the largest diversity of performance-based games have been released to date.

[18]See http://www.florian.ca/index.php?id=35 for one unusual alternative usage.

Where the home experience differed the most from the arcade was game modes, which were far more plentiful at home than in the arcade. The first home version of *DDR* included Game, Workout, Lesson, and Training modes. Game Mode is the main mode for *DDR* and is identical to the difficulty level found in the arcade version. Workout Mode adds fitness goals while counting the number of calories burned during play. Lesson Mode enables novice players to learn the game's basics in a more relaxed tutorial setting. Training Mode allows players to practice and master the game's more difficult songs. Future games in the series and the various clones and knock-offs would continue to expand on the intricacies of these core modes and add slightly to the play mechanics, such as requiring players to hold a foot position for a set period of time.

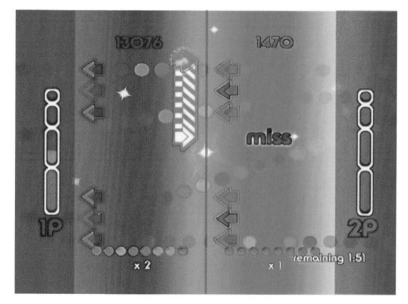

Screenshot from Codemasters' 2006 *Dance Factory* for the Sony PlayStation 2, which allowed gamers to use their own music CDs to create custom dance steps.

The success of the Bemani series and of course *DDR* would inspire other attempts at using special peripherals and add-ons to enhance the gameplaying experience.[19] Some, like Sega's *Samba de Amigo* (1999; Arcade, Sega Dreamcast), where the player used maracas to play the game, and Sony's EyeToy (2003, Sony PlayStation 2), a motion-sensing camera used with a variety of games, never really caught the public's attention,[20] while others like

---

[19]Prior to the Bemani series, most peripherals that weren't included with a system, including light guns and other specialized controllers, received limited support due to too few owners, making more aggressive forays into this area by developers few and far between.

[20]Although Sony's EyeToy has chalked up respectable worldwide sales and has a wide variety of game support, including many in the performance-based category, the concept has yet to capture the imagination of mainstream media and nongamers.

RedOctane's *Guitar Hero* (2005; Sony PlayStation 2), which features a guitar controller, and MTV Games' *Rock Band* (2007; Nintendo Wii, Microsoft Xbox 360, and others), which features a guitar, drum, and microphone, have become cultural phenomena.[21] Others still, like Konami's own microphone-based *Karaoke Revolution Party* (2005, Microsoft Xbox, Sony PlayStation 2, and others), allow incorporation of the basic *DDR* gameplay and dance pad as an adjunct

Promotional screenshot from 2004's *Dance Dance Revolution Extreme* for the Sony PlayStation 2, which—among other features—added support for Sony's EyeToy camera.

to their own main modes of play.

With the continued popularity of *DDR* and the even more popular *Guitar Hero* and *Rock Band* series,[22] performance-based gaming is a genre to be reckoned with for the foreseeable future. After all, combining popular music with the fun of performing is a concept that transcends many of the social biases against

---

[21]As Cravens states, "Since the Bemani line of games included *Guitar Freaks* and *Drum Mania* (not just *DDR*), there was obviously a huge influence. *Guitar Hero* and *Rock Band* are more popular than *DDR* because Harmonix [developer of *Rock Band*] took the *DDR* formula and made it for a more mainstream audience. Instead of jumping around on a lit stage, you are now 'looking cool' with a hunk of guitar-shaped plastic or a 'drum kit' in front of you while you played songs that were familiar and accepted by American audiences. The Bemani line of games proved that the concept would work; it just took a company that was more in tune with American pop culture to [really] make it explode."

[22]As well as Konami's own, newer multiperipheral band game, *Rock Revolution* (2008; Nintendo Wii, Sony PlayStation 3, and so on).

Karaoke has proven a popular subgenre in the performance games category, with Konami's own *Karaoke Revolution* series of games one mainstay. Box back for *Karaoke Revolution Presents American Idol Encore* for the Microsoft Xbox 360 shown.

the idea of videogames, particularly as games like *DDR* and Nintendo's exercise-centric *Wii Fit* game and Wii Balance Board (2008, Nintendo Wii) continue to rack up weight loss and fitness-related successes in otherwise sedentary individuals. As Cravens summarizes, "*DDR* is a series that is so positive, grandparents are aware of it and they can endorse it for their family. It is a wholesome game (save for a few stray lyrics) that is healthy for the players and it is not a game that was made entirely for 25-year-old men. Mainstream media have parodied it and embraced it for being an oddity that does not seem to lose much steam."

DIABLO (1996): THE ROGUE GOES TO HELL

4

Perhaps the handiest way to illustrate *Diablo*'s (Blizzard, 1996; Apple Macintosh, PC, Sony PlayStation) impact is by comparing it to another breakout hit of the 1990s: id's first-person shooter *Doom* (1993; Apple Macintosh, Atari Jaguar, PC, and others; see Chapter 5, "*Doom* (1993): The First Person Shooter Takes Control"). The two games have much in common. First, they both introduced critical innovations that established new genres. Second, they were staggeringly successful in their own right, inspiring other developers to shamelessly duplicate their formula. Both games offer similar plots (go to hell, confront demons). Finally, and perhaps most importantly, both games took full advantage of the tremendous graphics and networking potential of the PC. Simply put, *Diablo* did for the action role-playing game (RPG) genre what *Doom* did for the first-person shooter. Like all the games in this book, they have helped shape the videogame industry as we know it today.

Diablo-inspired games are still produced today, and the major game sites and magazines wax endlessly over highly anticipated games like Ascaron's *Sacred II: Fallen Angel* (2008, Microsoft Xbox 360, PC, Sony PlayStation 3) and Blizzard's own *Diablo III* (2012; Apple Macintosh, PC). Although *Sacred II* and *Diablo III* boast terrific graphics and interesting innovations, they still have much in common with the original—which was still being sold a decade later as part of Blizzard's *Diablo Battle Chest*.

Before going into detail about the game, let's explain the differences between conventional computer role-playing games (CRPGs) and action RPGs. The key difference is how the games handle time. Conventional CRPGs like Sir-Tech's *Wizardry: Proving Grounds of the Mad Overlord* (1981; Apple II, Nintendo Entertainment System, and others) and Origin's *Ultima* (1981; Apple II, Atari 8-bit, and others; see Chapter 23) are turn-based, much like their table-top role-playing cousins. This means that the gameplay is periodic; the game pauses at key periods to allow players time to make decisions and devise tactics. The advantages of this setup is that battles can be more intricate; the player has time to weigh more variables and assign complex tasks to her hero or party members.

Games like *Wizardry: Proving Grounds of the Mad Overlord*, box back and front shown, have a very different design philosophy than games like *Diablo*, relying more on careful planning and strategy than quick fingers.

In real-time games such as FTL Games' *Dungeon Master* (1987; Atari ST, Commodore Amiga, PC, and others) and Westwood's *Eye of the Beholder* (1990; Commodore Amiga, Nintendo Game Boy Advance, PC, and others), the monsters don't stand around waiting for the player to make a move. Instead, they roam about freely, and the player has to respond immediately to threats. Combat in these games tends to be reduced to clicking on monsters rather than wading through complicated menus; there simply isn't time to devise elaborate tactics once battle has commenced. Some games, such as Bioware's *Baldur's Gate* (1998; Apple Macintosh, PC) or New World Computing's *Might and Magic VI* (1998, PC) offer hybrids of real-time and turn-based gameplay, but *Diablo* and other action-RPGs are purely real-time.

Another defining characteristic of action RPGs is the emphasis on rapid dexterity with the mouse. Typically, this means moving the mouse pointer over each enemy and quickly pressing the left or right mouse button—taken to extremes, the game becomes a "clickfest" and a true test of hand-eye coordination. Later action RPGs such as Gas Powered Games' *Dungeon Siege* (2002; Apple Macintosh, PC) reduce the clickfest aspect, automating many tasks that formerly had to be manually executed by the player.

Finally, unlike older real-time games such as the aforementioned *Dungeon Master*, action-RPGs are depicted in third-person, isometric view. This means that players see their avatars, rather than viewing the action from a first-person perspective. Although other action RPGs differ markedly in their details, they all adhere (at least to some degree) to these basic paradigms.

One of the major breaks that *Diablo* made with conventional CRPGs concerns complexity. Conventional CRPGs, especially venerable old classics such as SSI's *Wizard's Crown* or Interplay's *The Bard's Tale* (both 1985; Apple II, Commodore 64, and others), tend to be far more difficult to learn than *Diablo*. This fact is apparent from the start of the game. In *Diablo*, the player simply picks one of three premade characters (warrior, rogue, sorcerer) to serve as the avatar, then the gameplay begins. *Wizard's Crown* and *The Bard's Tale* require players to build a whole party of characters from scratch, making dozens of critical and esoteric decisions that have a crucial, permanent impact on the gameplay. A few bad choices can make winning the game difficult or even impossible. Making smart decisions means reading the often-lengthy instruction manuals, and having a solid background in pen-and-paper *Dungeons & Dragons* and fantasy novels is helpful if not mandatory. Players are likewise challenged to make their own maps or risk becoming lost in dungeons. In short, these games require far more preparation and patience than many modern gamers are willing or able to commit. They simply are not casual games.

Unlike many CRPGs, which require lengthy character or party creation sequences, *Diablo* asks players to make a single choice before the game begins.

Blizzard's strategy was to keep what was fun about CRPGs intact, but move the complex and often intimidating statistical and literary elements under the hood. All fans of CRPGs enjoy watching characters "level up," becoming stronger and more proficient as the game progresses. They also enjoy the visceral nature of defeating increasingly tougher monsters and exploring dangerous and mysterious places. However, standard CRPGs can take days or even weeks for novices to master, whereas any reasonably intelligent person can get *Diablo* up and running in minutes. Indeed, the single-player campaign can be beaten in under 10 hours. Blizzard also added a brilliant online component through *Battle.net*, which ensured that avid fans would continue to enjoy the game long after they had completed the single-player campaign. The new formula was a tremendous success for Blizzard, and many of the innovations we see in the *Diablo* series were carried over into the even more successful massively multiplayer online game, *World of Warcraft* (2004; Apple Macintosh, PC). In this chapter, however, we focus on *Diablo* and its impact on the industry.

The action begins in this foreboding village. Lovely but slightly disturbing guitar music sets the mood. Note the red and blue orbs indicating health and mana (magic power), respectively. A comparable setup is seen in Blue Sky's critically acclaimed first-person-perspective role-playing game *Ultima Underworld: The Stygian Abyss* (1992; PC, Windows Mobile, and others).

Blizzard was not the first developer that attempted to inject more adrenaline into what many considered an overtly nerdy and contemplative genre. FTL's *Dungeon Master* offered real-time dungeon crawling from a first-person perspective, and was itself inspired by the earlier wireframe game *Dungeons of Daggorath* (Tandy Corp, 1982) for the Radio Shack Color Computer. Origin and SSI had also released some intriguing action-based CRPG titles such as *Moebius: The Orb of Celestial Harmony* (Origin, 1985; Apple II, Commodore Amiga, and others) and *Hillsfar* (SSI, 1989; Commodore Amiga, PC, and others). *Moebius* is a hybrid beat 'em up (see Chapter 17, "*Street Fighter II* (1991): Would You Like the Combo?") and CRPG, whereas *Hillsfar* is a simplistic CRPG with a series of action-based minigames. There were even some real-time games that offered a similar third-person iso-metric view featured in *Diablo*, such as *Shadow Sorcerer* (SSI, 1991; Atari ST, Commodore Amiga, PC), *The Four Crystals of Trazere* (Mindscape, 1992; Atari ST, Commodore Amiga, PC), and *The Summoning* (SSI, 1992; PC). However, none of these games attracted as much attention as *Diablo* and are seldom played today. Without question, the most enduring of these pre-*Diablo* games is Origin's *Ultima VII: The Black Gate* (1992; PC, Super Nintendo). This richly interactive game was well received by crit-ics and fans of the series, and remains a fan favorite.

Action-oriented RPGs were far more plentiful on consoles than computers. In particular, Nintendo's *The Legend of Zelda* (1986, NES), which is covered in Chapter 21, "*The Legend of Zelda* (1986): Rescuing Zeldas and Uniting Triforces," is worth mentioning here. Although the first Zelda game isn't a true role-playing game (it lacks a statistical system for leveling and is referred to as an "action adventure"), it nevertheless shares many of its features, and few developers could ignore the profits it reaped. Origin seems to have been thinking along these lines with *Ultima VIII: Pagan* (1994, PC), which added precision jumping sequences reminiscent of a Super Mario game (see Chapter 19, "*Super Mario Bros.* (1985): How High Can Jumpman Get?") to the venerable old series. However, reactions to the games were mixed. Writing for *Computer Shopper* magazine, Barry Brenesal remarked, "*Pagan* is certainly harder to play than any previous *Ultima*, and its mouse-based combat may frustrate fans of earlier releases."[1]

Brenesal's comment brings us to an important point regarding computer and console games: modern computers are far more likely to have mice and keyboards than game pads, a factor with serious implications for gameplay. Game pads are designed with arcade-like gameplay in mind; keyboards and mice are primarily intended for productivity. Although it was easy enough to buy a game pad or joystick for PCs, few outside the hardcore gaming community ever bothered to do so, and not all games supported them anyway. Furthermore, computer gamers (particularly CRPG fans) were thought to be older and more sophisticated than their console cousins. They thrived on complexity, not dexterity. The common assumption was that, at least on computers, role-playing and action games were mutually exclusive, and the long

---

[1]*Computer Shopper* (June 1994).

line of failed action-CRPGs seemed to attest to that fact. Blizzard finally proved, once and for all, that they were wrong.

Perhaps the most significant feature of *Diablo* is its highly polished, instantly addictive gameplay. In many ways it is comparable to *Rogue* (see bonus chapter, "*Rogue* (1980): Have @ You, You Deadly Zs"), a very old but still widely played CRPG that originated on university minicomputers.

Like *Diablo*, *Rogue* offers procedurally generated dungeons and bite-size, quick-fix style adventuring—a vast change from the drawn-out and even laborious campaigns of other CRPGs. A procedurally generated dungeon is one that relies on predefined algorithms to create dungeons on-the-fly; it's important not to confuse this process with purely random dungeons. After all, no one wants to play a dungeon that has no exits, or has hordes of the highest-level monsters roaming about the first levels. The major advantage of procedurally generated dungeons is replay value; as the dungeons will always be fresh, there is no need for the adventure ever to end. Indeed, several other CRPGs took advantage of the same technique; examples include *Telengard* (Avalon Hill, 1982; Commodore PET, TRS-80, and others) and *Sword of Fargoal* (Epyx, 1982; Commodore 64, Commodore VIC-20).

As with *Rogue* before it, characters gain levels quickly and frequently in *Diablo*. With each level, the player gains points to distribute among four attributes.

However, though randomizing the dungeons may improve replay value, it seems to diminish the opportunities for narrative and creative level design. What usually happens is that the gameplay descends into a simple yet addictive "hack 'n' slash" style, similar to the gameplay in the multiplayer arcade classic *Gauntlet*

(Atari, 1985),[2] in which the objective is only to kill the next wave of monsters with little thought to plot or long-term planning. If your character dies in *Rogue*, for instance, it's painless enough to create a new character and begin anew; little is lost in the process, and many versions lack any way to save a character anyway. Compare this to a game such as *Pool of Radiance* (SSI, 1988; Commodore 64, Commodore Amiga, PC, and others), which offers a huge campaign that takes weeks and hundreds of hours of gameplay to complete. Although *Diablo* has a plot and a mission for the character, it also lacks the long and drawn-out character creation sequence of most other CRPGs, and dying is a relatively trivial affair. As with *Rogue*, the idea is to get the player up and hacking as quickly and painlessly as possible, and although it is possible to save the current game, the player cannot save and restore multiple games.

Battles tend to be over and done with quickly, though the character can face dozens of enemies at once. Note here the transparent map overlay that can be turned on and off.

By far the most obvious difference between *Diablo* and *Rogue* is the audiovisuals. Whereas *Rogue* is based on simple character-set graphics and has only rudimentary sound, if any, *Diablo* offers quality graphics, full-motion video, and some of the best music of its era. Every spell and attack is fully animated, and a semitransparent overlay provides an onscreen map to help navigate the dungeons.

---

[2]Games like *Dandy* (APX, 1983; Atari 8-bit), *Gauntlet,* and their direct sequels and numerous clones focus almost entirely on direct action rather than any type of exploration or role-playing, mitigating their ultimate in uence on *Diablo*'s design.

Diablo's storyline is probably the least remarkable thing about it. As with *Doom*, the goal of the game is to battle wave after wave of demonic forces, ultimately battling it out with Diablo, Lord of Terror. Many of the game's most raving reviews, such as Trent C. Ward's for GameSpot, make no mention of the plot whatsoever. Nevertheless, the game and its sequels have inspired a series of six novels by Richard A. Knaak, and there have long been rumors of a movie based on the franchise.

Like *Doom*, *Diablo* also took advantage of the by-then exploding network multiplayer scene, and its massively popular *Battle.net* server became the first such project to turn a profit.[3] *Battle.net* stood out in stark contrast to other online gaming offerings of its era by focusing on its excellent player-matching service. First, anyone who had bought *Diablo* could use the service for free, without any monthly fees or obligations whatsoever. Although Blizzard was able to fully recoup the losses by advertising revenue, the service was mainly intended to boost sales of the game itself. According to Paul W. Sams, spokesman for the service, "We don't look at *Battle.net* as a profit center. We look at it as a value add to our customers that is justified by increased retail sales." Sams estimates that *Battle.net* led to a 10% boost in sales.[4] The genius of *Battle.net* was that game data wasn't channeled through Blizzard's servers. Instead, the service functioned as a matchmaker, connecting gamers directly. However, this setup opened the door wide for cheaters, who could modify their data files to gain an unfair advantage. Blizzard struggled mightily with this problem, regularly issuing patches to stymie the cheaters.

Even though *Battle.net* was free to use, that didn't stop a group of programmers from reverse-engineering the code and releasing *bnetd*, a free alternative to Blizzard's own service. Blizzard moved quickly to shut down *bnetd*, arguing that it promoted piracy. After all, Blizzard required users of *Battle.net* to verify their purchase by entering a special code printed on their game discs. The rival service offered a refuge to gamers who, for whatever reason, were unable or unwilling to provide a legitimate code. After a series of court battles, Blizzard ultimately prevailed.

Rather than design their own expansion to *Diablo*, Blizzard North outsourced to Synergistic Software, a company with roots going back to some of the earliest CRPGs produced for home computers. Their *Diablo* expansion, *Hellfire*, was released in 1997 to lukewarm reviews. Although it added plenty of new content and two new character classes, it lacked multiplayer support and was not nearly as well received as the original. Writing

---

[3] See Greg Costikyan's "Online gaming's store-self chains" article on Salon.com: http://www.salon.com/tech/feature/1999/04/21/battlenet/.

[4] See Barbara Walter's interview with Sams at http://www.gamasutra.com/features/19971128/battlenet_01.htm.

for GameSpot, "Desslock" wrote that the expansion "fails to provide as compelling an experience as *Diablo*" and that fans of multiplayer ought to pass on it.[5] However, Blizzard's first official sequel, *Diablo II*, released in 2000, became another smash hit for the company—and this despite what one reviewer described as

Diablo II offered superior graphics, more classes, and outdoor areas to explore. However, the core gameplay remained the same.

Diablo II offered a more sophisticated leveling system than the original. This branching tree system would show up in later games such as *World of Warcraft*.

5See http://www.gamespot.com/pc/rpg/hellfire/review.html.

"somewhat outdated" graphics.[6] The sequel maintained much of the gameplay that had proven so successful, but added several welcome features. These included large outdoor areas to explore, a more linear quest structure, new classes, and a branching tree system for leveling. Blizzard also improved its online experience for *Diablo II*, now storing all the private data on their own servers. This change greatly curtailed the cheating that had been such a problem for fans of the first game.

Diablo's impact on the industry was immediate and has proven long-lasting. Though simplistic compared to classics such as *Wizard's Crown* or *Pool of Radiance*, the game compensates with highly polished gameplay, attractive audiovisuals, and a highly intuitive interface. It was easy enough for even total novices to learn, but certainly challenging enough to keep from getting boring—and the randomized dungeons and highly active multiplayer options upped the replay value substantially. Its legacy is seen today in the aforementioned *Sacred II* and *Diablo III* games, but developers took the concept in wildly different directions; consider Iridon Interactive's *Dink Smallwood* (1998; PC), a comedy set in a typical fantasy setting; Interplay's *Fallout: Brotherhood of Steel* (2004; Microsoft Xbox, Sony PlayStation 2), set in a post-apocalyptic wasteland; or Activision's *Marvel: Ultimate Alliance* (2006; Nintendo Wii, Sony PlayStation Portable, and others), where the familiar fantasy paradigms are replaced with a contemporary superhero setting.

Other noteworthy *Diablo*-in uenced games include *Gauntlet Legends* (Atari, 1998; Arcade, Sega Dreamcast, and others),[7] *Darkstone* (Delphine Software, 1999; PC, Sony PlayStation), *Revenant* (Cinematix Studios, 1999; Apple Macintosh, PC), *Nox* (Westwood Studios, 2000; PC), *Baldur's Gate: Dark Alliance* (Interplay, 2001; Microsoft Xbox, Nintendo GameCube, and others), *Divine Divinity* (Larian Studios, 2002; PC), and *Champions of Norrath* (Sony Online Entertainment, 2004; Sony PlayStation 2). Blizzard has also gotten back into the *Diablo* business with *Diablo III*, which has a richer single-player story with multiplayer integration possibilities. As Leonard Boyarsky, Lead World Artist for *Diablo III*, says, "It's kind of like, 'I'm playing a single-player experience, but I can share that with my friends. There are going to be things like class quests that only certain classes go on, but my friends can get experience from going on those and helping me.'"[8] Though differing in their details, all of these games—and

---

[6]See Desslock's review at http://www.gamespot.com/pc/rpg/diablo2/review.html.

[7]After the original's release, the *Gauntlet* series of titles continued refining the original game's scope by introducing an increasing number of exploration and RPG elements until the latest releases had little to differentiate themselves from the myriad of *Diablo*-like clones.

[8]http://www.gamasutra.com/php-bin/news_index.php?story=19259.

ultimately all modern action-CRPGs—derive their core gameplay elements from the original *Diablo*.

Although the commands in games like *Champions of Norrath* (box back shown) tend to be executed in a more direct manner than *Diablo*, the influence from Blizzard's classic game is clear.

Although *Diablo* may not have inspired quite as many derivatives as *Doom*, there's no doubt that it belongs in anyone's list of historically significant games. The in uence it exerted on CRPG developers is striking, comparable only to the blow made by *Dungeon Master* and *Ultima* before it. Even prior to its release, there were few games attracting more attention than *Diablo III*, and even if that game is little more than a relatively minor overhaul of the first, no one doubts that Blizzard will continue to reap enormous profits from the series' immense, dedicated fan base.

All kinds of themes have been explored in the myriad games inspired by *Diablo*'s style of play, ranging from superhero to military to comedy, such as in the well-acted single-player fantasy spoof, *The Bard's Tale* (Vivendi Universal, 2004; Microsoft Xbox, PC, Sony PlayStation 2), box back shown.

5

DOOM (1993): THE FIRST-PERSON SHOOTER TAKES CONTROL

On December 10, 1993, the "Two Johns"—John Carmack and John Romero[1]—unveiled the infamous *Doom* for PC,[2] described in its manual as "a lightning-fast virtual reality adventure where you're the toughest space trooper ever to suck vacuum." The game was an instant success, catapulting Carmack and Romero's company, id Software, to the short list of the world's most eminent shareware game developers. It also spawned a genre now labeled the "first-person shooter" (FPS) or just "shooter," a genre that is still dominating the industry. *Doom* offered gamers visceral 3D-like graphics and intense, arcade-like action that could be soloed or enjoyed simultaneously against their friends in a mode affectionately dubbed "Deathmatch," now a commonly used term. Although it wasn't the first FPS, it was by far the most successful and influential PC game of the 1990s, if not of all time.

Doom puts players in the role of a bullet-chewing marine who's sent to Mars after assaulting an officer who ordered an attack on civilians. The Martian post was mind-numbingly boring, at least until the researchers on the Martian moons began making headway in their interdimensional space travel project. You and your combat troop were sent to Martian moon Phobos to secure the situation; they rushed in while you guarded the perimeter. However, you've now lost radio contact with the troop, who are likely dead, and have no way off the moon. Your only hope is to re-enter the station, facing the waiting terror with nothing more than a pistol—though there's every indication that more formidable firearms are to be found in the base.

This story, which seems inspired by such sci-fi and horror classics as *Alien* (1979) and *The Evil Dead* (1981), is well suited to the

---

[1]Other important figures at id at the time included Tom Hall, Adrian Carmack (no relation to John Carmack), and Sandy Petersen.

[2]Since the game's original release, official and unofficial ports of *Doom* have been created for nearly every capable platform.

Doom begins in a room free of monsters to give players a chance to master the interface.

gameplay. However, although the game did serve as the basis for a series of novels and a movie, no one bought this game for its story-line. The game's success was owed, in part, at least, to the developers' marketing as well as their technical savvy. Before moving on to the game's technical achievements, we should reflect on id's unusual marketing strategy.

Doom took advantage of two revolutionary trends in software distribution and production: shareware and user-generated content. The first of these was a well-established practice by 1993, and id had tried it before to great success with their earlier PC games *Commander Keen* (1990) and *Wolfenstein 3D* (1992), a vital predecessor that we'll discuss shortly. Then, as now, the majority of commercial software was published by traditional publishers, who did everything in their power to prevent others from illegally copying and distributing their products. Shareware publishers, however, encourage users to copy and share their programs, then employed a variety of methods to generate revenue. Usually these amount to a screen or message that displays while the program loads, asking users to send a donation to the developer. Sometimes trivial or even crucial features are unavailable until the user has paid a fee to receive a "registered copy" or a special key code. In the case of the original *Doom,* the user received a fully working game, but only the first part—to see the rest of the game, users were asked to send money. However, the free version included one pivotal feature: multiplayer gameplay over a local area network (LAN). This fact made it much easier for large groups of gamers to organize LAN parties, as they would otherwise have had to purchase an individual copy for each machine.

The shareware method proved exceptionally successful for id, but it took some doing to get the game uploaded to the University of Wisconsin's FTP server, where id had planned to release the game.[3] According to David Kushner, author of *Masters of Doom*, ten thousand users swarmed to the server, generating enough demand to crash the network.[4] Fortunately for id, many users weren't satisfied to own just the shareware version and eagerly sprang for the full registered version. According to estimates at the Doom Wiki, *Doom* and its sequel *Doom II* have sold over two million copies each.[5] Kushner's lively narrative describes in vivid detail the hectic bliss at id when hundreds of thousands of dollars ooded into the tiny company, swelling the bank accounts and egos of its team. id would later abandon shareware, though they still seem committed to the open source and free software movements, eventually releasing the full source code to *Doom* and other games to the public, greatly extending the life of the titles beyond their original platforms.

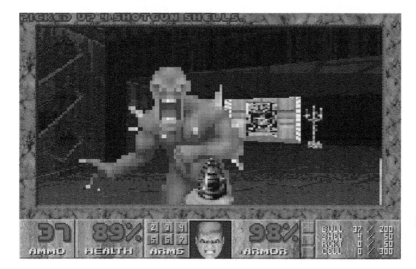

Several types of demons roam *Doom*'s levels, eager to make you an ex-soldier.

The other innovation—user-generated content—made perhaps a more significant contribution to the gaming industry. Again, id was certainly not the first game developer to encourage and even create tools to help gamers expand or modify their products. However, *Doom*'s immense popularity and the tools' impressive capabilities drew wads of dedicated and creative

---

[3]Internet usage was not yet widespread, so shareware games depended upon a wide variety of distribution methods. These methods included individually dialed Bulletin Board Systems (BBS) and mail order companies whose sole business model was selling disks filled with shareware and demo software.

[4]Kushner, David. 2004. *Masters of Doom* (ISBN: 0-8129-7215-5). Random House.

[5]See http://doom.wikia.com/wiki/Sales. The figure considers other estimates from a variety of published and online sources.

talent to the task. As a result, hundreds of gamers happily went to work designing new levels or taking the engine in unexpected directions. These user-built levels are called WADs, an acronym that stands for "Where's all the data?" id had specified in their licensing agreement that these WADs would be distributed free; makers were not allowed to charge for them. However, that fact didn't stop shady dealers from collecting WADs and selling them at unscrupulous or ignorant outlets. id countered by offering their own compilations via retail.

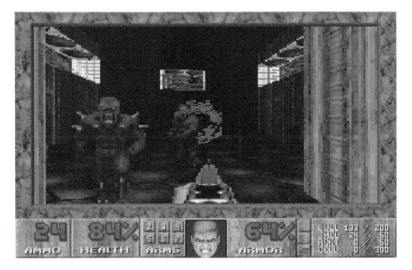

Ah, *Doom*'s boomstick, one step closer to the BFG (Big Fucking Gun).

Some of the better WAD makers eventually got involved with commercial game development. These include Tim Willits, later lead designer at id, and Dario Casali, whose work attracted Valve Software. Some of the more notable WADs include *Eternal Doom*, which offers 34 giant levels to explore, and *Hell Revealed*, an intensely difficult WAD designed to test an expert's prowess. A few off-the-wall WADs include *Chex Quest*, a game that served as a promotional tie-in for the cereal, and *Mockery*, a WAD that Scott Cover made specifically to illustrate the errors made by novice WAD makers. However, the wad became popular enough to inspire a subgenre of "joke mods." There are also programs such as *SLIGE* that can create randomly generated WADs.[6]

Before continuing the discussion of *Doom*, we should take a moment to examine id's 1992 game *Wolfenstein 3D*. This game, loosely based on the much older *Castle Wolfenstein* (see Chapter 2, "*Castle Wolfenstein* (1981): Achtung! Stealth Gaming

---

[6]The top 100 WADs of all time have been collected and reviewed at Doom World, a must-see site for anyone interested in WADs. Visit http://www.doomworld .com/10years/bestwads/.

Steps out of the Shadows"), prototyped many of the critical graphical and gameplay elements that would show up in *Doom* and later shooters, sans the familiar FPS control scheme, ability to significantly modify and extend the game,[7] and critical multiplayer components. The game puts players in control of William "B. J." Blazkowicz, a soldier trying to escape a Nazi stronghold. Although its graphics are somewhat crude compared to *Doom*, it still allowed gamers to experience 3D-like graphics rendered on-the- y with a first-person perspective. According to Kushner, Romero and Carmack were inspired by Blue Sky's *Ultima Underworld: The Stygian Abyss* (Origin, 1992; PC, Windows Mobile, and others), an incredibly ambitious role-playing game doomed by its steep hardware requirements. Carmack was convinced he could achieve similar effects on lower-end PCs, and proved it with *Wolfenstein 3D*.[8]

Blue Sky's (later known as Looking Glass Studios) *Ultima Underworld: The Stygian Abyss* beat id to the feature punch in many respects, but its steep hardware requirements and relatively complex interface may explain its relative obscurity.

Of course, *Wolfenstein 3D*'s impressive performance was not entirely without precedent, as id's two earlier titles, *Hovertank 3D* and *Catacomb 3D*, both from 1991, were pioneering games in their own right and formed the foundations from which the far-better-known shooter was built and greatly extended.[9] In *Hovertank 3D*, the player controls Brick Sledge, a merce-

---

[7]*Wolfenstein 3D* did allow for some modification of its graphics and maps, but not to the extent found in *Doom*.

[8]It's important to note, however, that although *Wolfenstein 3D* looked great and moved smoothly, the original *Ultima Underworld* still featured a far more advanced engine, with features like oor and ceiling textures, terrain of varying height, and lighting effects that would not be realized in an id creation until *Doom*.

[9]See http://www.idsoftware.com/games/vintage/hovertank/.

nary hired by an unknown organization to rescue people from enemy-filled cities under the threat of nuclear attack. The game used a combination of scaled sprites and rendered walls, much like *Wolfenstein 3D*, but the walls in *Hovertank 3D* were untextured and solid in color. *Catacomb 3D*, where the player, as the high wizard of Thoria, must save the troublesome but useful Nemesis of Kelquest from his suspended animation in magical amber, showed the character's hands and added other, now familiar, character-based features, along with textured walls. Both of these mostly forgotten early games—with their extremely modest system requirements, relative to their groundbreaking features—contributed greatly to *Wolfenstein 3D*'s emergence as such a polished product and ultimately to the even greater success of *Doom*.

id's *Hovertank 3D* (left) and *Catacomb 3D* (right), could be considered the earliest testing grounds for technology and concepts later used to popular acclaim in *Wolfenstein 3D* and *Doom*.

Now let's turn our attention back to the actual gameplay of *Doom*. At the start of the single-player campaign, the player is presented with a view of a futuristic room (the moon base) and a hand pointing a pistol. At this point, the player is offered a variety of control schemes, though most will tend toward the character's line of sight. A combination of mouse and keyboard control that is popular today. A typical configuration is to move with the arrow keys (this configuration later conformed to the standard W, A, S, and D keys) and aim and fire with the mouse. Spinning the mouse around changes the view; holding down the Alt key allows the arrow keys to strafe (locked in left and right movement).[10] Holding down the right shift key and the arrow keys makes the character run—an often-vital skill. Though moving and aiming can be terribly confusing and disorienting for the novice, most gamers will likely master the interface in a few minutes. To this end, id placed no monsters in the first room, so players are free to experiment with the control schemes until they feel ready for their first encounters. Other controls are for opening doors and operating switches. All of the action is depicted from "first-person perspective," meaning that the player is seeing from the character's

---

[10]Use of the mouse often negates the need for a strafe modifier key.

point of view. This setup is intended to make players feel a more immediate connection to the action.[11]

After leaving the first room, players will begin fighting demons and possessed soldiers. These enemies are dispatched readily with a shot or two from the pistol. However, the player must be careful not to waste ammo—an empty gun is merely a paperweight. There are also armor pickups, radiation suits, and health packs, a.k.a. "stimpacks," a "booster enzyme that make[s] you feel like a new man," to quote from the manual. By far the most welcome of all these powerups was a bigger and badder weapon. Persistent players eventually replace their pistol with shotguns, chainguns, rocket launchers, plasma ri es, and eventually the infamous BFG 9000, which can clear an entire room of monsters. Each weapon requires a specific type of ammo, and rationing out the ammo is an important part of the strategy. For instance, since pistol clips are far more plentiful than shotgun shells or rockets, it's better to use them for wimpy demons and save the rarer ammo for more powerful enemies. There's also a berserker rage powerup that greatly boosts the character's muscles, turning his fists into weapons of mass destruction.

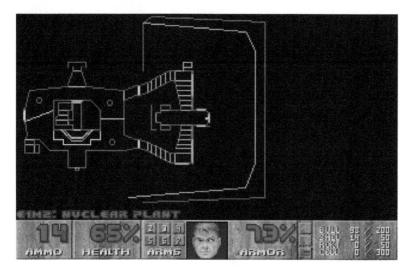

Doom's built-in automapper helps keep players on track.

Monsters aren't the only perils awaiting the player. Ceilings can cave in, slime/lava is radioactive, and barrels can explode. Indeed, the manual suggests (and any observant player will quickly discover) that these explosive barrels can be used to quickly clear a

---

[11]As author Loguidice recalls, "Playing this game for the first time on a fast Pentium 90 computer up close to a 15" at-screen CRT monitor created one of those 'wow' moments in gaming for me that are few and far between. The immersive effect was particularly stunning when walking down the game's dimly lit interior corridors."

room of enemies—simply wait until they are near the barrels and shoot them from a safe distance away.

At the bottom of the screen is the character's "mug," an animated face that changes upon receiving damage. The face winces when the character takes a blow, for instance, and quickly becomes bruised and bloodied as his health declines. This feature is important, because it helps balance out the first-person perspective; it's a constant reminder that the player is controlling an actual character rather than a oating camera.

In the mid-1990s, it seemed all but a prerequisite to have a *Doom* game for your system. Back of the box for the single-player-only version of *Doom* for the Sega 32X shown, which was often compared to the superior multiplayer-capable, though music-less, Atari Jaguar version. *Doom* was at home on a wide range of computers, consoles, and handhelds, including the 3DO, Nintendo Game Boy Advance, Super Nintendo, Sega Saturn, and Sony PlayStation.

id was quick to follow the original *Doom* with many upgrades, sequels, and spin-offs. *Doom II: Hell on Earth* appeared on

October 10, 1994, and featured the same basic gameplay as the original, though with a larger area to explore. The critical difference was that *Doom II* was intended for the retail market; it was never released as shareware. This game received official expansion packs that were based on levels designed by users, including *Master Levels for Doom II* (1995) and *Final Doom* (1996).[12] The retail versions of *Doom* were quite profitable for id, who soon found themselves awash with cash.

The *Doom* games have been ported to an amazing array of platforms, both popular and obscure, like this conversion of *Doom II* for the Palm OS–based Tapwave Zodiac handheld, back of box shown.

---

[12]*The Ultimate Doom* (1995) was a retail version of the original *Doom* that featured a new, fourth episode, "Thy Flesh Consumed."

id has also published spin-off games that utilized their *Doom* engine. These include Raven Software's *Heretic* (1994) and *Hexen* (1996), well-received games with a fantasy setting.[13] These games are noted for introducing a more sophisticated inventory system and the ability to look up and down. In 1996, id released *Quake*, another FPS that became a definitive series of the genre. This tremendously successful game and its sequels again put players in command of a soldier, and the plot is also based on a

Although for many it took the release of the Microsoft Xbox platform to legitimize FPS gaming on consoles as an alternative to using a computer, the genre had seen several strong console releases years earlier, though often with compromised performance and control schemes. The Nintendo 64 was a favorite target for id's properties, with the release of games like *Quake* and *Hexen* (back of box pictured). Below *Hexen* is the back of the box for Rare's original creation from the James Bond film, *GoldenEye 007*, one of the most popular console FPS titles prior to 2001's *Halo: Combat Evolved* for the Xbox.

---

[13]These games could be said to have taken inspiration from id's earlier *Catacomb 3D* games.

similar contrivance to the *Doom* games: government officials experimenting with teleportation technology ("slipgates") have unwittingly granted access to a race of vicious "death squad" marauders. It's up to the player to enter the slipgate and dispatch "Quake," a mysterious and powerful enemy who is responsible for the death squads.

Quake II, released in 1997, is a much different game than its predecessor. The game employs a science fiction setting. The player's character, a marine named Bitterman, is sent with a team to the home planet of a cybernetic race called the Strogg. Their mission is to destroy Makron, the Strogg's leader. As we might expect, Bitterman's team is quickly liquidated at the start of the game, and it's up to him to single-handedly complete the mission.

Perhaps id's most radical departure from the *Doom* setup is *Quake III Arena* (1999), which is entirely focused on multiplayer gameplay. After the first *Doom*, many gamers found themselves much more interested in playing with other humans rather than computer-controlled opponents. Because these early games existed in the early days of the Internet, mutiplayer sessions took place over LANs. This setup required that gamers assemble in the same physical location, then plug all of their computers into the same local or private network. This activity soon became a cultural phenomenon known as "LAN parties," and many games besides *Doom* were enjoyed during these events. LAN parties ranged from as little as two to four connected computers to the massive DreamHack party of Jonkoping, Sweden, which holds the Guinness Book of Records with 10,638 computers all connected to the same network. LAN parties have contributed much lingo to modern gaming culture, such as the term "frag" for killing one's opponents. The next *Quake* game, *Quake IV* (2005), returned to the story in *Quake II* with a long single-player campaign. Of course, there are also multiplayer options.

id's *Doom 3* (2005) was a highly anticipated release that pushed the boundaries of the then-current 3D graphics technology, particularly in regard to the use of light and shading. Unlike previous *Doom* games, the third lacks black humor and dark wit. Instead, the game strives for pure horror, placing players smack in the middle of a situation reminiscent of an *Alien* movie. Speaking of movies, it was around this time that the franchise received its first (and so far only) film treatment: Andrzej Bartkowiak's *Doom* (2005). This film, like so many games based on movies, did not fare particularly well at the box office.

Of course, id and its licensed partners are not the only developers who have produced first-person shooters worthy of note. Indeed, one could easily write an entire book covering the evolution of the genre. Two of the most popular are Valve's

Quake III Arena took a purely multiplayer approach to its design, allowing for lots of great human-on-human conflict, as seen here in a screenshot from the Sega Dreamcast version.

Despite selling well, *Doom 3* received a relatively lukewarm reception for its focus on improved audiovisuals over advancing the series' play mechanics.

Half-Life (1998) and Bungie's *Halo: Combat Evolved* (2001). *Half-Life* introduced several ambitious innovations to the genre, but is perhaps most notable for weaving in a more sophisticated narrative. Its sequel, *Half-Life 2* (2004) is even more story-focused, with characters and a plot that rivals that of a good science fiction film. *Halo: Combat Evolved* is also acclaimed for its excellent story and writing, but is also noteworthy for successfully adapting the genre to the console market. Although there had been plenty of earlier attempts (including many ports of *Wolfenstein 3D* and

Doom), with the key exceptions of Rare's *GoldenEye 007* (1997) and *Perfect Dark* (2000) for the Nintendo 64, these largely failed to make much of an impact. The precision control and sometimes complex control schemes demanded by the genre seemed to necessitate a keyboard and a mouse. Bungee and Microsoft solved this problem admirably; the game's control scheme took full advantage of the Microsoft Xbox's well-designed game controller. Indeed, now there are as many fans of the genre who prefer game controllers to the keyboard and mouse setup, making development of FPS games for every conceivable platform commonplace.

There are, of course, a multitude of other games we could mention, such as Looking Glass Studios' *System Shock* (1994; Apple Macintosh, PC), 3D Realms' *Duke Nukem 3D* (1996; PC, Tiger game.com, and others), Red Storm Entertainment's *Tom Clancy's Rainbow Six* (1998; PC, Sega Dreamcast, Sony PlayStation, and others), Dynamix's *Starseige: Tribes* (1998; PC), Valve's *Counter-Strike* (2003; Microsoft Xbox, PC), Crytek's *Far Cry* (2004; PC), and Monolith's *F.E.A.R.* (2005; Microsoft Xbox 360, PC, Sony PlayStation 3).[14] All of these games contributed new ideas and are well worth playing today. However, they are all variations on the model introduced by id's *Doom*, which is most certainly the progenitor of the incredibly successful FPS genre.

---

[14]*First Encounter Assault Recon*, or *F.E.A.R.*, is arguably considered a survival horror FPS. For more on the survival horror genre, see Chapter 1, "*Alone in the Dark* (1992): The Polygons of Fear."

6

DUNE II: THE BUILDING OF A DYNASTY (1992): SPICING UP STRATEGY IN REAL TIME

Westwood Studios' *Dune II: The Building of a Dynasty*[1] (1992; Commodore Amiga, PC, RISC OS, Sega Genesis) is widely regarded as the first modern real-time strategy (RTS) game. Although certainly not the first, it was highly successful and in uential, inspiring later games that eventually became one of the major genres of the industry. Later hits such as *Warcraft* and *Command & Conquer* can trace their ancestry back to *Dune II*, which is still enjoyable to play—even more than a decade after its initial release.

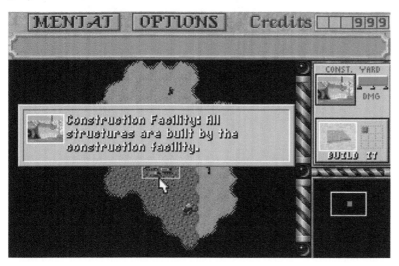

Dune II's gameplay is instantly recognizable by anyone familiar with the RTS genre.

Prior to *Dune II*, most strategy games were turn-based. They included classics like MicroProse's *Civilization* (1991; PC, Nokia N-Gage, Sony PlayStation, and others), a multilayered title that

---

[1]Subtitled *Battle for Arrakis* in some territories. The game also received a remake and pseudo update in 1998 as *Dune 2000*, for the PC and Sony PlayStation.

launched a series of turn-based strategy (TBS) games that is still going strong today.[2] Although *Civilization* is probably the most well known today, there were dozens of lesser-known strategy games, many based on tabletop wargames from the likes of Avalon Hill. With a few notable exceptions, such as Danielle Bunten Berry's[3] groundbreaking 1982 release, *Cytron Masters,* and Sir-Tech's hybrid, *Rescue Raiders* (1984; Apple II),[4] these earlier games broke the gameplay into discrete turns, during which only a single player (or computer opponent) could make any moves. *Dune II* popularized a form of gameplay in which the action was continuous; just because the player decided to break for coffee didn't mean that the computer-controlled opponents weren't steadily building up their resources. Although we'll have more to say about real-time versus turn-based games in a moment, for now let's just say that Westwood's game introduced a new facet to strategy gameplay by considering the passage of "real time," that is, the actual time the player spent playing. This fact meant that the player's physical ability to select units, scroll the map, and so on became vital. Westwood addressed this issue by integrating intuitive mouse control into the computer versions—a key innovation that sets *Dune II* apart from previous efforts at RTS games.[5]

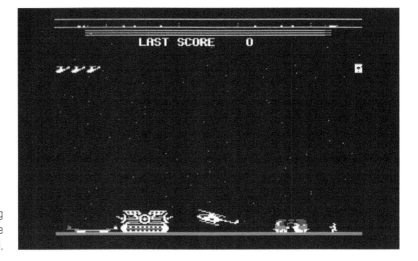

Screenshot from the intriguing hybrid, *Rescue Raiders,* for the Apple II.

---

[2]See Chapter 15, "*SimCity* (1989): Building Blocks for Fun and Profit," for more on this game.

[3]Dani Bunten Berry is also known as Dani Bunten and Dan Bunten. Born Daniel Paul Bunten, she changed her name after undergoing gender reassignment surgery.

[4]*Rescue Raiders* would be released by Three-Sixty Pacific in a slightly updated form for the Apple Macintosh and PC as *Armor Alley*. With superficial similarities to Dan Gorlin's *Choplifter* (1982, Broderbund; Apple II, Coleco Adam, and others), the 2D side perspective game puts the player in direct control of a helicopter, while releasing a variety of armored, autonomous ground forces in an attempt to get an explosives-filled van to the enemy base.

[5]It's important to note, however, that a mouse, though highly recommended, is not required.

Why did the elements found in *Dune II* prove so in uential? For many gamers, the constant action and immediate responses of RTS games are more appealing and easier than planning one or more moves a turn and then waiting for the results to be calculated and displayed, as in TBS. This feature became important as the potential buying population grew along with the industry; the new breed were often less enamored with the traditional wargame, with its complex strategy, statistics, and concern with historical accuracy. Titles like Chris Crawford's *Eastern Front (1941)* (Atari, 1981; Atari 8-bit), Hudson Soft's *Military Madness* (1989; NEC TurboGrafx-16, and others),[6] MicroProse's *X-COM: UFO Defense* (1993; PC, Sony PlayStation),[7] SSI's *Panzer General* (1994; Apple Macintosh, PC, Sony PlayStation), and Irrational Games' *Freedom Force* (2002; Apple Macintosh, PC) were well-designed, approachable, critically acclaimed, and ultimately sold well. Nevertheless, those games and others like them never allowed the TBS to reach the same critical mass in both depth and breadth of mainstream titles as RTS.

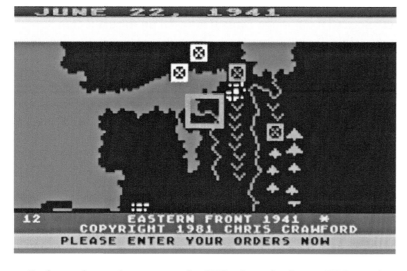

Screenshot from Chris Crawford's user-friendly TBS game, *Eastern Front* (1941).

Perhaps the main reason why RTS triumphed over TBS gaming is that it's a purely electronic creation. The only real analog is taking command of a real-life army, an activity probably best engaged in virtually. Although the top TBS games add slick and logical interfaces, automate the complex statistical calculations automatically behind the scenes, and may even feature impressive audiovisual elements, there is nothing inherent in such a game that can't be done between two or more dedicated players sitting at a table with a well-designed board game.[8]

---

[6]Also known as *Nectaris*, depending upon territory and/or platform.

[7]*UFO: Enemy Unknown* in Europe and Australia.

[8]Sometimes referred to as "pen-and-paper" games.

Dune II's optional mouse-driven interface enables fast yet precise input that works well with the real-time gameplay.

As its name implies, *Dune II* was represented as a sequel to an earlier game, Cyro Interactive's *Dune* (1990; Commodore Amiga, PC, Sega CD). Although *Dune II* is based on the same franchise, it is a vastly different experience. The original *Dune* is an adventure/strategy hybrid closely based on David Lynch's film *Dune,* which is itself based (or perhaps "inspired by") Frank Herbert's novel by the same name. Cyro's *Dune* is noted for easy, hand-holding gameplay, which guides the player (who takes on the role of the novel and movie's main character, Paul Atreides) along a path similar to the movie's. Paul must recruit help from the Fremen, a mysterious race of desert dwellers who have somehow managed to survive and even thrive in the harsh environment of the planet Arrakis. Arrakis is the only known source of Melange, also known as Spice, a mystical substance required for space travel and quasi-immortality. Arrakis was formerly the sole domain of vile House Harkonnen, who aren't in the least pleased with Atreides' arrival on the planet. Without spoiling the story, the gist of the game's plot is that Paul has mystical powers and must fulfill his role in an ancient prophecy. Although the game seems mostly concerned with keeping the player headed toward that goal, there are some basic strategy components as well. Players must specify which of the converted Fremen will mine ore and which will fight, and must equip and train them. In other words, the germ of what would become *Dune II* is present in the original, though the all-important strategic elements are buried underneath a fairly linear adventure game.[9]

---

[9]On a side note, *Dune's* soundtrack, composed by the French game composer Stéphane Picq, is considered some of the best music ever heard in a Commodore Amiga or PC game. It's been frequently remixed and updated, and remains a staple on sites that offer downloads of classic game music.

The first *Dune* has a few things in common with its sequel, but is far more focused on adventure and story than strategy.

Dune II differs most notably from its predecessor in its far greater emphasis on action and strategy over plot. Indeed, Westwood even dared to alter Frank Herbert's story, introducing a third house (House Ordos) and omitting the characters from the novel. The story here is that the emperor is low on funds, and has essentially improvised a contest to see which of the three houses can harvest the most Spice from Arrakis. The player begins as a military commander of the house of his or her choice, gradually building up Spice and eventually fighting for sole supremacy with the other houses and even the emperor.

Dune II's gameplay is instantly familiar to anyone who has played modern RTS games, and it's easy to forget how revolutionary it felt in 1992. For instance, clicking on a unit causes it to play a sound sample; "Yes, sir," for example. This convention would be carried over into most later RTS games such as *Warcraft*.[10] More important, though, is how the passage of "real time"—that is, the actual time the player interacts with the game—affects the gameplay. Though we've discussed a parallel issue with role-playing games in Chapter 4, "*Diablo* (1997): The Rogue Goes to Hell," it's worthwhile to raise it again in the context of strategy games.

The essential difference between RTS and TBS games is the gameplay. TBS games can be compared to a game of chess or checkers, in which each player can theoretically take as long as he or she wants to make a move. The other player cannot legally move until the first has moved.[11] If we wanted to make chess more like an RTS, the players would not wait for each other, but

---

[10]*Warcraft*'s implementation of speech took a more humorous slant; for instance, grunts that would grow increasingly agitated after repeated clicks.

[11]Unless the game is specifically designed to allow other players, typically remote-human or computer-controlled, to perform certain activities in the background for expediency's sake.

Blizzard's first foray into RTS, *Warcraft*, proved decisive for the company.

would move their pieces as frequently as they could. However, the differences between RTS and TBS are a bit more profound than this analogy suggests. Indeed, a set of real-time rules for chess would probably also include penalties for moving across certain squares, or a "cooling off" period for certain pieces. For instance, whereas in traditional chess the queen can move an unlimited number of spaces per turn, in a real-time version, she might only move one square every 30 seconds, whereas a pawn could only move one square every five minutes. Obviously, such factors would be impractical, if not impossible, to account for in the board game, but computers can easily track such variables, making for some very interesting strategic possibilities. Most fans of RTS games feel that the real-time aspect makes them more intense, whereas TBS fans can argue that their preferred setup allots more time for decisions and can thus seem much larger and more complex. Indeed, a single turn in *Civilization IV* (2K Games, 2005; Apple Macintosh, PC) can easily take 15 minutes or more.

Another important consideration is the number of computers one has available on the same network. Most multiplayer RTS games require at least two networked computers, whereas it's usually possible to "hot seat" a TBS. A hot seat game means that players literally take turns sitting in front of the computer; the seat is still warm when the next player takes over. Although *Dune II* is a single-player game, later RTS games would allow for multiple players over a LAN; a direct computer-to-computer connection via either serial cable or modem; and eventually, the Internet. These games include Blizzard's aforementioned *Warcraft: Orcs and Humans* (1994; Apple Macintosh, PC) and *Command & Conquer* (1995; Apple Macintosh, PC, Sega Saturn,

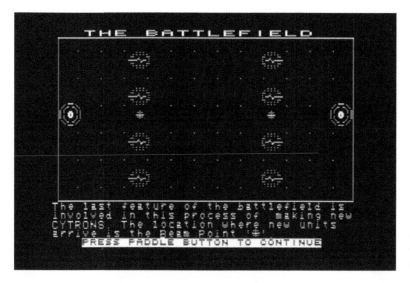

Screenshot from the animated tutorial from the original Apple II version of *Cytron Masters*.

and others), a deeply in uential game codeveloped by Westwood and Looking Glass Studios.

As we noted near the beginning of this chapter, *Dune II* wasn't the first attempt at an RTS, and it's worth taking a moment to examine the earlier pioneers. Perhaps the most cited games in this context are Dani Bunten's aforementioned *Cytron Masters*, Dan Daglow's *Utopia* (Mattel, 1981; Mattel Aquarius and Intellivision), and Technosoft's *Herzog Zwei* (1990; Sega Genesis).

Dani Bunten, perhaps better known for the Electronic Arts' multiplayer classic *M.U.L.E.* (1983; Atari 8-bit, Nintendo Entertainment System, and others) and the action adventure *The Seven Cities of Gold* (1984; Apple II, Commodore 64, and others), is certainly an intriguing developer worthy of a book of her own. *Cytron Masters*, published by SSI for the Apple II and Atari 8-bit computers, was a rather abstract war game with a real-time component. Two players[12] work to conquer each other's command centers by building cytrons, "cybernetic electronic units" that can perform different tasks. Bunten herself remarked in her memoirs that "rather than appealing to both action gamers and strategy gamers, it seemed to fall in the crack between them."[13] Bunten followed up these concepts in 1988 with *Modem Wars* (Electronic Arts; Commodore 64, PC). This revolutionary game took the important step of having the players connect to each other via modems; that way, each could have full control of his or her own machine and screen rather than

---

[12]Or one against a rather perfunctory computer opponent.

[13]http://www.anticlockwise.com/dani/personal/biz/memoir.htm. Additionally, a tribute in the October 1998 issue of *Game Developer* magazine by Brian Moriarty described *Cytron Masters* as a "two-player design [that] offered a curious conjunction of strategy and real-time action in a game that pushed the Apple II hardware to its limits."

having to share. Unfortunately, at the time, the lack of widespread modem use and long-distance telephone service costs for those that did prevented the game from achieving great sales, and, for all their innovation, neither *Cytron Masters* nor *Modem Wars* seem to have had much in uence on other RTS games.

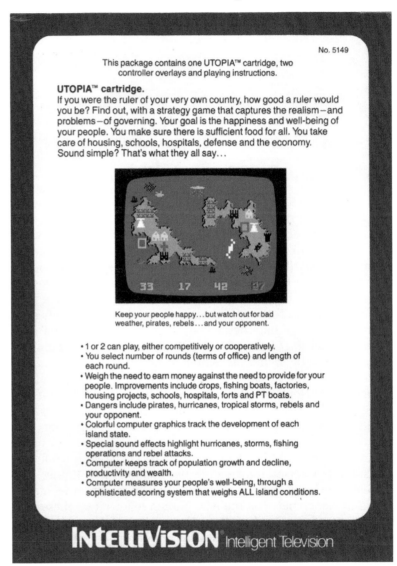

Box back from Mattel's *Utopia*, Intellivision version.

Dan Daglow's *Utopia* is another very interesting game from the early 1980s, often claimed as the predecessor of Maxis' *SimCity* and Bullfrog's *Populous* (both 1989 for various systems). A strictly two-player game,[14] *Utopia* put players in charge

---

[14]A single player could play for a high score if they so chose by simply leaving the other island abandoned.

of their own island economy. The goal is to construct buildings on the island, generating revenue and curtailing rebellion. However, since the players couldn't directly attack each other and combat was highly abstract, *Utopia* ultimately has more in common with *SimCity* than *Dune II* and later RTS games. *SimCity* and *Populous* were certainly better known than *Utopia*, and were widely admired by critics and gamers alike in the early 1990s. Although these games were not focused on combat, they did feature many of the elements that would become established conventions of the RTS genre. *Populous* is a "God game" that puts players in the role of a god who can manipulate land to aid followers and stymie the followers of the rival god. *SimCity* (Chapter 15), lets players plan and build a city, which develops in real time. As a parallel, *Dune II* takes both land and structures into consideration; for instance, players can build structures only on concrete foundations.

Screenshot from *Herzog Zwei*, a surprisingly forward-thinking console RTS.

According to the popular gaming website, 1up.com, *Herzog Zwei* is "in many ways the progenitor of all modern real-time strategy games," and claims that it laid the foundation for *Dune II* and later RTS games.[15] However, this rather obscure game by Technosoft didn't make it to Western shores until 1990 and is actually a sequel to *Herzog*, a game released only in Japan. Although the sequel is very popular among members of the Genesis community, for others it seems more of a historical curiosity, and there is little evidence to support 1up's claim. Regardless, *Herzog Zwei* is definitely

---

[15]See http://www.1up.com/do/feature?cId=3134179.

a forward-thinking game with many features commonly seen in later RTS games. It supports one or two players (via a split screen), who compete in real time to take over neutral bases, gradually producing the combat units necessary to destroy their enemy's base. Players directly control a ying transport ship that can transform into a robotic armor type combat unit. Although a very interesting game, it was not well received at the time and only later achieved cult status.

In short, while there were plenty of games that shared or introduced *Dune II*'s pivotal features, it stands alone as the first true modern RTS. It was the first to take advantage of the mouse and keyboard combo that had started to take over the computer gaming scene, and its high-resolution graphics made it possible to distinguish units and view a wider gaming map than ever before. Furthermore, its graphics were not abstract as in many earlier wargames, but representational—a trike looked like a trike, not a symbol. The vehicles even make trails in the sand they travel across. It's difficult to exaggerate the importance of mouse control as well, which made scrolling the map and selecting units far more efficient than ever before. However, even these innovations would have been for naught if the game hadn't been fun to play. Fortunately, Westwood's game offered some of the best gameplay of its era, coupled with high production values.

There could easily be an entire book on the many RTS games that followed in *Dune II*'s wake, including innovators like Chris Taylor's *Total Annihilation* (GT Interactive, 1997; Apple Macintosh, PC), which featured 3D units and terrain that in uenced gameplay; and Ensemble Studios' *Age of Empires* (Microsoft, 1997; Apple Macintosh, PC, Pocket PC), which combined the civilization-building elements from *Civilization* with typical RTS mechanics. Perhaps the two most enduring are the *Warcraft* and *Command & Conquer* series. *Warcraft: Orcs & Humans* was a tremendously successful game that helped establish Blizzard as one of the world's eminent game developers. Its gameplay is unmistakably in uenced by *Dune II*, though themed on fantasy rather than sci-fi. The game also featured popular options for multiple players over LANs, a pivotal feature that took advantage of the networking frenzy created by id's *Doom* (Chapter 5, "*Doom* (1993): The First-Person Shooter Takes Control"), which had penetrated to the core of the computer gaming industry. *Warcraft* spawned three sequels, and at least some of the gameplay seen in the massively multiplayer RPG, *World of Warcraft* (see Chapter 24, "*Ultima Online* (1997): Putting the Role-Play Back in Computer Role-Playing Games"), is borrowed from the older title (as well as the characters and stories). Of course, Blizzard's *StarCraft* (1998 for various systems) series of best-selling RTS games is also impossible to ignore.

Total Annihilation's key innovation was its 3D terrain, which influenced gameplay. For instance, units could move across hills, but at reduced speed.

Command & Conquer (1995; Apple Macintosh, Nintendo 64, PC, and others) was developed by Westwood, so it's certainly no surprise that many of *Dune II*'s best qualities show up in this long-lived series. This massive and many-forked franchise would take some time and space to describe accurately. Some of the games are based on sci-fi settings, whereas the *Red Alert* games (beginning 1996) are alternate history, in which Albert Einstein finds a way to travel back in time to assassinate Hitler. The *Generals* branch (beginning 2003) is not connected to the earlier games, introducing a storyline set in modern times.

The *Red Alert* series of *Command & Conquer* games pits the Allies against the Soviets.

In these and other RTS games, gameplay is based on building structures, generating units, managing resources, and engaging in strategic combat. This formula, first to see maturation in *Dune II*, has consistently proven successful with gamers, and there seems little doubt that RTS games will continue being produced and thrilling gamers worldwide for many years to come, particularly as efforts continue to streamline interfaces for play on gamepads.[16]

---

[16]Although every new console RTS seems to boast that it has at last overcome this challenge, computers remain the platform of choice for most fans of the genre.

FINAL FANTASY VII (1997): IT'S NEVER FINAL IN THE WORLD OF FANTASY

For countless gamers in the United States and Japan, the *Final Fantasy* series are more than just games—they're *the* games. Just hearing the word "Chocobo" or "Moogle"[1] is enough to tickle the thumbs of dedicated fans all over the world. Indeed, few video-game franchises in the history of the industry have enjoyed the popularity, longevity, and high acclaim of Hironobu Sakaguchi's epic series. The first *Final Fantasy*, developed during a financial crisis at Square, not only rescued the company but soon became

Final Fantasy VII offered an immense area to explore, including populated towns where players could buy equipment, talk to the locals, and advance the plot. The red triangles indicate possible exits, and the white glove makes it easier to spot the main character.

[1]Not to be confused with J. K. Rowling's word "Muggle," meaning a person not born in a magical world and lacking any sort of magical ability, in the 1997 U.K. book *Harry Potter and the Philosopher's Stone*.

a definitive console role-playing game—a reputation the series continues to enjoy. Because the series is much too lengthy and complex to cover adequately in a single chapter, we've decided to focus here on *Final Fantasy VII.*

Why the seventh game? Although fans and critics argue (often quite divisively) about which of the many *Final Fantasy* games are the best or most in uential, the seventh game is perhaps the most interesting from a historical perspective. It was the first to take advantage of the CD-ROM format, a decision that necessitated (or perhaps justified) Square's infamous break with Nintendo and new partnership with Sony. This exclusive partnership played an important role in the PlayStation's commercial dominance over the Nintendo 64. *Final Fantasy VII* is also notable for being the first of the series to receive an official PC Windows port, which expanded its audience and in uence considerably. It also made the transition from the 2D of its predecessors to 3D, polygonal characters on pre-rendered backgrounds.[2] Though the graphics may look primitive by modern standards, they were stunning in 1997.

Finally, and perhaps most importantly, *Final Fantasy VII* is arguably among the best games ever made. The highly polished gameplay, lavish production, intricate storyline, and well-developed characters all contribute to the game's high playability, then and now. It has won countless awards and remains at the top of many online and printed best-of lists. In August of 2006, GameSpot named it one of its "Greatest Games of All Time," remarking that "the game stands the test of time."[3] IGN's contemporary review called it a "cinematic wonder," the "RPG by which all others are to be measured."[4] There is even a computer animated film based on the game, *Final Fantasy VII: Advent Children*, released in the United States in 2006.[5] In this chapter, we'll explore the history of the game and touch on the series, paying particular attention to what makes it so different from most Western role-playing games.

Final Fantasy VII raises a number of contentious issues among fans of computer and console role-playing games. Some of these issues are technical and are concerned with how the game handles combat and leveling, the quintessential components of any role-playing game (henceforth, RPG; we'll ignore the table-top RPG and focus on electronic games only). The *Final Fantasy* series is famous for experimenting with combat and leveling systems, and because of or despite these many changes, the series has continued to please old fans and win over new gamers, year after year. Another major concern is the role of story and plot

---

[2]See Chapter 1, "*Alone in the Dark* (1992): The Polygons of Fear," for more on this technique.

[3]See http://www.gamespot.com/features/6155700/index.html.

[4]See http://psx.ign.com/articles/150/150494p1.html.

[5]The movie picks up two years after the events in the game.

in RPGs. Whereas most RPGs originating in the United States and Europe were focused primarily on tactics and statistics, the eastern RPGs of Japan distinguished themselves by railing their gameplay into tightly orchestrated, linear narratives. This convention turned off some fans of American RPGs, who preferred freedom to directorial control. A good example of this trend in modern RPGs is Bethesda's *The Elder Scrolls IV: Oblivion* (2007; Microsoft Xbox, PC, Sony PlayStation 3), a game praised for its open-ended, "sandbox"-style gameplay. What we'll see in our discussion of *Final Fantasy VII* is how its emphasis on character development and storytelling plays out in one of the most celebrated of all Japanese RPGs. However, the first issue we'll address here is the cultural differences between the American and Japanese gaming communities.

We see one crucial difference in the types of games preferred by the two markets, particularly as they stood in the late 1990s. Although the American audience for console RPGs was humble, this was completely untrue of the Japanese market, where Enix's *Dragon Quest* (*Dragon Warrior* in the West) and other console-based RPGs dominated the shelves. Indeed, an article in *Newsweek* about *Final Fantasy VII* condescendingly referred to American gamers as "vidiots [who would] rather twitch-and-shoot or fight hand to hand than explore and interact."[6] These and other critics hoped that *Final Fantasy VII* might at last inspire more U.S. gamers to turn away from the latest *Mortal Kombat* or *Street Fighter*[7] and engage in what they saw as a much more thoughtful and substantial genre. Although it's debatable whether *Final Fantasy VII* answered their prayers, many of the millions of gamers who purchased it for the PlayStation or PC became dedicated—even fanatical—fans of the franchise.

Another key cultural difference worth addressing is cuteness, or what Chris Kohler calls "kawaisa."[8] Although the majority of American RPGs are quite serious and even gritty in tone, most (if not all) Japanese RPGs prominently feature cute, comic-relief type characters, often juxtaposed (or clashing) with more mature themes and situations. It's likely this element of kawaisa that traditional RPG fans find so off-putting about *Final Fantasy VII* and other games. Though it is well beyond the scope of this chapter to analyze kawaisa in the Japanese context, it seems to be a defining characteristic of the manga style of comics and graphic novels that have so deeply permeated Japanese popular culture.

---

[6]Croal, N'Gai, and Rambler, Mark. 1997. "More game than guns." *Newsweek*, 07/15/97, Vol. 130, Iss. 11, p. 11.

[7]See Chapter 17, "*Street Fighter II* (1991): Would You Like the Combo?"

[8]For a much lengthier and insightful look at Japanese versus American gaming culture, see Kohler's *Power Up: How Japanese Video Games Gave the World an Extra Life* (Brady Games, 2004).

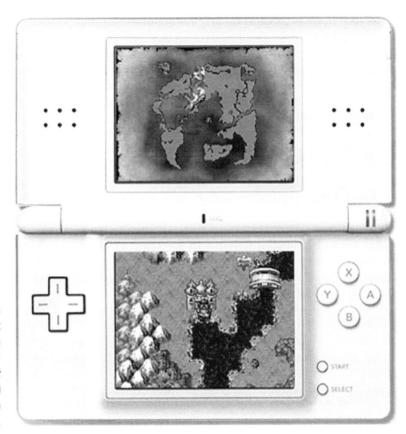

The *Dragon Quest* series has always been huge in Japan, but has had more modest success in the United States. Promotional image for *Dragon Quest IV: Chapters of the Chosen* (2007) from Square Enix for the dual-screen Nintendo DS.

Japanese audiences also seem less concerned with graphical realism than American gamers, many of whom value realism over the exquisite but highly stylized aesthetics of famous manga artists and the "super-deformed" style[9] of games like *Final Fantasy VII*. To put it simply, Western gamers raised on *Ultima* and *The Bard's Tale*[10] may have a hard time getting over kids with blue, spiky hair and enormous eyes, to say nothing of kawaisa-like talking kitties (Sega's *Phantasy Star*) and smiling slimes (*Dragon Warrior*). These gamers can seem prejudiced in their criticism of Japanese RPGs, which can seem quite juvenile to the uninitiated. Fortunately for Japanese developers hoping to tap into the U.S. market, this cultural rift has narrowed, thanks to the in ux of anime and manga, a growing movement that *Final Fantasy VII* might very well have sparked. More Americans than ever have been exposed to hit films from Hayao Miyazaki (2001's *Spirited Away* and

---

[9]Meaning characters drawn in an exaggerated manner, often with large heads and small, stocky bodies.

[10]See Chapter 23, "*Ultima* (1980): The Immaculate Conception of the Computer Role-Playing Game."

2004's *Howl's Moving Castle*) and rave about many of the anime programs now broadcast on outlets like the SCI FI Channel.

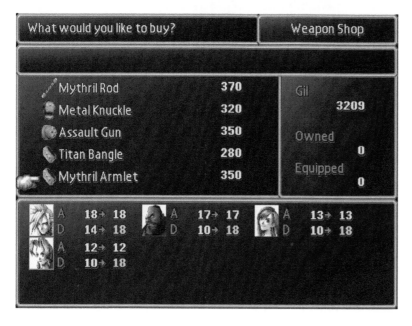

Like most role-playing games, *Final Fantasy VII* offered plenty of shops where characters can buy equipment. The bottom row shows how each character would benefit from the item, including characters that aren't currently in the party. Since characters can wear only one piece of armor (an armlet or bangle), these choices are very significant.

There is also the problem of language. As anyone knows who has even the most basic knowledge of linguistics, translation is a difficult and frightfully inaccurate process. Grammar and syntax aren't the only obstacles; a much larger problem is the cultural concepts and understandings expressed in language. For instance, games such as Shigeru Miyamoto's *Devil World* (Nintendo, 1984; Nintendo Famicom, NES) were not released in the United States because of their rampant religious imagery, which may well have offended some American gamers and brought negative publicity to Nintendo. Kohler gives several such examples in his book, but for our purposes it's enough to realize that even with superb translation, at least some important concepts will be lost. What seems confusing, inappropriate, or even incoherent to us may make perfect sense in the original language and cultural context. One characteristic quality of the pre-2000 *Final Fantasy* games is inaccurate—even laughable—translations. Thankfully, the later Nintendo Game Boy Advance (GBA) and DS ports have been retranslated and handled with care.

Much as Richard Garriott and Origin altered and even redefined the gameplay mechanics of each new *Ultima* title, the long-lived *Final Fantasy* series has itself often changed. However, this is not to say that the series has evolved in a linear progression. Instead, innovations that appear in one game may be omitted from the next, only to be restored later in altered form. Some of these

Here, the characters in *Final Fantasy VII* are given the chance to order a meal. The goal is to procure a coupon that can be turned in at the pharmacy.

changes fundamentally alter the gameplay, such as the Active Time Battle (ATB) introduced in 1991's *Final Fantasy IV* (released as *Final Fantasy II* in the West). ATB revolutionized combat with a hybrid turn-based system. Although it superficially resembled the turn-based games of its predecessors, now the characters' turns were timed and required faster reactions from players. ATB seemed the right system at the right time, appealing to the Super NES generation, who were far more familiar with classic action games like *Super Mario Bros.*[11] than legendary RPGs like *Ultima.* A seminal innovation introduced in the fifth *Final Fantasy* game is the refined job system, designed by Hiroyuki Itō.[12] This system offered vast customization options for characters, allowing them to train in more than 22 jobs that ranged from traditional classes (Thief, Knight) to some seen in no other RPG (Dancer, Mime). Each of these jobs eventually offered secondary abilities, such as the Dancer's irt, which reset the enemy's ATB timer. Characters could train in a job long enough to learn some of its secondary abilities, then switch to other jobs for some truly interesting and effective combinations. This incredibly exible and nuanced system was largely missing in the next installment, whose characters were limited to a single, prechosen job. The ATB and refined job system are only two obvious examples; a more comprehensive history could list many more important innovations, discussing at length how they affected gameplay.

[11]See Chapter 19, "*Super Mario Bros.* (1985): How High Can Jumpman Get?"

[12]An earlier job system had been introduced in *Final Fantasy III*, which was released in Japan in 1990. It was recently updated and released in the U.S. for the Nintendo DS in 2006.

Now that we've covered some of the background issues surrounding the series, let's delve into *Final Fantasy VII* itself. As the first of the series to break from the confines of cartridge onto the seemingly unlimited vistas of multiple CD-ROMs, *Final Fantasy VII* was intended to launch a bold new generation of console RPGs. The massive increase in storage space made it possible to incorporate full-motion video (FMV), or prerendered cut scenes that interrupted gameplay to advance the plot and character development. Interestingly, however, the developers did not incorporate digitized speech, having gamers instead read vast amounts of onscreen text. Voiceovers wouldn't appear until *Final Fantasy X*, released four years later for the PlayStation 2 (PS2).

Shown here is part of a minigame in *Final Fantasy VII* in which Cloud must perform more squats than his opponent. The minigames vary in their control schemes, but this one involves pushing a sequence of three buttons on the controller in rapid succession.

Though CD-ROMs offered much more storage space than cartridges, they were infamous for long loading times. Loading delays were commonplace for computer gamers, but console gamers had come to expect instant gratification. One of Square-Soft's main concerns was that *Final Fantasy VII* would suffer from the long loading times that dogged other CD-ROM games found on earlier platforms like the Sega CD, ruining the pace of the game and turning off gamers. Thankfully, Square devised clever programming feats that minimized or even eliminated loading downtime, pleasing gamers and impressing critics.

Sony's PlayStation was far better equipped to handle advanced 3D graphics than the Super NES had been, and SquareSoft (formerly Square, now Square Enix) meant to take full advantage

Shown here are Aeris and Cloud, dressed up as a girl in *Final Fantasy VII*. The cross-dressing is necessary to get past the Don's guards. The story suggests that many girls are being raped by the Don and his henchmen.

of the technology. Many games before *Final Fantasy VII* had very impressive cut scenes that featured far superior graphics to the in-game graphics. Although SquareSoft's game had the same type of disparity, *Final Fantasy VII* surpassed gamers' expectations by placing many of the best special effects in-game, making even routine battles superior to the cut scenes of other games. Battles are shown from an immense variety of camera angles, keeping these repetitive sequences fresh and appealing. The developers also blended the cut scenes carefully into the gameplay, lending the game a more coherent, film-like feel. In many games, the cut scenes tell a story that seems only marginally related to the actual gameplay. This rupture between gameplay and cut scene can make gamers feel little connection to the protagonist. *Final Fantasy VII* succeeds marvelously in bridging this gap, keeping players firmly tied to their onscreen persona.

Beyond all these important graphical innovations, *Final Fantasy VII* also offered two new gameplay features: Materia and Limit Breaks. One surprising aspect of the game is that the characters can wear only one piece of armor and a relic. This limitation is a substantial departure from other RPGs, which place great emphasis on finding and equipping dozens of various pieces. However, the game compensates for this simplicity with Materia, an evolved form of the "Esper system" seen in the sixth game. Materia can be inserted into slots on certain pieces of equipment. The manual breaks it into five color-coded categories:

- Independent (Purple): Enhances stats
- Support (Blue): Increases the effects of other Materia
- Command (Yellow): Grants new combat abilities

- Magic (Green): Lets character cast offensive or healing spells
- Summon (Red): Allows characters to summon monsters

Materia levels up along with the players, assuming it has been equipped. Higher-level Materia offers new or greater abilities. Furthermore, it can be swapped between items or party members, greatly expanding the possibilities for customizing characters. Materia also plays a critical role in the plot, which we'll discuss in a moment.

The Limit Break is a variation of the "desperation attack" that debuted in 1994's *Final Fantasy VI* (released as *Final Fantasy III* in the West). In the sixth game, characters gained special, powerful attacks when their health bars were low. The seventh game borrowed this concept, but now the effect's meter fills up with each enemy attack. Once the Limit Break is achieved, characters can use it immediately or save it for a future battle. Higher-level characters gain additional Limit Break attacks, and the regeneration rate is affected by the character's emotional state: fury increases it, and sadness slows it down. The Materia and Limit Break systems are a great way to add variety and complexity to what would otherwise become very tedious battle sequences.

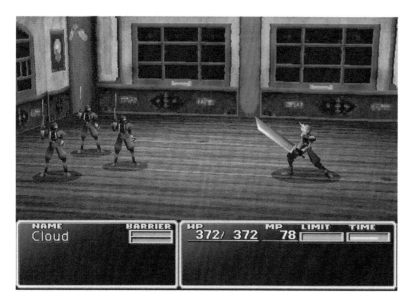

A typical combat scene in *Final Fantasy VII* has Cloud pitted against three opponents. When the "time" bar fills, Cloud is able to execute a move. When the "limit" bar fills, he can execute a "break," a special, super-powerful move.

A final technical consideration worthy of note is the highly acclaimed soundtrack composed by Nobuo Uematsu, perhaps one of the industry's best-known game composers. Uematsu realized that the PlayStation gave him many more channels of sound to work with than had been possible with the Super NES. Instead of that unit's humble eight channels, Uematsu now had 24, though eight of those were reserved for sound effects. However, Uetmatsu decided to use the PlayStation's integrated MIDI support rather than incorporate prerecorded sounds, which would have required longer loading delays. Nevertheless, the score is varied and effective, and has subsequently been rearranged and released on commercial audio CDs and remixed by dozens of amateur artists. However, Uematsu's decision to rely on the PlayStation's sound hardware was disastrous for the PC port, whose MIDI output tended to sound tinny and outmoded in many PCs. Fortunately for PC owners, a variety of unofficial patches and fixes are available to address this problem.

Although the game's graphics and audio may seem dated today, modern gamers can still appreciate the story and richly developed characters. Unlike previous *Final Fantasy* games, *Final Fantasy VII* is set in what can perhaps best be described as an alternative future of fantasy and sci-fi; factories and robots mesh with magic and swordplay. The game is set on Gaia, a planet being slowly destroyed by the giant corporation named Shinra. Shinra is killing the planet to acquire a mystical energy called Mako, though its ultimate purpose isn't clear until much later in the game. The main character, Cloud Strife, begins the game as a hesitant mercenary assisting a group of eco-terrorists named AVALANCHE. AVALANCHE is committed to destroying the Mako reactors, but they are opposed by SOLDIER, Shinra's elite squadron of fighters.

Eventually, Cloud finds himself embroiled not only with AVALANCHE but a girl named Aerith, a sweet " ower girl" who turns out to be much more important than anyone expects. Cloud agrees to be Aerith's bodyguard, and it's up to the player to decide how to handle her as a love interest. Aerith is being pursued by SOLDIER, who may be interested in what she believes to be useless white Materia. Because the game's story is often considered one of its most memorable features, it would be a shame to give away the many surprises for the sake of summary. Suffice it to say that many gamers came to love the characters and care about what happened to them, and the narrative turns out to be much darker and sophisticated than the typical RPG. Although the game certainly scores high in the fun department, it has also brought many tears to the eyes of sensitive gamers.

Final Fantasy VII was a grand success for SquareSoft, and it's hardly surprising that sequels would soon follow. The eighth game appeared in 1999, again for Sony's PlayStation. This game eschews the "super-deformed" in-game look of the previous games for a more realistic, Western aesthetic. Though still hugely successful, the sequel met with more negativity than its predecessor. Andrew Vestal of GameSpot wrote that "a large part of the game simply consists of proceeding from area to area with little or no impetus

This cut scene from *Final Fantasy VII* is an odd mix of humor and dread, because the Don clearly intends to rape Tifa. The odd juxtapositions of "inappropriate" humor and gritty realism are one of the more intriguing aspects of Japanese role-playing games.

to continue, and the main villain is almost assuredly the least threatening in the series' history," giving the game an 8.5 out of 10 point score.[13] IGN's David Smith had more praise, but still noted that "*Final Fantasy* may be showing its age, or perhaps more precisely a lack of evolution to suit that age."[14] Both reviewers criticized the audio, which they felt didn't rise to the series' own high standards. However, the bulk of the reviews in other publications had nothing but praise, and it's likely that SquareSoft had simply pushed the PlayStation's capabilities too far in the previous game. The technological leap from *Final Fantasy VI* to *VII* was immediately noticeable, but the next game simply didn't have much more to offer in terms of audiovisuals.

Final Fantasy IX, released in 2000 for the Sony PlayStation, abandoned the realistically proportioned characters of its prequel and dove back into traditional anime-style graphics. It was billed as a return to the series' roots—welcome news indeed to longtime fans of the series. By this point, the first PlayStation was showing its age; the PS2 had debuted the same year. Nevertheless, SquareSoft was able to push the original system to the limits, and critics were generally pleased with the result. IGN's David Smith wrote that the developers had built a fantasy world "he would be content to stare at," praising the graphics while wondering if the gameplay might be "showing its age."[15] Andrew Vestal

[13]See http://www.gamespot.com/ps/rpg/finalfantasy9/review.html.

[14]See http://psx.ign.com/articles/162/162190p1.html.

[15]See http://psx.ign.com/articles/162/162190p1.html.

of GameSpot felt that the game was "great" despite feeling like "a throwback" to earlier games in the series.[16]

Although the earlier *Final Fantasy* games have been rereleased on modern platforms, they were very different games from their later sequels, playing much more like traditional Western RPGs. Box back for *Final Fantasy I & II: Dawn of Souls* (2004) for the Nintendo Game Boy Advance shown here.

The tenth game, *Final Fantasy X*, debuted in December 2001 for the PS2. Meeting with near-universal acclaim, the tenth game abandoned the prerendered backdrops of its predecessors and replaced them with full 3D environments. Facial expressions are now more realistic and detailed, an apt innovation considering that this is the first game in the series to incorporate digitized speech. A direct sequel, *Final Fantasy X-2*, followed in 2003. This game features a female cast and was yet another commercial success for the company.

Final Fantasy XI marks a severe departure from the previous installments, abandoning the tried-and-true single-player campaign for the massively multiplayer online (MMO) model.[17] It debuted in 2002 in Japan for the PS2 and was released later

---

[16]See http://tinyurl.com/69rjxy.

[17]See Chapter 24, "*Ultima Online* (1997): Putting the Role-Play Back in Computer Role-Playing Games."

Japanese RPGs have gone in weird—and for many gamers, wonderful—new directions. Back of the box for *Kingdom Hearts* for the Sony PlayStation 2 shown here, which combines the worlds of *Final Fantasy* and Walt Disney into an enjoyable experience for fans of both properties.

in other territories, as well as in PC and Microsoft Xbox 360 formats. Although the game enjoyed initial success, the arrival of Blizzard's *World of Warcraft* in 2004 ended its dominance on the MMO charts. The criticisms and explanations for the game's performance are many, but most seem to agree on one point: Square Enix simply had neither distinguished itself from the competition nor learned from their successes. At first it didn't offer the Player-Versus-Player (PVP) options that popularized its rivals, and it suffered from the usual setbacks with lag and exploits that plagued other new MMOs. Greg Kasavin of GameSpot complained about the lengthy installation required for the Windows PC version, which took over an hour after all the necessary patching and updating.[18] According to the latest information available from MMOGCHART.com, a website dedicated to tracking MMO subscriptions, *Final Fantasy XI* commanded only 3.1% of the total market share in April 2008.[19] *World of Warcraft*, meanwhile, commanded 62.2% of the market during the same period, with more than 10 million active subscribers. Nevertheless, the game is the longest-lived MMO in the console market, where it can avoid direct competition from *World of Warcraft* and the many other computer-specific MMOs.

Given the developer's lengthy record of past successes and stunning innovations, the modest response to its first foray into the online world seems puzzling. Beyond the technical aspects already mentioned, perhaps the key failure is the lack of a solid, coherent narrative and memorable characters. Although the game did employ a variety of set quests and cinematics, these elements tended to get buried in the rather repetitive, exacting nature of the gameplay; this was no game for novices. A few American gamers also resented having to wait so long to enter the world, which had been colonized a year earlier by Japanese gamers, many of whom had already risen to the highest levels and were far more powerful than the U.S. immigrants. Despite several expansions, *Final Fantasy's* MMO simply hasn't managed to win the acclaim of its single-player cousins. Hiromichi Tanaka, Square Enix's producer, told *Electronic Gaming Monthly* that the next online incarnation will "aim for something different from the beginning," though it's unclear at this point what this entails.[20]

Perhaps in response to the relatively faint praise received for *XI*, Square Enix returned to the single-player model for its next sequel, *Final Fantasy XII*, which debuted in North America in 2006. This PS2 exclusive helped restore the series' former glory. The random encounters were gone, and story and character development took center stage. The game is also notable for its highly effective voice cast, which Greg Kasavin of GameSpot felt "deserved special mention" and Jeremy Dunham of IGN called "top-notch."[21] Perhaps the largest change to the gameplay is that now combat didn't involve switching to a different screen, one of several new features likely inspired or borrowed from the online game. This smoothed out the narrative by reducing the disruptions caused by the frequent random encounters of its predecessors. However, a more controversial change was the ability to

---

[18]See http://www.gamespot.com/pc/rpg/finalfantasy11/review.html. Surprisingly, the console versions also feature lengthy hard drive installs.

[19]See http://www.mmogchart.com for the latest charts.

[20]*Electronic Gaming Monthly*, September 2008 Issue 232, pp. 34–35.

[21]See http://www.gamespot.com/ps2/rpg/finalfantasy12/review.html and http://ps2.ign.com/articles/741/741991p4.html, respectively.

automate many of the tasks that formerly had to be managed for each character in the party. Some gamers felt that the result was hands-off gameplay; others thought it was a great leap forward. In any case, the game continues to sell well and is overall highly regarded. Of note, *Final Fantasy XII* is set in Ivalice, the game world explored earlier in the *Final Fantasy Tactics* games, among the most important in terms of the numerous *Final Fantasy* series spin-offs and compilations.

Released for the PlayStation in 1998 (a year earlier in Japan), *Final Fantasy Tactics* is labeled as a "tactical role-playing game," a subgenre that emphasizes strategic combat. In the case of *Final Fantasy Tactics,* this involves a fully 3D isometric battlefield that can be rotated to offer a better view. Though not as popular as the main *Final Fantasy* series, a spin-off named *Final Fantasy Tactics Advance* was released in 2003 for the Nintendo Game Boy Advance. A sequel to this game, *Final Fantasy Tactics A2*, followed in 2008. All of these games are set in Ivalice, Yasumi Matsuno's creation. The central idea behind Ivalice is that magic coexists with machinery. It's essentially a medieval world based loosely on Christian Europe, including a powerful religious institution named the Glabados Church.

The *Final Fantasy* franchise is so immense and diverse that it's easy to get lost in the many sequels, spin-offs, and cross-overs. However, it's important not to lose sight of *Final Fantasy VII*'s role in establishing this franchise in the United States. Although the series had always been popular among console RPG aficionados, it wasn't until the seventh game that it really hit the U.S. mainstream. Gamers who had never played an RPG, much less a *Final Fantasy* game, were drawn to the title by the media buzz and the game's own intense marketing campaign. This multimillion-dollar marketing campaign emphasized the 3D graphics and animation, intriguing gamers with its promise of film-like action and an

Blue Dragon (2007), based on a design by *Final Fantasy* series creator Hironobu Sakaguchi, who also supervised development and wrote the plot, is a role-playing game developed by Mistwalker and Artoon, and distributed by Microsoft Game Studios exclusively for the Microsoft Xbox 360 as an effort to make the American console more popular in Japan. The loose association with the *Final Fantasy* series was played up in all the countries the game was released in, though the game itself was only a modest commercial success.

epic storyline. Surprisingly, the commercials showed little actual gameplay—nary a single battle scene, in fact. This tactic suggests that the advertisers felt the thrilling cutscenes would sell the game better than the underlying gameplay mechanics. However, most fans of the series would likely agree that the graphics were merely the bait; the hook was the story and gameplay.

Final Fantasy VII's legacy is hard to overestimate. Its incredible popularity and record-breaking sales helped launch the RPG as a viable genre for the console market. Countless Japanese RPGs of varying quality followed in its wake, and nowadays it's common enough to see even top-rank American RPG makers such as BioWare targeting the console market first. Moreover, the game's impact wasn't limited merely to the gaming industry, but is likely one of the major forces behind the rise of Japanese manga and anime in North America. In short, *Final Fantasy VII* was a true cultural phenomenon that is without question one of the greatest games of all time.

8

FLIGHT SIMULATOR (1980): DIGITAL REALITY

There are two basic approaches to creating a videogame simulation: Casual and Strict. In the interest of providing the best possible gaming experience, the Casual Simulation Approach (CSA) purposely models only select aspects of the real world to provide a familiar framework or reference point. In other words, fun takes precedence over reality in situations where reality would get in the way of the fun. In the realm of flight simulation, this might take the form of automated take-offs and landings, for instance, or minimizing or eliminating in-flight stalls. The Strict Simulation Approach (SSA), on the other hand, models as many aspects of the real world as possible. The fun comes from allowing the player to mirror, as closely as possible, the real-world actions of something he or she might never get the chance to do in real life. In turn, as it relates to the earlier flight simulation example, this would take the form of often difficult manual take-offs and land-ings, and having to take aircraft performance into consideration to minimize in-flight stalls (and performing realistic maneuvers to hopefully pull the plane out of one when a stall happens).

The SSA approach has very real limitations—there are no holo-decks[1] as of yet. Even the most precise simulation isn't perfect, and consumer versions lack the budget busting custom controls and extended displays of military or commercial simulators.[2] Further, even an SSA-designed program needs to make concessions for both the platform and its respective technical limitations, as well

---

[1]Which *knowledgerush.com* defines as follows: "In the fictional *Star Trek* universe, the holodeck is a form of virtual reality. It is an enclosed room with force-fields (which are similar to shields and deflector fields), onto which light is projected, allowing the simulation of three-dimensional surfaces of objects (including people). The effect is a simulation of entire environments, with which the user can interact. Two of the main purposes of the holodeck are for recreation and training."

[2]It is important to note, however, that there always have been and always will be truly dedicated home enthusiasts who go to great lengths to bridge this gap, with elaborate cockpits, multiple displays, professional controls, and so on.

as its potential audience, often by allowing the end user to turn off various levels of realism or activate automated assists as a gateway (or form of training) for the full, unfiltered experience.

By the 1960s, after years of manual and electromechanical simulators that, at best, put pilots in realistic cockpits with minimal feedback and only a limited sensation of flight, digital computers were integrated and allowed for increasingly robust simulations, even playing a critical role in NASA's nascent space program. By the 1970s, the foundation was in place for today's full-flight simulators, which accurately replicate the cockpit and characteristics of a specific aircraft type, flight condition, flight dynamics, and navigation, with full outside vision and sound for other aircraft and meteorological variables.

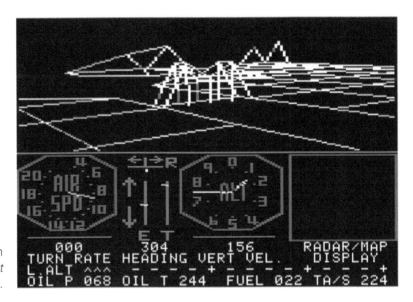

Screenshot of a later revision of subLOGIC's original *Flight Simulator* for the Apple II.

It was during this period in the 1970s that one man, Bruce Artwick, almost single-handedly established the market for realistic simulations in the fledgling home computer market. The website Flight Simulator History sums Simulator History, sums up Artwick's early history best:

In the mid-'70s Bruce Artwick was an electrical engineering graduate student at the University of Illinois. Being a passionate pilot, it was only natural that the principles of flight became the focus of his master's work. In his thesis of May 1975, called "A versatile computer-generated dynamic flight display" he presented a model of the flight of an aircraft, displayed on a computer screen. He proved that the 6800 processor (the first available microcomputer) was able to handle both the arithmetic and the graphic display, needed for real-time flight simulation. In short: the first Flight Simulator was born. In 1978 Bruce Artwick, together with Stu Moment, founded his own software company by the name of SubLOGIC and started developing graphic software for the 6800, 6502, 8080 and other processors. In 1979 he decided to take the model from his thesis one step further and developed the first Flight Simulator program for the Apple-II (based on the 6502 processor), followed shortly by a version for the Radio Shack TRS-80. Both versions were completely coded in their respective platform's machine-code. In January 1980 SubLOGIC FS1 hit the consumer market.... By 1981 Flight Simulator was reportedly the best selling title for the Apple. By the end of 1997 Microsoft claimed to have sold not less than 10 million copies of all versions of FS, making it the best sold software title in the entertainment sector. And in 2000 Microsoft Flight Simulator was taken up in the *Guinness Book of Records* with 21 million copies sold per June 1999. We certainly owe one to Bruce Artwick.[3]

Although visually crude to modern eyes, with a painfully low frame rate and rendered in only four colors, the original *Flight Simulator*, released on cassette for the 16K (RAM) Apple II in 1980, nevertheless contained all of the necessary elements to model flying an aircraft—in this case a slow, but maneuverable Sopwith Camel[4] biplane from World War I. The view was first-person, looking out of the front of the plane, which was represented on the top half of the screen, with the simplified cockpit display (instrument panel) on the bottom half. The graphics and collision detection were far from realistic. The scenery consisted of unfilled line drawings and players could fly right through mountains. Even crashing into the ground caused the plane to bounce back up rather than explode.

With the virtual world limited to a 6×6 grid, where each grid represented one square mile, Artwick chose to tie into the World War I theme with an option for aerial combat. At any time during a flight, the player could press the "w" key to declare war, which would immediately send five enemy planes into the air. It was then up to the player to engage the opposing planes and drop a bomb on their fuel depot before being shot down. Although not a great action game by any stretch of the imagination, the addition

---

[3]http://fshistory.simflight.com/fsh/versions.htm. It has also been suggested that *Airfight* (1974) for the PLATO networked computer system was an inspiration for the young Artwick. While Artwick would have had access to PLATO through the university, there is no evidence of any direct influence.

[4]A British single-seat fighter biplane that debuted in 1917 and was famous for its maneuverability (as well as being the plane that Snoopy from *Peanuts* imagined his dog house to be). According to Artwick's description in the manual for the first TRS-80 version, the plane was chosen for having similar flight characteristics to a modern Piper Cub 150.

of combat provided more incentive for the would-be player to try what otherwise might have been an intimidating simulation.[5]

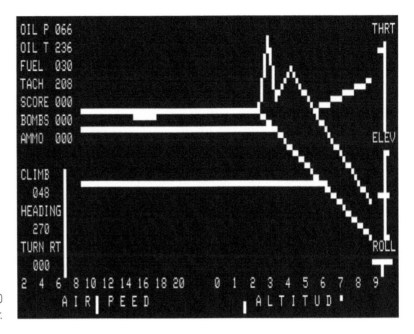

Screenshot from subLOGIC's TRS-80 version of *Flight Simulator.*

Shortly after the initial Apple II release, subLOGIC published a version on cassette for the technically inferior TRS-80 computer from Radio Shack (Tandy).[6] However, this did not stop Artwick from improving the program in at least a few key areas based on user feedback, a habit that would become a hallmark of subsequent *Flight Simulator* releases. Improvements included the frame rate, which was increased from three to six frames per second[7] and an additional overhead, or "radar" view. Of course, inherent to the platform, there was no sound and the visuals were black and white and blocky. The resolution was limited to the TRS-80's 128 × 48 display, which necessitated the removal of the graphical instrument panel. Nevertheless, as laughable as this sounds today, at the time what the program accomplished

---

[5]To be fair, the breakthrough visual display would certainly have been a big enough initial appeal, but this ultimately goes back to the earlier discussion of balancing realism with fun and would have been one of the factors that helped mitigate any potential monotony from just flying about, keeping players coming back for more.

[6]Also requiring 16K RAM, which—on a platform where configurations at the time could range from just 4K to 8K—was still a fairly reasonable requirement.

[7]As a point of reference, movies are generally shot in 24 frames per second, television in 30 frames per second, and modern videogames often 60 frames per second.

was groundbreaking, as this statement from a contemporary 1980 review by Roxton Baker indicates: "This is a superb program. It is so innovative and advanced that it must be praised in parts; its whole effect is beyond comparison with any existing TRS-80 software. First, FS1 is a highly realistic simulation of small aircraft flight. It combines with that a sophisticated, ingenious, and breathtaking 3D graphics display. Finally it provides an exciting and challenging real-time dogfight game. In any one of these aspects FS1 must be rated well ahead of its competition. Indeed for the graphics display, it has no competition."[8]

subLOGIC would release several more notable updates to *Flight Simulator:* two for the Apple II,[9] one for the TRS-80 and a fourth, a completely new version for the IBM PC, published through Microsoft. On the Apple II, version 2 added a crash graphic message if the player hit the ground too hard, a low altitude counter for a better sense of ground clearance, and the overhead view from the first TRS-80 version; version 3 expanded the size of the environment and added several new 3D objects in place of the previously flat landmarks. On the TRS-80, the update included a floppy disk version with enhanced frame rate and collision detection. The IBM PC version, released in 1982, would represent a second generation product and be the true blueprint for how the *Flight Simulator* series would look and perform right through to the present day.

Microsoft Flight Simulator first appeared in late 1982 to immediate acclaim. With modest requirements—64K RAM and a monochrome or CGA (four-color) graphics card—it was one of the few game titles that showcased what an expensive IBM PC was capable of at a time when even many low-end computers like the Commodore 64 had far greater audiovisual capabilities.[10] The simulated aircraft was a modern-day Cessna 182 (complete with retractable landing gear), and the interface featured an instrument panel with eight gauges, a new coordinate system, four different flight areas—Chicago, Seattle, Los Angeles, and New York/ Boston—with 20 airports, weather, and more. In other words, it took *Flight Simulator* to the next level. Regularly updated releases would follow, with Microsoft publishing the first of several initially black-and-white-only Macintosh versions, in 1986.

---

[8]http://fshistory.simflight.com/fsvault/fs1-trs80.htm.

[9]Check out Mark Percival's excellent introduction to each Apple II version update at http://fshistory.simflight.com/fsvault/fs1-apple.htm.

[10]In fact, it was common for both *Microsoft Flight Simulator* and the spreadsheet software *Lotus 1-2-3* to be used to prove how compatible an "IBM-compatible" computer really was. Microsoft would release a few additional versions of their original program for other IBM-like platforms that didn't have IBM PC compatibility but did run a version of Microsoft DOS, like the Texas Instruments Professional Computer.

Box back from *Microsoft Flight Simulator*. Note the modest system requirements.

In 1983, subLOGIC went back to the Apple II platform to release *Flight Simulator II*, which would later be ported to the Atari 8-bit,[11] Commodore 64, and Radio Shack Color Computer 3. It featured even more enhancements and innovations than *Microsoft Flight Simulator*, and was based on the Piper Archer aircraft. In 1986, *Flight Simulator II* was released for the advanced Atari ST and Commodore Amiga computers, and represented another audiovisual and feature leap for the series including the ability to fly different kinds of aircraft. Over time, the *Flight Simulator* series would receive expansions and complementary programs in the form of additional scenery, aircraft, and features, such as air traffic control or real-time weather.

subLOGIC and Microsoft would continue to release software titles independently of each other, including related simulations,

---

[11]Interestingly, *Flight Simulator II* would be one of Atari's pack-in cartridges with their XE Game System (XEGS), which was an Atari 8-bit computer with a detachable keyboard that was marketed against the Nintendo Entertainment System as a more sophisticated videogame console.

Screenshot of *Flight Simulator II* on the Apple II.

Flight Simulator II running on the transportable Commodore SX-64, shown with a custom controller and the program's detailed documentation.

like subLOGIC's *Jet* (1985; Apple II, Commodore 64, PC, and others) and *Microsoft Combat Flight Simulator: WWII Europe Series* (1998; PC). Today, only Microsoft has the rights to the *Flight Simulator* name and continues to release new, ever-more-realistic versions (like 2006's *Microsoft Flight Simulator X*), with full support for all kinds of expansions and third-party adjuncts to enhance the product even further, rivaling even the most advanced commercial systems of years past.

In 1988, Artwick left subLOGIC and founded BAO, or Bruce Artwick Organization, retaining the copyright to *Flight Simulator*, though the company and remaining rights were bought out by Microsoft in 1996. Artwick remained on as a consultant. BAO's

Box back for *Silent Service* (1985), Atari 8-bit version.

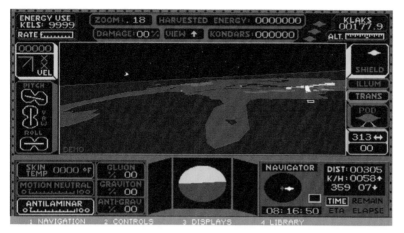

Simulations have often bordered on the fanciful, like subLOGIC's pictured *UFO* (1989) for the PC, which simulates control of an alien spacecraft.

most notable development was *Microsoft Space Simulator* (1994; PC), one of the first and so far only comprehensive mainstream general-purpose space-flight simulators, featuring different space-craft, space stations, missions, and intergalactic travel.[12] subLOGIC, which released *Flight Assignment: A.T.P.* (Airline Transport Pilot) in 1990 for PC,[13] was bought out by Sierra in 1995, who released the first of the short-lived *Pro Pilot* series of *Flight Simulator* competitors in 1997.[14]

By the mid-1980s, many competitive titles had been released, some taking *Flight Simulator* head on (*Solo Flight* [MicroProse, 1983; Commodore 64 and others]), with others focused on more targeted experiences, like pure combat (*Falcon* [Spectrum Holobyte, 1987; Atari ST and others]) or strict instruments (nonvisual) simulation (*BHXP1 Experimental Aircraft* [Bruce Hellstrom, 1987; TI-99/4a]). Of course, simulations, both of the CSA and SSA variety, were not limited to flight. Many other notable simulations were developed over the years, including *SCRAM* (Atari, 1981; Atari 8-bit), a nuclear reactor simulator by Chris Crawford; *Pinball Fantasies* (Digital Illusions, 1992; Atari Jaguar, Commodore Amiga, PC, and others), a pinball machine simulator with realistic physics; *C.P.U. Bach* (Microprose, 1993; 3DO), a simulation of Johann Sebastian Bach's music creation abilities by Sid Meier; *Gran Turismo* (Sony, 1997; Sony PlayStation), a sophisticated driving simulation with an arcade mode; *Baseball Mogul* (Sports Mogul, 1997; PC), which simulates managing an entire baseball franchise; and *Microsoft Train Simulator* (2001; PC), an

---

[12]See bonus chapter, "*Elite* (1984): Space, the Endless Frontier," for more on *Microsoft Space Simulator* and similar games.

[13]Modeling the Boeing 737, 747, 767, Airbus A320, and Shorts 360.

[14]Today, "subLOGIC Corporation" provides custom part-task or full simulations to industry or research organizations.

Box back for paper airplane simulator, *Glider 4.0* (1994), Apple Macintosh version.

add-on friendly train simulator. Like *Flight Simulator*, all of those games and more took great pains to model reality as closely as possible to create compelling experiences.

Surprisingly, in an industry best known for quick pick-up-and-play experiences, the arcade has also played a part in advancing the state-of-the-art for low-cost simulations. Outside of today's arcade games that mimic traditional activities like skateboarding, skiing, riding a motorcycle, or racing a car—almost like a mix of videogames and amusement park rides (see Chapter 3, "*Dance Dance Revolution* (1998): The Player Becomes the Star")—as far back as 1979, the arcade was providing immersive experiences, thanks in large part to Atari. In that year, Atari's *Lunar Lander* was released, an unforgiving vector-based simulation of landing a manned spaceship on the moon. The player must carefully manage fuel consumption and the effects of gravity and inertia while applying thrust in an attempt to carefully touch down on one of several landing areas. Atari would follow up a year later with *Battlezone* (mentioned in bonus chapter, "*Defender* (1980): The Joys of Difficult Games"), a vector-graphics action tank game

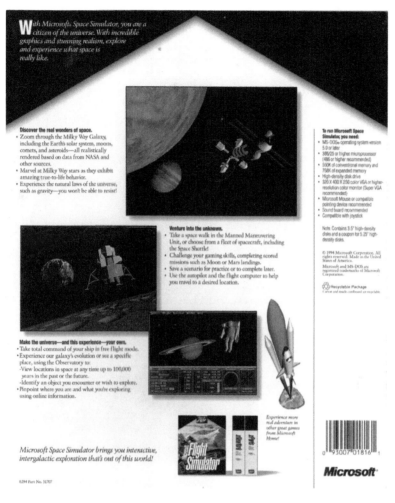

Some simulations, like *Microsoft Space Simulator* (box back shown), have amazingly ambitious scopes.

with realistic controls that the U.S. Army famously commissioned in a modified form for a simulation of their own. Atari would repurpose the *Battlezone* hardware themselves that same year for *Red Baron*, a first-person flight simulator skewed heavily toward action-packed dog fights.[15]

Perhaps more than any other genre of videogame, the simulation—and more specifically, the flight simulator—has pushed the boundaries of both hardware and software. A convincing simulation of flight requires an immense knowledge of both the real world and the technology to represent it. Once these technologies

---

[15]Not to be confused with Sierra's *Red Baron*, a 1990 game for the Commodore Amiga and PC (and now the Microsoft Xbox 360's Xbox Live Arcade). Sierra's game, which offered a story-based campaign mode, became a huge hit for the company, and is widely regarded as a classic of the genre. The game's own sequels failed to live up to the original.

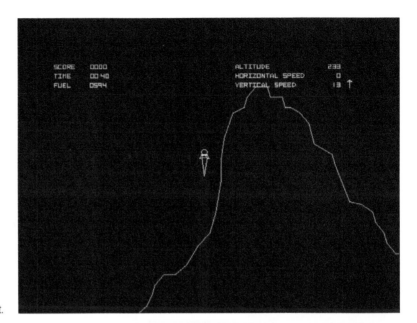

Lunar Lander screenshot.

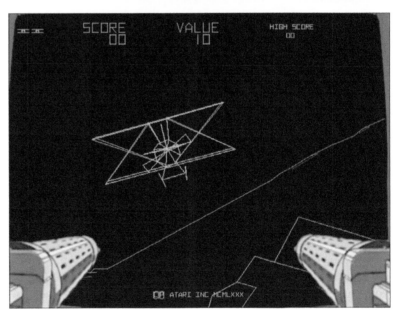

Red Baron screenshot, with simulation of the color overlay.

had been developed, they could be adapted for a wide variety of other types of videogames, such as the ubiquitous first-person shooters of today. However, as we've seen in this chapter, the most successful commercial developers of simulators had to carefully balance fun with realism, making trade-offs that would hopefully please more gamers than they turned off. Artwick's *Flight Simulator* certainly achieved such a balance, and thus stands as one of the greatest and most influential games of all time.

9

GRAND THEFT AUTO III (2001): THE CONSOLEJACKING LIFE

Although Rockstar Games' 2001 *Grand Theft Auto III*, or *GTA III*, for the Sony PlayStation 2 (PS2) was by no means the first open-ended or "sandbox" game,[1] it was the first with a believable, fully 3D world that was designed with Western audiences in mind. This fact may account for part of its blockbuster commercial success over Sega's innovative *Shenmue* (1999; Sega Dreamcast), which—while an amazing achievement—played out at times like a slow-paced Chinese soap opera. *GTA III* impressed gamers with its realistic simulation of a modern city and its inhabitants, as well as its almost comical, over-the-top violence and tongue-in-cheek parody and satire. Gamers enjoyed exploring this vibrant virtual world that seemed to react so convincingly to their every decision, even when that meant rewarding criminal behavior. *GTA III* was able to achieve a degree of unprecedented verisimilitude, a feature that distinguished the game and its sequels from the competition. However, it brought with it a rush of antigame hysteria from people who felt its morally neutral (or immoral) gameplay threatened to corrupt young minds.

GTA III benefited greatly from the technology of its era, which far surpassed what previous sandbox games had at their disposal. Brilliant games such as 1984's *Elite* (see bonus chapter, "*Elite* (1984): Space, the Endless Frontier") and 1990's *Ultima VII: The Black Gate* (see Chapter 23, "*Ultima* (1980): The Immaculate

---

[1] In this case, a sandbox game is defined as one that allows the player to move about a large environment and perform a wide range of typically realistic activities, but with a primary focus on accomplishing various goals and activities over creative or artistic production. Compare this to the primary goal of a "software toy," like in the *Pinball Construction Set* bonus chapter, "*Pinball Construction Set* (1982): Launching Millions of Creative Possibilities," which is to provide either the parts or allow the creation of the parts to build a game in a typically creative manner, and a "virtual playground", like *The Sims* in Chapter 22, "*The Sims* (2000): Who Let the Sims Out?," where the primary goal is to essentially play with or manipulate premade elements, with less focus on creativity and creation.

Grand Theft Auto III's gritty, realistic setting was certainly a big factor in the game's success.

Conception of the Computer Role-Playing Game") had offered amazingly detailed and interactive virtual worlds that gamers could spend weeks or even months exploring. Gamers marveled that they could plant seeds and sow grain in *The Black Gate*, actions that had no real effect on the game's plot. However, these optional activities were included in the game to make it feel more realistic; those seeds and tools weren't just there as decoration, but behaved the way we'd expect them to in the real world.

However, these games—while certainly ambitious—were nevertheless rigidly limited by the technology of their time. In other words, the verisimilitude of these games only extended so far. Players of *Elite* found that they couldn't leave their spaceships except when docked in spaceports, which amounted to a series of menus for buying and selling. Only the space ight segments were immersive, and even there monochromatic wireframe graphics for ships and asteroids demanded plenty of imagination to bring to life. *The Black Gate*'s world was densely populated with functional virtual objects of all sorts, but they were at, 2D sprites. You could click on a pair of pliers lying on a workbench to add them to your inventory, but their functionality was limited to very specific, predetermined usage. Despite the best efforts of the programmers, players of these games were constantly seeing the machinery at work behind the illusion.

GTA III's robust cause-and-effect physics engine and 3D graphics enabled players to interact with the game world and its objects like never before. Objects could be viewed from any

An Epic Quest in a Modern World

Seeking answers and vengeance, Ryo Hazuki arrives in the bustling metropolis of Hong Kong. Encountering new friends and foes alike, Ryo realizes he has much to learn and must master new martial art skills to prepare himself for his ultimate showdown with Lan Di, the man who killed his father. Each day brings Ryo closer to his goal of avenging his father's death and unlocking the mysteries of the Phoenix Mirror.

A massive, detailed 3D world! Walk the streets of a virtual Hong Kong and converse and interact with over 1000 unique characters.

Experience an epic adventure first-hand with all the drama, mystery, and intrigue of a live action movie.

Intense Combat — train hard and master real-time fight moves taken from the acclaimed Virtua Fighter™ series.

Xbox™ version includes a Snap-shot camera and Surround Sound cut scenes using Dolby® Digital 5.1!

Written and produced by Yu Suzuki, legendary creator of Virtua Fighter, Out Run™, Hang On™, & After Burner™.

Frequent fights, pulse-pounding chases, and intense action occur in a myriad of perilous encounters.

Box back from *Shenmue II* for the Microsoft Xbox. The technical accomplishments in the *Shenmue* series were impressive, but the games failed to inspire blockbuster sales.

angle. Furthermore, the game maintained the same level of detail during driving and ﬂying segments as when walking or fighting hand-to-hand. Whereas previous games had switched to different modes and interfaces for driving versus walking, *GTA III* made these transitions seamless and much more natural. Although there were still limits on what a player could do, the options seemed limitless.

As the roman numeral in its title indicates, *GTA III*'s development did not take place in a vacuum. There were important prequels, expansion packs, and related games. These earlier games were made by DMA Design, now known as Rockstar

North,[2] and included *Grand Theft Auto* (1997; Nintendo Game Boy Color, PC, Sony PlayStation), *Grand Theft Auto 2* (1999; same platforms, plus Sega Dreamcast), and *Body Harvest* (1998; Nintendo 64).

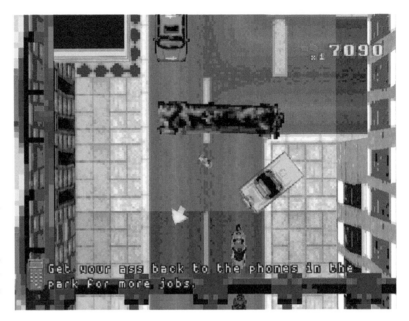

Grand Theft Auto could be played in "free play mode," or players could focus on fulfilling missions. Here, a mission has gone awry when a tanker blew up outside the building it was meant to destroy. Although the missions are often morally repugnant, the visuals and campy scenarios are typically more humorous than vile.

Grand Theft Auto or *GTA*, features a top down, bird's-eye view of the action. Depending upon the platform, the player takes on the role of one of four or eight different criminals. Each of these criminals vary only in appearance, and players can give them new names if they don't like the default (certain names act as cheat codes). Although the character is tasked with missions, he or she can freely roam the levels of one of three cities in the game: Liberty City, Vice City, and San Andreas,[3] each of which would become the settings for future titles in the series. In contrast to the greater exibility in later games, here the player must attain a certain number of points within a set number of lives before moving on to the next level. The player has some freedom in scoring points, like stealing and selling cars or causing general destruction, but by far the quickest path, worth the most points, is to complete the missions. Although the end result of a multiobjective mission is always the same, the player can usually make choices along the way, such as killing the police chief or rescuing

---

[2]Rockstar Games is a development division of Take-Two Interactive and presently comprises nine studios, all named for their respective locations, that is, Rockstar North (Edinburgh, Scotland), Rockstar Toronto, and Rockstar Japan.

[3]Loosely based on New York City, Miami, and Los Angeles, respectively.

a kidnap victim. The player can move about on foot, in a variety of cars, or even in a tank and boat, and has access to a variety of weapons, including a machine gun and amethrower.[4]

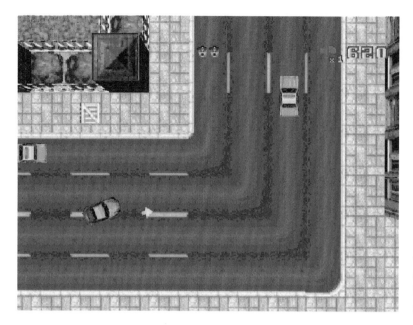

In *Grand Theft Auto*, whenever the player hijacks a vehicle, music or radio stations play. These infectious grooves add a great deal of value to the game.

Besides the general theme and fictional cities based on real cities, the original *GTA* established other series standards, including radio stations with original music, a police band, and the ability to play your own music.[5] The PC version of the game had limited network multiplayer support, an option that wouldn't be seen again until *Grand Theft Auto IV*. An add-on mission pack that required the original game was released in 1999 for both the PC and PlayStation called *Grand Theft Auto Mission Pack #1: London, 1969*, with a second following shortly thereafter, entitled *Grand Theft Auto Mission Pack #2: London, 1961*, though this time just for the PC. Both of these expansion packs eschewed the previous cities and time period for a trip back to London in the 1960s, though gameplay was still based on a criminal's climb up the ladder of a mob family.

Grand Theft Auto 2 or *GTA 2*, takes place in an unspecified near future ("three weeks") in an unspecified city ("Anywhere City") that consists of three distinct areas: Downtown (for example, casinos, hotels), Residential (prison, trailer park), and Industrial (seaport,

---

[4]The player also has the basic, nonlethal ability to punch.

[5]Features depended upon the version, with the PC having everything, the PlayStation having less, and the Game Boy Color having the least, with significant censoring of violence and language.

Grand Theft Auto II had improved graphics, but still depicted all the action from a top-down perspective. Players could not only steal cars, but actually earned points for running down pedestrians. The game seemed to take every opportunity to encourage players to break the law.

nuclear power plant). The player is cast as criminal "Claude Speed," who wants to be "King of the City" by game's end.

Although *GTA 2* plays and scores the same as the previous game, there were several key improvements. One was the option to work for different gangs; choosing sides inevitably brought hostility from the rival group. Furthermore, characters with a high enough "wanted" level garner interest from higher authorities than just the local police. City activity is a bit more robust, with pedestrians going about their normal activities, such as entering and riding in taxi cabs or buses—there is also more criminal activity going on than the player's own. One of the more popular additions is the option to carjack a cab or bus and then earn fares. Though still limited by its zoomed-out overhead perspective, all these additions (along with a greatly expanded selection of weapons and vehicle enhancements) made the game a much more realistic sandbox experience. *GTA 2*, like the rest of the series until the first downloads became available on Xbox Live for the Microsoft Xbox 360 version of *Grand Theft Auto IV*, did not receive any expansions or add-ons. However, a multiplayer patch for the PC version of *GTA 2* was incorporated when both that and the original game were released for free on Rockstar's website in 2004.[6]

Body Harvest, though not part of the official *GTA* series, was nevertheless the first time the developers took the gameplay concepts into 3D, albeit with a larger emphasis on action. Despite being "cursed with delays and development problems"[7] and the blurry graphics typical of all but the best games on the Nintendo 64, *Body Harvest* proved a critical success. Though limited to the capacity of

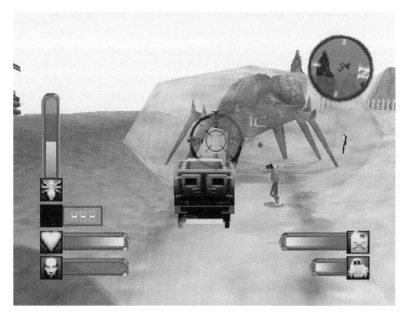

Body Harvest was DMA Design's first attempt at a 3D sandbox. Note the fleeing bystander.

the Nintendo 64's cartridge format, the game still delivered a large, relatively open Sandbox experience.

The player assumes the role of Adam Drake, a genetically enhanced soldier who must investigate and stop a time traveling alien attack force. Drake must battle in five different areas, covering Greece in 1916, Java in 1941, the United States in 1966, Siberia in 1991, and the alien homeworld in 2046. As players explore each of these time periods, they can talk to the locals and commandeer any vehicle they find. Like *GTA*, *Body Harvest* allows the character to move about on foot; drive various vehicles, including tanks, boats, and helicopters; and fire weapons. Unlike *GTA*, *Body Harvest* incorporates simple puzzles, such as finding parts to fix a boat, along with the usual rescue or assassination missions. In fact, *Body Harvest* is even more mission-based than the *GTA* games, requiring strict completion before opening up further levels.

---

[6]Each game also received necessary tweaks to run on most modern systems.

[7]http://ign64.ign.com/articles/150/150405p1.html; a reoccurring concept throughout the increasingly complex *GTA* series.

[8]The first version was released for the PS2 on October 22, 2001, giving DMA Design time to make minor cuts and modifications in deference to the series of coordinated suicide attacks by al Qaeda upon the United States on September 11, 2001, particularly on New York City, on which Liberty City is loosely modeled. A few other titles were affected around this time, as well, including Sega's promising air racing game, *Propeller Arena*, for their Dreamcast, which was never officially released in part due to the system's weak market position and in part because it featured a race that took place between skyscrapers.

This brings us back to the next game after *Body Harvest*, *GTA III*, released for Microsoft Xbox, PC, and PS2[8]. Despite the innovations of the previous games, no one expected all of the elements to come together as magnificently as they did in *GTA III*. The game garnered almost universal critical acclaim along with nearly unprecedented commercial success and numerous awards.[9] Legendary developer, Will Wright (see Chapters 15 and 22), raved about the game, describing it "as such an open-ended world…you can actually be very nice in the world and drive an ambulance around saving people, or you can be very mean. The game doesn't really force you down one path or the other unless you're playing the missions. For me, it's not really about the missions, it's about the open-endedness… going out and living a life in this little simulated city. It's like a big playground."[10] Improvements ranged from the now-iconic art style on the packaging and load screens to the addition of a 24-hour clock that featured true day and night cycles. Although not totally without aw, *GTA III* got a lot more right than it did wrong, and completed the developer's transition from 2D to 3D worlds in style.

The player is again cast as an unnamed thug[11] trying to move up the mob ladder in Liberty City. The plot involves double-crosses, revenge, and love triangles, all told through copious cutscenes that form the basis of the missions.[12] The game's design allows players to choose how involved they actually want to get in the various machinations, if at all. As Doug Perry of IGN put it in his review:

> I spent the first three hours of playing Grand Theft Auto III choosing some primary missions, but found myself constantly being distracted by random missions, side jobs, and simply exploring. My own personal raison d'etre was just to find the impressive insane stunt jump sections and to test the cars to their limits. After I got my fill, I then went back to playing the story in a more linear fashion. Players essentially can play the game as fast and as linear as their skills allow, or as distracted and as random as they feel. It's just another way in which Grand Theft Auto III offers freedom, nonlinear gameplay, and variety like never before.

---

[9]See http://tinyurl.com/42c8da for a small sampling.

[10]http://www.msnbc.msn.com/id/26630611/?pg=3#games_top5_080909_WillWright.

[11]Later revealed to be Claude in *Grand Theft Auto: San Andreas*, where he appears as a nonplayer character.

[12]*GTA III* has a notable voice cast, including veteran actors Frank Vincent, Michael Madsen, Michael Rapaport, Joe Pantoliano, Debi Mazar, Kyle MacLachlan, Robert Loggia, and Lazlow Jones. Future games in the series would follow suit.

One advantage to completing the story's missions and side missions is gaining access to more of Liberty City's domain,[13] which includes three large urban areas: industrial, commercial, and suburban. Each has a distinct look and feel. Even the demographics vary from area to area, populated with citizens of the corresponding demographic. Clearly, it is impressive stuff.

GTA III features cinematic opening credits that wouldn't be out of place in the latest Hollywood hipster gangster film. After the credit sequence and quick set of animated cutscenes, the player is immediately thrust into a fully playable tutorial—another hallmark of the series. The tutorial acts as a gradual introduction to the in-game controls and also sets the context for the story.

However, there are more signs of player progress than simply completing missions or advancing the story. The game tracks a seemingly countless number of statistics in real time. These stats are accessible any time, and let players know how much of the story they've completed and how many times they've attempted missions. Players can also find out how many people they've "wasted," number of hospital visits, and even how much distance they've traveled by car or foot, among many other statistics. All of this information gives players insight into their play style and overall ability.

The audio has been significantly enhanced, with better and more abundant speech, sound effects, and music, which now includes both original and licensed works. The songs are announced by talkative DJs, and there's even an all-talk station. The radio commercials are often quite funny, complementing the game's blend of humor and mature themes.

Some of the gameplay is identical to that found in many third-person shooters, but *GTA III* also involves a great deal of driving. These driving sequences have a significantly higher learning curve and difficulty level than the shooter mode. Driving doesn't work like typical racing games, which usually offer pinpoint control (see Chapter 14, "*Pole Position* (1982): Where the Raster Meets the Road"). Instead, the vehicles seem purposefully designed to crash into things, causing random destruction wherever one turns the wheel. Even stopping at stop lights or maintaining a consistent, law abiding speed can be challenging. It takes a lot of practice to acquire the skills needed to drive properly, and even the best players often fail to stay off the curb. Fortunately for poor drivers, obeying traffic laws is not the fun part anyway.

---

[13]*GTA III*'s excuse for initially limited access to certain parts of the city is that the particular access subway or bridge needs to be "repaired," which ties back into the believability aspect; that is, if a gamer is given a reasonable explanation for being restricted from going somewhere that they would easily be able to reach in real life, immersion in the gameworld is retained.

Controlling a vehicle can be a real challenge in *Grand Theft Auto III.*

Contemporary critics of *GTA III* tended to be very forgiving, overlooking many of its aws and harping on its litany of groundbreaking features. For instance, few criticized the repetitive missions, particularly those of the "drive from point A to point B" variety. These repetitive missions would show up (and be lambasted) in nearly every other open-world sandbox game, such as the otherwise inspired *The Simpsons Hit & Run* (Vivendi Universal, 2003; Microsoft Xbox, Nintendo GameCube, and others). This game placed more focus on its driving and platforming elements, but infuriated gamers with an excess of timed and very frustrating driving missions.

GTA III suffered the same standard technical issues seen in most games of the time, such as pop-in (objects suddenly appearing) and variable frame rate (smoothness). However, *GTA III* also had a surprising lack of variety in its character models: a startling omission, given the otherwise diverse world. It's disconcerting, for instance, to see small groups of the exact same hooker on different sidewalks—it's as though there's a city-wide clone convention. Furthermore, as is typical of 3D gaming (see Chapter 18, "*Super Mario 64/Tomb Raider* (1996): The Third Dimension"), even with a choice of multiple viewpoints, players could have difficulty finding just the right camera angle to view the action. Blind spots could affect everything from backing up in a car to being surprised by a police officer just out of the player's sight.

Despite these aws, *GTA III* is still as playable today as it was back in 2001. However, Rockstar North didn't rest on its laurels, releasing a steady stream of improved sequels, starting with 2002's *Grand Theft Auto: Vice City*, or *GTA: VC* (same platforms).

GTA: VC mined the rich pop culture references of the 1980s, going the *Miami Vice*[14] route, though with plenty of nods to iconic mob films like *Scarface*.[15] The player is cast as Tommy Vercetti, a mob hitman who is released from prison after serving 15 years for killing 11 men, and who is promptly sent to Vice City to undertake a series of cocaine deals. Naturally, complications arise. Tommy's ultimate goal is to become the crime kingpin of Vice City. Though *GTA: VC* retains the series reliance on mob themes, Vice City's more upscale, summery landscape is a pleasing contrast to Liberty City's drab and dirty environments.

Besides featuring a large selection of period music,[16] *GTA: VC* expands on its predecessor in several other areas, including both a larger weapon selection and a greater variety of law enforcement. The character can now steal and operate helicopters and fire trucks, the latter of which can actually be used to douse fires in the game. Players can also purchase building for hideouts or business purposes.[17] As expected, *GTA: VC* was another huge

Jacking a car in *Grand Theft Auto: Vice City*.

---

[14]A popular 1984–1989 NBC television series starring Don Johnson as a cool and stylish cop, drawing in uence from and defining 1980s fashion and pop culture.

[15]A violent film from 1983 starring Al Pacino as Tony Montana, who becomes a gangster against the backdrop of the 1980s cocaine boom.

[16]A hit multi-CD companion music compilation was sold separately.

[17]These properties can also generate missions of their own, such as eliminating certain competition.

Hand-to-hand combat with hookers in *Grand Theft Auto: Vice City.*

critical and commercial success, selling 15 million units as of September 2008, three million more than its predecessor.[18]

Rockstar North finally replaced the gangster (mob) theme with a similarly gritty gangsta (gang) lifestyle in 2004's *Grand Theft Auto: San Andreas*, or *GTA: SA* (same platforms). Cast as gang member Carl "CJ" Johnson, it's up to the player to unravel the plot behind his mother's murder. Achieving this goal requires reestablishing CJ's gang and expanding his business ventures. Although *GTA: SA* offered expanded environments, improved artificial intelligence, and a series-first ability to swim, the biggest innovation was the introduction of role-playing/character building elements.

Not only could CJ's hair, clothing, and tattoos be purchased and modified, these changes could also have a significant impact on his in-game relationships, both positive and negative. CJ's body is affected by diet and exercise; riding a bike instead of driving in a car, for instance, makes CJ increasingly muscular, whereas overeating can make him overweight. CJ can also acquire skills in various disciplines, such as driving, firearms, and martial arts. Finally, CJ can meaningfully interact with most pedestrians, who will react accordingly.[19]

---

[18]See http://tinyurl.com/4da24g.

[19]CJ can make more than 4,200 comments, which are separate from the 3,500 scripted comments and lines in the over two hours of motion-captured cutscenes. See http://tinyurl.com/475xfz.

Grand Theft Auto: San Andreas
protagonist CJ riding a bike.

Even with all of these impressive features, perhaps *GTA: SA*'s biggest claim to fame is the infamous "Hot Coffee" incident. Normally, when the player takes CJ's girlfriend home, she asks him to come in for "some coffee" and he walks inside. The camera, however, remains outside and comically sways back and forth as moaning sounds emanate from within. Enterprising hackers were able to either modify the game in the PC version or use cheating devices on the console versions to access unused game assets, which included a crude but blatant sex scene as a minigame sequence. Even though the content was not accessible by ordinary means and the game itself was already rated M for Mature by the ESRB[20], the usual public outcry over the content reached dizzying heights, with politicians looking for an easy cause to latch onto and calling for action. In response, publisher Take-Two gave stores the option of relabeling the game as AO, or Adults Only, a game designation most don't allow, or to send their remaining inventory back for replacement with an M version, with the offending content removed. Despite (or perhaps because of) the controversy, *GTA: SA* went on to sell over 20 million copies as of September 2008.[21]

Grand Theft Auto IV, or *GTA IV*, which bore no subtitle, was released in 2008 for the Microsoft Xbox 360, PC, and Sony PlayStation 3 (PS3). It takes place in a redesigned Liberty City.

---

[20]The Entertainment Software Rating Board.

[21]See http://tinyurl.com/4da24g.

The player stars as Niko Bellic, an Eastern European war veteran who comes to the United States with grand ambitions, but soon finds himself embroiled in a seedy criminal underworld. Besides the huge audiovisual leap expected for the move to the next generation of systems, *GTA IV* distinguishes itself from its predecessors with the long-awaited inclusion of an integrated online multiplayer mode, which consists of 15 different game types. For the creative (and dedicated), the PC version even allows players to modify the game well beyond what was possible with any of the previous games. It's hardly surprising that the game arrived amid a ood of positive reviews and sold more than six million copies in just a week after its release, earning Take-Two over $500 million— and that was just for the PS3 and Xbox 360 versions.[22]

In the years since *GTA III*'s release, several canon titles for portables were created, including *Grand Theft Auto*[23] (2004), for the Nintendo Game Boy Advance, an unevenly received variation of *GTA III* that mostly returned to the overhead perspective of *GTA 1* and *2.* The PSP saw *Grand Theft Auto: Liberty City Stories* (2005) and *Grand Theft Auto: Vice City Stories* (2006),[24] both of which maintained much of the look, feel, and scope of the console games. *Grand Theft Auto: Chinatown Wars* (2009) for the Nintendo DS uses an isometric perspective[25] and takes advantage of that platform's dual- and touchscreen functionality.

Of course, besides its own impressive list of sequels and offshoots, *GTA III*'s success inspired many other developers to build their own sandboxes. Examples include Sony's *The Getaway* (2002) for the PS2, which painstakingly modeled a portion of the city of London for its gangster-themed setting; Electronic Arts' *The Godfather: The Game* (2006; Nintendo Wii, PC, PS2, and others), which is based on the movie of the same name; Microsoft's *Crackdown* (2007) for their Xbox 360, a futuristic third-person shooter that casts the player as a cybernetically enhanced agent; Electronic Arts' *Mercenaries 2: World in Flames* (2008; PC, PS2, PS3, Xbox 360), a third-person shooter set in Venezuela that features destructible environments; and THQ's *Saints Row 2* (2008; PC, PS3, Xbox 360), a sandbox game with many similarities to the *GTA* series, but placing a greater emphasis on gang life and related customization. The various Rockstar studios would take inspiration themselves with the 2006 release of the imaginative *Bully* (PS2, PC, Xbox 360, and others), casting the player as a teenage rebel trying to survive a boarding school. However,

---

[22]http://tinyurl.com/5vfqmd.

[23]Also known as *Grand Theft Auto Advance.*

[24]Both were later ported to the PS2 as budget titles.

[25]This perspective features a similar overhead view like the first two *GTA* games, but with more 3D elements.

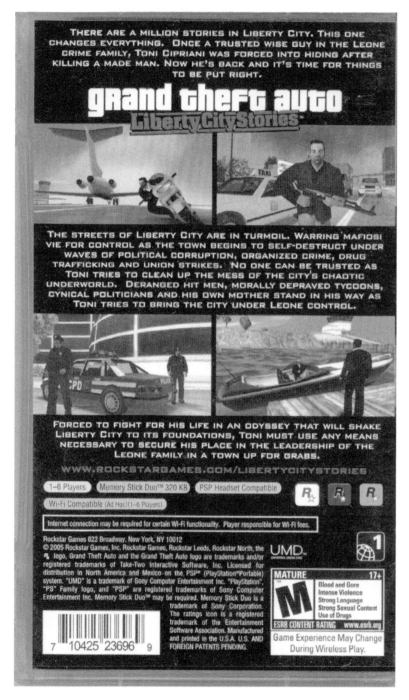

Box back for *Grand Theft Auto: Liberty City Stories.*

though many of these are good games in their own right, none lived up to Rockstar North's creations in either critical or commercial success.

Screenshot from *Mercenaries 2: World in Flames*, showcasing the destructible environments.

GTA III's in uence extends beyond sandbox games, with its open-world elements being incorporated into other genres, like racing games. These include Atari's *Test Drive Unlimited* (2006; PC, PS2, PSP, Xbox 360), which uses the modeled Hawaiian island of Oahu for its racing environment; and *Burnout Paradise* (2008; PC, PS3, Xbox 360), which is set in the fictional Paradise City. Both games allow players to challenge opponents, either of ine or online, to a race at nearly any point in the game.

The sandbox, open-ended, or open-world format has a lot of future potential as programming for realism (physics, destructible environments, and so on) continues to improve alongside the hardware. Although most critics praise Rockstar for making games with such rich possibilities for interaction, others—concerned but uninformed citizens—condemn it, blaming it for corrupting youth and valorizing violent crime and misogyny. Whereas Garriott's *The Black Gate* allowed players to commit unethical deeds, these were often cleverly (and decisively) punished later in the game; indeed, Garriott had long insisted that games should actively promote ethical behavior and strong moral values. Rockstar, conversely, seems to show no remorse for its products or how people play them, and it's hard to argue that "the public" disapproves of games that reap such enormous commercial rewards. There's perhaps an argument that allowing players to engage in *virtual* crime will make them less likely to commit *actual* crimes, though no legitimate psychological or sociological study to date has compellingly proven or disproven such claims. The lack of mutually acceptable evidence has in no way silenced critics of either camp, and we've certainly seen similar unscientific diatribes raised over other pop-culture icons like the tabletop role-playing game *Dungeons & Dragons* and comic books.

Although it's tempting to view the less savory aspects of the *GTA* series as evidence of its developer's immorality, we might also see it as rather cynical social commentary. Given the choice, would most people prefer to play the game as a Christian or a criminal, a Jesus or a Machiavelli? Rockstar can always fall back on the position that they merely create possibilities—it's up to the player to enact them. If living the life of a criminal is more fun than being a law-abiding citizen, what does that say about our society?

10

JOHN MADDEN FOOTBALL (1988): MODERN SPORTS VIDEOGAMES KICKOFF

Although this chapter focuses on the highly influential and commercially successful *Madden* series of football videogames, it's also concerned with sports videogames in general.[1] As the sports videogame industry grew and developed, so too did the *Madden* series—sometimes innovating, sometimes liberally borrowing ideas from others. To put it simply, what's good for *Madden* is good for the genre as a whole.

Some critics might wonder whether all videogames can be considered sports. After all, nearly all of them have some type of competitive and scoring element. We certainly find a strong sports influence in the earliest videogames. The first true videogame translations of sporting activities are discussed in bonus chapter, "*Pong* (1972): Avoid Missing Game to Launch Industry," and include William Higinbotham and Robert Dvorak's *Tennis for Two* (1958), a custom analog computer game; the sports games for Ralph Baer's Magnavox Odyssey console from 1972 (*Table Tennis*, *Tennis*, *Hockey*, *Football*, and others); and of course, Atari's arcade *Pong* from later that same year. *Pong*'s great success with such humble technology inspired more imitators than innovators, and it took a while for sports videogames to expand beyond tepid paddle and ball variations in which designers could simply change the number and size of paddles and balls and call it a different sport. Nevertheless, expand it did, culminating with the *Madden* games, which became perennial bestsellers and challengers for the top spot on the sales charts every year.

With all of that in mind, first we'll take you through a quick tour of the history of some notable games based on traditional sports:

---

[1] With the exceptions of vehicle racing, which are discussed in Chapter 14, "*Pole Position* (1982): Where the Raster Meets the Road," and casual and extreme sports games, which are discussed in bonus chapter, "*Tony Hawk's Pro Skater* (1999): Videogame Ollies, Grabs, and Grinds."

baseball, basketball, boxing, golf, soccer, hockey, tennis, and of course, football, as well as how they evolved, getting into more detail on what makes the *Madden* series what it is today. Let's begin then with a look at baseball games over the years.

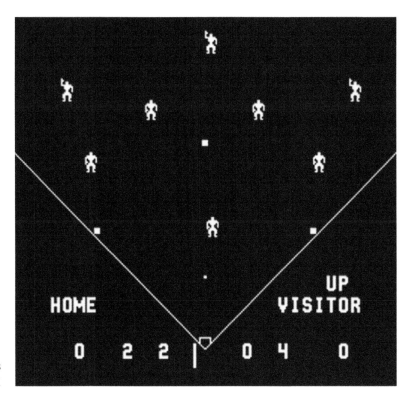

Screenshot from Midway's *Tornado Baseball*.

The first major baseball videogame was *Tornado Baseball*, released to the arcade in 1976 by Midway. The game featured an overhead view of the playing field that became the standard for a number of years. The black and white players, foul line, and scores were mirrored against a color overlay. Like many early games, *Tornado Baseball* required two players. The game's audiovisuals were quite simple: besides the movement of the ball, there was only minimal animation of the stick-figure players and just a simple bat to represent the batter. What the game did have was a nifty control panel, complete with a mini bat-like lever for hitting. The simple two-player gameplay and perspective would reappear in various simplified and enhanced successors, such as the modest RCA Studio II's *Baseball* (1977) and the Mattel Intellivision's classic and relatively sophisticated *Major League Baseball* (1980), which was one of the earliest examples of obtaining an official sports association license, though it affected only branding.

The next major change in presentation and perspective came with the 1983 release of Gamestar's *Star League Baseball* for the Atari 8-bit and Commodore 64. *Star League Baseball* presented the action from the right-field stands, offering the player a type of isometric view of the action. Unlike overhead views, which typically avoided up-down ball movement in either pitching or hit balls, *Star League Baseball* embraced it. Several other games would copy this perspective, but the one drawback to this point-of-view, much like overhead, was the relative lack of detail in

Electronic Arts' *Earl Weaver Baseball* (1987) was one of the early efforts to associate a famous name with a game, hoping to give it an edge with fans. The Commodore Amiga version of this game used the computer's built-in speech synthesis instead of digitized speech.

the pitcher-batter interaction critical to the sport. Games like *Hardball!* and *R.B.I. Baseball* would address this issue.

Hardball!, first released by Accolade in 1985 for the Commodore 64, presented the battle between the pitcher and batter from a television-style point of view, which is behind the pitcher, more or less from the perspective of the second baseman. Though this point of view proved popular and was particularly good for pitching, it was not quite as ideal for hitting because it was easy for batters to judge location, but not necessarily depth. *R.B.I. Baseball*, first released by Tengen in 1987 for the Nintendo Entertainment System, reversed the perspective and made the point of view that of the home plate umpire just behind the catcher. Though modern baseball games typically allow for a myriad of perspectives in their 3D engines, this point of view remains the default because it provides the best balance of visibility for both pitcher and batter. Though *R.B.I. Baseball* did not have a Major League Baseball license, which would have allowed it to use official branding and team names, it did have a Major League Baseball Players Association license, which allowed it to feature well-known players. Games like *World Series Major League Baseball* (1994) by Sega for their Genesis console would eventually bring it all together, with every license and top-notch gameplay and visuals. Games like 3DO's *High Heat Major League Baseball 2004* (2003; Microsoft Xbox, PC, Sony PlayStation) and Sony's *MLB 09: The Show* (2008; Sony PlayStation, Sony PlayStation 3, Sony PlayStation Portable) would eventually bring it all together in 3D, which was a boon for sports gaming, as the action could be rendered from nearly any angle necessary.

The first notable basketball game was Atari's trackball-controlled *Atari Basketball*, released to the arcade in 1979. *Atari Basketball* was a one- or two-player one-on-one full-court basketball game, shown from an angled side view. The side view would be a commonly used perspective over the years, though some games showed the full court at all times and others showed half or scrolling courts. Electronic Arts would release *Julius Erving and Larry Bird Go One-on-One* in 1983 on the Apple II (later for many other platforms), which featured an angled top-down half court game of one-on-one. Although the game played great and had neat touches, like a breakable backboard that caused an angry janitor to come out and sweep up the debris, it was most famous for being one of the first sports games to both involve and use the likenesses of actual sports stars, taking into consideration the strengths and weaknesses of each. The success of the game

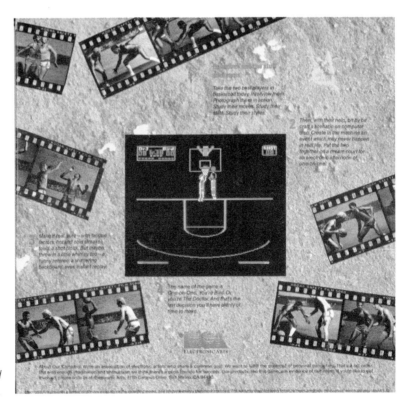

Box back for *Julius Erving and Larry Bird Go One-on-One*.

certainly predicted the demands of future sports videogame fans in regard to the modeling and usage of their favorite athletes. Of course, there have been many team-based basketball games over the years, including Konami's *Double Dribble* (1986) arcade game, famous for its scrolling court and cutscenes showing spectacular plays, and Electronic Arts' long-running *NBA Live* franchise, which besides the typical assortment of current teams, players, and signature moves, in the 2009 edition features daily player updates that modify tendencies, rosters, and hot and cold streaks based on their real-world counterparts.

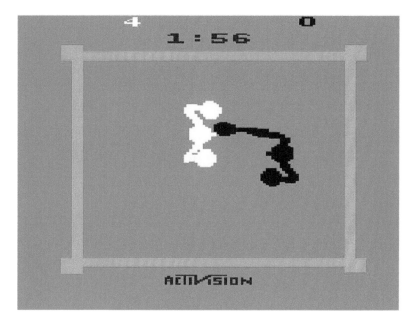

Screenshot from Activision's *Boxing* for the Atari 2600 Video Computer System.

Boxing has been one of the most consistently translated sports, making an appearance on even the most obscure platforms, though it has never achieved anywhere near the popularity of its close cousin, the fighting game (described in Chapter 17, "*Street Fighter II* (1991): Would You Like the Combo?"). Notable titles include Activision's *Boxing* (1980) for the Atari 2600 VCS, which displayed the action from an overhead view; Mattel's *Boxing* for its Intellivision, which displayed the action from the side; *4-D Sports Boxing* (1991; Commodore Amiga, PC, and others) from Distinctive Software, which featured a crude, but effective freeform 3D fighting engine; and Sega's *Greatest Heavyweights* (1993) for their Genesis console, which featured licensed likenesses of famous boxers, a close-up side view of the top half of the boxers, and a rotating ring. Of course the biggest challenge with boxing games is balancing button-mashing action with the sport's inherent strategic elements, and one of the best at combining these has been Electronic Arts' *Fight Night* series, which began back in 2004.

Fight Night sets the bar for boxing videogames high, offering a robust and responsive 3D fighting engine, custom and licensed boxers, career modes, and the usual polish of EA Sports titles.[2]

Box back for INTV Corporation's surprisingly advanced successor to Mattel's *PGA Golf*, *Chip Shot: Super Pro Golf*, released in 1987 for the Intellivision.

Golf would seem at first glance to be one of the more difficult sports for early hardware to simulate, with its myriad clubs,

---

[2]Though considered sports entertainment rather than an actual sport, the evolution of wrestling games have many parallels to both fighting and boxing videogames, with a similar important and beneficial transition from 2D to 3D. One of the best 3D evolutions of wrestling has been the *WWE SmackDown!* series, which began back in 2000 and featured the usual mix of licensed wrestlers, customization, and assortment of moves.

distances, and long and short driving and putting games. Of course, as our discussions throughout this book have shown, it is not always necessary to re-create a complete experience to have a fun videogame, and in fact golf titles were available fairly early on. Atari's *Golf* (1978) for their VCS and Mattel's *PGA Golf* (1979) for their Intellivision are two good examples. In Atari's title, there are nine different full screen holes that switch to a closer view when it becomes necessary to putt. Mattel's title, besides having licensed

LINKS THE CHALLENGE OF GOLF

(c) 1992 ACCESS SOFTWARE INC.

Golf Simulation so Realistic, You'll Think You're There!

It's a beautiful spring day as you prepare to tee off. You gaze down the fairway and notice every detail of your surroundings ...the location of each tree...the contour of each hill and slope...the lie of the ball. a day at your favorite course? Not quite, but it's the next best thing — LINKS the Challenge of Golf—is a totally realistic golf simulator for your VIS that is a quantum leap ahead of any other golf game you've seen!

Reviews on LINKS...

"LINKS graphics [are] far superior to any other computer golf game. LINKS' trees look like trees." *—Golf World*

"...a golfer's dream, a chance to play what feels like real golf without ever having to leave home. *—COMPUTE*

"...unequaled by other golf simulators currently on the market." *—Computer Gaming World*

Winner of *Computer Gaming World*'s **Best Action Game of the Year for 1991** as well as *SPA*'s **Best Sports Simulator in 1990!**

Hardware Required—VIS Player

This disc is fully compatible with all VIS players displaying the VIS logo.

This disc is for school and private use only. Any other use or copying, in whole or in part, without the express written permission of ACCESS Software Inc. is strictly prohibited.

© ACCESS Software, Inc. 1992. All rights reserved.

For customer service call or write:
ACCESS Software, Inc.
4910 W. Amelia Earhart Dr.,
SLC, UT 84116
Tel: 801-359-2900, **800-800-4880**

Featured in LINKS is the Torrey Pines Golf Course in San Diego, CA reproduced in exacting detail.

Actual VIS screen captures

Other Courses Available—

Barton Creek, Bayhill, Bountiful, Dorado Beach, Firestone, Pinehurst and Troon are also available for your VIS! These *LINKS Championship Courses* are **sold separately** and require *LINKS The Challenge of Golf* for the VIS. Call 1-800-800-4880 for details.

LINKS features include:

- *Stunning full color motion graphics*
- *Incredible 3-D contoured terrain*
- *Accurate physics of the flight and impact of the golf ball*
- *Actual digitized individual trees and buildings*
- *Three levels of game play— Pro, Amateur, and Beginner*
- *Instant replays*
- *Choice of male or female golfers*
- *All the sounds of true golf—from commentary and wildlife to the sound of your swing and the whack of the ball!*

Radio Shack   Cat No 25-6114

Custom Packaged in U.S.A. for Radio Shack
A Division of Tandy Corp. Ft. Worth TX 76102

25-6114

Box back for *Links: The Challenge of Golf* (1992) for the Video Information System (VIS) platform. The multiclick swing system was the de facto standard until fairly recently.

branding, takes a similar approach to Atari's, save for changing the point of view when putting. What really differentiated *PGA Golf*, however, was its surprisingly advanced features for the time, including aiming, swinging (don't slice!), and ball trajectories—all in the interest of avoiding standard hazards like sand traps, roughs, and trees. The videogame golf experience would remain virtually unchanged until Access' *Leader Board Golf*, first released in 1986 for the Commodore 64. *Leader Board Golf* featured a third-person behind-the-golfer viewpoint, with the course redrawn each time the ball changed its resting location. *Leader Board Golf* would eventually morph into the long running *Links* series. Incredible Technologies' *Golden Tee* series of popular arcade games debuted in 1989, eventually making the successful transition from 2D to 3D gameplay. With its intuitive trackball controls and solid pacing, the *Golden Tee* games continue to be popular bar fixtures, even inspiring regular tournaments. Like many of the other sports in this chapter, Electronic Arts presently has the strongest showing in golf videogames with their *PGA Tour* series, which started back in 1990 on the PC. It later became the *Tiger Woods PGA Tour* series starting in 1998 on the PC and Sony PlayStation. The latest *Tiger Woods* games feature an assortment of control schemes, tournaments, and real-time events based on the platform's internal clock and showcases the expected group of licensed professionals.

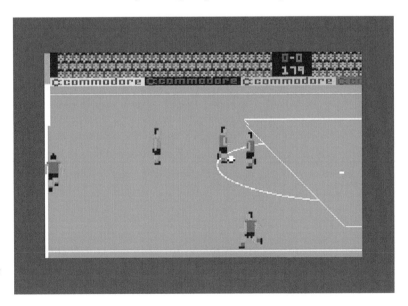

Commodore's *International Soccer* for the Commodore 64.

Soccer, better known outside North America as football, has of course received countless treatments over the years. One of the earliest recognizable videogame conversions was Atari's *Atari Soccer* (1979), which—like their other early sports titles—made excellent use of the trackball for more realistic control. Supporting up to four simultaneous players, Atari's game presented the black-and-white action from an overhead left-right perspective, and featured well-paced two-on-two (plus goalies) play. A good portion of the playfield was shown onscreen at one time, with scrolling as needed. Commodore's colorful *International Soccer* (1983) for the Commodore 64 used a similar scrolling technique, but this time presented the action from an angled side perspective, which allowed for the ball to bounce in a more realistic-looking fashion, as well as increased the number of players on the field. The popular *Sensible Soccer* series from Sensible Software, first released in 1992 on platforms like the Atari ST and Commodore Amiga, used a zoomed-out, top-down overhead view, and offered full season, quick play, and management modes. Electronic Arts' *FIFA* series debuted in 1993 and initially featured a zoomed-in, angled, isometric perspective, though on the marquee 3DO version, it sported greatly enhanced 2D graphics and a pseudo-3D camera. Perhaps the most popular soccer game today is Konami's *Pro Evolution Soccer* series, which was also known by the name *Winning Eleven*. The latest versions of the game, which include a bewildering array of features, continue to receive accolades. IGN's Alex Simmons mentions the series' "instinctive controls, the way you almost feel at one with your team when you're playing well."[3]

Hockey was perhaps the most popular sports variation on *Pong* outside of tennis, so there were of course many games released

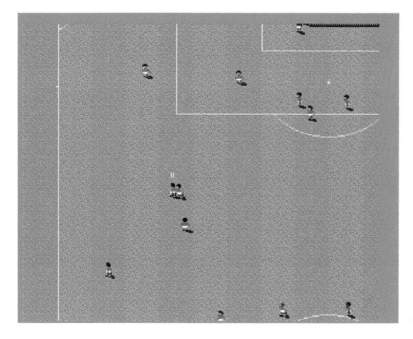

Sensible Soccer was one of the more popular games for the Commodore Amiga platform. Its smooth animation, superb audio, and bright graphics even made it popular with many gamers who didn't enjoy the sport.

---

[3]See http://ps3.ign.com/articles/828/828327p1.html.

Konami's *Blades of Steel* arcade game from 1987.

in the paddle and ball format both in the arcade and at home that called themselves "hockey." However, the first major realistic hockey game appeared on the Intellivision in 1980, in the form of Mattel's visually rich *NHL Hockey*. It was a two-player game of three-on-three hockey, plus goalies, all shown from a single-screen angled side perspective. Nintendo's *Ice Hockey*, released in 1988 for the NES; Bethesda Softwork's 1989 *Wayne Gretzky Hockey* (Commodore Amiga, NES, and others); NHL 2K (starting in 2000 on the Sega Dreamcast); and Electronic Arts' long-running *NHL* series (starting in 1991 on the Sega Genesis) competed for the affections of hockey fans. Although *NHL* started out as a popular companion to the *Madden* series on the Sega Genesis with a similar top-down overhead view, eventually morphing into the feature-rich 3D experience it is today, *NHL 2K* was always based on a 3D engine.

Tennis videogames often made use of a left-right overhead perspective that became increasingly popular, though in its more

Electronic Arts' *NHL Hockey* series has proven a videogame mainstay. Shown is *NHL 95* (1994) for the Sega Genesis.

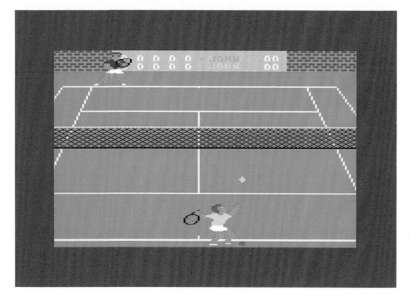

Gamestar's *On Court Tennis* (1984) was a highly accessible game, mostly because the computer automatically controlled the competitors' movement about the court. All the player had to do was focus on hitting the ball.

common top-down form. Tennis videogames are often thought of as "*Pong* with window dressing," but that's a bit unfair to the freedoms many such interpretations of the sport (particularly later ones) offer. We again turn to the Atari VCS and Mattel Intellivision for two very different early interpretations. On the VCS, Activision released *Tennis* (1981), which features a simple angled top-down view of the action for one or two players. Although there are no out-of-bounds shots and each of the players automatically hits the ball, the angle can be controlled based on player location. On the Intellivision, Mattel released *Tennis* (1980), a two-player game with an angled side view that offered full control over each player, as well as ball velocity and placement. Many future games would experiment with both the viewpoint and level of interaction, with most choosing some type of modified top-down view and full control over both the player and racket. There are two main series worth talking about that are still going strong today: *Virtua Tennis* and *Top Spin*. Sega's *Virtua Tennis* started out as an arcade game in 1999 and soon made its way home. The series is known for its quick, intuitive gameplay and—in the home versions—its quirky training minigames. PAM Development's *Top Spin* started out in 2003 for the Microsoft Xbox before seeing release on other platforms, and featured a robust create-a-player mode and online

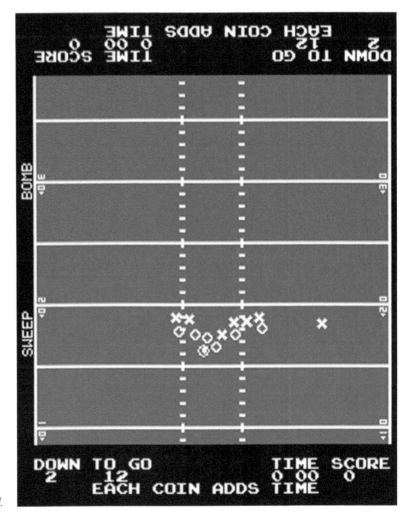

Screenshot from *Atari Football*.

play. Both series make a point of licensing the likenesses of famous tennis players to round out their feature sets.

The first major football videogame was another black-and-white Atari arcade game with trackball control, *Atari Football*, released in 1979. Supporting two or four players controlling Os (offense) and Xs (defense) from an overhead, scrolling left-right perspective, the game offered quick action and a choice of plays. Mattel led the way at home again with *NFL Football*, another two-player 1980 release for the Intellivision that featured the same field perspective as *Atari Football*, but showed its colorful animated players from the side. *NFL Football* also featured a large number of plays to choose from. Tecmo's *Tecmo Bowl* arcade game, released in 1987, utilized the same type of perspective and look as *NFL Football*, except with a closer, more zoomed-in camera, and far better graphics and sound. *Tecmo Bowl's* most notable feature in its fast-paced gameplay was the ability to shake off would-be tacklers. However, it would be its first home release for the NES in 1989 that gave the *Tecmo Bowl* series legendary status among competitive arcade sports game fans, who would make shaking off defenders into an art form. In fact, the stir that *Tecmo Bowl* created on the NES contrasted sharply with the release of a game from Electronic Arts for

Imagic's *Touchdown Football* was a popular six-on-six football game for multiple platforms. IBM PCjr version shown.

computers called *John Madden Football* from the previous year that went mostly unnoticed.

At the time of *Madden's* development and release, the computer gaming market was not in a position to support a breakout hit computer game as we think of them today. The primary development platform, the Apple II, though still popular, was no longer a particularly lucrative market. The even more popular Commodore 64 was also in decline, and the PC was still not a particularly capable audiovisual platform. With Electronic Arts not yet heavily vested directly in the console market, a system like the NES was not an option. That left a year or two until Electronic Arts' investment in the Sega Genesis platform as their direct entry point into consoles (i.e., as a big fish in a small pond) would really pay off with the system that *Madden* became most identified with and first became a best seller on.

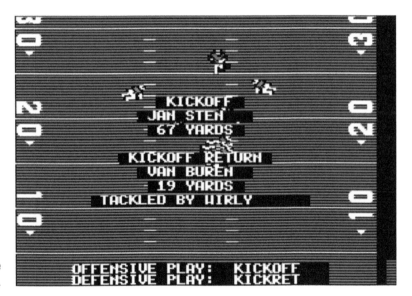

John Madden Football on the
Apple II.

Famously, even on the modest Apple II platform, John Madden insisted that for him to lend his name, the game must have full 11-member football teams facing off against each other, which was no small feat for any platform, let alone the aging 8-bit technology. By the time the game made it to the Sega Genesis in 1990 (ports for the Commodore Amiga and Super Nintendo would follow), the game's famous view from above and behind the quarterback would be set,[4] along with audibles, variable field conditions, and password-protected games. However, the game still lacked any other license besides Madden himself.

John Madden Football '92, released in 1991 for the Sega Genesis,[5] introduced instant replay, weather conditions, two-player

---

[4]Contrasting the mostly overhead perspective of the previous versions.

[5]*John Madden Football II* would be released independently for the PC the same year, with impressive updates of its own, but it did not receive the same notice as the Sega Genesis version.

Screenshot from *John Madden Football '92* for the Sega Genesis. John Madden is forever associated with football videogames. The franchise bearing his name still represents the cutting edge of sport-to-console adaptations.

cooperative play, injuries, and additional play modes. There was still no NFL or NFL Players Association license, so the developers were able to take liberties with the property, including having a reckless ambulance appear to cart off an injured player. The terms

John Madden Football (1993) for the 3DO was a high point for the platform.

of future licensing agreements with the professional football associations meant that humorous touches like that would no longer be an option.

John Madden Football '93 (1992) and *Madden NFL '94* (1993),[6] both for the Sega Genesis and Super Nintendo, continued adding features, with the latter release finally getting a full NFL team license—hence the change in name. *Madden NFL '95*, released in 1994, was the first version to feature the full names of most NFL players (not just their numbers), with full-season stat tracking. It was also the first version in a while to see release on multiple platforms again, including the Nintendo Game Boy, Sega Game Gear, Sega Genesis, and Super Nintendo.

Even the NEC Turbo Duo received *John Madden Duo CD Football* (1993). Similar to the 3DO version, the NEC release featured occasional video cutscenes.

Madden NFL '95, released in 1995 for the Nintendo Game Boy, PC, Sega Game Gear, Sega Genesis, and Super Nintendo, added classic teams and a create-a-player feature. Interestingly, a Sony PlayStation version was planned, but was canceled when Sony demonstrated an early version of the surprisingly advanced *NFL GameDay*, a series that would remain competitive through the PlayStation 2 era before being canceled.

---

[6]An advanced one-off version for the 3DO platform was produced this same year, with the title of *John Madden Football*, as well as a one-off version for the NEC Turbo Duo, titled *John Madden Duo CD Football*.

Box back for Sony's *NFL 98* (1997) for the Sony PlayStation.

Madden NFL 97 (1996) was the first version to be created for the Sega Saturn and Sony PlayStation, though versions were released for the Nintendo Game Boy, PC, Sega Genesis, and Super Nintendo as well.[7]

Madden NFL 98 (1997) was the last version released for the Sega Genesis, Super Nintendo, and Sega Saturn platforms, with Electronic Arts continuing to produce new versions for the PC and Sony PlayStation, and adding the Nintendo 64 with the release of *Madden NFL 99* (1998). Most notable in those releases was the addition of a franchise mode, which allows play across multiple seasons and involves off-season draft picks and trades. *Madden NFL 2000* (1999) added the Apple Macintosh and Nintendo Game Boy Color to the platform mix.

With the release of *Madden NFL 2001* (2000), Electronic Arts would begin the tradition of featuring a current athlete on the cover instead of John Madden.[8] Year after year, new games and platforms would follow, with online features, presnap adjustments, special defensive hits that might cause fumbles, and

---

[7]A one-off version for the Nintendo 64, *Madden Football 64*, was released in 1997 and was a step back for the series, containing only a player license.

[8]Do a web search on "Madden curse" for some fun trivia regarding each game's cover athlete.

Box back from Visual Concepts' *NFL 2K1* for the Sega Dreamcast. Sega's sports games were extremely well done, but the lack of support from Electronic Arts helped doom the Dreamcast.

many other features added to the mix to make each new year's release sound more exciting than what cynics basically called "the same game with just a few graphical tweaks and roster updates." The biggest addition to *Madden NFL 09* (2008), for instance, besides greatly improved graphics and expected gameplay tweaks, is the option to play in online leagues, allowing up to 32 players to compete in a simulated season.[9]

Madden NFL is the bestselling videogame sports franchise in history, spawning countless competitive tournaments and television competitions. It's no wonder that we chose *John Madden Football* as the greatest and most influential in its class. Although critics will argue that the "Madden Model" of typically incrementally improved new annual releases has hurt video-games in general,[10] the simple fact of the matter is that Electronic Arts has hit on a formula that works. As long as *Madden*'s rabid, foaming-at-the-mouth fanbase continues to clamor for each new release, other videogames and their creators will have no choice but to look to the series for how to release new versions of their

---

[9]Microsoft Xbox 360 and Sony PlayStation 3 versions only. The other releases for the Microsoft Xbox, Nintendo DS, Nintendo Wii, Sony PlayStation 2, and Sony PlayStation Portable are all different games.

[10]Perhaps the biggest offender pointed to is the *Tony Hawk's Pro Skater* series discussed in bonus chapter, "*Tony Hawk's Pro Skater* (1999): Videogame Ollies, Grabs, and Grinds."

own games on a regular basis. Even if *Madden*'s development did not happen in a vacuum, it's been as successful as any single game or series at giving the public exactly what they want, in this case evolving sports videogames to fall in line with the public's tastes from anonymous arcade fare to big-name-licensed sports simulations.

11

KING'S QUEST: QUEST FOR THE CROWN (1984): PERILOUS PUZZLES, THORNY THRONES

Roberta Williams' *King's Quest: Quest for the Crown*, published first in 1984 for IBM's short-lived PCjr platform, established many of the features we take for granted in modern adventure games. It's hard to exaggerate its importance on the development of the genre, to which it introduced brightly colored animated graphics, a navigable, pseudo-3D environment allowing for three axes of movement, and the quirky, irreverent humor that would dominate the adventure scene until Cyan's *Myst* exploded onto the world in 1993 (see Chapter 12, "*Myst* (1993): Launching Multimedia Worlds"). Sierra On-Line, the software publishing company formed by Williams and her husband Ken, would soon become the world's preeminent publisher of adventure games, releasing many highly popular and in uential games based on

Critics and gamers alike were blown away by the colorful animated visuals of the original *King's Quest* on the IBM PCjr.

the *King's Quest* model. Although few serious critics would claim that *King's Quest* is without aw, it represented a huge leap forward and is still played in various versions by adventure game fans today.

The history of *King's Quest* begins rather inauspiciously. Instead of releasing the game directly to the dominant computer platforms of the era (Apple II, Atari 8-bit, and Commodore 64), Sierra arranged an exclusive licensing deal with IBM for their upcoming PCjr platform. The PCjr, as the name implies, was intended as a cheaper, more family-friendly personal computer than the business-oriented IBM PC, and offered better sound and graphics, as well as built-in joystick ports. However, the PCjr's high price and a combination of other factors (awful keyboard, limited memory, compatibility issues) made it uncompetitive in the marketplace. Even with IBM's golden reputation, heavy advertising budget, and costly efforts to avert disaster (including a new and better keyboard), the PCjr failed miserably. Thankfully for adventure game fans, Sierra soon rereleased the game for other platforms, including the Tandy 1000, a much more successful IBM PC–compatible computer inspired by the PCjr. Sales of the game soared as scores of gamers ooded into software shops, eager to play the game that all their friends and magazines were talking about.

Roberta Williams was no stranger to the adventure game market, having already established a name for herself with *Mystery House*, *The Wizard and the Princess* (both 1980), and *Time Zone* (1982). All three of these games were among the firsts for their genres. *Mystery House* was the first graphical adventure game, and—though laughably primitive by today's standards—this Apple II game was tremendously progressive. Despite its crudely drawn monochrome graphics, poorly edited script, and one of the worst text parsers in the business, it still sold more than 11,000 copies in its first year of release.[1] *The Wizard and the Princess* upped the ante with color graphics and sold even better than its predecessor. *Time Zone* was by far the most ambitious graphical adventure game produced by anyone prior to that time; it shipped on six double-sided oppy disks at a time when many games fit comfortably alongside many others on one side. Unfortunately, the exorbitant cost of the game (over $100 in 1982 dollars) prevented its success, despite the immense size and somewhat improved graphics. Williams and Sierra produced several other "Hi-Res Adventures" during this era, but certainly none to rival their later *King's Quest*. We should note, too, that the company was called "On-Line Systems" during these early years, changing to "Sierra On-Line" later on to avoid confusion with another company.

---

[1] See The Dot Eaters' coverage of the game at http://www.thedoteaters.com/p4_stage2.php.

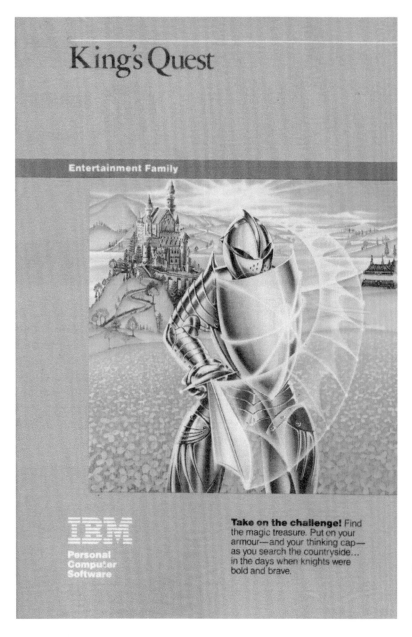

IBM's traditionally stuffy packaging and cover art for the original IBM PCjr version of *King's Quest* contrasted with the game's whimsical, storybook setting.

IBM made a smart decision in asking Sierra On-Line to create one of its popular adventure games for its PCjr. Roberta Williams was determined to up the ante yet again, producing a game that would not only look better than the competition but offer a much freer range of movement. Although Williams maintains in several interviews that she prioritizes plots and characters over interface, *King's Quest* was a technological marvel. Not only were the 16-color animated graphics superior to Sierra's earlier works,

Although *Time Zone*'s scope was impressive, the visuals were anything but.

but this time the player controlled a character that could move in three dimensions, all in real time. Williams' earlier games had been shown in first person, and it's interesting here to note that the designer felt that a third-person perspective would be more realistic—we'll see that line of thought reversed in the next chapter, when we discuss *Myst. King's Quest* isn't true 3D—the character does not shrink or expand as he moves toward the foreground or background, but could go behind or in front of objects on the screen. It was still an impressive feat for the time.

King's Quest simple parser worked in conjunction with real-time character movement to heighten the sense of interaction in the gameworld.

Simplicity was one of Sierra's main goals while designing the interface, but the game still relied heavily on textual input. As with Sierra's earlier games, the text parser was woefully dumb compared to Infocom's *Zork* (see Chapter 25, "*Zork* (1980): Text Imps versus Graphics Grues"), a fact that the legendary text adventure developer exploited ruthlessly in its magazine ads. A bigger problem, though, was that the relatively low resolution of the graphics made it difficult to identify certain objects; what looked like a stone might actually be a walnut. Typing "TAKE STONE" would simply result in the same error message over and over; only "TAKE WALNUT" would work. Although savvy players found ways to deal with these problems (such as typing "LOOK GROUND" to learn the name of the object), others were forced to rely on hint books or advice from friends. The cumbersome and vexing text parser was dropped in later Sierra adventure games (including *King's Quest V*), though some fans objected that doing so inhibited their (perceived, at least) freedom and creativity.

Even though *King's Quest*'s interface was easy for novices to master, the game itself was often quite difficult. The character, Graham, was easily and frequently killed in the adventure, so frequent saves were necessary to prevent tedious repetition—another factor that the game's diehard fans offer as a "feature," since it extends the time it takes to complete the game and thus ups the "play value."

A nastier problem was that it was also quite easy to get the game into an unwinnable state, so that even though Graham wasn't dead, there was no way to complete the game without restoring to an earlier save point. Sometimes it wouldn't even be obvious to players that they'd reached such a state; they'd simply continue trying things for hours or even days until finally giving up. Roberta Williams earned a reputation during these years for creating hard puzzles and obscure or even misleading clues.

One such puzzle in the game concerns a condor. The idea is to stand in a certain spot on the screen (walkthroughs have gone so far as to offer close-up screenshots to help) and enter "JUMP" into the parser at just the right moment. The precise timing and placement, combined with the somewhat obscure command to jump (why not catch or grab?) stumped many gamers. Another puzzle is based on the old fairy tale about Rumplestiltskin, but with a twist—when players were asked to name the gnome, they might not have realized that an earlier clue to "think backwards" meant they had to transcribe the name Rumplestiltskin using a backwards alphabet, yielding "IFNKOVHGROGHPRM." Williams admitted that this was an "awfully nasty puzzle," but defended it as a "typical 'advanced' puzzle in those days."[2] Yet perhaps the most infamous and frustrating "puzzle" has the player climbing

---

[2] See Joppe Bos's review of the game at http://www.adventureclassicgaming.com/index.php/site/reviews/120/.

a beanstalk. The climb involves careful coordination with the keyboard, since Graham will fall to his death at even the slightest deviation from the preestablished (and difficult-to-find) path. Even seasoned veterans were forced to save and restore countless times to finally get to the top of the beanstalk. Fortunately for modern adventurers, these and other puzzles have been simplified in later remakes of the game, and of course the diehards maintain that the challenge is what makes the game fun in the first place.

As we've alluded to several times already, the difficulty of the game is a point of contention among fans of the series and genre. Later adventure games, such as those from LucasArts, were much more forgiving; players were encouraged to explore without fear of dying or making the game impossible to beat. Some fans of the older style disliked these changes, claiming that gamers simply weren't patient or intelligent enough to meet the challenge. Sharply disagreeing with this opinion is Ron Gilbert, designer of LucasArts' breakaway comedy hit *The Secret of Monkey Island* (1990). His 1989 diatribe, "Why Adventure Games Suck," has been widely quoted and is worth partially quoting here:

> Some people say that following [my] rules makes the games too easy to play. I disagree. What makes most games tough to play is that the puzzles are arbitrary and unconnected. Most are solved by chance or repetitive sessions of typing "light candle with match," "light paper with match," "light rug with match," until something happens. This is not tough game play; this is masturbation. I played one game that required the player to drop a bubble gum wrapper in a room in order to get a trap door to open (object names have been changed to protect the guilty). What is the reasoning? There is none. It's an advanced puzzle, I was told.

Gilbert's essay is very much still relevant today, and it's easy to think that one reason the adventure game genre has declined somewhat in recent years is that not enough developers have read and applied it. In *King's Quest*'s defense, there are usually at least two possible solutions to the puzzles, and there are, of course, many diligent gamers who have completed it without any outside help.

Cynics might point out that, whether by design or not, the difficult puzzles created a healthy niche market for Sierra's own set of hint books. However, Sierra didn't seem to object to others' hint books, and both Roberta and Ken Williams had high praise for Peter Spears's *The King's Quest Companion*, which offered hints integrated into a novella based on the games. A historian would do well to pay attention to the hint book industry, as they were widely read and applied by adventure game fans.

According to Roberta Williams, the *King's Quest* series is primarily about personalities and stories: "Trying to come up with mind-bending puzzles and brain-twisting plots was never something that I strived for."[3] As you may have inferred from the earlier description of the puzzles, most of the stories and personalities involve popular folk and fairy tales, though usually with a twist to throw off gamers familiar with the outcomes. Whether one enjoys these games depends on their willingness to be charmed by the stories and characters, aspects that stand in stark contrast to Cyan's revolutionary *Myst* series.

The goal of *King's Quest* is to recover three stolen artifacts for the Kingdom of Daventry. These items are a shield that makes its bearer invulnerable, a chest that never empties of gold, and a mirror that shows the future. The mirror, which will play a strong role in later *King's Quest* games, was taken by a wizard who promises in exchange to "bring an heir" to the king and queen, who have been childless throughout their long and otherwise happy marriage. Rather than bear a child, however, the queen becomes deathly ill. Now a dwarf shows up who offers to cure the queen in return for the shield. The dwarf takes the shield, but the queen dies shortly after. The miserable king, however, manages to rescue a beautiful princess, whom he takes for his wife. When she learns about the chest, though, she runs away with it, leaving the king without a bride and the kingdom without its last magical artifact. The player's character, Sir Graham, shows up to help, and is promised the throne of Daventry if he can restore the three artifacts.

The low-resolution graphics sometimes made identifying objects quite difficult, as seen here in *King's Quest II*. Thankfully, typing "LOOK TREE" causes a pop-up window to appear that offers a text description of the object (a stake). Sierra relied on its text parser to both control the game and supplement the graphics technology.

---

[3]See Philip Jong's 2006 interview with Roberta Williams at http://www.adventure-classicgaming.com/index.php/site/interviews/198/.

King's Quest II: Romancing the Throne, released in 1985, continues the story introduced in the first game. Graham is now King Graham, and adventure ensues after he uses the mirror to find a suitable bride and queen for his kingdom. He is teleported to the land of Kolyma, where Hagatha the witch has trapped Valanice in a quartz tower. Graham sets out on a quest to save the damsel in distress, but rescuing her means searching all over Kolyma for the three missing keys and, of course, solving many puzzles along the way. The game's title, by the way, is an allusion to *Romancing the Stone*, a lighthearted 1984 action film/romantic comedy starring Michael Douglas and Kathleen Turner.

The second *King's Quest* game was written with AGI (Adventure Game Interpreter), a tool comparable to Infocom's Z-Machine (see Chapter 25, "*Zork* (1980): Text Imps versus Graphics Grues"). AGI, introduced in the 1984 multiplatform release of *King's Quest*, allowed writers and graphic designers to work independently of programmers, focusing on story and puzzle design rather than the game engine. It also made it easier to offer ports to the platforms of the day; once an AGI port was available for a given platform, Sierra could offer its entire library to its owners. AGI allowed Sierra to quickly develop and release not only later *King's Quest* games, but a plethora of popular spin-offs (which we'll discuss in a moment). The downside of Sierra's reliance was that many AGI games look and feel quite similar, and major innovations were a long time coming. An upgraded engine called SCI, or Sierra's Creative Interpreter, was introduced in 1988 for *King's Quest IV*. The superior audiovisuals of SCI offered 320×200 resolution (AGI was limited to 160×200), and support for sound cards and mice, two innovations that were rapidly being adopted by PC gamers. We'll discuss these issues later in this chapter.

King's Quest II is often considered one of the weaker games in the series. Harry Kaplan of *Adventure Classic Gaming*, for instance, calls it a "virtual carbon copy of the original title in both concept and style," and a sequel that has "lost both the charm and freshness of the original."[4] There were again objections to the puzzles, which some found illogical, and criticisms of the story, which some found hopelessly cliched. What's interesting from a historical perspective is the tension between the need for innovation and continuity: here, the sequel was too similar to the prequel, and suffered for it. Later games, especially the last one, would vary too widely from the model, again disappointing or even enraging loyal fans. Williams has stated in several interviews that she always carefully read and considered criticism of her games, which ranged from the highest   attery to the grossest insult. In

---

[4]See http://www.adventureclassicgaming.com/index.php/site/reviews/132/.

any case, even the "worst" games in the series tended to sell more copies than previous entries, though that fact might be explained by the broadening market and rising demand in general.

KING'S QUEST III

To Heir is Human

THE EAGERLY AWAITED SEQUEL!
With over 50,000 units sold in its first six weeks of release (on just one computer), King's Quest III was the best received software sequel of the year. As the game moves to other computers, it is quickly becoming the bestselling 3-D Animated Adventure Game in history.

A WHOLE NEW LEVEL OF INNOVATION.
Like its predecessors, King's Quest III breaks new ground in the development of adventure games as an art form. "Questbusters - The Adventurers' Journal", praises the "several exceptional innovations introduced in King's Quest III", including the addition of pull-down menus", special self-mapping features and an advanced parser.

THE MOST SOPHISTICATED PLOT YET.
King's Quest III also breaks new ground in the area of puzzles and plot. The complexity of the storyline, and the intricate game puzzles, make for a game that will challenge even the most experienced adventurer. Subplots include an escape from slavery, piracy on the high seas, and the mastery of powerful magic.

A COMPUTERIZED SCREENPLAY.
King's Quest III is a graphics extravaganza with plenty of color, animation and quick screen changes. The locations and characters of King's Quest III are the most lifelike and interactive to date. The soundtrack, which includes well-choreographed music and funny sound effects, adds new dimensions to the viewer's enjoyment. In fact, King's Quest III was nominated for "Best Music in Computer Software" by the Software Publishers Association.

THE MOST FUN YOU CAN HAVE PLAYING ADVENTURE GAMES!
In 1983, Roberta Williams and her team of programming artists designed the original King's Quest playing system. Four years later, King's Quest games are still the most enjoyable adventure games available.

Roberta Williams is designer of the King's Quest series. Over the last half decade, Roberta has worked closely with The Walt Disney Company and Jim Henson in the development of computer software. Her games have sold more copies than any other woman in computer software history.

⚠ SIERRA

Can you escape the bondage of the evil wizard Mannanan?

Learn to use magic...but don't get caught!

Find the amazing truth to your real identity.

Take to the high seas with fierce pirates.

TANDY   Cat. No. 26-3285
Color Computer 3
512K

Box back for *King's Quest III.*

The third game, *King's Quest III: To Heir Is Human*, debuted in October of 1986, and again found a ready audience of fans eager to return to Daventry. However, they must have been shocked to discover the game is not about Graham or Daventry, but rather a boy named Gwydion who has been kidnapped by Manannan, an evil magician. However, Gwydion does eventually make his way to Daventry, where he rescues Princess Rosella and saves the kingdom. Some fans were disappointed that the game didn't continue the storylines established in the earlier games, but most of the complaints focused on the difficult, frustrating gameplay.

Roy Wagner, writing in the June 1987 issue of *Computer Gaming World*, recommended that players buy the hint book immediately, since "there will be very few that can get through this game without a lot of help." Again, the problems were illogical puzzles and the expectation that players would recognize objects on the screen, which, as Wagner quips, are "drawn with two colors and a few pixels." There were also plenty of difficult climbing sequences, which seemingly only a true zealot would ever hold up as a selling point. Another controversial issue was Sierra's decision to integrate a copy protection system that expected players to have access to the printed manual. At certain points, players were asked to type in portions of the manual. Unfortunately, these weren't always accurate, as Emily Morganti of *Adventure Gamers* describes: "You're supposed to follow the directions in the manual to the letter, space, and period, but even then, some don't work. For example, typing 'Mold the dough into a cookie,' as written in the game manual, yields the response 'What's a mold?' (I took a lucky guess and found that Gwydion needs to 'pat' the dough instead.) Even without typos, it's very easy to mess up these spells, and it's game over if you do."[5] Fortunately for Sierra and fans of the series, these problems weren't bad enough to stymie sales, and modern gamers can find all the necessary manuals and codes easily enough online. After *King's Quest III*, Roberta Williams took a break to produce *Mixed-Up Mother Goose* (1987), a popular edutainment title designed for young children. The box cover showed Roberta Williams herself, surrounded by a group of children, including her own.

King's Quest IV put players in control of a female character, Princess Rosella. One of the starting puzzles involves this unicorn, who shyly retreats each time Rosella gets too close.

[5]See http://www.adventuregamers.com/article/id,590/p,2.

The fourth *King's Quest, The Perils of Rosella* (1988), makes an even more radical break from the series than its prequel. The most talked-about change concerns the protaganist, who is now female. King Graham's daughter, Princess Rosella, is whisked by the fairy Genesta to Tamir, where a magic fruit grows that can cure her father (who has recently suffered a massive heart attack). As we noted previously, this is the first *King's Quest* built with SCI, and critics made much of the improved audiovisuals and interface. However, they were again aggravated by the often illogical, obscure puzzles. The tedious and frustrating climbing segments are back, but another oft-criticized puzzle concerns a bridle. Scorpia writes about the puzzle in her December 1988 review of the game published in *Computer Gaming World:* "Finding [the bridle] can be a frustrating experience, since it is not visible on the screen, and you would never know it was there unless you had Rosella search every possible spot on the screen. There are no clues at all to this, therefore you might not even search very long, if at all. And as the location itself is not easy to reach (you have to do some swimming, among other things) it makes the situation that much more exasperating." Again, gamers hoping to finish the game sprang for a hint book, and it truly seems difficult to accept that such challenges make the game more fun to play—no matter what the zealots claim.

King's Quest V made a tremendous leap in graphics technology, making the older games look primitive by comparison. It also integrated full support for the mouse. The greatly simplified interface may have been more intuitive, but some fans objected, claiming that the older text parser allowed for more creative and fulfilling approaches to problem solving.

The next game in the series, *King's Quest V: Absence Makes the Heart Go Yonder* (1990), made another leap forward in graphics, this time to 256-color VGA. In her March 1991 review of the game in *Computer Gaming World*, Scorpia remarked that "this is the game to boot up when you want to show off your VGA system," a sentiment shared by plenty of other gamers and critics at the time. An updated version released a year later on CD-ROM went a step further by offering digitized voices, but shoddy voice acting raised some question whether this was really an upgrade to the original. Another big change is a switch to icon-based interaction, with the cumbersome and oft-lamented text parser finally laid to rest. This design made the game much more accessible to newcomers, and also reduced the frustration associated with trying to find the right word that would satisfy Sierra's hopelessly limited parser. However, again gamers were burdened with illogical puzzles and tedious action sequences (several of which were timed).

King's Quest VI: Heir Today, Gone Tomorrow, released September 1992, is usually regarded as the finest game in the series, and it shows up on several "greatest game" lists. GameSpot, for instance, includes it on its "Greatest Games of All Time" list, describing it as a "clever, beautiful, and unique adventure game [that] is truly one of the best games that the genre has ever had to offer, and reminds us sadly that adventure gaming may be dying rapidly, but it's never going to be forgotten."[6] Adam Rodman wrote for *Just Adventure* that "I, the reviewer, personally believe that *King's Quest 6* is the best adventure game Sierra has ever produced, and it would be one of my top candidates for the best adventure game of all time."[7] Indeed, it is hard to find any serious fan of the genre who can't appreciate the title, and it's certainly a worthy introduction for anyone new to the series.

Adventure game fans note *King's Quest VI* for bringing together two of Sierra's most celebrated designers: Roberta Williams and Jane Jensen, the designer responsible for the hugely popular *Gabriel Knight* series. Although fans will of course recognize the familiar blend of folk and fairy tales that are one of the series' trademarks, they seem more thoughtfully and artistically explored here than before. What appears at first to be a very basic plot (Prince Alexander sets off to find Princess Cassima) expands rapidly. Alexander must contend with four different islands in the Land of the Green Isles, each with its own theme and personality. What makes the story worthwhile are the characters: neither Alexander nor Cassima act in the stereotypical ways we might expect from the previous games, and the people of each island have a unique theme and personality. Finally, and perhaps most importantly, the puzzles are much less frustrating than in previous games, and the game is much more forgiving of mistakes, thus encouraging experimentation. It's quite accessible to novices, especially when compared to previous entries.

---

[6] See http://www.gamespot.com/features/6144989/index.html.
[7] See http://www.justadventure.com/reviews/KQ6/KQ6_Review.shtm.

The biggest change graphically was a lengthy introductory 3D cutscene; it was cutting edge for its day and provided gamers with a new "tech demo" to show off their systems. The intro is particularly impressive in the later CD-ROM release, which features professional-quality voice acting. Both versions boast full 3D animation and dramatic music. The introduction sets up the context of the game and introduces the characters. Though of course the actual game is less impressive than this cinematic introduction, everyone knew it was only a matter of time before graphic technology caught up with the imagination of visionary designers like Williams and Jensen.

One of the best puzzles involves five gnomes, each with a single, highly amplified sense organ (and no others). The player must find objects for Alexander that will fool the gnomes into thinking he's not human. For instance, one gnome has an acute sense of smell, and must be fooled by waving a ower under his nose. Clever and original puzzles such as this abound in the game, and have delighted the countless gamers who have managed to solve them.

The series seemed to decline after the sixth game, perhaps because Williams was by that point engrossed in her *Phantasmagoria* project, an adult-oriented game that incorporated large amounts of full-motion video. *King's Quest VII: The Princeless Bride* appeared November 1994, and seems to be an effort to create a game in the style of Disney's *Aladdin* and similar animated features. It featured cell animation and SVGA graphics, qualities that still give the game a distinctly modern look, despite its age. The protagonists are Queen Valanice and Princess Rosella, who has been resisting Valanice's requests that she seek a suitable husband. Rosella leaps into a magic pool

King's Quest VI: Heir Today, Gone Tomorrow, is widely regarded as the best game of the series. Shown here is the memorable gnome puzzle. Each gnome has only a single sense organ, and it's up to the player to find ways to exploit this fact to convince them he's not a human being. For this game, Roberta Williams was joined by Jane Jensen, who went on to create the best-selling *Gabriel Knight* series.

King's Quest VII brought the visual quality up to that of an animated film.

and is followed by a dumbstruck Valanice, but the two are transported to a realm named Eldritch. The game shifts from Valanice to Rosella as the two search all over Eldritch for each other. The rather cutesy nature of the story, characters, and animation style seemed a rather sharp contrast to the previous game, which seemed to cater more to mature gamers. *The Princeless Bride* also offers a simplified interface reminiscent of Cyan's *Myst*, which had debuted the year before. The puzzles were also far easier (or more intuitive) than ever before, naturally with zealous fans of the "hard" puzzles of previous games objecting.

In 1996, Sierra On-Line was purchased by CUC International, an event that signaled the beginning of the end for the developer's prominence. Because Sierra was a publicly traded company, the decision wasn't up to CEO Ken Williams, and he found afterwards that "I had no power to control things, and they got out of hand. I transferred out of the games division, primarily because I couldn't stomach watching my company being ripped apart."[8] Although Sierra would continue making games for some years, it's hard not to imagine how this tragedy behind the scenes was affecting morale and, subsequently, the quality of the final *King's Quest* games.

While some fans may have found *The Princeless Bride* disappointing, the final game, *Mask of Eternity* (1998), aroused much greater controversy. The boldest change to the gameplay was the introduction of role-playing elements. Sierra had achieved great success with Lori Ann Cole's *Quest for Glory* (also known as *Hero's Quest*) series of adventure/RPG hybrids, but many fans

---

[8]See Philip Jong's interview with Ken Williams at http://www.adventureclassic-gaming.com/index.php/site/interviews/197/.

Mask of Eternity went 3D and bears little resemblance to the previous games, a fact that upset many fans. The main character, Connor, can run, jump, and fight, arcade elements that were intended to make the series more accessible to modern gamers. Whether these innovations helped or hindered the game is controversial, though designer Roberta Williams thought they were essential to revitalize the genre.

were appalled to find them in a *King's Quest* game. Sierra had been doing poorly for some time, and Williams felt that a drastic change was necessary: "I was trying to bring new blood into the genre . . . thereby trying to keep it from dying. Times change, and tastes change . . . they just do, and you've gotta do what you've gotta do to try and reach the biggest possible audience to keep a genre alive. . . . The old-style adventure game that we all know and love will just not cut it in today's world."[9] Williams had also been quoted in other interviews claiming that because computers were now more affordable, the audience for games had become less sophisticated—many of them just couldn't handle a difficult game like *King's Quest*.

Reactions to the game were mixed. IGN's Tal Blevins called it a "welcomed addition" to the series, though acknowledging that "more traditional fans of the genre will probably scoff at this one.[10] Vince Broady of GameSpot was likewise favorably disposed: "Sierra should be applauded for trying something new, even if its reach somewhat exceeds its grasp."[11] However, two of the Internet's biggest adventure game sites, Quandary (defunct) and Adventure Gamers, gave it failing scores. Josh Roberts's review for Adventure Gamers describes a game "caught between two genres, unable to fully succeed in either," and complains

---

[9]See Randy Sluganski's interview with Roberta Williams at http://www.justadventure .com/Interviews/Roberta_Williams/Roberta_Williams_Interview_3.shtm.
[10]See http://pc.ign.com/articles/153/153529p1.html.
[11]See http://reviews.cnet.com/pc-games/king-s-quest-mask/4505-9696_7-30976333 .html.

about the uneven graphics, "complicated" controls, and the "stiff, boring, and frequently just plain irritating" protagonist.[12]

It's easy to compare the controversy surrounding the final *King's Quest* with the final *Ultima* game (See Chapter 23, "*Ultima* (1980): The Immaculate Conception of the Computer Role-Playing Game"); both Roberta Williams and Richard Garriott felt that the tried-and-true models established by their earlier triumphs just weren't compatible with the modern industry. The two icons had always striven not just to be on the leading edge, but rather the bleeding edge of game design. They played a vital role in establishing higher standards for PC games. Countless gamers upgraded their graphics and sound cards—if not their whole systems—just to play the latest *King's Quest* or *Ultima,* and it's quite possible that their risky efforts in these areas laid the foundation for the modern PC industry. Now that their games had been overshadowed by the next generation of top-tier developers—Cyan, id, and Bethesda, to name just a few—they no doubt felt something drastic had to be done. Unfortunately for both, this drastic action served more to alienate existing fans than win new ones.

Mask of Eternity deviated from its predecessors in several key technological aspects, the most noticeable being the shift to full 3D graphics. It also offered a choice of perspectives: third-person or first-person. This ability to shift perspectives proved vital, as so many of the puzzles involved precision running and jumping sequences reminiscent of *Tomb Raider* (see Chapter 18, "*Super Mario 64/Tomb Raider* (1996): The Third Dimension"). The world was very massive, consisting of seven regions, each with its own look and theme. The story introduced a new protagonist named Connor, who accidentally turns the entire citizenry of Daventry to stone when he picks up a mysterious object (a shard of the titular mask). Connor's quest, naturally, is to restore their freedom, a task that requires exploring nearly every inch of the sizable gameworld.

King's Quest legacy is immense, particularly regarding the adventure game genre. As we mentioned earlier, the early adoption of the multiplatform AGI and SCI engines made it easier for Sierra to quickly develop and release games. The first of these was *Space Quest,* a 1986 game developed by Mark Crowe and Scott Murphy. This zany and irreverent game was rife with parody and satire of popular science fiction, and launched a highly successful series that lasted for five sequels. A more controversial spin-off series is Al Lowe's *Leisure Suit Larry,* a notorious 1987 game intended for mature audiences. The game's protagonist, the nerdy Larry Laffer, remains one of the most recognizable characters in all of adventure gaming, and games based on the franchise are still in

---

[12]See http://adventuregamers.com/article/id,96.

production today, though Lowe himself is no longer involved. Jim Walls's *Police Quest*, a shorter-lived series that also debuted in 1987, is notable for being designed by an actual highway patrol officer. In 1989, Lori Ann Cole's *Quest for Glory* series debuted, which was a tremendously popular hybrid adventure with role-playing and action elements. Unlike *Mask of Eternity*, this earlier attempt to blur genres was a rousing success, and remains one of the most beloved of Sierra's many games and series. Although the look and feel of the games depended on the SCI or AGI engine, they pushed it in wildly different creative directions.

Box back for the *Space Quest Collection.*

Box back for *Police Quest III: The Kindred.*

Beyond in uencing other developers at Sierra, Roberta Williams' ideas spread far and wide across the industry. Although there are literally hundreds of games we could mention, by far the most important are those developed by LucasArts (earlier Lucasfilm Games). In particular, these include two classics designed or codesigned by Ron Gilbert: *Maniac Mansion* (1987) and *The Secret of Monkey Island* (1990), which are indisputably two of the greatest adventure games of all time. Like Sierra, LucasArts created its own in-house development tool called SCUMM, or "Script Creation Utility for Maniac Mansion," and countless best-selling games were composed with it. *Maniac Mansion* offered a purely icon-based interface (no text parser), and was much more forgiving than Sierra's hits. *The Secret of Monkey Island* further refined the formula, making it impossible for the protagonist (Guybrush Threepwood) to die except in one place. Because players no longer had to be worried about sudden death or getting the game into an unwinnable state, they were much more comfortable exploring and experimenting, savoring the story and witty dialog. Gilbert's masterpiece has been translated into five languages and is certainly worth the attention of any *King's Quest* fan. LucasArts would go on to produce many best-selling graphical adventure games, giving Sierra a run for their money (or, rather, a run for their customers' money).

Nevertheless, LucasArts only refined what Roberta Williams and Ken Williams created. The in uence of *King's Quest* still lives on today, surviving even the onslaught brought on by Cyan's *Myst*. After all, the bulk of adventure games still being produced today for computers, consoles, and handhelds are in third-person perspective, not first-person, and many are loaded with characters, humor, and plots that all make them much closer to *King's Quest* than *Myst* in spirit. We also see a revival of the genre in the latest *Sam & Max* games from Telltale Games (starting 2006), available in episodic form online and in a combined "season" on disc. Although many critics seem to think the adventure game is dead, *Sam & Max* and similar projects like 2008's *Penny Arcade Adventures: On the Rain-Slick Precipice of Darkness* (Hothead Games) and *Strong Bad's Cool Game for Attractive People* (Telltale Games and Videlectrix), demonstrate that gamers will always find time (and funds) for games with well-written stories, intriguing characters, and clever puzzles.

MYST (1993): LAUNCHING MULTIMEDIA WORLDS

Cyan's *Myst*, first released in 1993 for the Apple Macintosh and later for the PC and countless other platforms, is one of the most in uential adventure games ever made. It was so financially successful, in fact, that it helped spur the widespread adoption of CD-ROM technology, a critical development that changed the surface of the computer gaming industry. It also offered some of the best graphics of the era, offering a viable alternative to the often cartoony, pixilated, or blocky raster[1] or polygonal graphics of its contemporaries. Beyond these technological factors, *Myst* also ushered in a new type of graphical adventure game, one that deviated sharply from past adventure game hits such as Infocom's *Zork* (see Chapter 25, "*Zork* (1980): Text Imps versus Graphics Grues"), Sierra's *King's Quest* (see Chapter 11, "*King's Quest: Quest for the Crown* (1984): Perilous Puzzles, Thorny Thrones") or Lucasfilm's *Maniac Mansion* (1987; Apple II, Commodore Amiga, and others). Unlike these games, which emphasized story, character, and humor, *Myst* is primarily about ambiance, exploration, and complex logic puzzles. It is timeless and surreal, comparable to a quiet day spent wandering about a Zen rock garden.

However, *Myst* is not without its detractors, who are often as vehement in their condemnation as others are in praise. Despite its bold innovations in graphics, *Myst's* game engine is mundane and even primitive, often likened to an interactive slideshow. Even the prerendered, static graphics that were so compelling in the early 1990s looked fairly dated only a few years later, eclipsed even by Cyan's own sequel, *Riven*. Furthermore, the difficulty of the puzzles and lack of clear objectives frustrated many gamers, who eventually either gave up or were forced to consult hint books to finish the game. The severest critics lump *Myst* along with *The 7th Guest* and other early CD-ROM games as mere

---

[1] In reference to bitmapped graphics, which are the representation of a digital image as a matrix of pixels or, more simply, tiny squares.

A recurring theme throughout the *Myst* series is books and writing, specifically the ability to create worlds merely by writing about them. The series explores the complex relationship between writing, video, and gaming, blurring the boundaries among these supposedly discrete media.

historical curiosities; important in context, perhaps, but certainly not worth playing today. In this chapter we'll embark on our own exploration of *Myst*, keeping these criticisms in mind, but pointing out why we include it as one of the greatest and most in uential games of all time.

This *Myst* opening shot, one of the most canonical in all of computer gaming, gives the player a good idea of what the game will be about: mysterious machinery in surreal settings. It's up to the player to figure out where to go and what to do, but the primary joy is simply exploring these highly artistic environments.

Academic studies of *Myst*, such as the one found in Jay David Bolter and Richard Grusin's book *Remediation: Understanding*

New Media, tend to focus on how the game seems to re ect on the relationship between books and games, offering itself, perhaps, as the future of storytelling. This aspect of *Myst* is evident from the beginning; after all, the adventure begins when the Stranger (the player's avatar) is literally sucked into a mysterious book about an island. As the Stranger learns more about the world of *Myst*, he (or she) learns about its creators, powerful beings who create whole worlds with a magic script. The central dilemma of this game—which was principally developed by two real-life brothers (Rand and Robyn Miller)—concerns two brothers and their father. All are trapped in books; it's up to the player to collect the missing pages of these books and restore their freedom. Actually, these "books" contain blurry and distorted full-motion video segments; each restored page sharpens these videos and eventually lets the player hear and see the brothers.

The brothers accuse each other of murdering their father, but a savvy player will soon discover that neither is trustworthy. However, *Myst* spells out nothing; instead, players must piece the story together themselves, considering what they see and hear as they explore the large gameworld. Although there is no way for the Stranger to die, only one of the game's possible endings is a happy one.

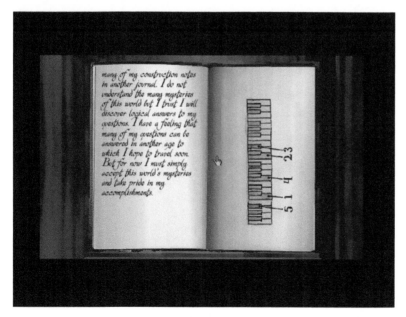

Many clues in *Myst* are hidden within journals and other writings sprinkled across the worlds, though their purpose is seldom clear initially. For instance, players will likely stumble upon this clue long before they discover the machine it corresponds to.

The game is represented through the Stranger's eyes in a first-person perspective, but is not free-roaming like modern 3D games. Instead, the player clicks "hot spots," which are special locations on the screen that enable possible actions. For instance, clicking on an exit will move the perspective to a new location, whereas clicking on a lever may raise or lower it. The interface is deliberately minimal and is easily controlled entirely by the mouse (or in other versions, gamepad or stylus). This setup was radically different from most adventure games of the era, which are usually represented in third-person perspective. The player sees the avatar and can move him or her around the screen by clicking the mouse, pushing the arrow keys, or (rarely) moving a joystick or gamepad. This is not to say that first-person adventure games were unheard of; indeed, the first commercially available graphical adventure game, On-Line Systems' *Mystery House* (1980; Apple II) was first-person, and ICOM Simulations' *Deja Vu* (1985; Apple IIGS, Atari ST, Nintendo Game Boy Color, and others) offered first-person perspective and mouse control. Nevertheless, the great majority of successful graphical adventure games were third-person point-and-click games such as Lucasfilm's *The Secret of Monkey Island* (1990; Apple Macintosh, PC, Sega CD, and others) and the aforementioned *King's Quest*. Both Lucasfilm (later LucasArts) and Sierra (was On-Line Systems and Sierra Online) took similar approaches to the genre, weaving witty, self-effacing narratives around scores of puns and puzzles.

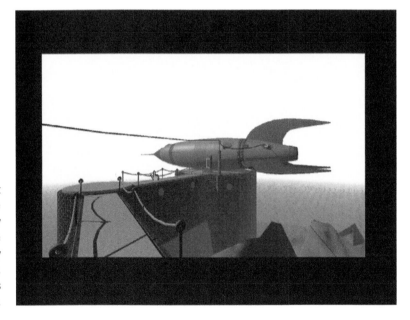

This *Buck Rogers*–style rocket ship is a good example of the creativity, artistry, and diversity of the worlds in *Myst*. The desire to explore the ship more fully (to find a way to open the door, for instance) helps keep players invested in the game.

Nevertheless, *Myst* differed sharply from these games, and not just in terms of perspective. Another significant difference is the lack of clear objectives, especially in the crucial first stages of the game. There is no orb to recover, no wizard to slay, no princess to rescue. Indeed, it's not at all clear what the player is *supposed* to do at all; the plot and characters are only revealed after hours of diligent exploration and experimentation. Of course, there are plenty of puzzles to solve, most involving strange machinery—a theme that shows up in later *Myst* games. Gameplay consists mostly of finding such machines, manipulating them, observing (or listening to) the results, and eventually discovering how one machine interacts with another. Clues are sprinkled around the gameworld, and only the most observant players will find them all. In short, it's a game of tinkering and exploration.

One good example of a puzzle (or "friction," as the game's developers are wont to say) involves a locked chest at the bottom of a ooded lighthouse. Opening the chest requires several steps. First, players must empty the lighthouse of water by manipulating a lever in an area called the Umbrella Crow's Nest. Then they must travel to the chest and drain it of water by opening a small valve, resealing the valve, then re ooding the lighthouse. The chest will now oat up to the top of the lighthouse, where a key is chained nearby that can (at last) unlock it. Puzzles of this sort abound in *Myst*. Note how this puzzle doesn't involve carrying or collecting items; *Myst* deliberately avoids the inventory systems that continue to be a staple of the genre. The only items the player can collect in *Myst* are the pages from the brothers' books.

A classic *Myst* dilemma: how does one get across the water to reach the switchbox? Clearly, the controls have something to do with it, but what? Is the time on the clock significant?

The best moments in *Myst* occur when the player begins to grasp the purpose and function of the various machines; the "aha!" moments that justify the hours of trial and error. However, sensitive players will also savor the lush environments and relaxing ambiance created by the visuals and the superb audio. The music, composed by Robyn Miller, is what might be described now as new age electronica, soothing synths that are occasionally dark and foreboding. Miller's 40-odd minutes of music fits the game perfectly, but it has also been released, along with some bonus material, as a standalone album by Virgin Records. Later games in the series would continue to uphold the high standard set by Miller's score; *Myst IV: Revelation* (2004), for instance, boasts a soundtrack by Jack Wall and Peter Gabriel.

Myst was a phenomenal success for Cyan, appealing to gamers of both sexes. Indeed, it was the best-selling computer game of all time until *The Sims* (see Chapter 22, "*The Sims* (2000): Who Let the Sims Out?") finally surpassed it in 2002.[2] Most critics raved about the product. Jeff Sengstack of GameSpot wrote that "if you own a PC, you owe it to yourself to try *Myst*," and Philip Jong of Adventure Classic Gaming calls it the "second coming of graphical adventure games."[3] Some recent reviews have been less kind. In a review of the 2008 Nintendo DS version of the game, Jack DeVries of IGN wrote, "Even when it's free, *Myst* is barely worth playing, so charging $30 for a portable version is just ridiculous, especially since the port absolutely ruins the game. No amount of nostalgia can make this pixelated, boring, sorry excuse for an adventure fun."[4] DeVries is certainly not the only critic to bash the game's fuzzy graphics and miserable interface. However, the industry as a whole has seemed to turn away from the graphical adventure game genre. The majority of recent releases are imported and often poorly translated games from Eastern Europe. We'll explore some possible explanations for this shift in a moment.

To better understand *Myst*'s legacy, it's worthwhile to compare it to a contemporary game, Trilobyte's *The 7th Guest*, released in 1993 for PC and later ported to the Apple Macintosh and Philips CD-i platforms. Superficially, *The 7th Guest* and *Myst* have much in common. Both pioneered the use of CD-ROM to create a more cinematic gameplay experience. Both weave a thin narrative around a series of difficult logic puzzles. Like *Myst*, *The 7th Guest* was also a tremendous financial success, sending hordes of gamers to the computer store to purchase a CD-ROM drive and updated graphics card. However, unlike *Myst*, *The 7th Guest* has not withstood the test of time, and very few people would care to play it today. Trilobyte's game simply relied too heavily on its ashy graphics and trendy live action segments to dazzle gamers. Such gimmicks were exciting enough in the early 1990s to compensate for lackluster gameplay

[2] See Trey Miller's "The Sims Overtakes Myst" at http://www.gamespot.com/pc/strategy/simslivinlarge/news_2857556.html.

[3] See http://www.gamerankings.com/itemrankings/launchreview.asp?reviewid=255087 and http://www.gamerankings.com/itemrankings/launchreview.asp?reviewid=922115, respectively.

[4] See http://ds.ign.com/articles/874/874807p1.html.

and mediocre acting, but the reign of full-motion video (FMV) in games was short-lived. Dozens of lesser developers surged in, rushing even the most decrepit FMV products onto the shelves in hopes of luring customers before the fad died out. These projects typically employed cheap, rightfully unknown actors, though a few managed to recruit faded stars.[5] In any case, the decline of FMV games after 1995 was severe, and nowadays it's rare to find any game with footage of live actors.

An iconic scene from *The 7th Guest*. *The 7th Guest* was a hugely popular and award-winning computer title back in its day, but lacked the staying power of *Myst*. The *7th Guest*'s direct sequel, *The 11th Hour* (1995), was ironically late to market and had only modest sales.

Unlike *The 7th Guest*, *Myst*'s reputation was able to survive the onslaught and general discrediting of FMV as a viable technique. It certainly helped that *Myst* relied much less on FMV than its contemporaries, but we shouldn't forget its intricate puzzles and the great attention to detail paid by the Miller brothers. Playing *The 7th Guest* today feels like roaming through an empty and decaying theme park; all that was once bright and shiny is now rusted and dirty. *Myst*, by contrast, may look dated by modern standards, but its gameplay is still enjoyable today.

Modern gamers will probably want to play one of the remakes of the game. These include *Myst: Masterpiece Edition*, released in 1999. In addition to greatly improved graphics (24-bit color depth instead of 8-bit), it also includes a handy in-game hint guide. A more ambitious remake released in 2000 is *realMyst*, a fully 3D game that allows players to freely roam about the world. Because both games include the exact same puzzles, a modern gamer would do well to sample both interfaces before committing to one.

---

[5]For instance, Amazing Media's *Frankenstein: Through the Eyes of the Monster* and *Mummy: Tomb of the Pharoah* (both 1997) starred Tim Curry and Malcolm McDowell, respectively.

Riven offers more upfront story and structure than *Myst*. Shown here is Rand Miller portraying Atrus, a recurring character throughout the series.

Cyan followed *Myst* with five sequels, which, with one exception, have been generally well regarded by critics and gamers. The first of these, 1997's *Riven*, was undoubtedly the most highly anticipated computer game of that year. By that time, *Myst* had sold more than 3.5 million copies, and game sites and magazines had been buzzing for months about the upcoming sequel.[6] When it was finally released, critics praised it and over 1.5 million gamers purchased it. Again, most of the praise focused on the audiovisuals; Cyan had a much larger team and budget to work with, and had even recruited a former Disney designer who had worked on the hit animated film *Aladdin* (1992). The game also offered much more FMV than *Myst*, though as we've seen the enthusiasm for this technique was waning by 1997. The story picks up after the first game, and has the player chasing down Gehn, a villain who has captured Atrus's (the father in the first game) wife Catherine. Along the way, of course, the player will   esh the story out by exploring and examining the machines, journals, and other artifacts placed throughout the massive gameworld. After *Riven*, the Miller brothers went their separate ways. Rand stayed on at Cyan, while Robyn left to pursue writing and music.

The next *Myst* game was entitled *Myst III: Exile*, a project outsourced to Presto Studios and released in 2001. Cyan was busy developing *Uru*, which we'll discuss in a moment, and didn't have the time or resources to allocate to the sequel. Presto Studios had earned a solid reputation with *The Journeyman Project* (starting

[6]See Jeff Sengstack's review of the game at http://www.gamespot.com/pc/adventure/riventhesequeltomyst/review.html.

Shown here is one of *Riven's* celebrated, full-screen gondola sequences, a sort of desktop rollercoaster that made good use of the era's graphic capabilities. These noninteractive but nevertheless thrilling rides also helped players learn the layout of the land.

in 1992) series of adventure games for the Macintosh and other platforms, and seemed a good choice for the project. *Exile* proved to be another successful game in the series, with good production values, well-designed puzzles, and decent acting. The game sold well, though it didn't generate the media sensation brought on by its prequels. If the game suffers, it's from being too faithful to its predecessors; there is little here to make the game stand out. The general consensus seems to be that if you loved *Myst* and *Riven*, you'll love this game.

The next wrinkle in the tale takes us down the steep slope of *Uru: Ages Beyond Myst*, an ill-fated project released in late 2003. Developed by Cyan Worlds, the idea was to bring the *Myst* concept to a massively multiplayer online (MMO) format, which had become a vital sector of the games market. The potential of the product was substantial: individual players would be able to create their own realms and puzzles, adding value to the game far beyond Cyan Worlds' initial investment. It is also the only *Myst* game to offer third-person perspective and the ability to create a unique avatar. Unfortunately, the developer ran out of time and money, and the resulting product was a half-hearted effort to salvage the material for use as a single-player game. Brass Lantern's reviewer Murray Peterson was aghast, remarking that "Cyan and Ubisoft have completely ruined the *Myst* experience for me. I won't be playing the online version of *Uru*, and unless things change, I won't be playing any future *Myst* games."[7] Like many

---

[7] See http://www.brasslantern.org/reviews/graphic/urupeterson.html.

Back of the box for *Uru: Ages Beyond Myst.*

other reviewers, Peterson objected to the cumbersome control scheme, limited save game options, and the many tedious puzzles involving running and jumping. Although the sterling reputation of the franchise was enough to guarantee good sales initially, word soon spread of the bugs and substandard gameplay. Later, Cyan Worlds worked out a deal with GameTap, an online games subscription service, to offer the game in a format closer to the original vision, but it again failed. Sadly, the failure of *Uru* paints a gloomy picture for the future of adventure games of this style, which have proven very resistant to the MMO format.

The back of the box for *Myst IV: Revelation*.

Myst IV: Revelation was developed by Ubisoft Montreal and released in 2004. Critics were impressed with the quality of this single-player game, which boasted the best audiovisuals and some of the best puzzles yet seen in the venerable series. The major game sites rated it highly, but the reception still paled in comparison to the first two games. That said, it is still the best-looking *Myst* game, with immaculate backgrounds and skillful direction.

For the final entry in the series, Cyan Worlds' Rand Miller again took the helm. For 2005's *Myst V: End of Wages*, the series at last abandoned prerendered graphics for real-time 3D. The end result may not have been as pretty as *Revelation*, but was still well

Myst IV reintroduced the gondola sequence, but surpassed all expectations by making it more interactive—and even incorporating a live actor! During the ride, the player can move the camera without distorting the animation of the girl or the terrain.

received by many critics, who admired its detailed models and quality voice acting. Despite glowing accolades, however, some reviewers bestowed mediocre ratings on the game. GameSpot commented that it was "not as immersive as it could have been," and the *New York Times* commentator argued that the game "does less with its real-time 3-D engine than 1997's *Riven* did with prerendered backgrounds and some clever animations."[8] In any case, *End of Ages* is a quality entry that any true fan of the series would be foolish to miss—if for no other reason than it brings a long-awaited resolution to the gaps left by the earlier games.

The impact of *Myst* is substantial, and it is no exaggeration to say that *Myst* brought about a paradigm shift in graphical adventure games. The extent of the in uence ranges from dozens of derivatives such as Dreamcatcher's *The Crystal Key* (1999), Knut Muller's *Rhem* (2003), and Detalion's *Sentinel: Descendants in Time* (2004), to more creative offerings like Her Interactive's *Nancy Drew* series (starting in 1998), XXv's *Dark Fall* (2003), Omni Adventure's *Riddle of the Sphinx II: The Omega Stone* (2003), and Kheops Studio's *Return to Mysterious Island* (2004). The type of gameplay pioneered in *Myst* is a touchstone for the genre, and countless reviews of modern games inevitably compare the new product to the venerable classic.

---

[8] See http://www.gamespot.com/pc/adventure/mystvendofages/review.html?page=2 and http://www.nytimes.com/2005/10/01/sports/othersports/01game.html?_r=1 &page, respectively.

Cyan went to great lengths to make *Myst IV* feel less lonely and more populated, carefully integrating footage of live actors in compelling and unobtrusive ways.

Unfortunately for fans of *Myst* and its derivatives, the number of new adventure games produced each year has steadily declined, and even big-budget games like FunCom's *Dreamfall: The Longest Journey* (2006) get lost in the buzz over the latest crop of violent shooters. The majority of new adventure games are imports published by The Adventure Company and Dreamcatcher Interactive. However, few of these are first-person games, relying instead on the third-person perspective popularized by Sierra and LucasArts. Third-person is a popular choice because it allows the player to see the facial expressions and body language of the avatar, a particularly important aspect of humorous games. Indeed, one of the most common complaints heard about *Myst* is that it feels alienating; even in later games that feature live actors more prominently, the somewhat detached first-person perspective and total anonymity of the avatar can make for a decidedly disconnected experience.

If *Myst* was such a huge financial success, why don't we have more *Myst*-like games on the shelf today? Steve Meretzky, author of several of the greatest text adventure games of all time, blames the big budgets and corporate-style decision making of the modern industry. "I like violent games as much as the next non-psychopathic gamer—but with the whole range of human experience, is there nothing else, nothing else that we can concentrate on?" Meretzky asked in a 2008 interview.[9] *Myst* certainly offered an alternative to violent games like *Doom*, id's seminal shooter released the same

---

[9]See http://www.gamesetwatch.com/2008/08/opinion_meretzky_lets_loose_on.php.

Rhem, primarily the product of a single person (Knot Muller), is distinctly *Myst*-like, which seems to be its primary appeal. *Myst* inspired countless other games.

year (see Chapter 5, "*Doom* (1993): The First-Person Shooter Takes Control"). Nevertheless, that game, not *Myst*, has come to dominate modern gaming. Perhaps developers simply found it easier to follow in id's footsteps than Cyan's, as designing ingenious puzzles seems infinitely more challenging than throwing together a bunch of monsters for players to shoot. Likewise, the tranquil nature of *Myst* stands in stark contrast to the fiery explosions and adrenaline-pumping action of *Doom*. Apparently, the number of gamers, developers, and publishers who prefer the latter are just much greater. Nevertheless, just as Hollywood produces sophisticated films as well as action-packed blockbusters, there seems little reason why gaming can't do both as well.

Speaking in a 2007 interview with Adventure Classic Gaming's Philip Jong, Rand Miller described what he thought made *Myst* special: "First was the attempt on our part to make it feel like a real place. We were fairly certain that the interface and game-play should be simple and intuitive enough to fade into the background. You should not have to be distracted with interface elements, and the game-play had to be built to support that. So no inventory, no on-screen arrows or menus, no points or timers—just the world. Second was the idea to step away from dying. We felt that dying was simply a brute force level of game-play friction to keep players from completing games too quickly. *Myst* would be large enough that we wouldn't have to depend on starting over to provide gaming value."[10]

---

[10]See http://www.adventureclassicgaming.com/index.php/site/interviews/269/.

Miller's analysis seems quite astute, and it seems fair to say that the Miller brothers succeeded in creating a plausible world and intuitive interface. Still, although *Myst* remains one of the best-selling games of all time, its in uence has not proven as long-lived as fans would have liked. Nevertheless, it spawned its own subgenre of adventure games that is still active in its own niche today, and Cyan Worlds seems eager to produce remakes and new compilations of the epic series.

13

PAC-MAN (1980): JAPANESE GUMPTION, AMERICAN CONSUMPTION

Now that we're awash with countless videogame mascots, it's hard to imagine when there was only one—a little yellow pizza with a missing slice, named Pac-Man. Yet long before the days of Master Chief, Lara Croft, Sonic, and of course Mario, this humble pie guy chomped out of the arcades and into public consciousness.[1] Here was proof that videogames were more than the sum of their parts; they could have personality and charisma. Pac-Man eventually found his way onto lunchboxes, breakfast cereal, Saturday morning cartoons, a hit song, toys, and pretty much anything else that could be affixed with his image and sold in a store. Indeed, the cavalcade of collectibles eventually grew large enough to warrant a book of its own, Deborah Palicia's *Pac-Man Collectibles* (Schiffer Publishing, 2002), which offers more than 400 photographs of Pac-Man products. Americans were as eager to gobble up Pac-Man as he was to chow down on power pellets!

But what made this game so overwhelmingly popular, and what were the repercussions for the edgling gaming industry? In this chapter, we'll explore the history of one of the most important and definitive games in the videogame canon, Toru Iwatani's 1980 masterpiece for Namco, *Pac-Man*.

According to legend, the inspiration for *Pac-Man*—or *Puck Man*, as it was originally known—came from a pizza. Iwatani looked down at his pizza after removing a slice, and wondered if the shape could work as a videogame character. Unfortunately for the many journalists and historians who have told this story, it is only "half-true" according to Iwatani. He claims the shape was

---

[1]See Chapter 5, "*Doom* (1993): The First-Person Shooter Takes Control," for more on Master Chief; Chapter 18, "*Super Mario 64/Tomb Raider* (1996): The Third Dimension," for more on both Mario and Lara Croft; and Chapter 19, "*Super Mario Bros.* (1985): How High Can Jumpman Get?" for more on both Mario and Sonic.

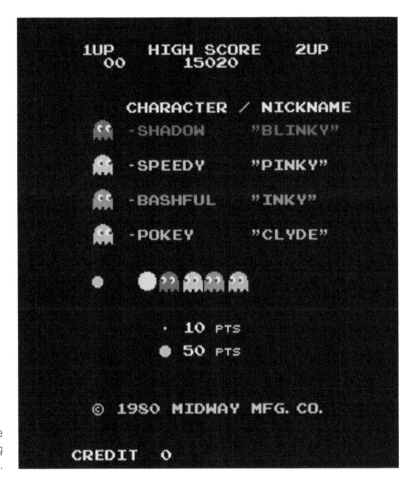

Title screen from the arcade version of *Pac-Man*, showcasing the emphasis on its characters.

simply a rounded version of the Japanese word for mouth (kuchi).[2] The game's title has a similar origin; in Japanese slang, "paku paku" represents the mouth opening and closing during eating; it was a small stretch to *Puck Man*. What the popular myth does get right, though, is the centrality of eating, or consumption rather than destruction. After all, everyone enjoys a good meal. Then as now, it was speculated that one reason more girls weren't into gaming was the overwhelmingly violent or serious nature of most games. A cute, accessible, and addictive maze game might help the industry expand to other demographics. At the time, arcades in both Japan and the U.S. were dominated by *Space Invaders* and its clones (see Chapter 16, "*Space Invaders* (1978): The Japanese Descend"). Although these games were tremendously successful, Iwatani still felt the industry was too narrowly focused and wanted to do something about it.

---

[2] See Marty Goldberg's "Pac-Man: The Phenomenon" at http://classicgaming .gamespy.com/View.php?view=Articles.Detail&id=249.

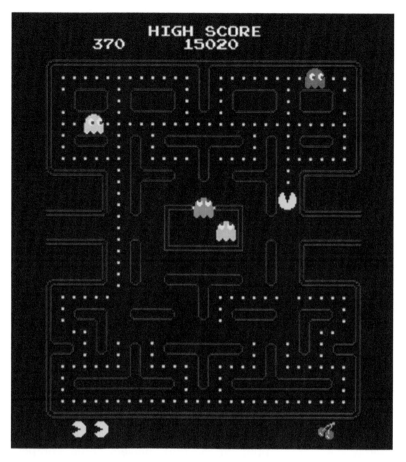

Pac-Man's legendary maze.

Unfortunately, Iwatani's *Puck Man* wasn't initially a hit in Japan; Namco's *Galaxian*, a colorful *Space Invaders*–style shooter, fared much better. Midway Manufacturing imported both games into the United States, altering *Puck Man*'s cabinet to make it both cheaper to produce and more eye-catching (bright yellow instead of white). They also changed the name to *Pac-Man*, fearing that pranksters would have too much fun rendering *Puck Man* into something far less appropriate. Fortunately for Midway and Iwatani, the game hit Western shores like a tsunami,   ooding first into arcades, then the wider market. Soon, every pizza parlor, supermarket, and drug store in the United States had to have one. It was all Midway could do to keep up with the demand for the quarter-munching machines, churning out a hundred thousand of them in 1980 (three times that number were produced over the next seven years). The machines were well worth the investment; in total they raked in over a billion dollars worth of quarters in the first year alone.[3] Iwatani's desire

---

[3]See Steven L. Kent's book, *The Ultimate History of Video Games* (Three Rivers Press, 2001).

to appeal to nontraditional gamers succeeded: *Pac-Man*'s appeal went far beyond young men; small kids and their moms could all enjoy *Pac-Man*. The 2005 edition of the *Guinness Book of World Records* even awarded *Pac-Man* the designation of "most successful coin-operated game" in history.

Pac-Man's initial success seemed to rest mostly on its unique gameplay, which is most often described as a "maze chase game," a designation that emphasizes the geometrical layout of the screen. *Pac-Man* was certainly not the first game in this early genre; precursors include Magnavox's 1972 two-player game for its Odyssey home system, *Cat and Mouse*, a very simple game that used an overlay (a mostly transparent screen placed over the television screen) to show a maze. Players, represented by white dots, moved about the maze, being careful not to hit the walls—if they did, the game reset their position at the start. One player controls a mouse, which must get through the maze to a "mouse house," erstwhile avoiding the cat, controlled by the other player. Likewise, there was *Gotcha*, a 1973 arcade game designed by Atari. This simple two-player game had players chasing each other through a maze shown from a top-down perspective. However, it never really caught on, with the game arousing little more than controversy—versions of the game's controllers featured two skin-tone bulges that resembled female breasts. Interestingly, Midway had released its own arcade maze game in 1976, *The Amazing Maze Game*. Though hardly as impressive as the title implies, the game improved on *Gotcha* in several ways. First, players were challenged to escape the maze rather than merely catch the opponent. Second, players could compete

There were many maze game precursors to *Pac-Man*, even on the most modest systems, like 1978's *Tunnel Vision and Kat and Mouse* by Michael Riley for the Commodore PET computer.

with each other or a computer-controlled opponent. None of these games, however, are played much today, having long been eclipsed by *Pac-Man* and its descendants in terms of playability, personality, and popularity.

Although *Pac-Man* has much in common with these earlier games, it relies entirely on computer-controlled opponents (the "monsters" or "ghosts"); the game's two-player mode simply has players alternating turns. Competition is thus indirect and limited to the high score table. Indeed, the artificial intelligence of the ghosts is perhaps the game's most-discussed feature. The ghosts do not wander randomly throughout the game's single maze, but follow programs that ostensibly give each one a unique personality. Savvy players quickly learned that following a certain path through the maze, called a "pattern," allowed them to achieve very high scores. Players who knew the patterns could play indefinitely on a single quarter, as they caused the game to react in a predictable manner every time. This fact no doubt displeased the owners of the machines, but magazines and eventually books happily published the patterns for anyone who cared to master the game.

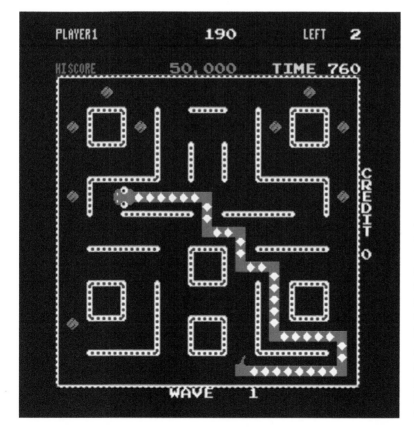

Nibbler was a 1982 arcade game by Rock-Ola where the player, as the titular snake, grows longer every time he eats. The player must be careful to avoid having the snake collide with himself. Broderbund's *Serpentine* (1982; Apple II, Commodore 64, and others) and Magnavox's *K.C.'s Krazy Chase!* (1982; Odyssey2) created excellent home variations of this alternate type of maze chase gameplay. Earlier forms of the basic gameplay mechanics include Gremlin's *Hustle* (1977; Arcade) and Atari's *Surround* (1978; Atari 2600 VCS), though many gamers will recognize it simply as "Snake" or some variation thereof.

However, modern fans who wish to truly dominate the game might want to emulate Billy Mitchell,[4] the world's first perfect *Pac-Man* player: rather than devise or follow patterns, Mitchell worked out methods to manipulate the ghosts into the corners of his choice. "I chose to do it this way because I wanted to demonstrate the depths of my abilities," says the reigning champ, defying anyone else to duplicate his amazing feat.[5] However, players who take the game as seriously as Mitchell are in the extreme minority. For most modern gamers, *Pac-Man* is a casual game; it's something you can play for five minutes while waiting for a pizza. If you have to leave before the game is over, who cares? For this reason, among countless other platforms, the game has made its way onto most games-capable mobile devices, including cell phones.

Pac-Man also features a small set of cutscenes or "intermissions," one of the first games to have this often controversial enhancement.[6] These humorous sketches star Pac-Man and Blinky, the red ghost. Unlike modern games where long cutscenes often interrupt a game's pacing, these charmingly brief segments in *Pac-Man* gave gamers a chance to relax their wrists, while also helping to establish personalities for what would otherwise have been fairly abstract characters.

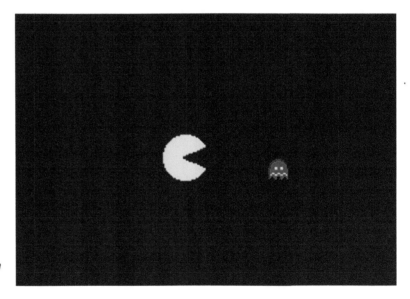

A scene from the first *Pac-Man* intermission.

---

[4]See the 2007 movie, *The King of Kong: A Fistful of Quarters*, or Joshuah Bearman's article "The Perfect Game" in the July 2008 issue of *Harper's Magazine*, for more on the colorful Mitchell.

[5]See GameSpot's interview with Mitchell at http://www.gamespot.com/features/vgs/universal/hist_pacman/p11_01.html.

[6]See Chapter 7, "*Final Fantasy VII* (1997): It's Never Final in the World of Fantasy," for more on cutscenes.

Naturally, Atari and other console manufacturers were eager to cash in on the *Pac-Man* craze, but efforts to adapt the arcade game to the consoles of the day were mixed at best. The most infamous is Atari's *Pac-Man* (1981) for its Atari 2600 VCS console. The popularity of the arcade game had generated a huge demand for this home version, but developer Tod Frye's company mandated effort to rush the game's completion by the all-important Christmas season resulted in one of the worst ports of all time.

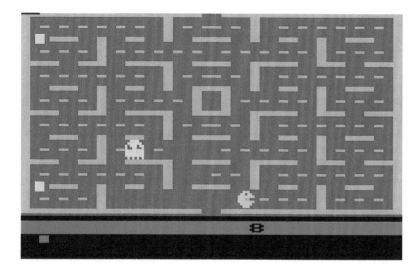

Although Atari would rectify the issues on both the Atari 2600 VCS and other platforms with future *Pac-Man* and *Pac-Man*-family releases, the original VCS adaptation, pictured, was a technical disaster.

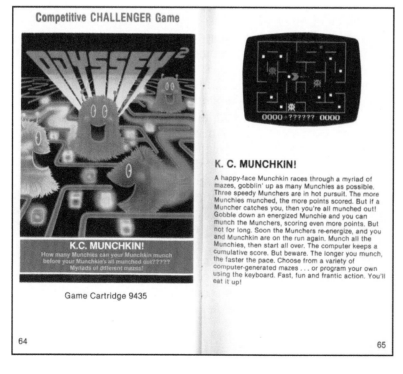

Competitive CHALLENGER Game

0000 → ?????? 0000

K. C. MUNCHKIN!

A happy-face Munchkin races through a myriad of mazes, gobblin' up as many Munchies as possible. Three speedy Munchers are in hot pursuit. The more Munchies munched, the more points scored. But if a Muncher catches you, then you're all munched out! Gobble down an energized Munchie and you can munch the Munchers, scoring even more points. But not for long. Soon the Munchers re-energize, and you and Munchkin are on the run again. Munch all the Munchies, then start all over. The computer keeps a cumulative score. But beware. The longer you munch, the faster the pace. Choose from a variety of computer-generated mazes . . . or program your own using the keyboard. Fast, fun and frantic action. You'll eat it up!

K.C. MUNCHKIN!
How many Munchies can your Munchkin munch before your Munchkin's all munched out?????
Myriads of different mazes!

Game Cartridge 9435

64

65

Magnavox's catalog entry for their superior maze game, *K.C. Munchkin!*.

Even by the standards of the Atari 2600's humble capabilities, the audio, visuals, and gameplay were dismal. Although millions of unsuspecting or desperate Atari 2600 owners purchased the cartridge, word quickly spread, and Atari was soon overwhelmed with unsold inventory. Though this is an oversimplification of the market dynamics at the time, together, the Atari 2600 versions of *Pac-Man* and the equally rushed *E.T. the Extra-Terrestrial* (1982) are often blamed for the sharp decline in videogame sales in 1983 and The Great Videogame Crash the following year. Nevertheless, most other ports, such as Mike Winans' for the Mattel Intellivision in 1983, published under Atari's Atarisoft label, adhered more faithfully to the original.

Having paid millions for the exclusive home translation rights, Atari was determined to stop competitive maze chase games from reaching market, particularly on non-Atari hardware. Even though programmer Ed Averett took obvious pains to distinguish 1981's *K.C. Munchkin!* Magnavox Odyssey2 game from Namco's *Pac-Man*, providing four mazes, moving dots, and user-programmable playfields, Atari felt it was close enough that it infringed on its exclusivity. Magnavox's game sold briskly at first and was far superior to what would be Atari's weak attempt for the 2600. *Pac-Man*-reminiscent cover art on *K.C. Munchkin!*'s box and manual aside, there were enough differences and enough danger in Atari's attempt to corner the entire home maze chase genre that Magnavox won in court. Unfortunately, Magnavox became complacent in victory, and Atari eventually won on a hard-fought appeal. Despite the abundance of other maze chase games far more derivative that remained on the market going forward, it was *K.C. Munchkin!* and Magnavox that would ultimately be the most damaged. With *K.C. Munchkin!* off store shelves, the void was filled by its voice-enhanced sequel, *K.C.'s Krazy Chase!* (1982), which—although generally considered less fun—again took the maze chase concept in a slightly different direction while still retaining the unique ability for gamers to create their own mazes. As Averett put it, "*K.C.'s Crazy Chase* was designed soon after the *K.C. Munchkin!* court exercise and did a good job of capturing the moment at Magnavox. There was something about the adversary biting the behind of little K.C. that appealed to everyone at the moment. I had another result planned when the bad guys bit K.C., but that is one time I did not get my way in the design or in the real world."[7]

In 1981, Midway released an unauthorized sequel to *Pac-Man* in the arcade called *Ms. Pac-Man*, which was itself based on *Crazy Otto*, an unauthorized *Pac-Man* conversion (mod) kit developed by engineers at the General Computer Corporation. Midway adopted the game as a sequel to *Pac-Man*, altering its appearance to make

---

[7]See http://www.dadgum.com/halcyon/BOOK/AVERETT.HTM.

it more in line with the original. Now celebrated as one of the best games ever designed, *Ms. Pac-Man* improved on its predecessor in several key areas. First, the character was less abstract, now sporting a bright red bow, lipstick, and a beauty mark. Many critics claim this change made the game more appealing to women, though the game was popular with men as well. The sequel also added new mazes, new behavior for the ghosts, and new intermissions concerned with the budding relationship between Mr. and Ms. Pac-Man. *Ms. Pac-Man* was widely admired by fans of the original, many of whom concluded that it was superior. Some legal wrangling followed between Midway and Namco, who was rightfully concerned about Midway's questionable conduct. Nevertheless, the popularity of the game eventually persuaded Namco to adopt *Ms. Pac-Man* as an official sequel, and in a combination cabinet with *Galaxian* sequel *Galaga*, remains among the most commonly spotted arcade games today. This time around, Atari took more care in porting the game to the 2600 in 1982, and the results were comparatively impressive in terms of playability and overall faithfulness to the arcade release.

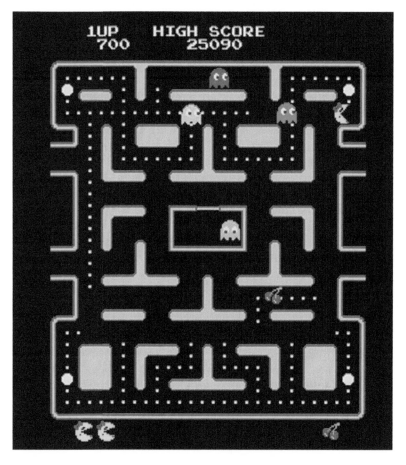

Screenshot from the still-popular *Ms. Pac-Man.*

A few months after *Ms. Pac-Man*'s debut in arcades, Midway released *Super Pac-Man*, Namco's official and long-awaited sequel. This sequel substantially altered the gameplay of the original. Most noticeably, Pac-Man no longer eats dots, but fruits and keys. As the title suggests, Pac-Man can now gain super powers by munching a "super pellet." In super form, Pac-Man is twice as big and invulnerable, but cannot eat ghosts. Despite these innovations, the game isn't nearly as popular as *Ms. Pac-Man*, though it has its share of loyal fans. Bally and Midway (later Bally Midway) released other unauthorized *Pac-Man*-related games throughout the early 1980s, including *Pac-Man Plus* (1982), a minor alteration of the original that manipulates the effects of power pellets; an innovative, but notoriously difficult pinball/videogame hybrid named *Baby Pac-Man* (1982), and a poorly received trivia game called *Professor Pac-Man* (1983). Towards the middle of the decade, the franchise drifted further away from the familiar maze game setup, opting instead for platforming. Though innovative at the time of its 1984 release, *Pac-Land* was a lackluster side-scrolling platformer (see Chapter 19, "*Super Mario Bros.* (1985): How High Can Jumpman Get?" for more) that had little in common with its predecessors. Similarly, Namco released *Pac-Mania* in 1987, which took the maze game into an isometric perspective and featured boards that were much larger than a single screen. The key innovation was Pac-Man's ability to jump at any time, including over enemy ghosts.

Perhaps the oddest Pac-Man game is *Pac-Man 2: The New Adventures*, released in 1994 by Namco for the Nintendo Super NES and Sega Genesis. Again eschewing the maze layout for a side-scrolling game, *Pac-Man 2* had players using a slingshot to try to keep Pac-Man from stumbling into trouble. The oddball gameplay failed to impress critics and gamers. Namco followed up that same year with *Pac-in-Time*, which is a rebranded version of Kalisto's *Fury of the Furries* (1993), for Apple Macintosh, Commodore Amiga/CD32, and PC. The high production values made the game more popular than *Pac-Man 2*, and helped extend the life of the venerable franchise, despite its tenuous connection to the earlier games.

In anticipation of *Pac-Man*'s twentieth anniversary, Namco released *Pac-Man World* for the Sony PlayStation in 1999, a 3D mix of adventure gaming and simple problem solving that retains many of the maze, and pac-dot-, fruit-, and ghost-eating elements of the original. *Pac-Man World* was followed by several sequels, including *Ms. Pac-Man Maze Madness* (2000; Sega Dreamcast, Sony PlayStation, and others), which was more puzzle-oriented and even more faithful to the original source.

The latest true *Pac-Man* maze game worthy of mention is *Pac-Man Championship Edition* (or *Pac-Man C.E.*), released by

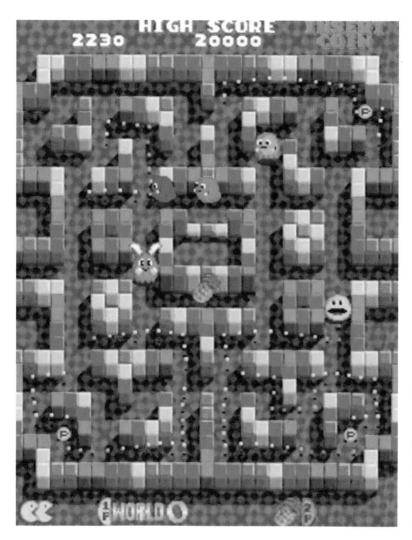

As part of the Namco Classic Collection Volume 2, the fast-paced *Pac-Man Arrangement* was released to the arcades in 1996 (home ports followed) and included two-player simultaneous play, additional enemies, updated graphics and music, and a true ending. Besides the original version of *Pac-Man*, other Namco classics included in the collection were *Rally-X* and *Dig Dug*.

Namco Bandai in 2007 for Xbox Live Arcade on Microsoft's Xbox 360. Iwatani designed the game as his last project before entering retirement. Despite trippy, high-definition visuals and sound combined with wild new game modes, the game stays faithful to the original game's concepts and timing. *Pac-Man C.E.* was well received and proved a worthy tribute to its legendary namesake—a distinction that few other classic game updates and remakes can claim.

As mentioned earlier, despite the risks, there were countless clones, knock-offs, and derivatives of *Pac-Man* throughout the 1980s, some of which tried to advance the depth-of-play mechanics. One such title was Data East's *Lock 'n' Chase*, published by Taito in 1981 for the arcade and later by Mattel for a variety of home console and computing platforms. The player's character is a thief

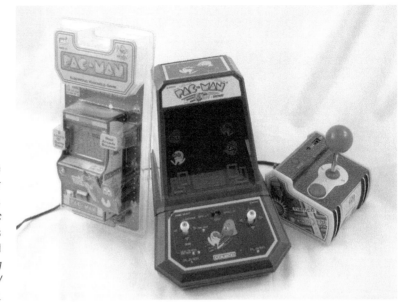

The Pac-Man games have always been popular targets for alternative videogame products, like MGA's *Pac-Man Electronic Handheld Game* (2005), Coleco's *Pac-Man Tabletop* (1981), and JAKKS Pacific's *Namco Featuring Pac-Man Plug It In & Play TV Games* (2004).

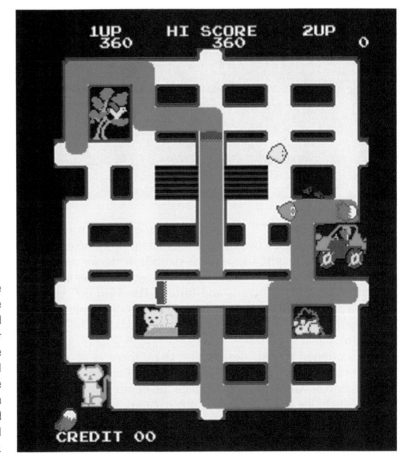

Make Trax is a 1981 arcade game by Williams that reverses the consumption paradigm. Instead of picking up pellets or other objects, the player's task is to use a paintbrush to color the level, all the while avoiding fish (the game is set in an aquarium). Though certainly based on an odd and illogical premise, the game is still charming and quite fun to play.

Universal Games' *Lady Bug* (1981; Arcade) is, as the name implies, based on an insect theme. The player guides a ladybug through a maze, eating dots and bonus objects while avoiding other insects. One nice innovation here is a gate system. The player can shift these gates to divert enemies, but they can always find a way around.

who can open and close doors to collect coins and treasure while avoiding policemen. On the other hand, *Piranha*, a 1981 game by GL, despite a visual overhaul, more or less replaced Pac-Man with a piranha and the ghosts with squids. Others took more of a middling approach to their design considerations, like Commodore's *Cosmic Cruncher* (1982) for their VIC-20 computer, a game in which Pac-Man had been replaced by the company's logo, but balanced its lack of innovation with a large number of levels and mazes.

Ultimately, what may be even more important than *Pac-Man*'s gameplay is its cultural impact. Rarely has a game managed to attract so much mainstream attention; even today's biggest and best-known franchises, such as *Halo* and *Madden* (see Chapters 5 and 10, respectively), pale in comparison. Although the reign of the maze chase game was relatively short-lived, *Pac-Man*'s legacy continues to this day, as few other videogame characters are as universally recognizable as the little, yellow, and different, circular wedge who was almost named Puck Man.

Exidy's *Mouse Trap* (1981; Arcade) shares *Lady Bug*'s gate system, but is slightly more complex: the colored gates can only be activated by tripping a corresponding button located elsewhere in the maze. In this game, the player controls a mouse on the run from cats; the power pills turn the player's mouse into a dog who can eat them.

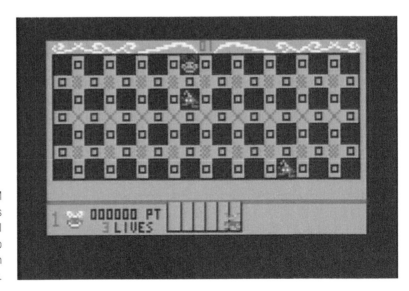

1983's *Ms. Candyman* by L&M Software and Bit Fiddlers was one of the Bally Professional Arcade's (Astrocade) answers to the *Pac-Man* craze; every platform had to have its maze chase game.

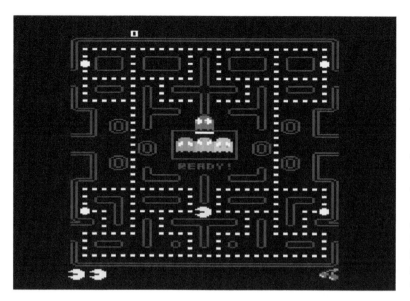

The *Pac-Man* family of games continues to be a favorite target of homebrew authors on a variety of platforms. Bob DeCrescenzo's hack of the original Atari 7800 version of *Ms. Pac-Man* (1984, but released 1986) has resulted in 2006's *Pac-Man Collection*, which contains well over a half-dozen different games and variations, filling a glaring hole in the system's software library. A similarly titled and even more impressive *Pac-Man Collection* homebrew cartridge from Opcode Games was released in late 2009 for the Coleco ColecoVision.

14

POLE POSITION (1982): WHERE THE RASTER MEETS THE ROAD

"Prepare to qualify!" What gamer of the 1980s could forget these words? Certainly none of those whose souls still carry some trace of rubber, some hint of those skid marks left there by Namco's *Pole Position.*[1]

Screenshot from the Japanese version of *Pole Position.* Note the billboard advertising a brand of cigarettes. When the game made it to the United States, the billboards were changed to advertisements of other games.

Introduced to the United States by Atari in 1982, *Pole Position* is arguably the most important racing game ever made. Although it wasn't the first, it was far more successful than its predecessors and established the conventions of a genre that has ourished

---

[1]Just in case you don't recognize the allusion here, watch Atari's infamous television commercial for the home version of *Pole Position* at http://www.youtube.com/watch?v=Om84Zc4-KcQ.

ever since. Of particular note are its audiovisuals and physics, which steered mightily toward realism. Whereas most previous arcade hits had been abstract or fictitious, *Pole Position* seemed to follow *Pong* in simulating a recognizably human activity. The game became a key title for Atari's 2600 VCS console, but was eventually ported to almost every viable platform of the era.

Pole Position was widely imitated, and naturally other developers were eager to launch their own racing games and franchises. As we'll see, these efforts eventually splintered into several subgenres of racing, with different vehicles, objectives, perspectives, and gameplay. First, though, let's talk about the racing games that came before.

Modern gamers might be surprised to learn that the first arcade racing games were introduced as early as the 1940s.[2] Games like *Drive Mobile*, made by International Mutoscope Reel Company in 1941, operated purely on "electromechanics." Although not technically "videogames" (there was no video display!), these games used electrical and mechanical components like relays, resisters, belts, and bells to simulate the driving experience. The basic idea was that players controlled a small metal car by moving a steering wheel. The car hovered above a road or map printed on a cylinder that rotated and moved from side to side as the game progressed. It was the player's job to keep the car positioned above the road while avoiding any obstacles. Though woefully primitive by today's standards, these games still earned tidy profits for their owners—even though players inserted pennies rather than quarters!

Auto Test, a driving simulation released in 1959, was—as the name implies—intended more to help student drivers than entertain children. Nevertheless, it offered a nice innovation—the road was shown in a film projected onto a screen located directly in front of the player. There were plenty of similar machines produced throughout the 1960s and 1970s, gradually introducing innovations and refining techniques. Perhaps the pinnacle of this genre is Namco's *F-1*, manufactured in the United States in 1977 by Atari. The "deluxe" model offered a cabinet that resembled an actual race car and was quite popular with gamers. Unfortunately for modern collectors and anyone who'd like to try these machines, their fine, complex assemblies of moving parts made them anything but durable—particularly after years of abuse by overenthusiastic children.

The first true racing videogame to show up in arcades was Atari's *Gran Trak 10*, which debuted in 1974. The cabinet featured

---

[2]The material for this section comes mostly from Lance Carter's excellent *History of Racing Games*, which features lots of photos and scans of vintage hardware and advertisements. This highly recommended book is available for free at http://historyofracinggames.wordpress.com.

a steering wheel, accelerator and brake pedals, and even a gear shift. However, the graphics consisted of a fixed screen, with the player's car shown from a top-down perspective. Since there were no other cars besides the player's, the game was really only a race against time. Unfortunately, an accounting error caused Atari to lose quite a bit of money manufacturing the machine. Atari offered a scaled-down version in 1974 called *Trak 10.* A more ambitious project was *Gran Trak 20*, which allowed two players to simultaneously race about the track. Perhaps the most ambitious of all such games was Atari's *Indy 800*, a 1975 game that allowed eight simultaneous players. The players' wheels surrounded a screen located in a pit in the center. It was also the first video-game to use full color, boasting a 25" display. There were even mirrors that let bystanders watch the race! Atari's much later release, the popular *Super Sprint* (1986), is somewhat of a spiritual successor to this game.

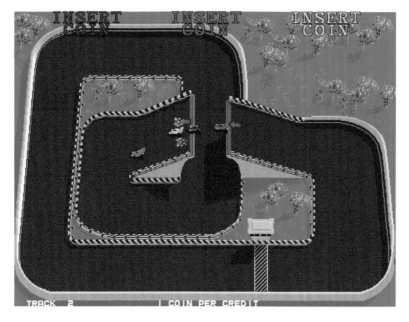

Screenshot from Atari's *Super Sprint.*

The Japanese got into the top-down racing craze at this time as well. A great example is Taito's *Speed Race*, which made its way in 1974 to U.S. arcades via Midway, who rebranded it as *Racer.* Its key claims to fame were vertical scrolling and great collision detection. This model would prove quite in uential. We can definitely see its in uence in Atari's 1975 game *Highway*, the first racing videogame to feature a sit-in cabinet like the old electromechanicals. In passing, we should mention Exidy's *Death Race* (1976), a top-down game that aroused some controversy for its gameplay that consisted of running over people (later called "gremlins") to earn points. An otherwise utterly forgettable game, *Death Race* attracted the attention of the mass media, and the resulting controversy marred the image of the neophyte arcade industry. Such hysteria is still with us today, as any fan of *Grand Theft Auto* (see Chapter 9, "*Grand Theft Auto III* (2001): The Consolejacking Life") can easily attest.

Screenshot from Atari's *Night Driver* with simulated plastic overlay.

Some of the leftover cabinets from *Highway* were used for Atari's *Night Driver*, released in 1976. *Night Driver* was a different kind of racing game. Superficially, it resembled the older electromechanical games, which offered a scrolling road rather than a fixed view. Atari's game was black and white, and the car was merely a plastic overlay glued to the bottom of the screen. The "night driving" aspect of the game was a brilliant design decision, as it justified the sparse graphics, which consisted of rectangular re ectors that demarcated the road. The challenge came from taking sharp turns at high speeds; there were no other cars. Despite all these limitations, the game deserves some respect for offering some semblance of the first-person perspective that would become such an integral part of later racing games.

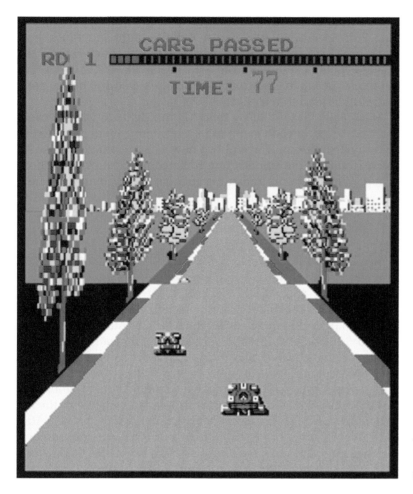

Screenshot from Sega's popular *Turbo*. Coleco would bundle a home conversion of *Turbo* for their ColecoVision with Expansion Module #2, which consisted of a steering wheel and pedal.

Perhaps the next big step came in 1981 with Sega's *Turbo*. Like *Night Driver*, *Turbo* offered a first-person perspective of the road. Besides the obvious addition of color and other cars to compete against, the game also offered a third-person ("above and behind") view of the player's vehicle on the screen. The objects alongside the road (buildings, trees, and so on) also scaled and whizzed by as the race progressed. However, the game isn't won by reaching a finish line, but only by staying on the road and passing 30 other cars before a time limit runs out.

As this brief history shows, by the time *Pole Position* appeared on the scene in 1982, gamers had come to expect some sort of racing game at every major arcade. However, it would blaze past the competition like a Formula One against a Model T, establishing itself as the future of the genre. But what was so great about *Pole Position*?

For one thing, its graphics made other racing games—even those released months earlier—antiquated by comparison. The animation was much smoother and more realistic, and the sound effects were varied and clear. It also offered an actual racetrack (the Fuji Speedway) that had a definite start and finish line. Another novel feature was a "qualifying lap" that determined the player's "pole position" for the actual race. Players who couldn't complete the lap in 73 seconds were disqualified and had to pony up another quarter to try again.

Atari really lucked out by securing the rights to what became the best-selling arcade game of its year. Namco had given Bally/Midway first dibs on which of two new games it would license for manufacture in the United States. The company lucklessly chose *Mappy*, a cutesy jump-and-run game that achieved nowhere near the success of *Pole Position*. Atari later licensed *Pole Position* for its own platforms and several of its competitors. There was even a version for the Intellivision, whose eager owners could at last put the arcade pedal to the Mattel.

Namco released *Pole Position II* the following year, which offered two new racetracks and improved graphics, and of course there was no shortage of derivatives and clones for arcade, computer, and console markets. One of the most innovative of these is Epyx's *Pitstop*, a 1983 game for the Atari 8-bit, Coleco ColecoVision, and Commodore 64. The big innovation here is the titular "pitstops," where players took control of a pitcrew to refuel their racecar and change its tires. A sequel released in 1984 offered split-screen modes so that two players could compete simultaneously. Perhaps the ultimate customizable racing game of the era was Rick Koening's *Racing Destruction Set* (1985), for the Atari 8-bit and Commodore 64, a popular but often-overlooked computer racing game that let players design their own tracks, then race on them (alone or with a friend) using a selection of modifiable types of vehicles (see bonus chapter, "*Pinball Construction Set* (1982): Launching Millions of Creative Possibilities" for more).

1986 saw the release of Sega's *Out Run*, an in uential arcade game itself with much in common with *Pole Position*. However, here the player controls a Ferrari Testarossa convertible, and the game seemed to take itself much less seriously than many of its rivals. Players could select from among three different songs to listen to while driving, and could choose which route they took through the course. One version of the cabinet introduced a hydraulic system that would become in uential in later arcade racing games; it moved along with the car on the screen, greatly heightening the feeling of immersion.

Another great innovation came in 1988 with Atari's *Hard Drivin'*, which the company billed as "the world's first authentic driving simulation game." It offered a racing environment composed entirely of 3D polygons, a highly realistic gear shift, and a steering wheel with "force feedback," which made it bump and vibrate in a manner that corresponded to the car's situation in the game.

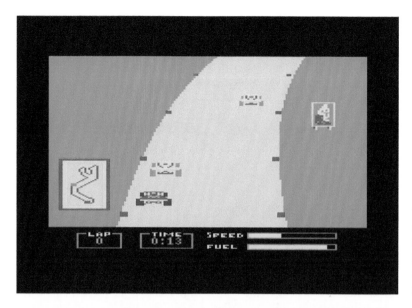

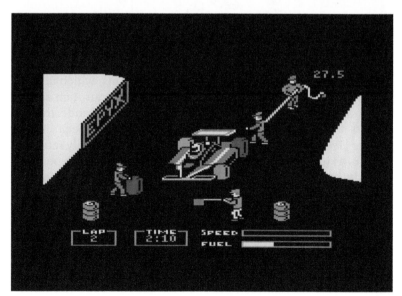

Pitstop added a crucial new feature to the *Pole Position* model: the pit stop (below), where players had to move quickly to refuel their vehicle and replace worn tires. Commodore 64 version shown.

The game's most impressive feature was its accurate simulation of actual driving, but also boasted a fun stunt track. The "above and behind" perspective of *Pole Position* and *Out Run* was replaced with a first-person or "windshield" view.

The trend toward increasingly realistic driving games continued in 1989 with Papyrus' *Indianapolis 500: The Simulation*, a game released for Apple Macintosh, Commodore Amiga, and PC computers. Like *Hard Drivin'*, it offered a first-person view and focused on realistic physics and detailed graphics. However,

Screenshot from Atari's *Hard Drivin'*.

what really set it apart was its "car setup" options, which allowed players to make all sorts of adjustments to their car, such as gear ratios and tire pressure. It also offered a replay mode that let players study a race from six different perspectives. Sega's *Virtua Racing* (1992) took things a step further by offering fully rendered 3D cars as well as environments and the ability to switch perspectives during the race. It was left behind a year later when Namco's *Ridge Racer* rolled into arcades.

If games like *Hard Drivin'* and *Indianapolis 500: The Simulation* were racing toward realism, other games of the era strove to incorporate elements from other genres. We certainly see this in Bally Midway's 1983 arcade hit *Spy Hunter*, which combined a vertical-scrolling racing game with elements from shoot 'em ups. We can also find alternatives to realism in Rare's *R.C. Pro-Am* for the Nintendo Entertainment System, a 1987 game that put players behind remote controls instead of steering wheels. As with *Spy Hunter* before it, the gameplay was focused not just on racing but on collecting powerups for battling one's opponents. This trend would continue in later games like Nintendo's *Super Mario Kart* (1992), for the Super Nintendo, which would inspire a whole series of clones itself, and Silicon & Synapse's *Rock N' Roll Racing* (1993; Nintendo Game Boy Advance, Sega Genesis, Super Nintendo).

None of these games would likely appeal to someone wishing to simulate an authentic racing experience, though they are certainly fun and many are in uential. We might be better off

Indianapolis 500: The Simulation, Commodore Amiga version shown, allowed players to fine-tune their cars, then instantly try out the results on the track. It was a definite move toward more realistic, simulation-style racing games.

thinking of them as "simulations of driving simulations" rather than driving simulations in their own right. Indeed, some games get so far off track, so to speak, that they defy classification. This is certainly the case with Sega's *Crazy Taxi* (1999), an innovative action arcade game whose similarity to *Pole Position* is superficial at best. *Crazy Taxi* is one of many vehicle-based games that focus more on stunts and destruction than realistic racing; other examples include Re ection's *Destruction Derby* (1995; Sony PlayStation) and Angel Studios' *Midtown Madness* (1999; PC).

Unlike some of the genres we've discussed in this book, the racing sim's best days seem to be ahead of it rather than behind. Modern fans have a number of superb franchises to choose from, such as Atari's *Test Drive* (first Accolade release, 1987; Atari ST,

Box back for *Mario Kart: Super Circuit* (2001) for the Nintendo Game Boy Advance, one of several entries in the popular and influential franchise.

Commodore 64 and others), Electronic Arts' *The Need for Speed* (starting in 1994 for the 3DO), and Polyphony Digital's *Gran Turismo* (1998; Sony PlayStation), to name just three. Big budget racing games are still able to command the attention of the gaming media, and the genre shows no signs of slowing down. Indeed, if anything, it is rapidly expanding, with high-profile games available for nearly every type of vehicle—real or imagined.

But what is it about games like *Pole Position* that made and continue to make them so fun for so many people? Some obvious explanations are that they offer a viable alternative to the many violent games on the market. Although some of the games we've discussed in this chapter do contain violence, most racing sims punish players who intentionally or accidentally crash into other vehicles. Another appealing aspect of the genre is its emphasis on cinematic realism; the best of these games look almost identical to a race one might see on television. There is also some pleasure to be found in competing, either against the clock or against other cars, particularly when those other cars are controlled by one's friends.

Finally, and perhaps most importantly, driving games seem more familiar to many gamers than other genres. After all, most of us will at some point drive a car or at least ride in a motorized

Box back for the original 3DO version of *The Need for Speed*.

vehicle. Americans, in particular, seem obsessed with their vehicles, and many (if not most) of us have fantasized about driving as recklessly (yet skillfully) as the many action heroes we see in the movies or on the NASCAR track. Of course, trying to do so in reality will likely get one killed, or at least handed a nasty ticket. These games give us a safe opportunity to explore these fantasies, performing the delicate maneuvers that we would love to initiate each time we're stuck in traffic. Thus, racing and driving sims offer, on one hand, an intimately familiar experience. On the other hand, they offer the exotic—the chance to qualify as a true speed racer.

15

SIMCITY (1989): BUILDING BLOCKS FOR FUN AND PROFIT

Maxis' *SimCity*, first published in 1989,[1] is one of those games whose premise doesn't sound much fun at all. Only the most open-minded of gamers would have found a game about city planning anything to get excited about, and Will Wright had to work hard to find a publisher. Who wants to be mayor of a virtual town, overseeing seemingly tedious matters as constructing highways and power grids? On paper, the game looks like some disgruntled developer's idea of a joke. Yet Wright was able to use these atypical gameplay concepts to make one of the most critically acclaimed games ever, launching a best-selling series of sequels and spin-offs that is still vibrant today. *SimCity* not only established Wright as one of the world's foremost game developers, but introduced a new subgenre of strategy games typically called "god games" or "system simulation games," though "management games" might be the best descriptor. Such games focus on simulating complex systems, such as the ecosystem in Maxis' *SimEarth: The Living Planet* (1990) or the railroad transportation system in Microprose's *Railroad Tycoon* (1990).

The fun of these games doesn't come from obliterating enemies or rescuing princesses. Instead, they're about observing the results of one's decisions played out on a grand scale. They are system games that encourage tinkering and experimentation, and the grounding in everyday reality adds to the thrill. Few of us have firsthand experience ying to outer space or gunning down enemy soldiers, but almost all of us have spent some time in a city. Many of us have wondered why cities are the way they are, and what would happen if someone came along and changed things. These games offer precisely the opportunity to be in

---

[1] It was released in 1989 for PC, Commodore Amiga, Commodore 64, Apple Macintosh, and Amstrad CPC. It was later released for a number of other platforms including the Atari ST and Nintendo's Super NES.

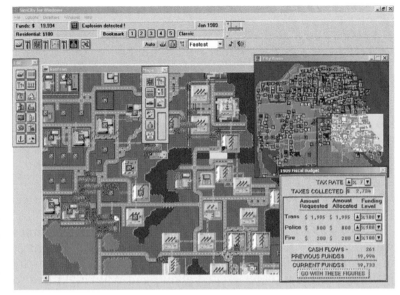

SimCity appears quite intimidating, with an array of windows stuffed with information. However, the tidy graphics and catchy music suggest a less serious, more playful tone. Players could either build a new city from scratch or take control of one based on a historical scenario. Shown here is the San Francisco setting.

charge—to make the big decisions that have a real impact not just on our own lives, but on all the citizens in the community.

These games are also wonderfully educational, encouraging us to see the world as a collection of complex, intertwining systems; a constantly evolving mosaic whose pieces interact with one another in often surprising ways. They can model anything from economics to evolution. Will raising taxes stimulate or stall the economy? How should a mayor plan and respond to natural (or even extraterrestrial) disasters? How does an intelligent, sentient being evolve from a unicellar organism? *SimCity* and its many sequels, clones, and derivatives vary widely in theme and content, but they're all about managing a complex, intricate system. They are both virtual laboratories and electronic playgrounds.

Before moving on to a specific discussion of *SimCity*, it's worthwhile to mention some games that predated or may have in uenced its development. As usual, even a highly original game like *SimCity* has its precedents: its gameplay concepts didn't spontaneously come into being. We've already discussed Don Daglow's *Utopia* in our discussion of *Dune II* (see Chapter 6, "*Dune II: The Building of a Dynasty* (1992): Spicing up Strategy in Real Time"), but it's worth mentioning again here. This 1981 game for the Mattel Aquarius and Intellivision put players in charge of a small island economy. The goal was to generate revenue by constructing buildings and pacifying the populace. It was intended for two players, who would simultaneously work to build up their respective island while inciting rebellion on the other's. Occasionally the computer would generate a random natural event, such as a tropical storm or hurricane.

Box back for the Commodore 64 version of *SimCity*.

Critics such as William Cassidy of GameSpy and T. Byrl Baker of GameSpot have described it as an unsung hero, a progenitor of both Wright's *SimCity* and Sid Meier's *Civilization*, a turn-based game mentioned in Chapter 6 that we'll discuss again later in this chapter. However, it's not clear whether Wright or Meier ever played the game, and similarities could be coincidental. Daglow began work in 1987 on a computer game version of the boardgame *Civilization* from Avalon Hill, but was promoted to an executive position at Broderbund and never completed the game that established Meier's legend. He also signed the original distribution deal for *SimCity* with Maxis and Broderbund, defending Wright's vision against "bureaucratic meddling."[2]

---

[2]See http://www.gamasutra.com/php-bin/column_index.php?story=8450.

Back of the box for Coleco's impressive *Fortune Builder*.

A slightly later and even more obscure predecessor is Circuits and Systems' *Fortune Builder*, a 1984 game for the Coleco ColecoVision. This game has much in common with *SimCity*. Players began with an empty map, then built roads and all manner of buildings whose earning potential depends on their proximity to other kinds of buildings (i.e., a hotel next to a factory will not do well). The goal is to generate a specified net worth before reaching the time limit. It also offered a two-player mode, which used a split-screen to let players compete in real time. As with *Utopia*, there were also natural disasters that could affect gameplay.

Although *Utopia* and *Fortune Builder* both have features found in later sim games, neither achieved the staggering success of *SimCity*. One reason could simply be a matter of bad timing; both were console games, a market that collapsed in 1984. By 1989, few gamers cared about old ColecoVision or Intellivision games.

It's interesting to speculate, though, what might have happened if these enterprising games had been ported to the Apple II or Commodore 64.

If Will Wright wasn't inspired by *Utopia* or *Fortune Builder*, where did he get his ideas? Wright himself often credits his wide reading and research interests. These include Jay Forrester's urban planning theories (*SimCity*), James Lovelock's Gaia theory (*SimEarth*); and Christopher W. Alexander, an architect concerned with "pattern languages" (*The Sims*, see Chapter 22, "*The Sims* (2000): Who Let the Sims Out?"). According to Wright, "I'll find some subject that I'm reading about that fascinates me. It will pique my interest and then I'll slowly become obsessed with it. About half of those subjects I'll end up seriously pursuing as a game project."[3] This approach has seemed to work well, and no doubt at least some fans of the games have found themselves interested enough in the ideas behind them to conduct their own research.

A more immediate inspiration for *SimCity* was *Raid on Bungeling Bay*, Will Wright's first game. It was released in 1984 for the Commodore 64 and later ported to the Nintendo Entertainment System and MSX platforms. *Raid on Bungeling Bay* is an action game set in a war zone; it's the player's task to y a "helicraft" around a 2D map, dropping bombs on six different factories. The gimmick was that the factories evolved over the course of the game, developing more powerful weapons to use against the player and eventually a super weapon—a battleship—to destroy civilization itself.

Although *Raid on Bungeling Bay* is considered a classic by many, Wright himself had more fun creating a map editor to aid in the game's development. With that, an odd idea occurred to him: could the process of making a map (or, by extension, a full- edged city) be fun for other people? It was this question that led Wright to his research on urban planning. Besides the emphasis on urban planning, the game would also have another novel feature—there was really no way to win or lose. Wright describes the experience quite aptly himself: "My games are more like a hobby—a train set or a doll house. Basically they're a mellow and creative playground experience."[4]

Not surprisingly given its radical nature, Wright had a hard time finding a major publisher after he completed a version for the Commodore 64 in 1985. Wright described his experiences trying to get Broderbund interested in the concept: "They kept saying,

[3]See Melanie Cambron's interview with Wright at http://www.gignews.com/ goddess_wright.htm.

[4]See Geoff Keighley's "Simply Divine: The Story of Maxis Software" at http:// www.gamespot.com/features/maxis/page2.html.

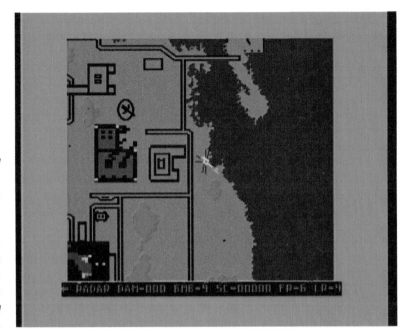

Taken on its own, Wright's *Raid on Bungeling Bay* is a classic action game with depth, but its most significant historical role would be in influencing *SimCity*'s development. *SimCity*'s final terrain model would look very similar to what is seen in this screenshot from the Commodore 64 version of *Raid on Bungeling Bay*.

'Where's the ending? When do you win or lose?' And they wanted to have an election where you got kicked out of office or not. And I was like, 'No, it's even more fun if you're doing it badly.' And they just parked it. They decided they weren't going to release it."[5] Wright ended up having to form his own publishing company, Maxis, with Jeff Braun. Broderbund finally published the original Commodore 64 version and ports for the Apple Macintosh and Commodore Amiga in 1989, with a PC version following shortly after.[6] Let's take a look now at the game itself.

SimCity puts players in charge of a city, either one they build from scratch or an existing one that requires some type of reform (a "scenario"). Players are allocated a budget for setting up buildings, basic utilities (electricity and water), and highways. Cities must be divided into three zones: Residential, where the citizens or "Sims" live; Industrial, which houses factories and warehouses; and Commercial, where the Sims go to shop and tend to business. Players can adjust the tax rate to receive more income, as well as set a budget for police, fire, and transportation departments (the Super Nintendo version adds a casino and amusement park for generating additional revenue). All of these factors affect other factors; for instance, densely populated areas with low property

---

[5]See Brandon Sinclair's "Spot On: Here's the Pitch" at http://www.gamespot.com/ c64/strategy/simcity/news.html?sid=6183997 for this and other fun stories of great developers who struggled with timid publishers.

[6]Other versions would continue to be released over the years.

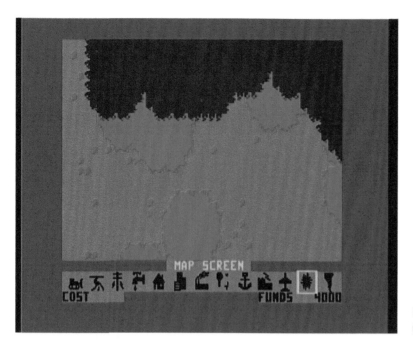

Screenshot from the Commodore 64 version of *SimCity*.

values have an increased crime rate. Such a situation might occur in a city with too many factories and not enough or poorly situated residential zones. Likewise, the player has to make sure that the city is properly powered; natural disasters can cause blackouts that, if untended, quickly lead to drastic problems.

However, the gameplay isn't necessarily about building a wealthy or well-ordered city, and it's even possible for players to introduce their own natural disasters (such as an earthquake or Godzilla-like monster attack) just to view the awesome consequences. This is a point Wright has made frequently in interviews: sometimes, doing poorly in this game is as much fun as doing well.

For the first few months after its release, sluggish sales indicated that Broderbund's executives were justified in their skepticism. Fortunately for Wright and Maxis, however, word began to spread. The game received its big break when *Newsweek* covered it in a full-page story, instantly catapulting it from the fringe to the mainstream. The game enjoyed a tremendously broad appeal, winning over large audiences who had formerly cared very little for computer games. The game was viewed as not just fun but educational, and it found its way into 10,000 classrooms.[7] The game eventually sold millions of copies, a fact that made a sequel practically inevitable. However, the next few "Sim" games would not be direct sequels, but a plethora of mediocre spin-offs. The

---

[7] See "Inside Scoop: The History of SimCity" at http://simcity.ea.com/about/ inside_scoop/sc_retrospective02.php.

first was *SimEarth: The Living Planet*, a game released for a range of platforms in 1990.

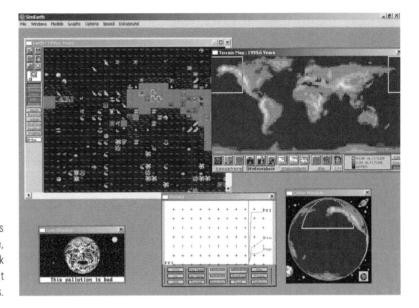

SimEarth is a planetary ecologist's game. The dense interface, steep learning curve, and lack of immediate feedback made it inaccessible to most gamers.

SimEarth, which was never as well received as *SimCity*, put players in control of a planetary ecosystem that they could affect by altering its temperature, atmosphere, and landmasses, then observing how these conditions in uenced the evolution of living organisms. The game was based on James Lovelock's famous Gaia hypothesis. The hypothesis describes the earth itself as a living organism; its organs are living and nonliving entities, who interact in powerful and dynamic ways. Although this idea is certainly intriguing, the game's steep learning curve and complex interface (described in the manual as a "planetary spreadsheet") turned away gamers looking for a more *SimCity*-like experience. Lovelock himself contributed to the game's manual, a 212-page document loaded with facts, theories, and even the occasional one-liner, such as "is this a random world or did you planet?".

The next Sim game was *SimAnt*, released in 1991, also for a variety of platforms. This ant colony simulation attracted a bit more attention than *SimEarth*, probably because of its less intimidating interface and subject matter. This game was followed by another abstract/scientific title called *SimLife*, a 1992 game that focused again on ecosystems. However, this time players could modify the genetic code of plants and animals. Wright would return to this theme in 2008 with *Spore* (discussed later), though in a much more accessible fashion. In 1993, Maxis released *SimFarm*, a game that, as the title suggests, had players managing a farm.

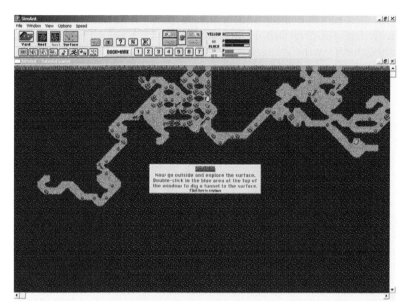

SimAnt put players in charge of an ant colony. The colorful graphics and zany situations (such as being destroyed by the "evil lawnmower") made the game more accessible than other sim titles, but it never attained *SimCity*'s level of success.

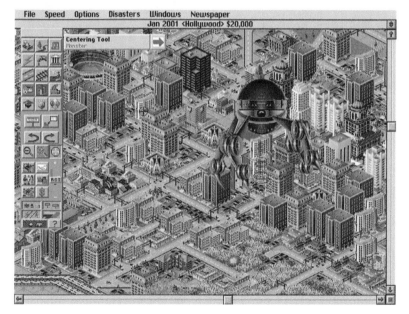

SimCity 2000 offered a substantial leap in audiovisuals, along with new buildings and events. Shown here is a disaster caused by a giant robot.

None of these spin-offs achieved anywhere near the popularity of the original, which finally received a true sequel, *SimCity 2000*, in 1993. This game marked a huge leap forward in audiovisuals, with the city now shown in isometric perspective instead of the top-down view of the original. This angled perspective made the structures look more realistic; taller buildings visibly looked taller. The sequel also added many new structures and options, such as subways, airports, and seaports. Although all the new bells and whistles pleased fans and critics, others were more impressed with the *SimCity Urban Renewal Kit*, which allowed players to alter the in-game images to represent particular buildings or settings. The award-winning game reestablished the franchise and was widely discussed in gaming circles and beyond.

SimCopter is one of the more unusual sim-games, casting players in the role of a helicopter pilot. The gimmick was that maps from *SimCity 2000* could be imported into the game, allowing players to fly through a 3D re-creation of their own cities.

Nearly a dozen other spin-offs followed *SimCity 2000*. Two of the most intriguing of these are *SimTunes* and *SimCopter*. *SimTunes* (1996), designed by Toshio Iwai, is a musical game for children. Players draw a picture using dots of various colors, each of which represents a certain musical note. Then up to four "bugz" crawl over the picture, playing the notes of the resulting composition. Players could also add functions, such as having the bugz turn or jump. *SimCopter* (1996) is a 3D game that puts players in the cockpit of a helicopter. Gameplay consists of redirecting traffic, apprehending criminals, fire fighting, rescues, and (naturally) transporting people. One nice innovation was the ability to import maps from *SimCity 2000*. However, Maxis was later embarrassed when it was discovered that a disgruntled designer named Jacques Servin had inserted some unauthorized code. The code caused mobs of shirtless male "himbos" with uorescent nipples to appear on certain dates, hugging and kissing each other. Maxis quickly removed the code, but the word had spread.[8]

_____

[8]See Ben Silverman's "Controversial Games" article at http://videogames.yahoo.com/feature/controversial-games/530593.

Streets of SimCity, released in 1997, was a racing and "vehicular combat" game that also allowed players to import maps from *SimCity 2000*. However, the game is now considered the black sheep of the Sims line, mostly because of its poor collision detection, driving simulation, and quality assurance.

Along with better audiovisuals and more buildings, *SimCity 3000* was significantly more complex. Players could now negotiate with neighboring cities, selling or buying services like water or power.

The third official sequel, *SimCity 3000*, appeared in 1999. By this point, 3D games had taken over the industry, and Maxis's management "wanted the game to be 3D so much that it wasn't receptive to the people who were actually making the game telling them it wasn't going to work," according to Ocean Quigley, Maxis's art director.[9] Unfortunately for Maxis, the intricate detail of the *SimCity* series made a move to full 3D difficult indeed; the graphics and processors of the era simply couldn't handle it. The long line of so-so Sim titles had cost Maxis much of its credibility and revenue, and the oundering company was finally acquired by Electronic Arts. Luc Barthelet was named the general manager, and the young French engineer faced a difficult job salvaging the project. One of his first decisions was that *SimCity 3000* would not be a 3D product, a choice that finally brought focus back to the project.

SimCity 3000 may not have been 3D, but it did boast great graphics and even more sophisticated gameplay. Naturally,

[9]See http://www.gamespot.com/features/maxis/page7.html.

there were more structures to build, which now included farms and wastewater management services. Players could also interact with neighboring cities to work out business deals or purchase services. There was also a greater emphasis on land values. A jazzy score by Jerry Martin rounds out the package. Incidentally, *SimCity DS* (2007) for the Nintendo DS is based on this version of the game.

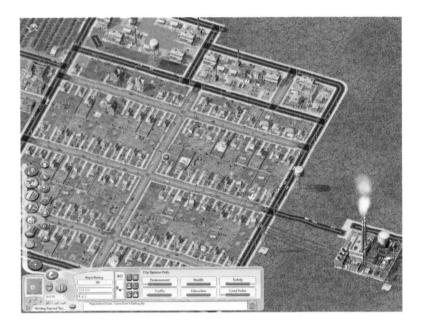

SimCity 4 is one of the latest official SimCity games for the PC. The audiovisuals have been enhanced for modern hardware, with an interface reminiscent of *The Sims.* Shown on the bottom is the "night mode."

SimCity 4, released in 2003 for Apple Macintosh and PC, is the fourth game in the long-lived series. This release finally brought the game up to 3D graphics. It also allowed players to shape land (terraforming) before establishing their city, creating mountains, canyons, and mesas as desired. Neighboring cities and towns played a greater role, and day and night cycles were finally depicted graphically. Perhaps the most interesting innovation, though, was the ability to import Sims from *The Sims*, who could afterwards "tell" players about their personal lives in the new city. Although most critics had positive things to say about the game, a few glitches and performance issues cropped up that dampened their enthusiasm. Greg Kasavin of GameSpot remarked that while the game "does a fine job overall of living up to its name, ... [s]ome players will invariably get soured on the experience due to some of the bugs and the missing or underdeveloped features and options."[10]

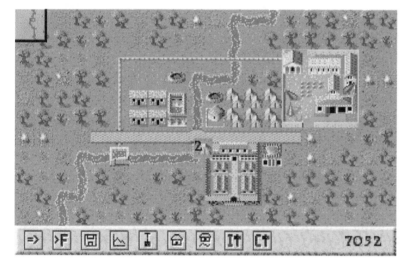

Caesar is essentially *SimCity* set in ancient Rome, though with emphasis on military strategy.

In 2007, a game called *SimCity Societies* by a developer named Tilted Mill Entertainment debuted for PC. Tilted Mill had achieved some recognition for its *Caesar IV* (2006), the fourth game in a series that we'll discuss in a moment. With *SimCity Societies*, Tilted Mill strived to create a "social engineering simulator" rather than another mayor or god game. Players work to balance three competing ideals: Creativity and Authority, Knowledge and Productivity, and Prosperity and Spirituality. The balances are affected by buildings, which either increase or decrease the levels. The gimmick is that the look of the city will change depending

---

[10]See http://www.gamespot.com/pc/strategy/simcity4/review.html.

on its core values. Despite an interesting premise, the game was widely criticized for counterintuitive gameplay and performance issues. Steve Butts of IGN called it "fun … for a short period but you'll constantly be battling the developers' decisions about how the game should work," and Kevin VanOrd of GameSpot wrote that "unlike most city builders, there's nothing to keep you engaged."[11]

Screenshot from *SimCity Creator*.

Although *SimCity Societies* may have been a disappointment to some, fans were more receptive to *SimCity Creator*, a 2008 release by Hudson Soft for the Nintendo Wii platform. The game takes advantage of the Wii Remote to allow players to "draw" roads and tracks. Another interesting feature is the ability to view the city from a helicopter or airplane.

Wright's most ambitious project to date, *Spore*, debuted in 2008 for the Apple Macintosh and PC. This high profile project hearkens back to 1992's *SimLife*, though Wright was careful to make this game more accessible to the general public. The player begins with a species of unicellular organisms, guiding its development through the stages of evolution until it becomes a member of a spacefaring culture. One much-talked about feature of the game is "asynchronous sharing," which allows players to download and import creatures from other players. Once they reach the spacefaring stage, they can visit the planets and civilizations of other players as well.

---

[11]See http://pc.ign.com/articles/834/834720p3.html and http://www.gamespot .com/pc/strategy/simcitysocieties/review.html, respectively.

Obviously, Maxis and later Electronic Arts exploited the *SimCity* brand as much as they could, producing dozens of spin-offs and four direct sequels. However, other developers and publishers were also eager to create their own Sim-like games. One of the most successful and perhaps enduring of these is Impressions Games's *Caesar*, which debuted in 1992 for the Apple Macintosh, Atari ST, Commodore Amiga, and PC. Essentially *SimCity* set in Roman times, *Caesar* focused more on military combat and real-life history. The game was popular enough to warrant three sequels, the final one being the aforementioned *Caesar IV*. Impressions also developed city-building games based on Ancient Egypt, Greece, and China.

Another branch of *SimCity*-style games are called "business management simulations," which focus more on business and commerce. Perhaps the most in uential of these is Enlight's *Capitalism*, published by Interactive Magic in 1995 for Apple Macintosh and PC. Designed by Trevor Chan, *Capitalism* is about founding and growing a thriving corporation in retail, manufacturing, research and development, or farming. While the game attracted mainstream media attention for its highly detailed and realistic gameplay, its steep learning curve was not suitable for the casual gamer, but did appeal to teachers and professors. Chan remarked in an interview with *GameSpot* that "for the *Capitalism* series, I attempted to immerse myself in the academic world by reading an extensive list of academic books on the subject during the early stage of development. On the other hand, the gaming perspective came relatively effortlessly, as I have always been a gamer."[12] An expanded version called *Capitalism Plus* appeared in 1995, and a full sequel, *Capitalism II*, was published by Ubisoft in 2001. Chan also introduced the "Empire" franchise of business simulation games, beginning with *Restaurant Empire* in 2003. Other games in this franchise include *Zoo Empire* (2004) and *Marine Park Empire* (2005). As their titles suggest, these popular games are focused on a single business sector.

An earlier attempt at a business simulation was *Railroad Tycoon*, a 1990 game designed by Sid Meier. This series, focused on the train industry, was successful enough to warrant a scad of sequels. The latest is *Sid Meier's Railroads!*, a 2006 game published by Firaxis Games. Of course, there are plenty of other "Tycoon" games with different themes, such as Chris Sawyer's *RollerCoaster Tycoon* (1999), Holistic Design's *Mall Tycoon* (2002), and Blue Fang Games' *Zoo Tycoon* (2001). Bullfrog Productions also developed two popular games in this subgenre: *Theme Park* (1994) and

---

[12]See http://www.gamespot.com/pc/strategy/capitalism/news.html?sid=2833574&mode=news.

Box back for the Atari Jaguar version of *Theme Park*.

Theme Hospital (1997). Business-simulation games seem to have become popular among casual gaming fans. A quick glance at the strategy section of Big Fish Games, a major distributor of casual games, turns up titles like *Fish Tycoon*, *Plant Tycoon*, *Virtual Farm*, *Restaurant Empire*, and even *Fairy Godmother Tycoon*.[13]

Sid Meier's Civilization (also known as *Civilization* or *Civ*), published by Microprose in 1991 for most viable platforms, takes a radically different spin on the genre. The two most noticeable

---

[13]For the whole list, see http://www.bigfishgames.com/download-games/genres/29/strategy.html.

differences are a much larger time frame and turn-based, rather than real-time, gameplay. Instead of starting players off in modern times, *Civilization* and its sequels begin in ancient times (the first begins in 4000 BCE). Players then work to build up empires that gradually become more technologically advanced, eventually reaching the Space Age. Like the *SimCity* games, players can adopt different gameplay styles. Some will prefer to build up a strong military and conquer rival civilizations, whereas others may take a more passive stance. However, the game can be won, though in different ways—by destroying all rivals, sending a spaceship to Alpha Centauri, or simply by earning the highest number of points when time reaches the modern age. One of the game's main appeals is that players must make choices about which technology to research next, with each new technology affecting the gameplay in fundamental ways. For instance, the civilization who first develops ight technology will have a tremendous military advantage over its rivals. The turn-based gameplay also makes a considerable difference. Gamers could take as long as they wanted to make endless micromanagement decisions, and it was easier to move troops and settlers. The *Civilization* series has been incredibly popular in its own right, leading to numerous sequels and spin-offs.

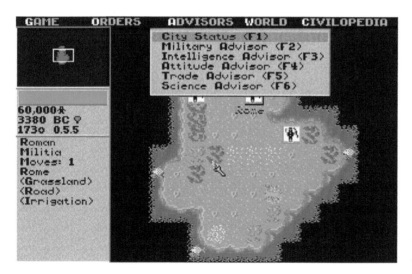

Civilization offers turn-based gameplay and individual units (settlers, soldiers, etc.) that can be moved about the map. The civilization eventually develops new technologies, forcing players to adapt their strategies to accommodate.

Will Wright's *SimCity* was one of the most important and in uential games at the turn of the 1990s, leading to hordes of sequels, spin-offs, clones, and derivatives that has represented a considerable slice of the gaming industry ever since. Although modern sim games are orders of magnitude more complex than Wright's original, his basic gameplay model has endured. Whether building theme parks or corporations, players seem to enjoy simulating wondrously interconnected systems. As computer, console, and handheld technology continues to improve, we are likely to see even more sophisticated and nuanced *SimCity*-in uenced games.[14]

---

[14]This development might well be spurred by Maxis's decision to release a free version of the original game under a GNU license as part of the One-Laptop-Per-Child initiative. The license allows other developers to see and borrow freely from the code, provided that they don't use Electronic Arts' trademarks. The first of the major projects to take advantage of the arrangement is *Micropolis* by Don Hopkins.

16

SPACE INVADERS (1978): THE JAPANESE DESCEND

Toshihiro Nishikado's 1978 masterpiece *Space Invaders* is on the shortlist of the world's most important videogames—another master stroke that truly brought the masses to the medium. A success in both the United States and Japan, *Space Invaders* would become

Screenshot from the original *Space Invaders* arcade game, with simulated color overlay.

one of the most widely imitated games of all time: endlessly cloned, copied, and modified right up to the present day.

Even if you've never actually played *Space Invaders* or even seen a working machine, chances are you've played one of its thousands of derivatives, such as Namco's ever-popular *Galaga* (1981) or Konami's *Gradius* (1986). Although *Space Invaders* is primitive even compared to these early games, its foundational in uence is unmistakable. *Space Invaders'* importance goes far beyond serving as the basis of so many "shoot 'em ups," however. Perhaps even more so than *Pong* (see bonus chapter, "*Pong* (1972): Avoid Missing Game to Start Industry"), *Space Invaders* appealed to the general public. Their quarters and 100-yen coins advanced into coin slots as relentlessly as the aliens themselves descended, making millions for Taito, inspiring hundreds of would-be developers, and exploding the market for videogames. It's hard to imagine what the modern arcade and console markets would look like were it not for Japanese games like *Space Invaders* and *Pac-Man* (Chapter 13, "*Pac-Man* (1980): Japanese Gumption, American Consumption")—assuming that it survived at all!

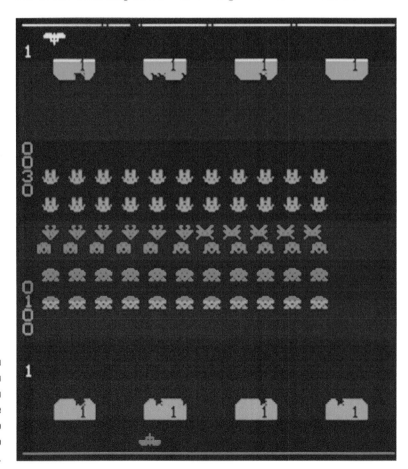

Arcade screenshot with simulated color overlay from *Space Invaders II* (1980), which featured a competitive mode where two players fight to destroy each other in addition to the advancing attackers.

Perhaps we should begin with some geography. How was Japan's gaming industry and pop culture different than those found in the United States, and why have so many Japanese games been so extraordinarily successful both here and abroad? *Space Invaders* was only the first of what would become an onslaught of Japanese imports that would become the foundations of the arcade and console industries. It's difficult to exaggerate the importance of Japanese games like *Pac-Man, Super Mario Bros.* (Chapter 19, "*Super Mario Bros.* (1985): How High Can Jumpman Get?"), *The Legend of Zelda* (Chapter 21, "*The Legend of Zelda* (1986): Rescuing Zeldas and Uniting Triforces"), *Street Fighter II* (Chapter 17, "*Street Fighter II* (1991): Would You Like the Combo?"), and *Final Fantasy VII* (Chapter 7, "*Final Fantasy VII* (1997): It's Never Final in the World of Fantasy"). It's likewise a mistake to question the relevance of Japanese consoles like the Nintendo Entertainment System, the Sega Genesis, and the Sony PlayStation.

Superstar American developers—such as Richard Garriott (Chapter 23, "*Ultima* (1980): The Immaculate Conception of the Computer Role-Playing Game"), Roberta Williams (Chapter 11, "*King's Quest: Quest for the Crown* (1984): Perilous Puzzles, Thorny Thrones"), and Will Wright (Chapters 15 and 22)—all got their start on home computer platforms like the Apple II and Commodore 64. Though there was of course the occasional modestly successful port (such as *SimCity* for the Super Nintendo), Japanese games dominated the console market. Jack Tramiel, president of Commodore, had always worried that cheap Japanese home computers would topple the American home computer industry, but that never happened. Although the Japanese never seriously challenged America's desktops, they first captured the arcades and later the living rooms of U.S. gamers, where they have dominated ever since.

Chris Kohler discusses the Japanese gaming industry in depth in his book *Power Up: How Japanese Video Games Gave the World an Extra Life* (Brady Games, 2004). Kohler thinks that the reason Japan's gaming industry ourished was the country's unique pop culture, which was (and is) saturated with cartoons and comics (anime and manga, respectively). Whereas such things were typically viewed as fit only for children in the United States, they enjoyed far broader appeal and acceptance in Japan. Furthermore, the highly stylized aesthetics of anime and manga lent themselves well to videogames, which were (at the time) too limited to represent anything approaching graphical realism. Nevertheless, Kohler points out that Japanese games became increasingly like movies, borrowing frequently from film and working to spin coherent narratives around the gameplay. Kohler argues that whereas American games like *Pong* and *Breakout* were abstract, Japanese games were more like movies, with identifiable characters and fictional scenarios. *Space Invaders*, for instance, gives us a recognizable threat (alien invasion), and the player is cast in a desperate and ultimately futile mission to save the world.[1] The cinematic nature of Japanese games would become even more pronounced with Shigeru Miyamoto's *Donkey Kong* in 1981, another dizzyingly successful Japanese import.

Are the Japanese simply better at making games than their American counterparts? Although Kohler makes some good points about the Japanese gaming industry, we could also posit more banal explanations for why Japanese games came to dominate the West—or, more specifically, our arcade and console industries. Perhaps the most glaring factor was the frequently mentioned Great Videogame Crash of 1984, which devastated the American console industry, creating a massive vacuum that no American manufacturer or retailer seemed willing or able to fill. It was Nintendo who finally resurrected the console, joined later by Sega, another Japanese company. Though there were, of course, many American games made for these systems, the most successful were typically imported from Japan. Furthermore, while games like *Super Mario Bros.* and *Final Fantasy VII* were smash hits in both countries, few games originating in the West were popular in Japan. Even today, it's a surprise to find an American game on the Japanese best-seller charts. Of course, in recent years, Western developers have had a renaissance in the United States, creating a wide range of innovative best-sellers, though they still have an uphill climb in a mostly indifferent Japan.

In 1978, many an American game developer must have felt like the laser cannon in *Space Invaders*, hopelessly outnumbered and watching dismally as the last defenses eroded (a process often aided by the player's own shot). On a more positive note, the popularity of *Space Invaders* was hard to miss. Whole arcades sprang up around the machine, offering row after row of identical machines to satiate the public's desire to blast aliens. Although *Pong* had enjoyed tremendous popularity, *Space Invaders* made it look primitive in comparison. Who wants to knock a ball back and forth when you can save the universe?

Steven L. Kent discusses the game at some length in his *The Ultimate History of Video Games* (Three Rivers Press, 2001), noting that it wasn't an instant success in its mother country. After a few quiet months, though, the game swept across the country—even small shops selling raw vegetables would shove aside their inventory to make room for more *Space Invaders* machines. According to Kent, when the game was exported to the United States, arcade owners found they could recoup the $1,700 it cost to buy a *Space*

---

[1]Though Kohler doesn't seem to recognize it, *Breakout* did have a recognizable, if abstract, story that was established through the cabinet art—help some crooks break out of a prison.

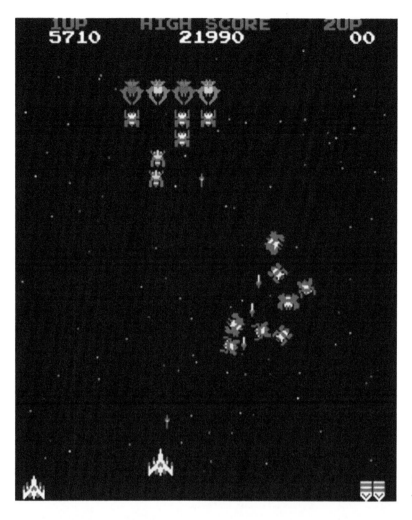

Screenshot from the arcade version of *Galaga*.

Invaders machine in a single month. Taito and its partner Midway ended up selling the United States more than 60,000 machines. Naturally, the excitement and piles of cash that built up around *Space Invaders* helped spur the growth of the broader arcade industry, which was still very much in its infancy in the late 1970s. Indeed, before *Space Invaders*, it was rare to find an arcade machine outside of bars and arcades; afterwards, grocery stores, pizza parlors, and even waiting rooms were often stocked with them, predating the coming ubiquity and even greater dominance of *Pac-Man* machines.

What made *Space Invaders* such a hit? Before we discuss the gameplay, let's pause to consider the historical context. Specifically, *Space Invaders* arrived on the heels of George Lucas' *Star Wars*, a 1977 science fiction film that became a true cultural phenomenon. That same year, Americans had also lined up to see Steven Spielberg's *Close Encounters of the Third Kind*, another high-profile science fiction film about visitors from space. The space program was also still in its heyday, and many children dreamed of one day becoming an astronaut. Coupled with these science fiction films were plenty of paranoid thrillers, such as Spielberg's earlier movie, *Jaws* (1975), whose ominous music served as the inspiration for so many other movies and games. Indeed, as we'll see, *Space Invaders* relied heavily on movies like *Jaws* for inspiration for its sound effects, which certainly added to the tension and dread of the descending aliens. In short, the pop cultural milieu of the late 1970s was perfect for a game like *Space Invaders*, which combined science fiction themes with a level of tension and anxiety comparable to the groundbreaking thrillers of the era.

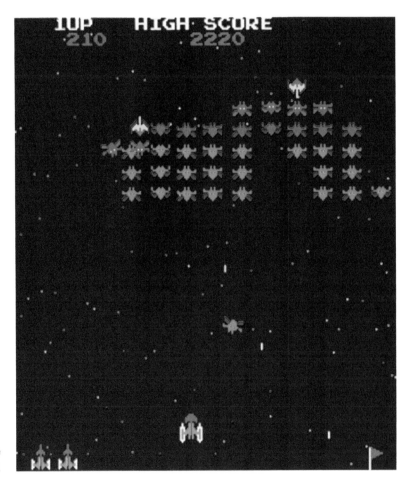

Screenshot from the arcade version of *Galaxian*.

Space Invaders' gameplay is not as simple as some take it to be. The player controls a laser cannon that can be moved left and right along the bottom of the screen; vertical movement is not possible. Pressing the fire button causes a shot to move rapidly from the cannon to the top of the screen, assuming it is not "intercepted" by an object or alien. Only one shot can be in the air at one time, so players either have to wait for it to hit something or reach the top of the screen. In the middle of the screen are five rows of invaders. In a movement reminiscent of a manual typewriter, the aliens move to the extreme left and right of the screen, dropping down one row each time they reach the border. Between the cannon and the aliens are four destructible fortifications that serve as (temporary) cover. The typical strategy is to duck in and out of cover, fire some shots, then use the cover to avoid the alien bombardment. The player can also try to shoot the aliens' bombs with the cannon; doing so renders the bomb harmless. The aliens speed up as they are eliminated; the last few move very quickly and can be very difficult to hit. The game also features a flying saucer that occasionally flies across the top of the screen. Hitting this target requires precision, timing, or just dumb luck.

The invaders come in three basic designs. Nishikado mapped these designs onto graph paper first, striving to create bit-mapped images that would resemble the alien monsters of H.G. Wells's *The War of the Worlds*. In a 2005 interview with *Edge* magazine, Nishikado said that his original idea had been to have the player battling against tanks or airplanes, but couldn't find a way to make these objects look recognizable with limited graphics technology. "Human movement would have been easier," said Nishikado, "but I felt it would be immoral to shoot humans, even if they were bad guys. Then I heard about a movie called *Star Wars* released in the U.S. which was coming to Japan next year, so I came up with a game based in space which had space aliens as targets."[2] Nishikado's challenge was great—he not only had to design the game itself, but the hardware to run it. It was an incredible achievement for the 34-year-old engineer.

Perhaps the single most-discussed feature of *Space Invaders* is its innovative use of sound. The most important of these is the "thump thump thump" that plays as the aliens advance, gradually rising in frequency like an over-excited heartbeat. Later games such as DynaMicro's *Dungeons of Daggorath* (1982) for the Radio Shack Color Computer would borrow or adapt this feature. Sounds also play when the player fires a shot or strikes a target. All of these effects make the game almost as fun to listen to as to see in action, and indeed, many gamers can easily identify the game by sound alone.

Besides the innovative sound and graphics, we might attribute some of *Space Invaders*' success to more basic impulses.

---

[2]See http://www.edge-online.com/news/the-creation-space-invaders.

For instance, most of us feel somehow responsible for the fate of the laser cannon (and the world under attack by the aliens). It *needs* us to save it; neglecting it for even a few seconds results in catastrophe. We might also compare destroying the aliens to rapidly popping the air pockets in a sheet of bubble wrap—an activity which, we might add, has recently made its way into several casual and Web-based games.

Another key aspect of the game's appeal was its high score indicator, an innovation that quickly became a mainstay of the arcade industry. *Space Invaders* didn't offer the more elaborate high score tables with initials seen in later games—only the single highest score was recorded and displayed. Nevertheless, this component added a vital competitive edge to an already engrossing game, and no doubt many an aggressive gamer spent that extra quarter to try once more to beat the existing score.

As everyone knows, *Space Invaders* was widely imitated, spawning a massive genre that eventually split into a variety of subgenres. Although it is well beyond this chapter to offer a comprehensive look at the thousands of games inspired by *Space Invaders*, we can't help but mention at least a few of the most celebrated.

Perhaps the most famous of all *Space Invaders* clones is *Galaga*, a 1981 shooter developed by Namco and manufactured in the United States by Midway. *Galaga*, which is still widely available today in almost any venue that offers arcade machines,[3] was based on an earlier game, from the same company, named *Galaxian* (1979), which we'll discuss first. *Galaxian* introduced several key innovations to the *Space Invaders* formula. Besides vastly improved audiovisuals (it was the first arcade game in 100% RGB color[4]), the aliens could now attack in kamikaze-style formations. The four destructible shields were gone as well, making the game even more difficult. *Galaga* is essentially an enhanced remake of *Galaxian*, offering stat tracking and better audiovisuals. The best innovation, though, is that the enemy's motherships ("Boss Galagas") can trap the player's ship in a tractor beam. If the player is out of ships, the game is over. Otherwise, the player can try to destroy the mothership that's holding the trapped ship; if successful, the captured ship is released. It then attaches to the side of the player's ship and doubles its firepower.

With *Space Invaders* and its clones causing so much commotion in arcades, it was only a matter of time before it swept into living rooms. At this time, the "console market" was almost entirely limited to self-contained *Pong* systems. Atari had released its famous

---

[3]*Galaga* is usually seen nowadays in a special combination cabinet with *Ms. Pac-Man*.
[4]RGB is a convenient Red, Green, Blue color model for computer graphics, because the human visual system works in a similar manner.

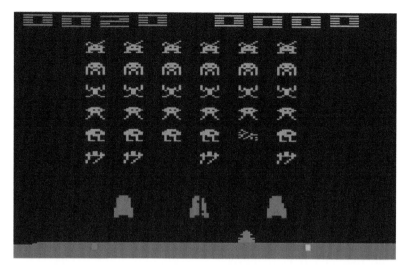

Screenshot from the Atari 2600 VCS version of *Space Invaders*, which was the first of several arcade-to-home conversions that put the system on the map. Though not necessarily a faithful conversion, *Space Invaders* for the 2600 was a great deal of fun and featured more than 100 play variations. Although this version is among the most famous home conversions, nearly every other platform during this era—no matter how obscure or limited—would receive at least one knock-off of this game, if not an official port.

Atari 2600 Video Computer System (VCS) in October of 1977, but success had proven elusive. Even though several of Atari's first game releases for its VCS were translations of their own arcade titles, none were true blockbusters that people wanted to play badly enough to buy the system. It wasn't until 1980 when arcade blockbuster *Space Invaders* was converted to the VCS that the first console killer app was born. It became the best-selling game of the year and helped establish the VCS as the definitive videogame console of its era.

Space Invaders–style games would eventually evolve into a plethora of styles. One of the first major innovations was scrolling. Instead of showing all the action on a single screen, games like Konami's *Scramble* (1981) and *Gradius* featured a background that moved horizontally as the game progressed. The player's ship

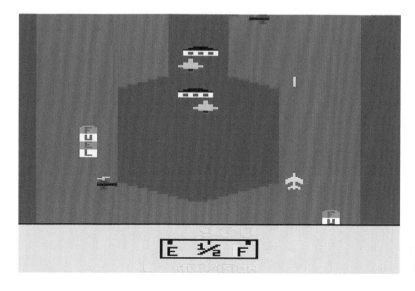

Screenshot from the Atari 2600 VCS version of *River Raid*.

could also move up and down as well as left and right, increasing the complexity considerably. *Defender* (bonus chapter, "*Defender* (1980): The Joys of Difficult Games"), introduced in 1980, is perhaps the most difficult and sophisticated of all such games. Instead of a background that moved independently of the player (as with *Scramble*), *Defender* let players move all over the map (and even gave them a radar to keep their bearings). Although such a setup was undoubtedly more advanced, games that continuously autoscrolled were far more common.

Namco's *Xevious* (1982) is often credited with being the first vertically scrolling shooter, though it was predated by Atari's arcade game *Sky Raider* (1978). In any case, vertical scrolling became quite popular. Activision's *River Raid* (1982) for the Atari VCS is an example of an early console game of this type. Other in uential arcade shooters of the 1980s include Capcom's *1942* (1984; vertical), Toaplan's *Tiger-Heli* (1985; vertical), and Irem's *R-Type* (1987; horizontal), just to name a few. As the years progressed, the audiovisuals improved dramatically, along with nice features like powerups, damage resistance, and boss fights. The genre seemed to peak in the 1990s with ambitious titles such as Konami's *Axelay* (1992, Super Nintendo), which featured both horizontal and vertical scrolling along with a bevy of impressive visual effects. The Atari ST and Commodore Amiga computers were also home to plenty of lavishly detailed shooters, particularly those from the British company Psygnosis, such as *Menace* (1988), *Blood Money* (1989), and *Agony* (1992). Game developers competed to see who could design the best-looking and best-sounding shooters, and even if the actual gameplay varied little, gamers looked forward to these

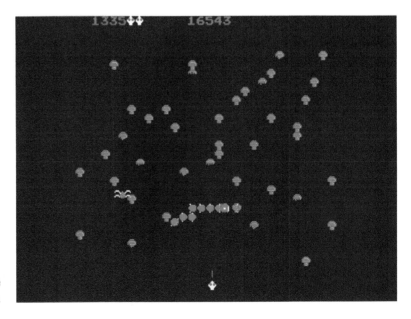

Screenshot from the arcade version of *Centipede*.

richly aesthetic experiences. For instance, though the shooters from Thalamus, *Sanxion* (1986) and *Delta* (1987), offered little-to-no innovation gameplay-wise, their superb musical scores (composed by Rob Hubbard) are still enjoyed today on Remix.Kwed.Org and other Commodore 64 music sites.

There were also plenty of exotic shooters that innovated even more radically from the *Space Invaders* model. These include Atari's *Centipede*, a fast-paced 1980 arcade game that utilized a trackball for more uid movement. Another 1980 arcade classic from Atari is *Tempest*, a 3D vector-based shooter that is rather difficult to describe. Essentially, players move a ship around the edges of a complex web that emanates outward from the center of the screen. The enemies begin at the center and move toward the outer edges, destroying the player's ship if they make contact with it. Instead of a trackball, this game used a spinner[5] to give players

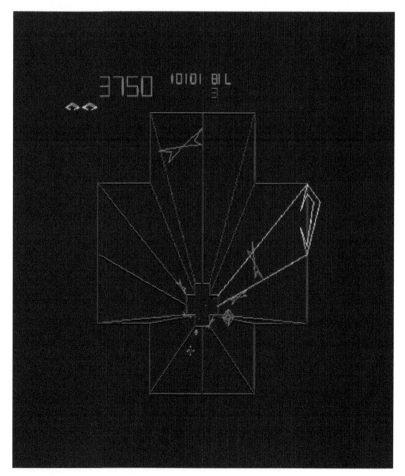

Screenshot from the arcade version of *Tempest*.

---

[5]A paddle or dial that spins freely. See bonus chapter, *Pong* (1972): Avoid Missing Game to Start Industry, for more information.

more precise control around the grid. Konami seems to have been inspired by *Tempest* to create the raster-based *Gyruss* in 1983. *Gyruss* lost the spinner in favor of a joystick and the abstract, grid-look of *Tempest*, but maintained its intriguing 3D look and feel.

It's tempting to try to lump all games that involve spaceship combat under the "shooter" designation. However, it seems more sensible to attribute games like Atari's *Asteroids* (1979) and Midway's *Omega Race* (1981) to an earlier in uence—namely, *Spacewar!* (bonus chapter, *SpaceWar!* (1962): The Best Waste of Time in the History of the Universe). Like *Spacewar!*, *Asteroids* and *Omega Race* employed realistic physics, complete with iner-tia and momentum. This characteristic seems to set it and games like it apart from the less realistic action of *Space Invader*–style games. Likewise, it seems ludicrous to group first-person games with light ight simulation elements like Atari's *Star Raiders* (1979) and *Star Wars* (1983) under the "shooter" label, as no one would confuse their gameplay with *Space Invaders*.[6]

What about "shooter" games that feature human or humanoid avatars rather than some type of ying craft? Often enough, "run 'n' gun" arcade games like Capcom's *Commando* (1985), SNK's *Ikari Warriors* (1986), and Nazca Corporation's *Metal Slug* (1996) end up in the same category as *Space Invaders*, though it's plain that these games have precious little in common with conventional shooters. Even though all these games involve shooting enemies, the control scheme (and thus the gameplay) is entirely different.

One might also wonder why games like id's *Doom* (Chapter 5, "*Doom* (1993): The First-Person Shooter Takes Control") are called first-person shooters, as though they shared a heritage with the shooters we've been talking about. Again, just because these games involve shooting enemies doesn't seem a sound reason for placing them alongside *Space Invaders* and *Galaga*; one might as well throw in Nintendo's *Duck Hunt* (1984) and Sega's *The House of the Dead* (1996)—arcade light-gun games—for the same reason.

But, we are at something of an impasse here if we try to nail down precisely what we mean by "shooter," "shoot 'em up," or, as they are known by their fans, "shmups." The only criterion that really seems to distinguish them is the player's *inability* to direct the avatar's (or ship's) progress through the gameworld. Instead, the player can navigate only within a designated area, and is either prevented or punished for violating those boundaries.[7]

For instance, *Space Invaders* and *Galaga* are fixed-screen games; the player cannot move the ship beyond the confines of the screen (though in *Galaga* the aliens can move out of sight).

---

[6]For more on *Star Raiders* and the *Star Wars* arcade game, see bonus chapter, *Star Raiders* (1979): The New Hope.

[7]Of course, even with this, there are exceptions, such as Sega's *Fantasy Zone* (1985; Arcade), where players can control the scrolling by moving right or left.

Box back from Opcode Games's 2003 homebrew release for the Coleco ColecoVision, *Space Invaders Collection*, featuring near-perfect ports of both *Space Invaders* and *Space Invaders Part II*. *Space Invaders* and its basic play style continues to be an inspiration for new games today.

Scrolling games may give players the freedom to move in all four directions, but players don't change the way the screen moves. It's comparable to a child bouncing around inside a school bus. Although the child may be free to move all around the vehicle, he or she is unable (hopefully, at least!) to change the direction the bus is moving. In fact, many games, like the aforementioned *River Raid* and *Blood Money*, actually punish the player for straying from the path. In the almost sadistically difficult *Blood Money*, for instance, contact with the walls damages the player just as much as colliding with an enemy ship or being hit by its fire.

In short, a conventional shooter constrains players' range of movement, forcing them into a sort of dodgeball match with the computer. Indeed, perhaps dodgeball is the closest physical analogy we have to these games, though with one exception—the player can throw balls as well (at enemies who seldom bother to dodge!).

Space Invaders is responsible for many "firsts" that came to define the arcade experience. It was the first mega hit from Japan, a country whose exports remain a vital part of the American gaming industry. It also represents a bold step toward representational (as opposed to symbolic) graphics; the aliens looked like aliens, not blocks or wedges. The sound effects were revolutionary, escalating the tension of an already intense experience. The high score added the all-important competitive spirit that would afterwards come to characterize the arcade era. Finally, the easy-to-learn yet hard-to-master gameplay of *Space Invaders* would be endlessly duplicated and refined in hundreds if not thousands of clones and derivatives. Practically any games-capable device in existence has some form of *Space Invaders.* We even find versions that rely totally on character-set graphics!

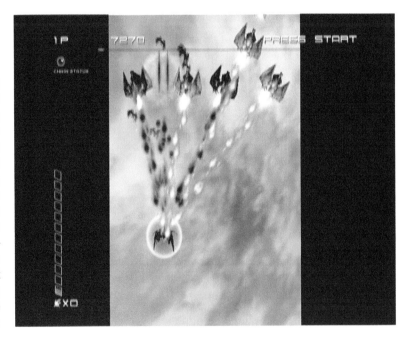

Treasure's *Ikaruga*, screenshot from the 2002 Sega Dreamcast version shown, is one of a long line of fast-paced shooters from Japan that continue to be released today. Their designs are in stark contrast to the relatively pedestrian pacing of classics like *Space Invaders*. Some critics argue that these later games were so difficult and elaborate—making it a point of pride to fill a player's screen with bullets—that casual fans turned away, leaving only hardcore enthusiasts in the cockpit.

With the possible exception of *Pac-Man*, no game seems to represent all of videogaming as well as *Space Invaders*. Even people who have never seen or played the game are familiar with its iconic aliens and trademark sound effects. Even if the industry has come a long way since the first eager teenager plunked in a quarter and blasted her first space invader, there's still something strangely satisfying about a good shmup. Let them come, wave after wave; we'll happily burst each bubble of the bubble wrap. Thankfully, the aliens are a fully renewable resource.

17

STREET FIGHTER II (1991): WOULD YOU LIKE THE COMBO?

Ryu, Ken, E. Honda, Guile, Chun-Li, Zangief, Dhalsim, Sagat and M. Bison—do they really need an introduction? If so, you're overdue for a serious Shoryuken.[1] The game: Capcom's *Street Fighter II*, probably the single most important arcade title of the 1990s.

Street Fighter II's cast of characters.

Although there had been several competitive fighting games before it, *Street Fighter II* trumped them all with its spectacular graphics and sophisticated—even artistic—gameplay. If the graphics were the bait, the gameplay was the hook. A seemingly endless line of teenagers lined up in front of these machines,

---

[1]A special attack in the *Street Fighter* series, of course, consisting of a jumping uppercut in which the user spins, knocking the opponent to the ground.

eager to demonstrate their virtual street fighting skills—or, at least their mastery of *Street Fighter II*'s esoteric combat system. For many boys (and no doubt many girls as well!) growing up in the 1990s, *Street Fighter II* wasn't just a game, but a rite of passage.

Street Fighter II joins the ranks of other Japanese games that overwhelmed American arcades: *Space Invaders* (Chapter 16, "*Space Invaders* (1978): The Japanese Take Over"), *Pac-Man* (Chapter 13, "*Pac-Man* (1980): Japanese Gumption, American Consumption"), and *Pole Position* (Chapter 14, "*Pole Position* (1982): Where the Raster Meets the Road"). All four games introduced critical innovations that would be shamelessly duplicated and endlessly refined. Although they perhaps had their greatest impact in the arcades, they also played a critical role in the console industry. Console makers competed fiercely for the rights to port these titles, as they knew countless fans would purchase their console specifically to play these games in their living rooms. Indeed, one of the recurring standards of console excellence throughout the 1980s and 1990s was the degree to which their ports of games like *Pac-Man* and *Street Fighter II* approximated the arcade experience.

However, there's little argument that what made *Street Fighter II* so popular was its competitive nature, which, like *Pong* (bonus chapter, "*Pong* (1972): Avoid Missing Game to Start Industry") before it, made it uniquely suited to the arcade. Though it was possible to play *Street Fighter II* and other fighting games against the computer, the real challenge was facing off against a skilled human opponent. The arcade owners of the early 1990s must have loved these fighting games, which filled their arcades with quarter-popping teens who otherwise would have stayed home to play videogames on their consoles and computers. Indeed, the only real competition that fighting games had at the arcades were driving simulations, which benefited from specially built enclosures and cabinets that would have been prohibitively expensive to have at home (see Chapter 14). Other arcade games didn't enjoy this advantage, and their graphical superiority gradually eroded as console technology improved. However, unless one had like-minded friends to play with at home, the arcades were still the best place to test one's mettle against other *Street Fighter II* fans. This fact helped keep fighting games ourishing in the arcades long after shoot 'em ups and platformers had faded from that venue to the family television.

Street Fighter II was certainly not the first fighting game, and we'll spend some time in this chapter describing its most in u-ential predecessors. However, it did offer some key innovations that came to define the genre, which we'll discuss in turn. There is some contention about what was actually the first true competitive fighting game. One very early contender is Vectorbeam's *Warrior*,

Vectorbeam's *Warrior*, shown with simulated color backdrop.

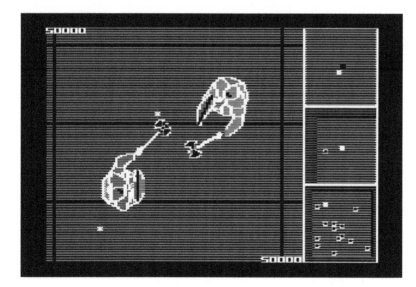

Marc Goodman's *The Bilestoad* (1982) for the Apple II was a superb expansion of concepts from *Warrior*. Using a sophisticated control scheme, players battle it out on a small island with limb-severing axes and protective shields.

a 1979 arcade game that showed an overhead view of two dueling knights with swords. It featured vector graphics, and the two players could win either by whacking their opponent with their swords or forcing them into a pit (solo play wasn't possible). However, the machine's hardware was unreliable, and poor collision detection and sluggish controls—two of the most critical aspects for a fighting game—certainly didn't help endear it to gamers. It faded quickly from the scene.

In 1984, John G. Avildsen's *The Karate Kid* debuted in theaters. This film smashed into theaters like a ying sidekick, raking in over $90 million and inspiring untold legions of boys to seek martial arts training at one of the new dojos popping up all over the country. Everyone seemed to be saying "wax on, wax off" in their best Mr. Miyagi accent. Needless to say, the time was ripe for a good karate game that would let players reprise Ralph Macchio's role as Daniel LaRusso.

Screenshot from Data East's *Karate Champ.*

Technos Japan Corporation's *Karate Champ*, released in 1984 by Data East, certainly gave them the chance. The original version was for a single player who fought against computer-controlled opponents. The interface relied on a pair of joysticks for control; the left was primarily for movement and the right for attacks. *Karate Champ* also offered the familiar side-by-side perspective that would become standard in almost every subsequent fighting game. Technos is also responsible for *Double Dragon*, a side-scrolling "beat 'em up" that we'll discuss later. In addition to the now-standard sparring mode, *Karate Champ* also offered a series of minigames to further test one's skill at the controllers.

Data East revised the game and rereleased it as *Karate Champ Player vs. Player* later in 1984, with home ports for a variety of systems following shortly thereafter. The arcade version featured two pairs of joysticks, and, as the title makes clear, offered competitive gameplay. Naturally, the ports had to make concessions for simpler control schemes, such as requiring players to hold down a controller button while moving the joystick (or operating

International Karate (top) and *The Way of the Exploding Fist* (bottom) were clearly based on the earlier *Karate Champ*, but courts ruled that they were different in the ways that mattered—such as background graphics and scoring systems. Both shots shown here are from the Commodore 64.

the d-pad) in a certain direction to execute a move. For instance, the rather inadequate Nintendo Entertainment System (NES) port required players to move right on the d-pad and simultaneously press the A and B buttons to leap right. All versions but the NES have the players fighting over a woman, who seems to prefer a boyfriend who can pulverize his rival. The NES version removed this aspect of the game, though it's unclear whether this was a move to make the game less sexist or simply to get the coding done faster. The sloppiness of the collision detection and control schemes suggest the latter.

A British company named System 3 developed and released a computer game in 1986 called *International Karate*. The game was quite similar to *Karate Champ*, but was available on far more platforms, including British computers like the ZX Spectrum. The game was published in the United States by Epyx. Data East sued System 3, accusing them of a complex set of copyright and trademark violations. The case was eventually decided against Data East, though the reasoning behind the judge's decision was somewhat complicated. Essentially, he believed that the many elements the games had in common were essential to the sport of karate and could not be copyrighted. On the other hand, the elements of *Karate Champ* and *International Karate* that were "creative contributions," such as scoring and background scenes, were quite different and did

Konami's *Yie Ar Kung-Fu* (1985) was a very popular single-player-versus-the-computer arcade fighting game. Though it lacks the depth of most other one-on-one fighting games, *Yie Ar Kung-Fu* was heralded for its fast action and colorful cast of opponents.

not violate copyright. Data East seemed to have learned from the experience, and tried something similar in 1993 with *Fighter's History*, which Capcom felt was similar enough to its *Street Fighter II* to warrant another trial. Again, the courts ruled in favor of the clone-maker, and Data East emerged victorious in the struggle.[2]

There were several other notable fighting games made in the *Karate Champ* style, such as Beam Software's *Way of the Exploding Fist* (1985), a popular Australian game that made its way to Britain and the United States for the Commodore 64 and most British computers of the time. However, arguably the best of the lot is Jordan Mechner's *Karateka*, a methodically paced 1984 side-scrolling fighting game for the Apple II published by Broderbund and ported to most other platforms of the era.

Karateka, like Mechner's later hit *Prince of Persia* (1989), was known for its realistic graphics and convincing animation of the human body. Unlike most fighting games, *Karateka* featured a comprehensive and cinematic storyline—the player must face a series of increasingly difficult fights to rescue princess Mariko from the evil Akuma. Interestingly enough, in most versions, the box art portrayed the player's character and Princess Mariko as blond Europeans; only Akuma looks Asian.

Screenshot from *Karateka* (the Apple II version).

Another early approach to the fighting genre is represented by Technos's side-scrolling *Double Dragon* (1987), often called the definitive "beat 'em up." *Double Dragon* and its imitators differ from competitive fighting games in several key ways. Most

---

[2]These legal battles are discussed at length in Steven L. Kent's *The Ultimate History of Video Games* (Three Rivers Press, 2001).

significantly, instead of all the action taking place on a single screen, the screen scrolls horizontally as the player (or players) progress through the game, battling increasingly tougher or more numerous enemies. Second, the controls are greatly simplified, with much fewer moves—a fact compensated for with the ability to pick up and use a variety of weapons (baseball bats, whips, and so on). Third, players usually cooperate with each other to fight computer-controlled thugs rather than duel one-on-one. Beat 'em ups like *Double Dragon* were popular in the arcades, but were also a hit on home platforms.

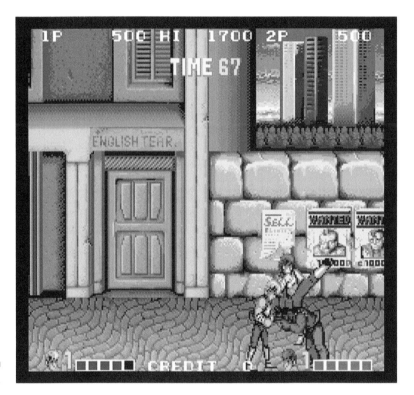

Screenshot from *Double Dragon*.

Double Dragon saw several sequels and even a typically mediocre film treatment in 1994. It also inspired a slew of quality clones, including Capcom's *Final Fight* and Sega's *Golden Axe*, both in 1989. There have also been several successful beat 'em ups based on comic book and cartoon characters, such as Konami's *Teenage Mutant Ninja Turtles: The Arcade Game*, yet another bestseller of 1989, and Konami's *X-Men* (1992), a quarter-gobbler that offered simultaneous gameplay for up to six players. The popular TV show *The Simpsons* also served as the basis for a classic beat 'em up, with Konami's unlikely *The Simpsons: The Arcade Game* in 1991.

There was a cavalcade of computer, arcade, and console games based more or less on *Karate Champ* released in the mid to late 1980s, but most of these were quickly forgotten. One such game that might have ended up in the dustbin of history was Capcom's *Street Fighter* (1987). Though it offered better audiovisuals than *Karate Champ*, the controls were inaccurate and often frustrating, and players only had two virtually identical playable characters to choose from (Ryu and Ken). The original controls were a joystick and two pneumatic pads. The idea was that the characters in the game would execute a strong or weak move depending on how hard players smacked these pads; needless to say, these machines were quickly ruined by abusive players. Later versions replaced these pads with the six-button setup that afterwards became a staple of the genre. It also featured three secret techniques (special moves) that players had to learn on their own. The game was eventually ported to many home platforms of the day, though sometimes with modifications, like the release for the NEC TurboGrafx-CD as *Fighting Street*.

Screenshot from *Street Fighter*. This unremarkable fighting game was the unlikely precursor to one of the most famous videogames of all time.

Capcom more than redeemed itself four years later with *Street Fighter II: The World Warrior*. The sequel represented a vast improvement over its prequel. Besides the expected improvement in audiovisuals, Capcom made some innovative changes to the gameplay that revolutionized the genre: eight unique playable characters, each with an extensive set of attacks, some of which could be combined into multihit combinations, or "combos." It also offered four AI-only "boss" characters and borrowed the competitive "loser pays" game system from the previous game; the winner of player versus player match could play another bout for free, but the loser had to ante up another quarter. This design gave gamers yet another incentive to master the combos!

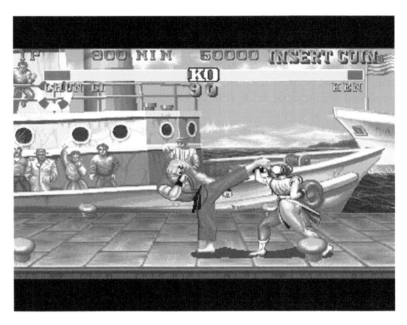

Screenshot from
Street Fighter II.

The huge number of moves made *Street Fighter II* the most sophisticated game of its kind. Players enjoyed trying out the different characters and devising strategies to deal with every possible situation. Although of course there had been strategy involved in earlier fighting games, *Street Fighter II* was substantially more complex. Players had to work hard to learn all the moves and then the right circumstances to execute them. Furthermore, the super-tight controls and detailed graphics made the game fun to play and impressive to watch. Players could either compete head-to-head or take on the game solo, in which case they'd fight all the other characters and the four bosses. Later versions made these bosses playable characters as well.

Although arcades had always been veritable arenas of competition, *Street Fighter II* took things to a new level. Dedicated players discussed moves and strategies with their friends, read magazines and guides, and spent countless hours practicing and tweaking their performance. Naturally, novice players facing a seasoned veteran often found themselves hopelessly outmatched, unable to last more than a few seconds or get off a single attack. Although some such players might accuse the other of cheating or playing "cheap," for the most part even the nastiest attacks and combos had their appropriate countermove.

Street Fighter II: The World Warrior was a staggering success for Capcom and the arcade industry as a whole. Capcom released multiple variations over the years, adding or revising content and tweaking or speeding up the gameplay. The game was also ported to most computer and console platforms. A Super Nintendo version appeared in 1992, but the NEC TurboGrafx-16 and Sega Genesis platforms didn't see the game until 1993 with the arrival of *Street Fighter II: Champion Edition*. Late 1993 saw the arcade release of *Super Street Fighter II*, which upgraded the audiovisuals and added new characters but slowed the gameplay down. In 1994, *Super Street Fighter II Turbo* added "super combos" and let players adjust the game's speed. *Street Fighter II* aficionados endlessly debated the merits and limitations of each port, sequel, and remake. Fans would have to wait until 1995, however, for the first true sequel with all new content—*Street Fighter Alpha*, which was set chronologically before *Street Fighter II* and had a younger cast of fighters. This was followed in 1997 by *Street Fighter III: New Generation*, which revamped the gameplay and got rid of all the original characters except Ryu and Ken.

Screenshot for *Super Street Fighter II Turbo.*

The enormous success of *Street Fighter II* spurred a huge number of clones and spin-offs. SNK added several key games to the genre, including *Fatal Fury: King of Fighters* (1991), *Art of Fighting* (1992), and *Samurai Shodown* (1993). A comprehensive list (much less description) of each such game would strain the energies of the authors and the patience of even the most devoted reader. Through it all, however, *Street Fighter II* remained the standard by which all others were measured.

Perhaps the most notorious of all is Midway's *Mortal Kombat*, a 1992 arcade game that aroused almost instant controversy for its cinematic realism and over-the-top violence.[3] It looked more realistic than *Street Fighter II*, because it was made with live actors who had been filmed over a bluescreen and digitized—a technique utilized in Atari Games's otherwise insignificant *Pit-Fighter*, released two years earlier.[4] Word quickly spread of the game's "fatality" system, which allowed victorious players to perform some particularly gruesome finishing moves on the fallen competitor. Perhaps the worst offender was a "spine rip" fatality performed by the character Sub-Zero. As we might expect, the publicity made the game even more popular.

Screenshot from *Mortal Kombat.*

The excessive violence made for plenty of drama when it came time to port *Mortal Kombat* to consoles. Nintendo had long had a decidedly family-friendly policy when it came to its games, and naturally *Mortal Kombat* would need a serious scrubbing before it satisfied their censors. For the 1993 Super Nintendo port, the fatalities were toned down or taken out completely, and the blood

---

[3]Though beyond the scope of this book, politicians such as U.S. Senator Joseph Lieberman conducted hearings during the 1990s regarding violent videogames, which—to his thinking—included titles like *Mortal Kombat*. It's partially from this sometimes unfounded political and social hysteria that today's Entertainment Software Ratings Board (ESRB) ratings and advertising guidelines came about.

[4]An even earlier example of digitized graphics is Gottlieb's *Exterminator* (1989), an otherwise forgettable shooter game that used 100% digitized graphics.

was recolored gray and referred to as "sweat." Meanwhile, Sega, who had long distinguished itself from Nintendo by projecting an edgier image, also had their Genesis version altered to make it less offensive to parents, but by entering a special code, gamers could bring back the violence. Needless to say, even though the Super Nintendo version featured better graphics and sound, once word got out about which version kept more of the arcade experience intact, the version for Sega's Genesis won the battle for most sales. No doubt due in no small part to this sales disparity, Nintendo would lower their censorship standards for the game's many popular sequels.

Due to their immense cultural impact, both *Street Fighter II* and *Mortal Kombat* received live-action silver screen treatments. The first was Steven E. de Souza's dreadful *Street Fighter*, a 1994 Jean-Claude Van Damme action vehicle. Richard Harrington of the *Washington Post* derided the movie, quipping that "fortunately, we're as unlikely to see a 'Street Fighter' sequel as we are to see one to the latest video/film fiasco, 'Super Mario Bros.'."[5] Paul W. S. Anderson's film *Mortal Kombat*, which debuted in 1995, fared much better both critically and commercially, with a solid story and excellent martial arts action, even spawning a few sequels.

As the 1990s continued, developers kept searching for ways to keep the fighting genre fresh. Sega had a surprise hit in 1993 with its arcade game, *Virtua Fighter*, a pioneering attempt to bring the third dimension to fighting games. Critics raved about its realistic fighting system and impressive 3D graphics. The series hit its seventh installment with *Virtua Fighter 5*, a 2006 arcade game released the following year for the Sony PlayStation 3 and Microsoft Xbox 360, with the latter allowing for online play. The *Virtua Fighter* series inspired several other 3D fighting games, including Namco's *Tekken* (1994) and Team Ninja's *Dead or Alive* (1996). Both games led to best-selling and long-running series. The *Dead or Alive* series gained some measure of fame for its scantily clad female characters, something of a staple in fighting games, culminating in 2003 in *Dead or Alive Xtreme Beach Volleyball* for the Microsoft Xbox—a volleyball game that starred the series' female cast in next to nothing.

There are, of course, plenty of other interesting and innovative one-on-one fighting games we could mention, such as Squaresoft's *Bushido Blade* (1997; Sony PlayStation), a realistic weapons-based game featuring one-hit kills, Arc System Works' *Guilty Gear* (1998), featuring beautiful anime-style graphics, and Namco's *Soulcalibur* (1998), a weapons-based fighter with greater freedom of movement—all of which can boast of sequels and loyal fanbases.

---

[5]See http://tinyurl.com/3lm9r3.

Screenshot from *Virtua Fighter Remix* (1995) on the Sega Saturn. *Virtua Fighter Remix* was a game Sega sent for free to all registered Saturn owners as a type of *mea culpa* for the lackluster first release on the platform.

An interesting trend in fighting games has been mixing together characters from different titles or even different genres, like 2008's *Soulcalibur IV* for the Microsoft Xbox 360 and Sony PlayStation 3 including Yoda and Darth Vader, respectively, from *Star Wars*. Often it seems like the cast of fighters is as important as the gameplay. We certainly see this in games like Sega's *Fighters Megamix*, a 1997 game that includes characters from the company's earlier *Virtua Fighter 2* and *Fighting Vipers* titles. There are also several unlockable characters such as Bark the Polar Bear and Bean the Dynamite, obscure characters from Sega's *Sonic the Fighters* (1996). Capcom and SNK also teamed up to create several fan-pleasing mashups. Other examples of crossover games are Capcom's *X-Men vs. Street Fighter* (1996) and *Marvel vs. Capcom* (1998), which pits warriors from *Street Fighter II* and other Capcom games against several of Marvel's most famous heroes, including Spiderman and Wolverine. Although some players found the idea of Spiderman going head to head with Megaman somewhat unsettling, others were delighted by the variety. These games were followed up with several sequels and spin-offs.

Perhaps the most famous modern game of this type is *Super Smash Bros.*, an approachable multiplayer Nintendo 64 game developed by HAL Laboratory and released in 1999. It features characters from many of Nintendo's franchises: *Donkey Kong*, *Super Mario Bros.*, *The Legend of Zelda*, and *Metroid* are represented, to name just a few. This critically acclaimed hybrid of fighting and platforming games sold nearly five million copies and spawned two sequels: *Super Smash Bros. Melee* (2001; Nintendo GameCube) and *Super Smash Bros. Brawl* (2008; Nintendo Wii). This latter title is the first in the series to introduce third-party creations: Solid Snake from Konami's *Metal Gear* series and Sega's famous Sonic the Hedgehog.

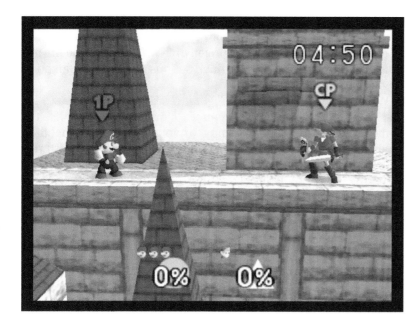

Super Smash Bros. is a popular Nintendo 64 game that included characters and themes from Nintendo's many successful franchises. Shown here is a battle between Mario and Link.

Despite the occasional smash hit like *Super Smash Bros.*, fighting games have fallen considerably from the position they enjoyed at their peak in the 1990s. Their decline was likely brought on by the sheer glut of these games, but also by the popularity of first- and third-person shooters in the 2000s.

First, whereas before gamers had to visit arcades to find worthwhile competition, the newer consoles offered easy networked and online gameplay. Thus, the type of hardcore gamer who was drawn to *Street Fighter II* in the 1990s is probably playing a deathmatch in some version of *Halo* or *Gears of War* today, which accommodates both competitive and cooperative gameplay styles. Even though modern fighting games like *Virtua Fighter 5* and *Tekken 6* offer online multiplayer gameplay, these often distant matches don't seem to stimulate quite the same competitive intensity of the old arcade games, where players literally stood only a few feet apart. Of course several classic fighting games, such as *Street Fighter II*, and new creations of both the one-on-one and side-scrolling variety, do see plenty of competitive online matches on the Microsoft Xbox 360's and Sony PlayStation 3's respective networks. Capcom's recent *Street Fighter IV* (2008), a high-definition reimagining of *Street Fighter II*, certainly proves the commercial viability of such a setup when paired with the right property.

Second, the learning curve required to play fighting games had risen to the point where only seasoned veterans could hope to master their incredible sophistication. If *Street Fighter II* had alienated some novices, *Street Fighter III*—with its myriad special moves and parries—was downright forbidding. Another factor, of course, is that consoles had caught up to the arcades in terms of audiovisuals; no longer did console ports seem like pale imitations of the real thing. Serious gamers left arcades, never to return.

What is the legacy of *Street Fighter II*? Although it's easy to get lost in the many revisions, sequels, clones, and spin-offs, the game's role in gaming history may turn out to be more social than anything else. The many gamers who became obsessed with this game, tirelessly discussing strategies and refining techniques, were the seeds of what we'd now call the "hardcore gamer" community.

Hit games of the 1980s like *Space Invaders* and *Pac-Man* were certainly in uential, but seemed more suited to individuals than communities of gamers. Competition was only indirect and based on the rather abstract high score table. *Street Fighter II* was, if nothing else, very clear about winning and losing. As players competed, they talked, either to taunt their opponent or compare notes. Serious players analyzed the game's ins and outs with the same dedication a sports nut might lavish on a favorite team. In short, fans of *Street Fighter II* didn't talk to each other the same way the fans of older games did. How much, really, can you say about playing *Pac-Man*? On the other hand, any competent *Street Fighter II* player can easily talk your ear off about the comparative merits of Ryu versus Guile—and probably still remembers how to pull off at least a few favorite combos. *Street Fighter II* defied the old paradigm of good game development: it was *not* easy to learn how to play well. Capcom took a serious risk by introducing such a complex and sophisticated game, but the gamers of 1991 and beyond welcomed the challenge.

18

SUPER MARIO 64/TOMB RAIDER (1996): THE THIRD DIMENSION

So far in our journey through the greatest and most influential games of all time—a list compiled with no small apprehension by your humble and well-meaning authors—we have yet to cheat. But, alas, we at last come to a tie that neither of us could break: was it *Super Mario 64* or *Tomb Raider* that finally established 3D as the new standard for videogames? Which of these two best-selling, trend-setting games can really be said to have rendered 2D obsolete? Unable to decide between Mario's mustache or Lara Croft's … pistols, we finally decided not to decide. Both of these critically acclaimed games established paradigms that are still guiding the industry today.

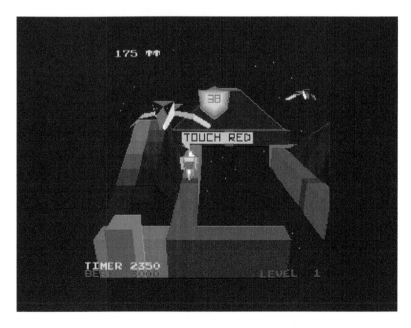

A scene from Atari's 1983 arcade game, *I, Robot*, which was the first commercial videogame with flat, shaded 3D polygonal graphics. Though ostensibly a shooter, *I, Robot* was a hybrid that featured maze and platforming (jumping) elements.

Clearly, *Super Mario 64* and *Tomb Raider* are two very different games, but still have much in common. They both, for instance, featured or came to feature two of the industry's most recognizable and beloved characters. Both games were widely praised and sold millions of copies, establishing or extending massive franchises that extended to Hollywood. Perhaps most importantly, however, is that these games offered some of the best 3D gameplay ever seen to that point. They demonstrated, conclusively, that 3D was the future of videogames.

Adding a new dimension to a game like *Super Mario Bros.* (Chapter 19, "*Super Mario Bros.* (1985): How High Can Jumpman Get?") wasn't just a matter of graphics; the real challenge was the interface. How could players accustomed to the 2D games learn to move a character in three dimensions, particularly in situations that required very precise control? In short, could the run-and-jump gameplay that practically defined the NES and Super Nintendo eras survive the transition to 3D? What sort of interface and controller setup would best accommodate these new games? Would novice and child gamers be able to cope with the added complexity?

Super Mario 64 consists of a number of highly diverse worlds, which Mario enters by leaping into paintings like these. Each world has its own theme and special challenges, making for highly varied gameplay.

Perhaps the biggest problem was "camera control," or perspective. This hadn't been an issue with 2D platformers, as the screen could simply scroll left and right (or occasionally up and down) as the character moved along the X (horizontal) and Y (vertical) axes. The third dimension meant that now characters could move along the Z axis, toward and away from the camera. This feature made the gameworlds feel much more realistic and immersive, but it came at a cost. The groundbreaking 3D game *Alone in the Dark* (see Chapter 1, "*Alone in the Dark* (1992): The Polygons of Fear"), for instance, was slow and sometimes difficult to navigate. The game was set up as a series of prerendered rooms or scenes, each with a "fixed camera." Although the arrangement worked well for a horror-themed game like *Alone in the Dark,* it certainly wouldn't have accommodated a fast-paced, cheerful run-and-jump game like *Super Mario Bros.*, where fast movement and accurate collision detection were critical. Furthermore, gamers now expected the backgrounds as well as the characters to be rendered on the fly, as they were in first-person shooters.

A more specific consideration is that the third dimension made jumps much harder to estimate; players might need to study the situation from several angles to properly aim and time a difficult leap. All of this hadn't been a problem with first-person 3D games such as id's *Doom* (Chapter 5, "*Doom* (1993): The First-Person Shooter Takes Control"), where the camera behaved as if it *were* the character, though more like a disembodied eye. Jumping had been limited in these games anyway and was not necessarily seen as a key inclusion, as in *Star Wars: Dark Forces* (LucasArts, 1995; Apple Macintosh, PC, Sony PlayStation). Such sequences called for third-person perspective; the player needed to be able to see the character and ledge from a distance. However, such a feat required a more dynamic camera than those seen in first-person shooters. In short, players would need an easy way to control both the character and the camera. As we'll see, though still working towards mastery, game developers found clever ways to make these cameras "smart," automatically maintaining a useful perspective and requiring fewer adjustments from the player.

Richly interactive 3D games like *Super Mario 64* and *Tomb Raider* were obviously quite demanding from a technological perspective, and by the mid-1990s the Super Nintendo and Sega Genesis were clearly not up for the challenge, even with extra hardware added inside cartridges like *Star Fox* (1993; Nintendo) or *Virtua Racing* (1994; Sega) to give them the ability to process small numbers of polygons. However, the major console developers seemed hesitant about placing their bets on 3D graphics technology. Were 3D games simply an expensive fad? Would they catch on with console gamers as they had with PC gamers?

Sega, which seemed to pride itself on beating its rival Nintendo to the latest technological standards, hedged its bets in 1994 with the Sega Saturn.[1] This system had originally been intended as the world's most powerful 2D console with modest 3D capabilities, but the plans changed after Sega learned of Sony's decision to enter the market with its PlayStation. Sony's device was said to

---

[1]Released in early 1995 in the US.

feature powerful support for 3D games, and Sega certainly didn't want to seem behind the times. The Sega Saturn ended up as a hodgepodge of 2D and 3D technology that proved difficult for developers to contend with. The system would end up flopping miserably outside of Japan, and the stigma carried over to Sega's final console, the Dreamcast.

The Sony PlayStation, built from the ground up as a 3D machine, would be amazingly successful, soon putting Sony in the enviable position of the world's biggest console producer. Nintendo, meanwhile, waited a year after the release of the PlayStation before launching its Nintendo 64 in 1996. However, the surprising decision to rely on cartridges instead of CD-ROM technology hindered its ability to compete squarely with Sony's juggernaut; though cartridges offered quick access, cost and storage capacity were serious issues. Nevertheless, the Nintendo 64 would see several successful and influential 3D games besides *Super Mario 64*: Nintendo's *Wave Race 64* (1996), Rare's *GoldenEye 007* (1997), and Nintendo's *The Legend of Zelda: Ocarina of Time* (1998; see Chapter 21, "*The Legend of Zelda* (1986): Rescuing Zeldas and Uniting Triforces").

Besides added support for 3D graphics, the newer consoles offered controllers with features that made them a better fit for 3D games. Perhaps the most important addition was an analog stick and extra buttons for adjusting the camera. Controllers with just a "d-pad" were limited to four directions: up, down, left, and right, and their diagonals, with no intermediate values. The analog stick allowed for nuanced, fluid movement in all directions and greatly improved the control of 3D games like *Super Mario 64*. We should note that neither the Sony PlayStation nor the Sega Saturn originally shipped with such controllers, but both would eventually have analog controllers as an option.[2] The Nintendo 64's controller was the only one equipped with an analog stick and buttons designated specifically for camera control from the beginning. It was designed with *Super Mario 64* in mind, which Nintendo knew would be its surest bet for promoting the system.

In short, the mid-1990s were the turning point from 2D to 3D, and it soon became obvious that the "best system" was the one with the best 3D games. The challenge was manifold—the system itself would have to be capable of handling the high demands of 3D gameplay, but a console with even the finest hardware would sit on the shelf without innovative games to harness its power. Fortunately, two such games were just around the corner.

---

[2] Few games on the Sega Saturn would support its analog controller, but a large number of games for the PlayStation came to support its famous DualShock, which eventually shipped as the default controller with all new systems (there were revisions before this model that were quickly discontinued).

The worlds in *Super Mario 64* are richly detailed and fun to explore, though getting a handle on the 3D control scheme might be a bit challenging at first for those more familiar with the 2D Mario games.

Perhaps the first major 3D platformer out the gate was *Jumping Flash!*, a game developed by Exact and Ultra and published by Sony Computer Entertainment (SCE) in 1995 exclusively for its new PlayStation. This highly innovative game didn't go unnoticed, but was all but forgotten after the arrival of *Super Mario 64* and *Tomb Raider*.

Jumping Flash! is one of only a handful of platform games depicted in first-person perspective.[3] Players can move the avatar (a robotic bunny named Robbit) in three dimensions and control the camera as they see fit. The bulk of the gameplay consists of Robbit leaping from platform-to-platform in fully rendered and quite colorful 3D worlds. As we'll see in *Tomb Raider*, the developers of *Jumping Flash!* were able to give the impression of extreme heights—no doubt, players with acrophobia found the game quite unsettling.

As we mentioned earlier, one of the big problems with jumping in first-person games is accurately judging the distance and aiming at a suitable landing spot. *Jumping Flash!* admirably solved this problem by automatically pivoting the camera down during jumps and showing Robbit's feet and shadow as he fell toward a landing platform. The game was successful enough to warrant a sequel in 1996, but even with its improved graphics, could not compete with Nintendo's *Super Mario 64*, particularly

---

[3]1997's *Montezuma's Return* from Utopia Technologies for the PC was another. The game was a well-received spiritual sequel to the classic Parker Brothers multiscreen platformer from 1984, *Montezuma's Revenge*, released for most contemporary platforms.

Jumping Flash! was a very playable first-person platform game with several innovations. Perhaps the best is allowing players to see the character's feet and shadow to help guide his landings.

as it was difficult to identify with the mostly unseen character. It's disheartening to think that *Jumping Flash!*'s innovative interface may never return, because it offers extraordinary possibilities for first-person games. GameSpy selected both games as part of its "25 Most Underrated Games of All Time" list, a well-deserved placement if there ever was one.[4]

On September 26, 1996, North Americans got their first taste of the game that would come to define the 3D platformer: *Super Mario 64*. The game was unsurprisingly a smash hit for both the *Mario* franchise and the Nintendo 64, which certainly benefited from the game's sensational publicity (understandably, it was also set up for play on countless in-store kiosks). The game is still widely admired and played today,[5] and was named as one of GameSpot's "15 Most Influential Games of All Time," arguing that it "set the standards for how 3D space would be navigated within video games," a bold claim, to say the least.[6] Contemporary reviews raved about the game. Matt Casamassina of IGN called it "possibly the greatest videogame achievement ever," though others seemed reluctant to give any cartridge-based game full scores now that CD-ROMs had become a standard.[7]

---

[4]See http://archive.gamespy.com/articles/september03/25underrated/index9.shtml.

[5]Nintendo DS (2004) and Nintendo Wii Virtual Console (2006) versions were also released to critical acclaim and robust sales.

[6]See http://www.gamespot.com/gamespot/features/video/15influential/p15_01.html.

[7]See http://ign64.ign.com/articles/150/150606p1.html.

What made *Super Mario 64* so super? Besides the vivid graphics, memorable music, and meticulous attention to detail that defines all of Nintendo's *Mario* and *Zelda* games, it's really the interface that stands as the game's greatest achievement. The integration of the analog stick was particularly impressive. Depending on how hard players pushed it one direction, Mario would either tiptoe, walk, or run. Although the camera would sometimes automatically switch to the "recommended view," players were "cinematographers" as well (to quote from the manual), utilizing the controller's four "c" buttons. Mario was followed by Lakitu, a camera "crew" that flew around on a cloud. The player could move the camera closer or further (zoom) and around to get a better view of the scene. Players could also see what Mario himself was looking at, a useful technique for spotting Power Stars and powerups.

The Power Stars, by the way, are what Mario needed to collect to win the game. The Power Stars, which protected Princess Peach's Mushroom Castle, have been stolen by Mario's famous nemesis, Bowser. It's up to Mario, of course, to find the stars. This meant traveling into a set of magical paintings, which were self-contained worlds full of puzzles and monsters.

These worlds are quite diverse, bringing welcome variety to both the aesthetics and challenges of the game. They also give Mario a chance to show off his many abilities, such as swimming, climbing, flying, and even launching himself from cannons. Mario also has a bevy of jumps and leaps available, such as wall kicks, long jumps, and side and back somersaults—in short, the skills of a master acrobat. In addition to his classic squashing technique to destroy enemies, Mario can now punch and kick them as well. Although all of these moves might seem intimidating, the game introduces them gradually, mostly by reading text on signs sprinkled throughout the worlds. Although it's naturally more difficult to control than the classic 2D *Mario* games, Nintendo streamlined the 3D interface to the point where even a child could master it with little struggle. Nintendo had brought 3D gaming to the public the right way.

Nintendo followed up *Super Mario 64* with several sequels and spin-offs. The first was *Super Mario Sunshine* in 2002 for their GameCube console. Besides the expected graphic enhancements, the game offered a new spin jump and FLUDD, a water tank that let Mario spray water or hover in the air. Although *Super Mario Sunshine* sold well, it didn't have quite the same critical impact as *Super Mario 64*.[8] The next game changed that, *Super Mario Galaxy*, released to a rousing critical reception[9] in 2007 for

---

[8]See, for example *IGN*'s review at http://cube.ign.com/articles/368/368539p1 .html.

[9]For example, *IGN*'s review: http://wii.ign.com/articles/833/833298p1.html.

Screenshot from Sega's *Sonic Adventure 2* on the Dreamcast. Despite Sega's best efforts, Sonic has not had the same successful transition from 2D to 3D like Mario or Link has.

the Nintendo Wii. It features levels that take the form of galaxies filled with a variety of minor planets and worlds, and gameplay is affected by gravity and new powerups.

If *Super Mario 64* was cute, family-friendly, and full of bright colors and bouncy music, *Tomb Raider* was sexy, dark, and hip. What it lacked in polish it made up for in spit—that is, the drool flowing from the mouths of so many men who found themselves in love with Lara Croft. *Super Mario 64* is to *Tomb Raider* what Kool-Aid is to Budweiser. *Tomb Raider* seemed to cater to every stereotypical male desire: guns, gold, and gazongas.

Lara Croft, guns drawn, running through traps in an early scene from the Sega Saturn version of *Tomb Raider.*

Let's start, then, with the topic most often raised in any discussion of *Tomb Raider:* Lara Croft's boobs. When Lara first bounced onto the scene in November 1996, critics seemed to expect a strong backlash from feminists and female gamers. IGN's review of the game, which awarded the game an "Outstanding" score, ran under the byline "IGN Staff," as if no individual critic wanted to be held responsible for praising the game so highly. The opening line of their review read, "*Tomb Raider* is bound to stir up lots of trouble with the feminists. Lara Croft's unrealistic proportions can only lead to further gender stereotyping and objectification of women." With these disclaimers out of the way, the staff went on to call it "one of the best games of 1996."[10] A similarly "anonymously" authored review in *The Economist* began with the question, "WHAT man could resist a creature like Lara Croft? This ravishing British heiress divides her time between acrobatic workouts in her stately home and dangerous expeditions to exotic ruins. She wears shorts everywhere, which show off her sprinter's legs, and a tiny waist draws attention to her gravity-defying bust. Then there is the small matter of the twin automatic pistols she straps to her bare thighs."[11]

Was *Tomb Raider* simply a sexist game that pandered to horny boys? Though some might think so, others point out that since the game put players in the role of a woman—and a strong, self-assured one at that—it perhaps did more to dispel sexist stereotypes than reinforce them, despite attempts to market the character in a sexual manner. In an interview with *Forbes* magazine, Eidos' spokesman Gary Keith argued that "it used to be that when we played videogames, it wasn't cool to be a girl," and suggested that Lara and her imitators had reversed the situation.[12] Although the game was ostensibly targeted at 18- to 35-year-old males, plenty of women enjoyed the game as well. "There was something refreshing about looking at the screen and seeing myself as a woman," said Nikki Douglas, a female gamer interviewed by Justine Cassell and Henry Jenkins for their book *From Barbie to Mortal Kombat: Gender and Computer Games* (MIT Press, 1998). Other female gamers and critics were less pleased. Even if Lara were a strong female character in a genre dominated by male characters (and weak women), she still presented a physical stereotype that ordinary women could not (and should not) equal. Espen Aarseth, one of the world's foremost game scholars, found the whole subject irrelevant: "When I play, I don't even see her body, but see through it and past it."[13]

---

[10]See http://psx.ign.com/articles/150/150097p1.html.

[11]Anonymous. 1997. *The Economist.* 2/22/97, Vol. 342, Iss. 8005, p. 74.

[12]See *Forbes*, 1/12/98, Vol. 161, Iss. 1, p. 39.

[13]See "Genre Trouble: Narrativism and the Art of Simulation" in *First Person: New Media as Story, Performance, and Game* (MIT Press, 2004).

Lara Croft in a temporary state of repose in the Sega Saturn version of *Tomb Raider.*

The game may have had some feminists gnashing their teeth, but it certainly had millions of gamers mashing their controllers. It certainly put its developer Core Design in the spotlight, and generated millions in earnings for publisher Eidos Interactive. Incidentally, these two companies were both based in the United Kingdom. The international success of *Tomb Raider* was a welcome boon to the United Kingdom's gaming industry, which had lagged behind that of the United States and Japan.

Although the game was better known on the Sony PlayStation and PC, it actually debuted on the aforementioned Sega Saturn platform.[14] This version, though one of the best-sellers on the platform, is understandably overshadowed by the later releases, which offered slightly better visuals[15] and a larger user base. All versions offer third-person perspective and a camera that follows along behind Lara (or over her shoulder). Like Mario in *Super Mario 64,* Lara can perform a wide variety of movements—walking, running, jumping, side-stepping, and swimming. She can also grip onto ledges and climb up, a feature that makes leaping from platform to platform much easier to master. Lara makes frequent use of her pistols to kill beasts or human enemies, but most of the gameplay is focused on avoiding traps and solving puzzles. Lara can push or pull objects, throw switches, and use items that she collects during the adventure. The game is a great deal more violent than *Super Mario 64,* with several grisly ways for Lara to meet her end, including being impaled by spikes.

---

[14]Apple Macintosh, Pocket PC, and Nokia N-Gage versions would be released later.

[15]The PC release came in versions supporting software-only and hardware-accelerated 3D rendering, as the latter was not a standard feature at the time. Naturally, those with supported 3D cards had the best-looking versions.

Perhaps the most important feature from a gameplay perspective is its superb control and response. There is no free-roaming camera, but players can force the camera immediately behind Lara and then use the direction buttons to look around (essentially seeing what she's seeing). This feature came in handy whenever the built-in camera was stuck at an awkward angle.

As the title implies, *Tomb Raider* is set in an ancient ruins, a theme comparable to that of the *Indiana Jones* movies. Like Indy, Lara is a brash adventurer, more than happy to risk her life in pursuit of some archaeological treasure or another. Indeed, the game's fast-paced plot reads very much like an *Indiana Jones* script, with plenty of intrigue, double-crosses, history, and travel to exotic locales (Peru, Greece, Egypt, and ultimately Atlantis).

Screenshot from the tutorial "gym" mode that takes place in Lara's home in the Sega Saturn version of *Tomb Raider*.

Another feature worth mentioning is the in-game tutorial system. Rather than thrust players directly into the adventure, *Tomb Raider* let players experiment first in a special level that takes place in Lara's home. Players could use Lara's home to familiarize themselves with the controls before embarking on the adventure. Later *Tomb Raider* games would elaborate on this concept, eventually offering lengthy in-game tutorials that not only taught players the controls, but filled them in on the backstory along the way. Perhaps the best example of this is seen in *Tomb Raider: The Last Revelation* (1999; Sega Dreamcast, Sony PlayStation, and others), the fourth game in the series. This game begins with Lara as a rather spunky teenager. Lara accompanies her mentor Werner Von Croy to a set of ancient ruins, where the experienced adventurer guides Lara through a series of traps and tests of agility. Along the way, Von Croy offers instructions and tips, but Lara needn't follow his directions to the letter. Indeed, deviating a bit can actually earn her some bonus points as well as the chance to try more difficult (and perilous) training sequences.

Tomb Raider may well have made more impact on the industry than *Super Mario 64*, if for no other reason than it was so much more widely available. It was a best-selling and definitive title for both the Sony PlayStation and the PC, and Lara's celebrity status seemed to ensure a grand future for the franchise. However, the series seemed to generally decline with each sequel or spin-off, which either lacked the originality or polish of the original. The worst offender was the sixth game, *Tomb Raider: The Angel of Darkness* (2003; Apple Macintosh, PC, Sony PlayStation 2), which critics lambasted for its glitchy gameplay and cumbersome control scheme. The seventh game, *Tomb Raider: Legend* (2006; Microsoft Xbox 360, PC, Sony PlayStation 2, and others) was developed by Crystal Dynamics, a California team. This game seems to have put the franchise back on track. The company also worked on *Tomb Raider: Anniversary* (2007; Apple Macintosh, Nintendo Wii, Sony PlayStation Portable, and others), an enhanced remake of the original. *Tomb Raider: Underworld* (2008; Microsoft Xbox 360, Nintendo Wii, Sony PlayStation 3, and others) offers the typical audiovisual improvements, but its most interesting feature is a gameworld that reacts dynamically to Lara's actions in a persistent manner—mud will stick to Lara until washed away by rain, enemies will remain where they were killed, and any environmental destruction is permanent.

The influence of *Super Mario 64* and *Tomb Raider* on both console and PC gaming has been immense. Indeed, it's hard to know where to start. Seemingly any 3D action-adventure game—particularly any with a third-person perspective—owes a debt to these trailblazers. It's also tempting to say that any later game featuring a sexy female avatar was probably inspired by Lara Croft. Would we have Joanna Dark of *Perfect Dark* (Rare, 2000; Nintendo 64), Cate Archer of *The Operative: No One Lives Forever* (Eidos, 2000; Apple Macintosh, PC, Sony PlayStation 2), Rayne of *BloodRayne* (Majesco, 2002; Microsoft Xbox, Nintendo GameCube, and others), or Nariko of *Heavenly Sword* (Sony, 2007; PlayStation 3) without Lara Croft? There's no doubt that the number of games with female main characters swelled after *Tomb Raider*.

Perhaps the three games that seem to have followed most closely in Nintendo's wake are Sega's *Nights into Dreams ...* (1996; Sega Saturn), Naughty Dog's *Crash Bandicoot* (1996; Sony PlayStation), and Rare's *Banjo-Kazooie* (1998; Nintendo 64). *Nights into Dreams ...* is an intriguing game from Sonic Team packaged with an analog controller that unfortunately arrived

Two screenshots from Eidos's *Tomb Raider: Underworld*, which again upped the ante on the popular series.

too late to save the Sega Saturn. It is essentially a "rail" 3D plat-former, meaning that while the graphics are rendered in 3D, the movement of the player's character is constrained to preestab-lished paths. Nevertheless, it was an impressive achievement, and remains one of the finest games ever made for the system. *Crash Bandicoot* is one of the best-selling games for the PlayStation, and its eccentric central character became a mascot of sorts for the platform, though many of the sequels and offshoots would come to appear on other platforms. As with *Nights into Dreams …,* the character's movement is a linear, "railed" game with intense jumping action. Perhaps *Crash Bandicoot's* greatest claim to fame is its polish and ability to capture a 2D side-scrolling platformer feel in 3D. Rare's *Banjo-Kazooie* is a closer derivative of *Super*

Mario 64, with nonlinear 3D worlds. However, *Banjo-Kazooie* expanded on the concept. The characters can transform into different creatures, for instance, and learn new moves as the game progresses. All three of these games are of course important and influential in their own right.

Screenshot from *Crash Bandicoot* for the Sony PlayStation, a character who appears to have been inspired in many ways by Sonic—complete with comical attitude.

Screenshot from Sega's cult favorite, *Nights into Dreams . . .* for the Sega Saturn.

Taken together, *Super Mario 64* and *Tomb Raider* represent a paradigm shift from 2D to 3D. They demonstrated not only that such games were technologically feasible, but that they could be intuitive and easy even for novices. After these games, any 2D game—even "railed" 3D games such as *Nights into Dreams ...* and *Crash Bandicoot*—would suffer the unflattering comparison to *Super Mario 64* or *Tomb Raider.* Naturally, the success of 3D platform and action games seems all but certain to continue well into the next decade.

19

SUPER MARIO BROS. (1985): HOW HIGH CAN JUMPMAN GET?

Mario. This mustachioed Italian plumber from *Super Mario Bros.*, a 1985 run-and-jump platform game for the Nintendo Entertainment System (NES), is one of the most recognizable videogame characters of all time. Indeed, his fame is rivaled only by *Pac-Man*. His humble, even comical image is the face of Nintendo and the unlikely hero of generations of American and Japanese videogamers. If any videogame character is truly worthy of the epithet "super," it's Mario.

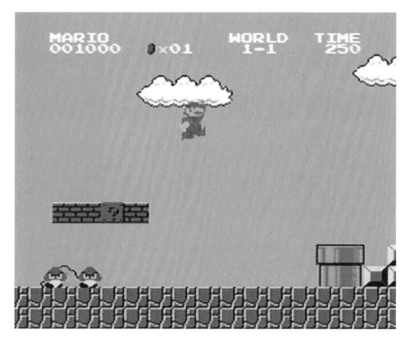

Screenshot from the famous World 1-1 in *Super Mario Bros.*

Mario made his debut in the 1981 arcade game *Donkey Kong*, in which he was known only as Jumpman. Nintendo of Japan had begun exporting coin-operated videogames to the United States approximately one year earlier, in December 1980. Their venture got off to a rocky start with   ops like *Radar Scope*, which interested Americans about as much as shrimp- avored breakfast cereal. To prevent the company from sinking, Nintendo's president, Hiroshi Yamauchi, decided to repurpose the *Radar Scope* machines, selecting game designer Shigeru Miyamoto[1] for the task. After the company failed to obtain the license to develop a game based on the popular *Popeye* comic strip,[2] it decided to create its own characters. The end result was *Donkey Kong*, one of the hottest arcade games of the 1980s.

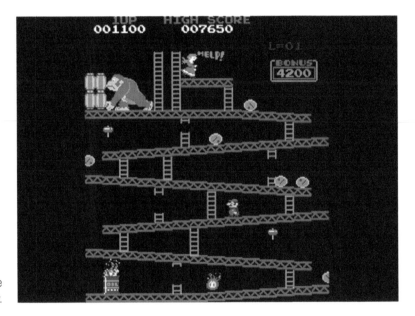

Screenshot from the arcade version of *Donkey Kong.*

The *Donkey Kong* franchise earned Nintendo over $280 million by 1983,[3] and encouraged them to develop other arcade hits like *Mario Bros.* (1983), a spin-off of *Donkey Kong*. It also gave them the capital to enter the home console business, starting with the Nintendo Family Computer (Famicom) in Asia, later modified

---

[1]Responsible for many classics and three primary games in this book. Besides *Super Mario Bros.*, he was also instrumental in the creation of *The Legend of Zelda* (Chapter 21, "*The Legend of Zelda* (1986): Rescuing Zeldas and Uniting Triforces") and *Super Mario 64* (Chapter 18, "*Super Mario 64/Tomb Raider* (1996): The Third Dimension").

[2]Something that Nintendo would rectify with the 1982 release of the popular single screen arcade platformer, *Popeye*.

[3]Based on adding figures from Steven Kent's book, *The Ultimate History of Video Games* (Three Rivers Press, 2001).

and introduced in the United States as the NES. The success of the NES and *Super Mario Bros.*, which has sold over 40 million copies worldwide,[4] are credited with resurrecting the moribund videogame market after The Great Videogame Crash of 1984 (see Chapter 13, "*Pac-Man* (1980): Japanese Gumption, American Consumption"). *Super Mario Bros.* played a decisive role not only in the revival of the console market, but in the expansion of the videogame industry as a whole.

Mario, the star of *Super Mario Bros.*, is a short and stocky Italian plumber who resides in the Mushroom Kingdom. His appearance had not changed much from his Jumpman days. He still had his prominent mustache and characteristic cap and overalls. These features, incidentally, were largely dictated by the limitations of the era's hardware and software; the mustache, for instance, was easier to represent than a mouth. Nevertheless, the image was endearing and accessible, and what Mario lacked in heroics he made up for with charm. He is a kind-hearted soul, always willing to help those in need (except in *Donkey Kong Junior*, the only game in which he is portrayed as a villain).

Mario's goal in *Super Mario Bros.* was once again to save a damsel in distress from an anthropomorphic creature. In *Donkey Kong*, Jumpman/Mario is a carpenter on a quest to save his girlfriend from his peeved pet ape, whereas in *Super Mario Bros.*, he is on an epic adventure to save Princess Toadstool (also known as

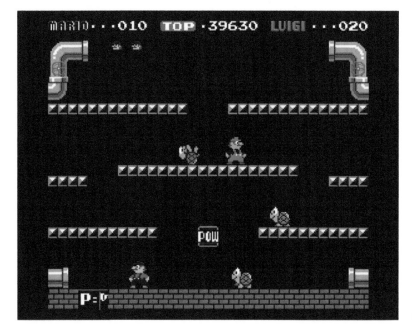

Screenshot from the *Mario Bros.* arcade game.

---

[4]http://gamers.guinnessworldrecords.com/records/nintendo.aspx.

Princess Peach) from the evil Bowser, a turtle-like creature who is king of the Koopas. In his quest, Mario encounters a series of enemies and obstacles, some of which had been previously introduced in *Mario Bros.* The most notable of these are the Koopa Troopas, which closely resemble the earlier game's Shellcreepers.

Super Mario Bros. can be played in one- or two-player mode, with players taking turns and advancing through each world independently. Player 1 is Mario and player 2 is Luigi, who was first introduced in *Mario Bros.* and is Mario's doppelganger in white overalls. The game consists of eight worlds, each of which has four subworlds. At the end of each world, Mario must defeat one of Bowser's henchmen. Along the way, Mario (or Luigi) collects coins, magic and "1-up" mushrooms, fire owers, and star men. Once 100 coins are collected or a 1-up mushroom is consumed, an extra life is awarded. Magic mushrooms cause Mario to grow in stature, becoming Super Mario, and allow him to take a hit from an enemy without dying, though afterwards he returns to his regular size. Fire owers turn Mario into Super Mario and also allow him to spit fireballs at enemies; star men provide temporary invincibility, acting much like power pellets in *Pac-Man*. The mission is to complete each board before the allotted time runs out. Otherwise, Mario loses a life and must restart the board at the beginning—or at roughly the midpoint, if the invisible checkpoint had been reached. Despite the time limit, there is still plenty of opportunity for exploration. There are subterranean worlds, which can be accessed through select pipes. These are generally self-contained areas that offer coin rewards. There are also sky worlds, which are accessed through vines that grow when certain blocks are nudged. These worlds tend to be larger and offer coin rewards or access to warp zones, which allow Mario to advance to other worlds. Besides defeating enemies, Mario must navigate his way over and under obstacles. Getting sucked into a "whirlpool" (bottom of the screen in a water world) or falling into a pit or into lava will result in instant death.

Super Mario Bros. came bundled with the NES and remained one of the best games ever made for the system throughout the platform's long shelf life. Although Nintendo had to make amends of sorts for the sins of others at retail for The Great Videogame Crash by promoting their system more as an electronic toy[5] than a console—explaining the inclusion of the basically useless Robotic Operating Buddy (R.O.B.) robot and avoiding the term "videogame" on packaging and promotional materials—*Super Mario Bros.* left no doubt in consumers' minds what the system was all about. The gameplay was superb, which is why the formula continues to be

---

[5]See http://archive.gamespy.com/articles/july03/25smartest/index22.shtml.

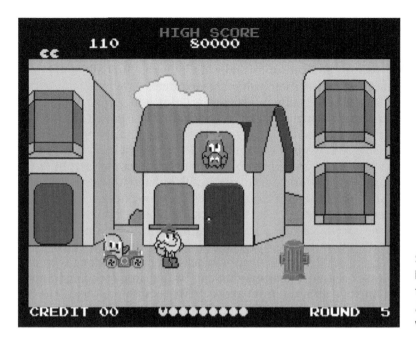

Surprisingly, maze-game maestro Pac-Man starred in one of the first side-scrolling platformers, *Pac-Land*, in 1984. Original arcade version shown.

popular today, as demonstrated by the release of games like 2006's *New Super Mario Bros.* on the Nintendo DS. The controls in *Super Mario Bros.* are straightforward and intuitive.

Unlike the previous generation of game consoles, which relied on joysticks for movement, the NES shipped with the now-common game pads. The NES controllers had a directional pad (d-pad) and A and B buttons. Each button had a main function and a secondary function, depending on the environment or status of the character. Players advanced left or right by pressing accordingly on the controller's d-pad, though the screen only scrolls to the right, preventing backtracking. Pressing down allows Mario to crouch or access hidden worlds in pipes. Pressing up is used to ﬂoat up in a water world or to climb vines. The A button is the jump button and also allows Mario to stay aﬂoat in an aquatic environment if pressed repeatedly. The B button allows Mario to accelerate and to shoot fireballs at his enemies, provided that he is fiery Mario. Usage of the buttons is ﬂexible; the longer the A button is held down, the higher Mario will jump, and the extent to which the B button is held down determines the pace at which Mario walks or runs. Although the new controllers were arguably easier to manipulate than joysticks, some gamers complained of "numb thumb" and even bought items of dubious value like special gloves to deal with the problem.

Besides its intuitive controls, *Super Mario Bros.* boasts superb physics. Objects interact with each other consistently and in a convincing manner. Also, each category of enemy has specific mechanics and requirements for being defeated. Piranha plants can only be eliminated with fireballs. Goomba mushrooms, the weakest of all enemies, can be jumped on. Turtle Koopas require a two-step process (unless they are hit with a fireball), and Mario must first render them vulnerable to attack.

This two-step attack concept was introduced in *Mario Bros.* by jumping under a oor with an enemy on top of it or with use of the "POW" block. Hitting this block, like hitting the oor from under them, would cause enemies to ip on their backs, allowing Mario or Luigi to dispose of them upon direct contact. In *Super Mario Bros.*, Mario is not powerful enough to destroy blocks unless he is Super Mario, but he is able to nudge them. If an enemy happens to be on the block that is nudged, it may be disposed of (such as the Hammer Brothers) or it may simply change the direction the enemy advances (for example, Goombas); however, Super Mario will destroy blocks on contact along with any enemy on it. Any enemies that can be defeated by being jumped on must be attacked from above. If Mario or Super Mario hits the enemy from the side or brushes against them, he takes a hit.

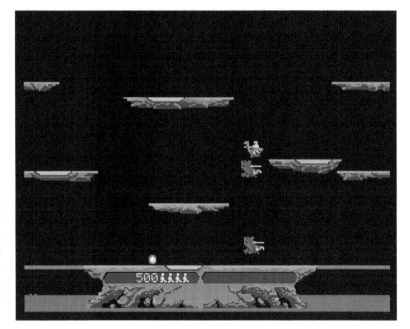

Screenshot from the arcade version of Williams Electronics' *Joust* (1982), which was perhaps the first time the play mechanic of being higher than your enemy to overcome them was introduced, a key concept when jumping on enemies in *Super Mario Bros.*

Besides avoiding or defeating enemies, players must master timing to successfully complete various running and jumping feats, such as advancing between moving platforms or those that straddle seemingly insuperable chasms. This gameplay is reminiscent of *Pitfall!*, a classic platformer published in 1982 for the Atari 2600 VCS by Activision. In this multiscreen, nonscrolling game,

Pitfall Harry must navigate a series of jungle obstacles to recover 32 treasures within a 20-minute period. To accomplish this, players must master various timing feats. Unlike *Super Mario Bros.*, there are no enemies to kill, so they must be avoided altogether or landed on in a spot where they are innocuous (e.g., the very tops of the crocodile heads). The jumping mechanics in *Pitfall!* are not as refined as they are in *Super Mario Bros.* In some cases, even when it appears an enemy has been avoided successfully, a hit is taken, leading to frustration. In *Donkey Kong*, Mario also had very limited jumping abilities; thus, what distinguishes *Super Mario Bros.* from other platformers is a very precise but flexible jumping mechanic that feels just right.

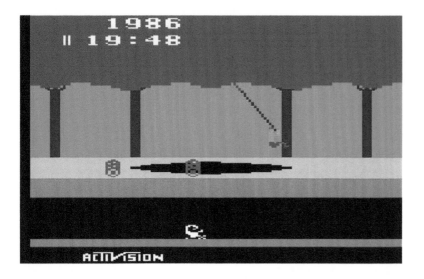

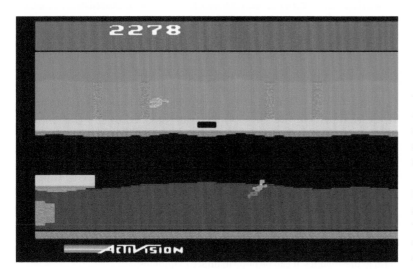

Pitfall! (above) was one of the first platformers, but did not scroll; as Harry passed through a screen edge, a new scene would appear. *Pitfall II: Lost Caverns* (1984), left, like the later *Super Mario Bros. 3*, would have extra hardware in the cartridge to give additional technical capabilities to its home platform and was an amazing technical achievement on the Atari 2600 VCS.

It is clear that a lot of thought went into the level designs in *Super Mario Bros.* Enemies and obstacles are placed so that the player is progressively challenged, unlike many other side-scrollers, which are notoriously difficult from the outset—*Mega Man* (Capcom, 1987; NES) comes to mind. Another element that adds to the appeal of *Super Mario Bros.* is that it can be played multiple ways. One can play it as an epic adventure, with the goal of racking up as many points as possible and collecting as much as possible in each world, or as a time trial by racing to the finish as quickly as possible.[6]

Screenshot from *Super Mario Bros. 2* from the Super Nintendo's *Super Mario All-Stars* compilation.

Super Mario Bros. 2—which was released in North America in 1988, in Japan in 1989, and in Europe in 1992—was not a direct sequel to *Super Mario Bros.*, but was actually a conversion of a Japanese game called *Yume Kōjō: Doki Doki Panic* (1987). The Japanese market, however, had received a true sequel to the game three years earlier in 1986, which was released to the U.S. market in 1993 as *Super Mario Bros.: The Lost Levels* as part of the *Super Mario All-Stars* compilation for the Super Nintendo (SNES). The reason that this version had not been initially released as the real

---

[6]Numerous videos on YouTube demonstrate how to defeat the game in a matter of minutes. Individuals have even raced each other by placing televisions side-by-side. The ability to race through the game is a feature that is maintained in *Super Mario Bros.* 2 and *Super Mario Bros.* 3. Although this feat takes a little longer to accomplish in these games, it can be done in under 15 minutes.

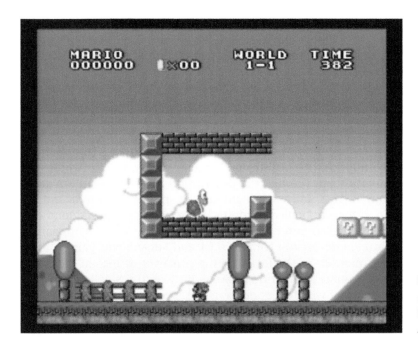

Screenshot from *Super Mario Bros.: The Lost Levels* from the Super Nintendo's *Super Mario All-Stars* compilation.

sequel in the U.S. market was that it had been deemed too difficult by some Nintendo of America employees.

The premise of the converted *Super Mario Bros. 2* game is actually a radical departure from *Super Mario Bros.* and 1990's *Super Mario Bros. 3*. In this game, Mario dreams of a kingdom called Subcon, which has been cursed by a character called Wart, and Mario is asked to return this kingdom to its "natural state." When he wakes up, he talks to the Princess, Toad, and Luigi about it, and they decide to go on a picnic, only to discover the world Mario dreamed about is real.

Super Mario Bros. 2 is a one-player game in which players can alternate playing as Mario, Luigi, Toad, and Princess Peach, each of which has different abilities (i.e., speeds) and jumping mechanics. Mario has average jumping power, which decreases slightly upon lifting an object. Luigi can jump higher and farther than Mario, but he is slow and his power is decreased more than Mario's when he carries an item. Toad has the least jumping power with very short jumps, but he is the quickest character and his abilities are not diminished when carrying objects. The Princess is the weakest character and third in jumping power, but she can oat in the air for roughly 1.5 seconds if the A button is held down. Players can also increase their character's jumping capacity by pressing down on the d-pad while pressing the A button. Once the character ashes, he or she will be able to jump 1.5 times higher than usual. *Super Mario Bros. 2* was one of the few Mario games in which the objective was not to rescue

Princess Peach; in fact she could be the hero. However, once the game is finished and Wart is defeated, we find Mario still sleeping, demonstrating this was in fact all a dream (which, as many angry *Dallas* fans know, is often a frustrating resolution).

Super Mario Bros. 2 introduced a menagerie of unusual and quirky characters, mainly because these characters were repurposed from *Doki Doki Panic*; however, many of these would appear in subsequent Mario games. The most notable of these is Ostro, also known as Birdo. This sweet character from Subcon is Nintendo's first full-fledged transsexual, and one would not know it except through the description in the first-edition game manual: "He thinks he is a girl and he spits eggs from his mouth. He'd rather be called Birdetta." Interestingly, subsequent edition manuals omitted the second line, and when he reappears in *Mario Tennis* for the Nintendo 64 and subsequent games, there is no mention of the fact that she was ever a "he." In fact there is affectionate interaction between Birdo and Yoshi, the dinosaur-like creature who first appears in 1991's *Super Mario World*.

Players defeat enemies by throwing vegetables at them, which must first be plucked from the ground. Enemies can't be stomped on, but certain ones can be picked up and thrown at others. To defeat Birdo, one must capture his eggs and throw them back at him. *Super Mario Bros. 2* is the first Mario game to feature a life meter. The player starts the game with three lives and a total of two units on the life meter, which can be increased to a total of four units, allowing four hits to be taken before death. As in *Super Mario Bros.*, however, falling into a chasm will result in instant death. This is also the first Mario game to use doors, including those requiring keys, as a means of entering other rooms and secret worlds. If a player uproots a magic potion from the ground and throws it down, a door to "Sub-space" will appear. If the player enters the door, he or she will find a nonscrolling world that is an unlit duplicate of the current screen sans the enemies. In this world, the music becomes the iconic *Super Mario Bros.* theme song and coins are uprooted instead of vegetables. If the magic potion had been used in just the right spot, a life-meter-increasing mushroom will appear. Unlike its predecessor, this game does not have a time limit and players can backtrack. Players may also uproot a stopwatch, which will suspend enemies in time for a certain period. It also introduced the "minigame" to the *Mario* franchise through the bonus slot machine game, through which a player can win more lives (up to a maximum of five if they get three cherries). There are a total of seven worlds with a combined 20 levels. As with *Super Mario Bros.*, there are warp zones, allowing players to skip worlds, though these are accessed only through select vases. Some of these vases are inhabited by cobras, reminiscent of piranha plants in *Super Mario Bros.*

Screenshot from *Super Mario Bros. 3* from the Super Nintendo's *Super Mario All-Stars* compilation.

Although *Super Mario Bros. 2* was radically different from its predecessor and is sometimes referred to as the "black sheep" of the series, it was still very successful. The game sold more than 10 million copies on the NES, making it the third highest grossing game on the system. The second highest selling game was *Super Mario Bros. 3* at more than 18 million copies.[7] This game was released in 1990 and hailed by some as the best Mario game of all time. *Nintendo Power* ranked it sixth in their list of the 200 Greatest Nintendo Games and it also made GameSpot's list of "The Greatest Games of All Time."[8] Stanford University History of Science and Technology released a list of the 10 Most In uential Games of All Time. Several industry insiders were consulted, each of whom picked some games. Christopher Grant, the editor of Joystiq.com, was one consultant, and when asked why he selected *Super Mario Bros. 3*, he said that the game was important for its nonlinear play, a mainstay of contemporary games, and new features like the ability to move both backward and forward (scroll left, as well as right). For many, what makes the game so appealing is that it stuck to the formula that made *Super Mario Bros.* so enjoyable, but improved upon this by adding an even better soundtrack and many exciting new features, such as more

---

[7]*Nintendo Power*, February 2006, pp. 58–66.

[8]See http://www.gamespot.com/gamespot/features/all/greatestgames/.

minigames and hidden items, an overview map outlining the levels in each world, and a two-player mode that allows players to take turns clearing levels or to compete against each other.

The antagonist in this game is once again Bowser, who has sent his seven children (known collectively as the Koopalings) out to disrupt the kingdoms that make up the Mushroom World. They have stolen the royal magic wands of each kingdom and turned the kings into animals. Mario and/or Luigi must recover the wands and return the kings to their true forms. There is a king to be saved at the end of each level; however, as with other *Mario* games, players can advance to distant kingdoms by using magic whistles. Once played, these whistles will bring forth a tornado, which transports Mario or Luigi to a distant world. This warping technique had been introduced previously in *The Legend of Zelda* (see Chapter 21, "*The Legend of Zelda* (1986): Rescuing Zeldas and Uniting Triforces"), and even the tune of this warp whistle is the same as the one that transports Link in *Zelda*.[9] The musical references in *Super Mario Bros. 3* also manifest in the names and likenesses of the Koopalings. Morton Koopa Jr., for instance, is named after the late controversial talk show host, Morton Downey Jr., but also has the trademark makeup of guitarist Paul Stanley from rock group KISS. The only female Koopaling is Wendy O. Koopa, and she is named after punk singer Wendy O. Williams. Larry Koopa is the only Koopaling for which the musical reference, if there is any, is unclear.

Super Mario Bros. 3 brings back many familiar enemies, including Goombas, Koopa Troopas, and Piranha Plants, but with a twist. For instance, in addition to there being the usual walking Goombas, there are now Para-Goombas, which y and unleash micro-Goombas that attack Mario by clinging to him. The familiar staples in Mario's arsenal from *Super Mario Bros.* are there, including the magic/super mushrooms, fire owers, and star men. Additional powerups include the frog suit, which increases his swimming abilities, as well as super leaves, which change Mario into Raccoon Mario. This powerup allows Mario to use his tail to attack enemies and to y short distances. If Mario uncovers the incredibly rare Tanooki suit, he appears in full Raccoon regalia and is granted the same abilities as with the super leaf, but he can now also turn to stone to defeat enemies.[10] Other useful items include

---

[9]The tunes can be compared at http://themushroomkingdom.net/games/smb3. As Shigeru Miyamoto and Koji Kondo had worked on both games, this similarity was unsurprising.

[10]"Tanooki" refers to the Japanese term "tanuki," which according to Japanese folklore are raccoon dogs. These mythical creatures are thought to be able to use leaves to shapeshift and cause chaos. Tanuki statues are found outside many temples and restaurants in Japan; thus, Mario or Luigi's added ability to turn into stone with the Tanooki suit is quite a clever play on the tanuki mythology.

a magic wing, a music box, a hammer, and a cloud. These items allow Mario to fly, put enemies to sleep, break through rocks on the map scene, and bypass an action scene, respectively. Powerups can be stored in an item box, which is accessible on the world map. At the end of most levels is a goal, which has three cards flashing in it—mushroom, flower, and star. Once Mario jumps to hit the goal, a card is gained. If three cards are eventually obtained, an extra life is granted. If three cards of the same type are acquired, even more lives are granted (two lives for three mushrooms, three lives for three flowers, and five lives for three stars). In two-player battle mode, Mario or Luigi are opponents and can steal these cards from each other or get rid of the ones that they do not want. Once the level goal is hit, any enemies on the screen will be turned into coins and a bonus will be added to the player's score, depending on how much time is left on the clock.

The game features several types of minigames, some of which appear on the map board. One is a spade panel, which is a slot-machine-type game in which the object is to line up the mushroom, flower, and star pictures. Lives are granted based on which pictures are aligned, and star again ranks highest in the hierarchy. There is also an N-mark spade panel, which is a memory-type card matching game. If two matching cards are uncovered, that item is obtained. The player is allowed to continue matching cards until there are two misses or all nine items are acquired. Another way to obtain booty is by visiting Toad's house, where Mario can select one of three treasure chests to open. The game also includes a true minigame, which is actually a version of *Mario Bros.* Players can access this minigame by entering two-player mode and selecting the other player's resting square on the world map. The player wins if he or she defeats five enemies or the opponent gets hit by an enemy.

Before we continue our discussion of the *Mario* series, you may be wondering how the competition responded to Nintendo's plat-forming masterpieces. The short answer is: not particularly well. Starting in 1986, Sega had the *Alex Kidd* and *Wonder Boy* series for their Sega Master System, but neither platformer had particularly broad appeal. Atari had three consoles out at the time—the VCS, XEGS, and 7800—but managed only the visually flat and late to the party *Scrapyard Dog* (1990) for the latter. NEC first tried on their TurboGrafx-16 console with the pack-in of *Keith Courage in Alpha Zones* (1989), which was an audiovisually rich action adventure platformer, but proved to be little fun. NEC then came back with the much more successful *Bonk's Adventure* (1990), starring a fun cartoon caveman, Bonk, who would go on to star in several additional games and represented the platform admirably, but could do little to improve sales in the United States.[11] In fact, it wouldn't be until 1991 that Mario met his match: *Sonic the Hedgehog*, for Sega's fledgling Genesis console.

Screenshot from *Bonk's Revenge* (1991) for the NEC TurboGrafx-16.

Although *Sonic the Hedgehog* became known for the cheeky attitude of its main character—for instance, Sonic would famously tap his foot in impatient frustration if the player took too long to move—it was the game's speed that really differentiated it from the competition. Whereas a game like *Super Mario Bros. 3* encouraged careful exploration, *Sonic the Hedgehog* encouraged running through its levels as quickly as possible, which was often the only way to make it through the loops to get the highest rings. With springboards and other high-speed launching devices, there was no shortage of encouragement to feed a player's need for speed. *Sonic the Hedgehog 2* was released the following year and sold even better than the best-selling first game, both of which separately came as pack-ins for a time with the system.[12] Like the *Mario* series, Sonic would see countless spin-offs, off-shoots, and clones, and would become a worldwide media icon himself.

In the same year as Sonic's first appearance, *Super Mario World* was released for the SNES, which once again Nintendo had bundled with a surefire hit. Mario and Luigi are back on a quest

---

[11]The console was a big hit in its country of origin, Japan, as the PC Engine, but had poor sales elsewhere in comparison to Nintendo and Sega.

[12]According to Wikipedia [Sonic_the_Hedgehog_(video_game)]: "As of November 19, 2007, [Sonic the Hedgehog] has sold 4 million copies, the second-highest amount for a Genesis game, behind Sonic 2, which has sold 6 million copies."

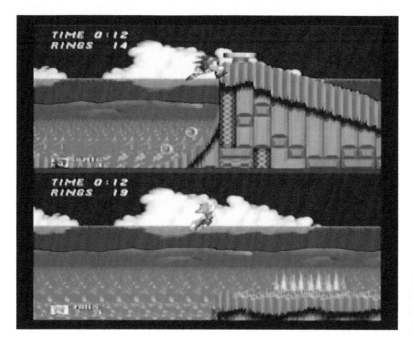

Screenshots from *Sonic the Hedgehog* (top) and *Sonic the Hedgehog 2* (bottom), both for the Sega Genesis.

to save the Princess from the Bowser, who captured her while the brothers were relaxing in a magical world called Dinosaur Land. During their search for the Princess, Mario and Luigi find a sealed egg, from which a dinosaur named Yoshi hatches. Yoshi tells the brothers that he and his pals were sealed in the eggs by evil turtles and proceeds to give them a magic cape. This starts the journey across seven worlds and two secret worlds, with a cumulative of 72 levels. In the game, Mario is able to pick up and throw items or place them down gently. In addition to super mushrooms and fire owers, there are now cape feathers, which allow Mario to y with a cape. When enemies are hit with a fire ball from fiery Mario, they turn into coins instead of being knocked off the screen. In the game, Mario is also able to ride the Yoshis. These come in various types and each has unique abilities; however, they all are able to eat enemies. If Mario finds a little Yoshi, he must feed it five enemies so that it becomes a big Yoshi. Most levels have one exit, but some have two, with the second being hidden.

Screenshot from *Super Mario World* for the Super Nintendo.

Super Mario World introduced many firsts to the *Mario* series. It was the first to allow players to exit a level without dying or having to complete it; however, this feature is activated only when replaying the level after completing it. It was also the first to have a visible marker, or checkpoint, in the level, so if a player reached that marker before exiting the board or dying, upon returning to the board, they would pick up at that marker instead of having to restart the level. The marker also serves as a powerup if Mario did not reach it as Super Mario. Although all levels do not need to be played or explored to complete the game, this was one of the first games to reward gamers who did.

Because of the increased capabilities of the SNES, *Super Mario World* features a more modern 3D effect, which is partially achieved through the use of parallax scrolling as well as Mode 7–style rendering in select boss battles, most notably those between Morton, Ludwig, Roy, and Bowser. The first technique employs multiple layers, and by moving the background layer slower than the foreground layers, creates the illusion of depth. The second technique uses texture mapping that allows the background layer to be rotated and scaled, also contributing to a 3D effect. The colors throughout the game are very vibrant, making the graphics aesthetically pleasing.

Of course, Nintendo was not alone in offering innovations; Sega introduced several of their own in the *Sonic* series. Unlike with Nintendo's, these did not necessarily involve gameplay, but came in the forms of *Sonic CD* and *Sonic & Knuckles*. *Sonic CD*, which was released first for the Sega Genesis's Sega CD add-on in 1993, was really the only epic side-scrolling platformer ever put on such an expansive storage medium. The main innovation of *Sonic CD* was allowing Sonic to time travel to the same game zone in the past, present, or future, with player actions in one period affecting the outcome and appearance of another. *Sonic & Knuckles*, released on cartridge for the Sega Genesis in 1994, featured lock-on technology that enabled another cartridge to be plugged in via the game's top or pass-through socket. *Sonic & Knuckles* allows play through the same game levels as either of the titular characters, with each having their own unique abilities

Screenshot from *Super Mario World 2: Yoshi's Island* for the Super Nintendo.

to interact with the levels differently. While Sonic has the speed and a type of shield, Knuckles the echidna can climb walls, break through blocked entryways, and glide in the air. By inserting either the *Sonic the Hedgehog 2* or *3* cartridge in the *Sonic & Knuckles* pass-through socket, extra areas and features are unlocked in the earlier games, including the ability to play as Knuckles.

Sonic, Sega's mascot, began the "animal with attitude" craze, of course, which Nintendo addressed in a way through the Mario franchise by introducing *Super Mario World 2: Yoshi's Island* in 1995. This was the first Mario game to allow Yoshi to be the main playable character. The premise is that baby Mario and Luigi are being delivered to their parents, when an evil Magikoopa intercepts the stork. He thinks he has captured both babies, only to find upon returning to his castle that he has only Luigi. Mario had fallen onto Yoshi's Island. The Yoshis decide that they will reunite Mario with his brother, using a relay system to do so, "not unlike the old pony express." Throughout the game, Mario rides on Yoshi's back, while Yoshi is used to defeat enemies along the way, who were sent out to capture baby Mario. Yoshi can take a lot of damage, but if he is hit, Mario is knocked off his back and encapsulated in a bubble, initiating a countdown timer. Yoshi must recover Mario before time runs out, otherwise Mario is captured by the Koopas and a life is lost. Unlike Sonic, the Yoshis do not have much "attitude" and are very laid-back creatures, but they do offer some whimsical moves to defeat enemies. As in *Super Mario World*, they can swallow up enemies and spit them out, but they can also make an egg out of them. Much of the game involves the collection and use of eggs to defeat enemies and solve puzzles. At various points in the game, a metamorphosis bubble will appear, which allows Yoshi to become another transportation vehicle, including a helicopter, mole tank, race car, train, or submarine. During these sequences, baby Mario is left behind, and Yoshi must reach a Yoshi block within a specified period of time, otherwise he returns to the point at which he started. However, if he reaches that block, Mario is warped there and reunited with him. If a Super Star is obtained, baby Mario becomes playable and can inflict a lot of damage on enemies. He becomes much like Sonic, with his ability to dash and "climb" walls. The game features many mini battle games, such as balloon and watermelon-seed-spitting activities. There are also bonus challenge games, many of which are lottery- and casino-style.

As technological capabilities increased, the thirst for 3D gaming also increased. Few 2D platformers made a successful transition to 3D, but Mario did it with style in the 1996 release of *Super Mario 64* for the Nintendo 64. Despite this success, there was still nostalgia for the 2D Mario platform games, leading to some interesting hybrids, most notably the *Paper Mario* series. *Paper Mario*

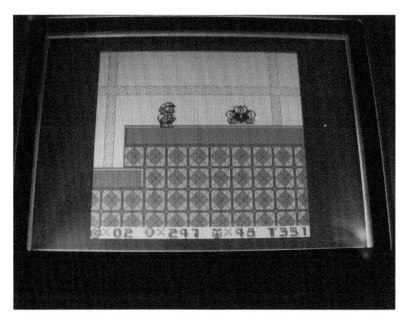

Photo of the Nintendo Game Boy's *Super Mario Land 2: 6 Golden Coins* (1992), shown running on a Nintendo Game Boy Advance. Most Nintendo systems featured great *Mario* series platform games.

was first released in 2001 for the Nintendo 64 and juxtaposed 2D character renderings with a 3D environment. The game is a role-playing platformer in which Mario is again on a quest to save the Princess from Bowser. The manner in which he progresses in this quest depends on how he interacts with the nonplayable characters. In 2007, Nintendo released *Super Paper Mario* for the Wii, which took the 2D/3D juxtaposition to the next level. To advance between levels, players must switch between 2D and 3D views to solve puzzles and pass obstacles. When switching from 2D into 3D, a " ip meter" appears and slowly starts decreasing. If a player is not cognizant of the time spent in this dimension, the meter will run empty, costing one health point. Although games in the *Paper Mario* series were well received and highly successful, the desire for traditional platformers did not cease. When *New Super Mario Bros.* was released on the Nintendo DS in 2006, it sold 500,000 copies in the first 35 days, or one copy every 20 minutes.[13] This game was largely in uenced by *Super Mario Bros.*, but incorporated elements from other *Mario* games.

The *Mario* games introduced innumerable innovations to gaming, right through to games like 2008's *Braid* for the Microsoft Xbox 360, which took significant in uences from both *Donkey Kong* and the main *Mario* franchise. *Braid*'s designer, Jonathan Blow, discussed his in uences on Independent Gaming: "As far as games go, the main in uence is *Super Mario Bros.,* which is

---

[13]http://www.gamespot.com/ds/action/supermariobrosds/news.html?sid=6153037.

obvious as soon as you start playing." Braid is a visually stunning platformer that requires the player to manipulate time to solve puzzles. The story is the timeless tale of a boy looking for a princess, but the narrative is cryptic and pieced together slowly much like a patchwork quilt.

The *Mario* series feature, some of the greatest videogames the world has ever seen, directly in uencing at least two generations of games and gamers. They have remained popular and in uential well beyond the technical shift from 2D to 3D. *Mario* games are platforming the way it should be, with no cut corners. The worlds are vibrant and alive and the critical jumping mechanics feel exactly right. Many games tried to follow in their footsteps with often-forced attempts at mascots, low-budget hacks, and the like, but none—save for *Sonic*—could get anywhere near that special *Mario* magic. To many, *Super Mario Bros.* is the quintessential videogame, and—based on the game's success and the amazing amount of reverence given to the series even today—who are we to argue? Besides his in uence on countless other videogames, Mario has permeated other media as well, like film, adventure books, and comics. Nevertheless, videogames are still clearly his home turf. With old and new gamers alike adoring him, Jumpman will no doubt continue to reach new heights.

TETRIS (1985): CASUAL GAMING FALLS INTO PLACE

Alexey Pajitnov's *Tetris*, created and introduced to the United States in the mid-1980s, is perhaps the greatest videogame ever to come out of Russia—or arguably anywhere else in the world, for that matter. It has been endlessly cloned and ported for almost every viable platform, and is still widely played today on all manner of devices, including mobile phones. *Tetris* is also a useful illustration of two important principles of good game design. The first is that it's easy to learn, yet hard to master. Second, despite its simple appearance, it's a game that could be possible (practically speaking, at least) only in electronic format. It's one of those games that we wish we had thought of ourselves; it seems so obvious, yet it took a computer engineer to invent.

Tetris later led to the rise of what is now called "casual gaming." This genre of videogames covers a broad array of gameplay styles, but is usually confined to low-tech games that can be run in a browser or low-budget hardware. They are also casual in the sense that they can be picked up, played for a few minutes, and put down without losing anything important—in stark contrast to most popular games for computers and consoles, which require a significant time investment to learn and play. In this chapter, we'll discuss the history of *Tetris*, its impact on the market, and the future of the genre that it helped create.

Tetris is usually described as a "sliding block" or, more generally, a "puzzle" game. The game consists of moving and rotating seven different pieces (called "tetrominoes") as they fall toward the bottom of the screen. The goal is to make the individual squares that make up the tetrominoes form a horizontal line; when this happens, the line is erased, lowering any incomplete lines above it. The player is also awarded points; most versions offer bonus points if the player is able to simultaneously clear more than one line at once (the maximum is four, which is

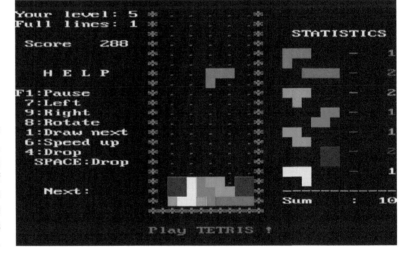

The IBM PC version of *Tetris* credits A. Pajitnov and V. Gerasimov. Despite the game's overwhelming popularity, Pajitnov himself wouldn't earn a dime from the game until a decade later, when he at last acquired the rights to his own program.

called the titular "Tetris"). Making clean lines is critical, because bungled efforts quickly result in stacks of unmatched pieces. The game ends if a new piece is blocked by such a stack and is unable to fall past the top of the playfield. In most versions, the pieces fall very slowly at first, gradually speeding up as the game progresses.

Why do so many people have so much fun playing such a simple game? Besides the competitive factor (most versions offer a high score table) and the increasing speed (which quickly ratchets up the intensity), the game seems to satisfy some basic desire to impose order on chaos; to "tidy up." We might compare this aspect of the game to blasting the aliens, one by one, in *Space Invaders* (Chapter 16, "*Space Invaders* (1978): The Japanese

Many of the countless original *Tetris* ports, like the one shown here on the Philips CD-i from 1992, added superfluous window dressing around the core gameplay model. In the CD-i version's case, it was the addition of full-motion video backgrounds. For most fans, all that mattered to them about a port or clone was whether the core gameplay remained intact, not the quality of the graphics or sound.

Descend"), which we likened to the joys of popping each bubble on a sheet of bubble wrap. It's tempting to bandy about terms like "obsessive-compulsive" to describe such behavior. Perhaps we could also talk about Freud's "anal stage," with the disappearing lines of tetrominoes analogous to our solid waste being ushed away in the toilet. Given this model, we might describe *Tetris*-fans as "anal-retentive," compulsively arranging those pieces in some futile quest to achieve the gratification they missed during toilet training. Pajitnov himself had designed some psychology-related games before *Tetris*, so it's possible he had such things in mind as he created his masterpiece. In any case, there's no denying the satisfaction one gets from seeing a stack of badly arranged tetrominoes organized and whisked away.

Pajitnov programmed the game on an Elektronika 60, a Soviet clone of the DEC PDP-11 mainframe. According to his friend and fellow game programmer Vadim Gerasimov, Pajitnov got the name by combining "tetramino" and "tennis," his favorite sport. Although Pajitnov's exposure to videogames was quite limited, he did get a chance to see *Pac-Man* (Chapter 13, "*Pac-Man* (1980): Japanese Gumption, American Consumption") and cube-hopping arcade classic, *Q*bert* (Gottlieb, 1982).[1] Pajitnov created the game purely for fun as a type of electronic variation of the

---

[1]See Kikizo's interview with Pajitnov for the source of these and other facts about *Tetris* at http://games.kikizo.com/features/tetris_iv_dec07_p2.asp.

pentomino puzzles he liked to solve,[2] but soon realized he had a hit on his hands when he noticed the game showing up on pretty much every Elektronika 60 in the country.

Pajitnov ported it to the IBM PC, upgrading the graphics along the way. This version spread just as quickly, and it wasn't long before foreign companies wanted to secure exclusive rights to distribute what was sure to be a multimillion dollar mega hit. Here's where the story gets quite murky and contested. In short, the Soviet Union didn't allow individuals like Pajitnov to own programs and make contracts with foreign companies concerning those programs. Instead, the government (and its agencies) were responsible for such matters.

Pajitnov seems quite touchy about the subject: "I don't really like to talk about that because when I think about those things I lose my sense of humour," he said in an interview posted on the website Kikizo. To make a long story short, Pajitnov lost control of the project, and several different foreign companies held (or thought they held) rights or even exclusive rights to the game. One of the first commercial releases was Spectrum Holobyte's version for the IBM PC, which debuted in 1986. Spectrum Holobyte had secured the rights from a British software company named Andromeda, who didn't really have any official authorization to do so (they had gotten the game from some Hungarians who had somehow managed to get a copy from the Soviet Union). Eventually Andromeda did secure official rights to license the game for the IBM PC and other home computers.

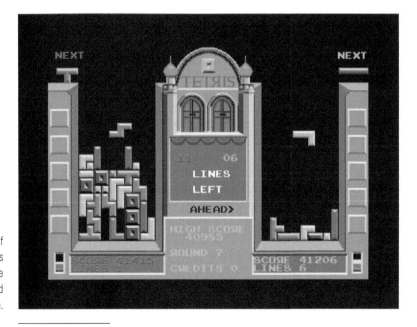

Atari's arcade conversion of *Tetris*, shown here, which was later ported to the NES before being pulled over rights, featured a head-to-head mode.

[2]A standard pentomino puzzle involves tiling a rectangular box with the differently shaped pentominoes by covering it without overlap or gaps.

The licensing arrangements got even more complicated (and dubious) after 1988, when the Soviet government set up the "Elektronorgtechnica," which was made responsible for marketing and licensing the game. However, by this point six different companies were claiming rights to *Tetris* for all manner of platforms. The government ended up giving Atari the rights to the arcade version and Nintendo rights to versions for consoles (except, strangely enough, in Japan) and handhelds.

Atari jumped the gun, however, and, under its Tengen banner, released a Nintendo Entertainment System (NES) version without permission. This version was considered to be superior to Nintendo's, because it allowed two players to play the game simultaneously on juxtaposed boards. Nintendo, however, took them to court and managed to get Tengen's game taken off the shelves.

Meanwhile, Nintendo was able to leverage its license to great success for its Game Boy handheld, released in 1989. The game sold millions of copies, and countless gamers bought a Game Boy specifically to play *Tetris*, which for a time came bundled with the system.

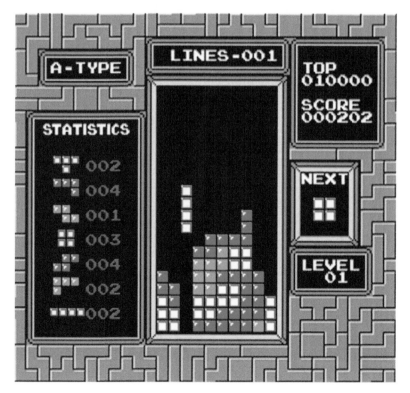

Nintendo's *Tetris* for their NES, shown here, was considered inferior to Tengen's conversion, which allowed for simultaneous two-player competitions.

In 1996, the rights reverted to Pajitnov, who had emigrated to the United States and teamed up with Henk Rogers. Rogers formed The Tetris Company with the goal of extracting some royalties from the many companies making *Tetris* games. However, although the company claims the exclusive right to the *Tetris* name, their control over *Tetris*-like games is not certain. The upshot is that people making unauthorized *Tetris* clones have called them by other names, such as Wolfgang Strobl's *Klotz* (1989; PC), to avoid litigation, and The Tetris Company hasn't been aggressive in shutting down these operations. Although Pajitnov may not have received any royalties when he made the game, he seems satisfied with the money he has received in conjunction with this new company.

Pajitnov created several other games based on *Tetris*, such as *Welltris* (1989). The game gets it name from its 3D setup; the pieces fall into the center of the screen as though into a hole (or a well). Although perhaps more cognitively advanced than *Tetris*, this game hasn't received nearly the same publicity. Pajitnov went on to make several other mind and puzzle games. Among his latest is *Hexic*, a colorful puzzle game inspired by *Bejeweled* (which we'll discuss in a moment).

Dr. Mario for the NES was one of many "themed" *Tetris*-style games, and one of the many examples of Nintendo's practice of repackaging its characters from one type of game for use in another. *Dr. Mario* also offered the popular side-by-side competitive play mode that was absent from Nintendo's original attempt at *Tetris* for the platform.

Although no derivative of *Tetris* has achieved the recognition or success of the original, there have been several noteworthy attempts. One of the best known is *Dr. Mario*, a 1990 game for the NES with branding from Nintendo's popular *Mario* franchise.

Here, the *Tetris*-style gameplay is given a medical theme. Instead of blocks, players guide pills (consisting of two blocks) that fall from the top of the screen to a set of viruses toward the bottom. Players win the game by matching up pills and viruses of the corresponding color (red, blue, or yellow). There was also a popular two-player mode available, which employed side-by-side simultaneous gameplay.

An even more radical derivative is Capcom's *Super Puzzle Fighter II Turbo*, released in 1996. The game pits players against each other in the same side-by-side setup we saw in *Dr. Mario* and Atari's version of *Tetris*. The players are represented by parodied versions of characters from Capcom's *Street Fighter* series (Chapter 17, "*Street Fighter II* (1991): Would You Like the Combo?"), who fight each other as the players match up gems. Like *Dr. Mario*, the falling bits consist of two blocks, and must be connected to other gems of the identical color. However, lining them up isn't enough; only a special exploding block of like color will clear the formations. Whenever this happens, the fighters will respond with one of the moves (or combos) that they used in Capcom's popular fighting games.

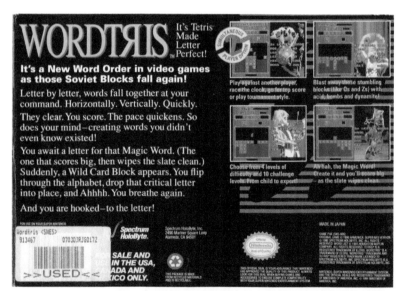

The main *Tetris* series has had a series of interesting offshoots, including *WordTris* (box back for the Super Nintendo version shown), in which the object is to build words of three letters or more using tiles that fall from the top of the playing area. Nintendo's platforms have always been home to popular puzzle games, including the unrelated—though extremely popular—*Tetris Attack*, which requires matching colored blocks.

It's likely that the staggering success of *Tetris* made publishers more responsive to similar puzzle games from other developers. Of these, perhaps the four most famous are Sega's *Columns* (1990), Compile's *Puyo Puyo* (also known as *Puyo Pop*, 1991), Taito's *Puzzle Bobble* (also known as *Bust-a-Move*, 1994), and PopCap Games's *Bejeweled* (2001).

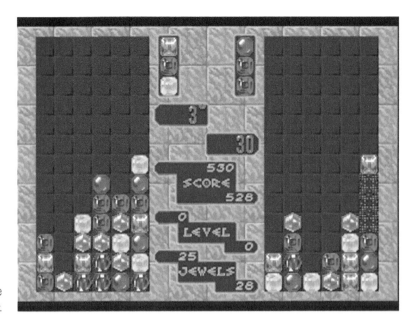

Screenshot from the arcade version of Sega's *Columns*.

Columns takes place inside a tall, rectangular playing field, similar to Tetris. Columns of three different colored jewels appear, one at a time, at the top of the screen and fall to the bottom, landing either on the oor or on top of previously fallen columns. After a column has fallen, if there are three or more of the same symbols connected in a straight line horizontally, vertically, or diagonally, those symbols disappear. The pile of columns then settles under gravity. Occasionally, a special column called

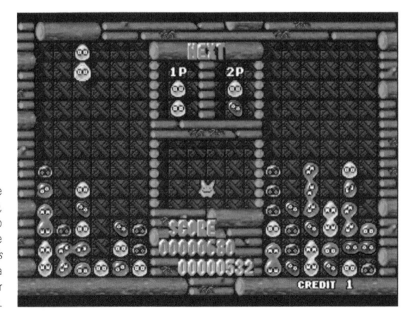

Screenshot from the arcade version of Compile's *Puyo Puyo*, which is probably better known to U.S. gamers in some of its home incarnations, like *Dr. Robotnik's Mean Bean Machine* for the Sega Genesis and *Kirby's Avalanche* for the Super Nintendo.

the Magic Jewel appears, which ashes with different colors and destroys all the jewels with the same color as the one underneath it when it lands.

Puyo Puyo's basic goal is for one of the players to defeat their opponent (computer or human) in a battle by filling their tall, rectangular playing field up to the top with garbage blocks. The gelatinous and expressive Puyos fall from the top of the screen in groups of two or more, and can be moved left and right and rotated. When four or more Puyos of the same color form together to create a group—whether vertical, horizontal, or in a *Tetris*-shaped piece—they form a chain, then pop and disappear. Because doing well in one playfield would send the garbage blocks to the opponent's, it was always an exciting race to execute a chain reaction big enough to completely bury the other player's Puyos.

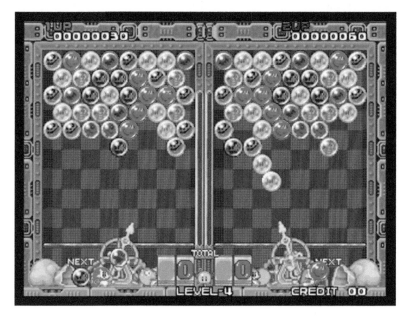

Screenshot from Taito's arcade version of *Puzzle Bobble* for SNK's Neo Geo platform.

Puzzle Bobble, based on the characters from single-screen arcade platformer, *Bubble Bobble* (1986), contains a rectangular playfield with a prearranged pattern of colored bubbles. At the bottom of the screen, the player controls a rotating pointer that can aim and fire a queued colored bubble at the top bubbles, preferably forming and clearing matching chains of three. The objective is to clear all the bubbles from the playfield before they eventually creep down to the bottom.

Bejeweled is one of the first major "casual games." It was created with Macromedia Flash, a Web programming language often used to make animated ads for websites. The game was so

Bejeweled is one of the most successful "casual games" ever made. Casual games are intended for so-called noncore (hardcore) gamers, who often have limited technical knowledge and little interest in investing their time in learning complicated games. Games like *Bejeweled* are known for being easy to learn, yet hard to master.

successful that it was eventually published as a best-selling multiplatform stand-alone game, but has continued to be a mainstay of online casual gaming sites. *Bejeweled*, like *Puzzle Bobble*, has its pieces already fill the board when the game begins. The goal is to swap adjacent gems around to make a chain of three gems of the same color. New gems fall only when players clear room for them on the board.

Highly addictive and well-crafted games like *Bejeweled* are no doubt responsible for the rise in "casual gaming" over the last few years. Although many of these games are available exclusively online, some also appear on store shelves alongside titles with bigger budgets. They are also popular choices for gaming on mobile phones. In general, though, these games seem to have the most appeal for "nontraditional" gamers with little interest in the latest *Halo* or *Madden* (Chapters 5 and 10, respectively). They are, as is often stated, quite popular among women and older gamers. For instance, all of author Barton's grandparents are avid casual gamers, spending hours and hours every evening engrossed in casual games like PopCap's aforementioned *Bejeweled* and *Bookworm* (2004). *Bookworm*, also known as *Bespelled*, is a fun variation on *Bejeweled*; instead of matching gems, players make words out of letter tiles. Interestingly, though ostensibly role-playing games, the *Puzzle Quest* series, starting with the 1997 release of *Puzzle Quest: Challenge of the Warlords* on the Nintendo DS and Sony PlayStation Portable, even uses a competitive *Bejeweled*-style playfield to resolve in-game combat and other activities as part of its hybrid gameplay.

This package contains one 4-TЯIS cartridge, two controller overlays, and playing instructions.

4-TЯIS cartridge

It is raining... BRICKS!!! Before you know it, you will be over your head in these things. There is only one way to get rid of them; row by row. Spin, shift and drop the bricks to manipulate how they align when they land. Successfully completing a row will make the bricks dissolve, thus shifting all bricks above the row down. As the game progresses, the bricks come down faster and faster. An umbrella is not going to help.

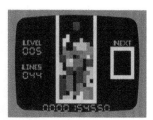

Move the pieces to keep the bricks at the bottom of the screen making for easier game play.

- For one player.
- Skill levels that continually advance.
- Start play on levels 1 through 10.
- Disable the preview window for higher points.

Game programmed by: Joe Zbiciak
Project Coordinator: David Harley
Box Design and Overlays: Oliver Puschatzki

As Pajitnov's original character-based version of *Tetris* proved, any platform with a display makes a suitable playing environment. Box back shown from a version of Joseph Zbiciak's *4-Tris* (2000) for the Mattel Intellivision, just one of a seemingly never-ending series of modern homebrew games based on *Tetris* for classic platforms.

When Emma Boyes of GameSpot UK asked Pajitnov whether people would play *Tetris* forever, he responded, "Yes. Technology may change but our brains don't. So basically, I don't know why not."[3] To many, this is what makes *Tetris* the "perfect" videogame— one that's at home on any platform in any setting. *Tetris* has never been about dazzling graphics or sophisticated gameplay; it's a simple diversion that somehow manages to stay fresh and compelling year after year. It's also a testament to the fact that great, best-selling games don't always require multimillion-dollar budgets and huge teams of professional game developers. As *Tetris* proves, what one really needs to make a great game is the imagination to conceive it.

---

[3]http://tinyurl.com/46c429.

21

THE LEGEND OF ZELDA (1986): RESCUING ZELDAS AND UNITING TRIFORCES

Like most of the games covered in this book, Shigeru Miyamoto's *The Legend of Zelda* needs no introduction. A gamer who'd never heard of *Zelda* would be as bizarre as a science fiction fan who'd never heard of *Star Wars*, or a fantasy buff who'd never read Tolkien. Love it or hate it, *The Legend of Zelda* is a foundational game, one of only a handful of titles that can truly be said to have helped to define the industry as we know it today. Its popularity and name recognition is rivaled only by the likes of *Super Mario Bros.* (Chapter 19, "*Super Mario Bros.* (1985): How High Can Jumpman Get?" also from Miyamoto) and *Pac-Man* (Chapter 13, "*Pac-Man* (1980): Japanese Gumption, American Consumption"). To say that it "in uenced" the games industry is like saying that the biblical Moses "in uenced" the Red Sea. It didn't just sell copies, it parted the Pacific Ocean, helping to open a critical link between Japan and America that has yet to close. If Miyamoto's *Super Mario Bros.* was the lure, *The Legend of Zelda* was the hook. It was a game that turned ordinary people into lifelong gamers.

But what was it about *The Legend of Zelda* that aroused such hyperbole? Maybe, you say, it was just a case of the right game at the right time, a simplistic action game with just enough role-playing elements to titillate the unwashed masses. After all, surely the plot—rescue Princess Zelda from the evil clutches of Ganon by assembling eight pieces of a magical artifact called the Triforce—is hopelessly cliché, more Mother Goose than Norman Mailer. And surely the gameplay is simplistic as well, having more in common with *Space Invaders* (Chapter 16, "*Space Invaders* (1978): The Japanese Descend") than *Ultima* (Chapter 23, "*Ultima* (1980): The Immaculate Conception of the Computer Role-Playing Game"). Perhaps the record-setting sales of *The Legend of Zelda* and its

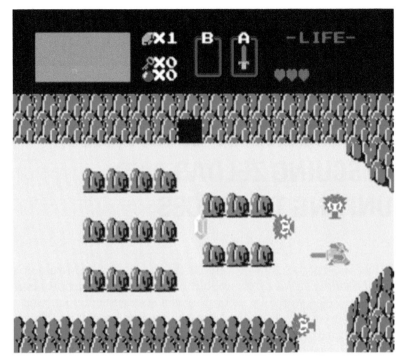

Amazingly, legendary *Donkey Kong* and *Mario* creator Shigeru Miyamoto designed yet another "mascot" game in the 1980s that would spawn a huge mainstream phenomena and franchise. Screenshot from the original *The Legend of Zelda* on the NES that started it all.

sequels say more about the naïveté of the buying public than the artistry of its creators: a masterpiece only of marketing.

But such claims, no matter how eloquently presented, would be as eccentric as a science fiction fan who hated *Star Wars*, or a fantasy buff who loathed Tolkien. They certainly exist. But nobody particularly likes them.

In this chapter, we'll explore the legacy of *The Legend of Zelda*, one of the most successful and long-lived franchises in the history of the industry. As we'll see, all of these games were instant best-sellers and were routinely given perfect or near perfect scores by all major critics. *Zelda*—at least in the eyes of its many fans—can simply do no wrong.

The first *Zelda* game debuted in 1986 for the Japanese version of the Nintendo Entertainment System (NES)—the Famicom—followed by a North American release in 1987. Often described as an "action-adventure," the game put players in the role of a courageous lad named Link. Link's quest is to reassemble the eight pieces of a powerful artifact called the Triforce of Wisdom, which Princess Zelda had separated and hidden to keep them away from the megalomaniac Ganon, Prince of Darkness. Ganon learned of Zelda's deed and imprisoned her, but not before the wily princess sent her nursemaid (Impa) to search for a hero. Link saves Impa and learns of the threat to the land of Hyrule. Fortunately for Link, there are some people willing to help him on his quest, and they provide vital but often cryptic clues.

The gameplay is usually described as "action-adventure," though some people wrongly consider it an RPG. Players spend most of their time exploring a tile-based map, shown from an overhead perspective comparable to early *Ultima* games. Many maps are swarming with monsters, who can be vanquished by swings from Link's sword. If Link's "life hearts" are at their maximum capacity, he can also throw the sword. Because the sword instantly reappears in Link's hand,[1] this aspect of the gameplay is similar to that found in the many "run and gun" games of the era, such as SNK's *Ikari Warriors* (1986; Arcade) and Konami's *Contra* (1987; Arcade). Link can also find an upgrade for his shield and a magical bow and arrows, as well as other character items that allow him to gradually access more areas, but there's hardly the emphasis on upgrading arms and armor found in most role-playing games.

Although *The Legend of Zelda* has much in common with many RPGs, such as a fantasy setting and the presence of magic, it lacks both a leveling system and tactical turn-based combat system, two of the quintessential features of the computer RPG genre. We can easily contrast it with contemporary games like Enix's *Dragon Warrior*, which debuted first in Japan as *Dragon Quest* in 1986 and a year later in North America under its new name. Though not nearly as popular here as it was in Japan, it still gave American NES owners a chance to play a true "Japanese role-playing game." *Dragon Warrior* offered both the point-based leveling system and tactical combat that has characterized much of the genre ever since. A similar point could be made of Square's *Final Fantasy* (1987), another classic console RPG, discussed in Chapter 7, "*Final Fantasy VII* (1997): It's Never Final in the World of Fantasy." Both *Final Fantasy* and *Dragon Warrior* were hugely successful in Japan, but didn't seem to attract much attention in North America, where console owners at the time seemed to prefer action-oriented games.

It's important to bear in mind the state of the console market in 1987. Although the NES was more advanced than the last generation of American consoles, the bulk of successful console games still tended to be rather simplistic action games. This situation was in stark contrast to the computer games market, where adventure, RPG, and strategy games were far more abundant. Furthermore, the NES seemed targeted primarily to children, an idea that Nintendo reinforced with its strict censorship policies, cartoony mascots, and family-friendly advertisements. Although plenty of adults could enjoy games like *Super Mario Bros.* and the light-gun game *Duck Hunt*, these were simple diversions indeed compared to the latest offerings from Origin or Sierra On-Line. No doubt

---

[1]In reality, Link's sword never really leaves his hand—it just shoots out a ashing replica.

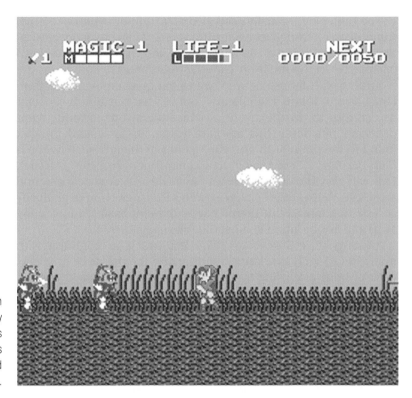

Zelda II for the NES had random encounters, like so many Japanese RPGs of its era. Players could try to avoid these monsters if they wanted, but Link would miss out on the experience points.

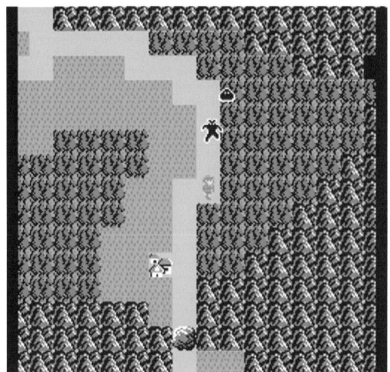

Zelda II offered a 2D, side-scrolling view during combat and some exploration modes. Even though the game sold well, many fans consider it the worst game of the series on a Nintendo system.

many publishers feared that a more sophisticated game would have oundered miserably in a market dominated by adolescents. On the other hand, Nintendo clearly needed more than run-and-jump games if it wanted to expand its North American user base.

The Legend of Zelda seemed destined to fill the gap. Like *Super Mario Bros.*, it was simple enough for kids, but still compelling for adults. Miyamoto confessed that he was initially nervous about the game, because it "forced the players to think about what they should do next. We were afraid that gamers would become bored and stressed by the new concept."[2] Fortunately for Miyamoto, console gamers were more than up for the challenge.

We've already alluded to the action sequences, which consist mostly of destroying or avoiding the roaming monsters with Link's sword or bow. Link also collects money as he slaughters foes, which can be used to purchase special items from merchants. The adventure elements are mostly finding keys and items, gathering clues, and navigating the large overland and dungeon maps. Naturally, magazines were quick to publish guides and maps, and there's no telling how many fans of the game compared strategies and shared insights with their friends.

The relative complexity of *The Legend of Zelda* raised the need for a key innovation: the battery backup system for cartridges. Before *The Legend of Zelda*, most console games were intended to be played in one sitting. If players quit and resumed hours or days later, they were forced to start over from the beginning. The only way around this limitation was a password system, but this was an often-cumbersome process. The battery in the shiny gold *Zelda* cartridges let gamers painlessly save their games, restoring them later with hardly any hassle. Although it's easy enough to trivialize such a detail, it was instrumental in narrowing the gap between console games and computers, the latter of which had the benefit of cassette and disk storage.

The success of *The Legend of Zelda* is hard to exaggerate. It not only sold millions of copies, but spawned a cavalcade of licensed consumer products like breakfast cereal and bedsheet sets. It also served, along with its first sequel, as the basis for a short-lived Saturday morning cartoon that ran in 1989. The game is still frequently played today in various incarnations and remains a popular entry on many of the Web's greatest game compilations.

The next *Zelda* game was *Zelda II: The Adventure of Link*, released in the United States in 1988. Although wildly popular at the time, this title is generally considered the black sheep of the series and has a number of features that are found in no other *Zelda* game. The most noticeable change from the original was a shift to a 2D, side-view perspective reminiscent of Nintendo's

---

[2]See http://www.miyamotoshrine.com/theman/interviews/230403.shtml.

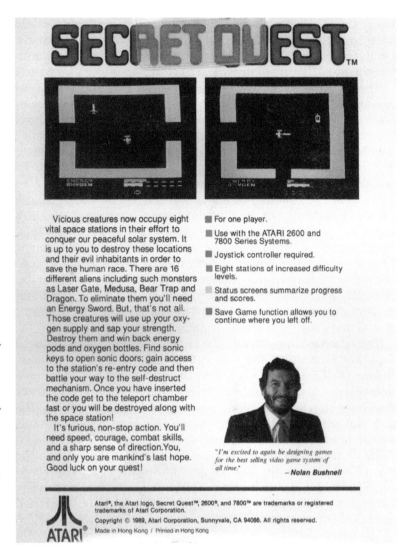

Box back for Atari's *Secret Quest* (1989), one of the last games released for the Atari 2600 VCS during its original commercial lifetime. Many feel that *Secret Quest*'s development and release was part of Atari's last-ditch attempt to demonstrate that the software library on their modest system from 1977 could still compete with more sophisticated systems like the NES and games like *The Legend of Zelda*.

popular run-and-jump games for combat and in-town scenes (the overhead perspective was maintained for overland travel). This is also the only *Zelda* game that qualifies as a true RPG, since Link now gains experience points and attack, magic, and life levels.

The third *Zelda* game and the first for the Super Nintendo (SNES) is *The Legend of Zelda: A Link to the Past*, published in the United States in 1992. It returned to the overhead perspective of the first game, but took advantage of the SNES's superior technology to offer substantially improved audiovisuals. The game's enormous sales undoubtedly helped Nintendo's new platform establish itself in the market and eventually outperform its rival, the Sega Genesis—which had beaten Nintendo to the 16-bit era.

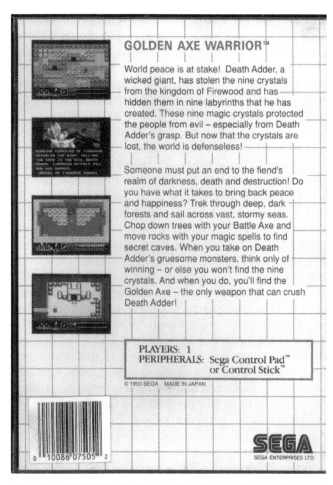

Box back (top) and screenshot (bottom) from Sega's *Golden Axe Warrior* (1991) for the Sega Master System. Though little known today, some fans of the game claim it is better than its obvious inspiration, *The Legend of Zelda*.

Sega, always struggling to outdo Nintendo, had also introduced a CD-ROM add-on for the Genesis in 1992, and new titles with full-motion video were attracting a great deal of buzz. Besides the Sega CD, there were several stand-alone CD-ROM consoles available, all of which proved to have minimal staying power. One of these was Philips's CD-i platform, released in 1991, which plays a small role in the *Zelda* story.

Nintendo famously wavered on the CD-ROM issue. On the one hand, CD-ROMs had enormous storage capacity and were very cheap to produce. On the other, Nintendo feared they would be much easier than cartridges to copy and distribute illegally. The company eventually decided not to release a CD-ROM add-on that it had commissioned from Philips,[3] but agreed to let them develop and release software using Nintendo characters for the CD-i platform. Philips moved quickly to exploit the arrangement and in addition to developing *Mario*-themed titles, released three low-quality *Zelda* games for its console: *Link: The Faces of Evil*, *Zelda: The Wand of Gamelon* (both 1993) and *Zelda's Adventure* (1994). Like most early CD-ROM games, these were loaded with noninteractive full-motion video sequences (the first two are animated; the third has live actors). All three of these games were poorly contrived and had none of the polish and attention to detail that characterized Nintendo's games. Few fans of the series consider these wretched games worth playing today.[4]

The next official *Zelda* game was *The Legend of Zelda: Link's Awakening*, a 1993 game for Nintendo's Game Boy. Despite its lack of color, the game was quite successful, selling millions of copies and receiving praise from nearly all major critics. Nintendo would continue to release *Zelda* games for its handheld platforms, such as *The Legend of Zelda: Oracle of Seasons* for the Game Boy Color in 2001, and *The Legend of Zelda: A Link to the Past & Four Swords* for the Game Boy Advance in 2002, which combined an update of the SNES game with a multiplayer game that could interact with the single-player game. One of the more recent handheld *Zelda's* is *The Legend of Zelda: Phantom Hourglass* for the Nintendo DS, which was released in 2007 and supported both local and online multiplayer. These games have not received as much media attention as the console versions, but are still must-haves for any serious fan and have all been top sellers.

---

[3]Nintendo initially contracted with Sony to develop the add-on, dubbed "Play Station," but for various reasons the deal fell through and the relationship between the two corporations soured. Sony reworked the concepts into an entirely new console entitled "PlayStation," becoming one of Nintendo's most powerful competitors.

[4]For a detailed overview of the CD-i games, see http://www.zeldaelements.net/cdiseries_foe.shtm.

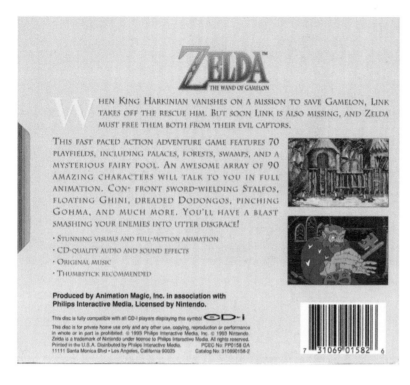

Box back for one of
the controversial Philips
CD-i releases: *Zelda:
The Wand of Gamelon.*

Sega's 1991 *Ax Battler: A Legend
of Golden Axe* for their Game
Gear, was very similar to *Zelda II,*
featuring a traditional top-view
overworld mixed with side-
scrolling action sequences.

The next game in the console series, *The Legend of Zelda: Ocarina
of Time*, was released in 1998 for the Nintendo 64 and is considered by many fans to be the best game in the series, if not of all
time. Even though it was released in November 1998, it still became
the bestselling game of that year, with more than 2.5 million units

The Legend of Zelda: A Link to the Past brought the beloved franchise to the Super Nintendo.

Nintendo was always eager to promote its new platforms by offering exclusive games based on its popular franchises, like *The Legend of Zelda: Link's Awakening* for the Game Boy.

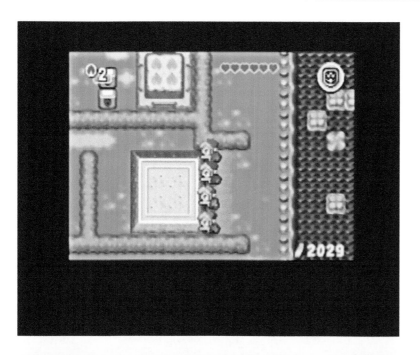

Screenshots from the multiplayer
Four Swords portion of *The Legend
of Zelda: A Link to the Past &
Four Swords* for the Nintendo
Game Boy Advance.

shipped.[5] The game raked in dozens of awards and even today
is one of the top downloadable purchases for the Nintendo Wii's
virtual console.

---

[5]See http://ign64.ign.com/articles/066/066340p1.html.

Ocarina of Time adapted the series for the 3D era, pioneered in Nintendo's earlier *Super Mario 64* (see Chapter 18, "*Super Mario 64/Tomb Raider* (1996): The Third Dimension"). However, it also refined the formula with "Z-Targeting," which let Link lock on to a target and perform strafing and other maneuvers without having to wrestle with the camera. Another nice feature was that the

Screenshots from *The Legend of Zelda: Ocarina of Time* rerelease for the Nintendo GameCube, which also contained *Ocarina of Time: Master Quest*, featuring rearranged dungeons.

function of the controller's buttons, which were always displayed onscreen, changed depending on the context of the situation, creating a versatile but intuitive control scheme. The game also contained many puzzles, including several based on the titular musical instrument. Contemporary reviews of the game read like overhyped ad copy. Peer Schneider of IGN, for instance, wrote that "if you're making games and you haven't played this game, then you're like a director who has never seen Citizen Kane or a musician who has never heard of Mozart."[6] Jeff Gerstmann of GameSpot was just as enthusiastic, writing that to call it anything but perfect "would be a bald-faced lie."[7]

Nintendo followed up *Ocarina of Time* in 2000 with *The Legend of Zelda: Majora's Mask*, another game for the Nintendo 64. As the title implies, the main theme is a collection of masks that grant Link different powers and abilities. Three of them actually transform him into different creatures. Though the game had some novel concepts and sold millions of copies, it wasn't as well received as its predecessor. Jeff Gertsmann of GameSpot complained about the tedious side-quests and "meaningless minigames."[8] IGN's reviewers were less critical, but knocked off a tenth of a point for lacking any major innovations, including a remedy for the "sometimes-sluggish framerate and occasionally blurry textures."[9] Some gamers resented that the game required the system's memory Expansion Pak to even play, one of only two games to do so along with Nintendo's 3D platformer *Donkey Kong 64* (1999).

There were two very different followups to the Nintendo 64 series: *The Legend of Zelda: The Wind Waker* (2002) and *The Legend of Zelda: Twilight Princess* (2006). Both of these were released for the GameCube, though a special version of the latter is available for the Wii. Perhaps the most noteworthy aspect of *The Wind Waker* is its distinctive and controversial aesthetic; its cartoon-like cell-shaded animation gives it a fresh appearance, though many gamers missed the darker tone of the previous games. There was also an option to connect a Game Boy Advance handheld. Once Link finds the "Tingle tuner," the handheld can be used to view maps and hints as well as activate exclusive in-game abilities. Unsurprisingly, this game was also a massive hit for Nintendo and received a direct sequel on the Nintendo DS in the form of the aforementioned *The Legend of Zelda: Phantom Hourglass*. *Twilight Princess*, which returned the series to a

---

[6]See http://ign64.ign.com/articles/150/150437p1.html.

[7]http://www.gamespot.com/n64/adventure/legendofzeldaoot/review.html.

[8]See http://tinyurl.com/3n4 3.

[9]See http://ign64.ign.com/articles/151/151933p1.html.

The Legend of Zelda: The Wind Waker for the Nintendo GameCube, featured a controversial art style.

darker and more traditional look, also boasted terrific audio-visuals and compelling gameplay. However, GameSpot's critic complained about its lack of innovation; it still relied on text for dialog, and the special features added for the Wii version seemed like afterthoughts. Of course, there are no shortage of supposedly critical reviews that declare it ﬂawless. IGN's video review, for instance, called it the "the best Zelda, period," and claimed that Wii controllers made the game feel more natural and satisfying.[10]

Although the *Zelda* series is one of the bestselling video-game franchises in the history of the industry, we have yet to see another developer successfully duplicate its formula with both critical and commercial success. Whereas other mega-hit titles like Nintendo's own *Super Mario Bros.*, id Software's *Doom* (Chapter 5, "*Doom* (1993): The First-Person Shooter Takes Control"), Cyan's *Myst* (Chapter 12, "*Myst* (1993): Launching Multimedia Worlds"), and many others have seen whole genres and subgenres form in their wake, *Zelda* seems to stand alone. This isn't to say there are *no* clones, just that games like Hudson Soft's *Neutopia* (1990, NEC TurboGrafx-16) and Nextech's *Crusader of Centy* (1994; Sega Genesis) have seemed to pose little, if any, challenge to the epic franchise. Surely, no one would seriously prefer such games to the real thing.

---

[10]See http://tinyurl.com/4geha8.

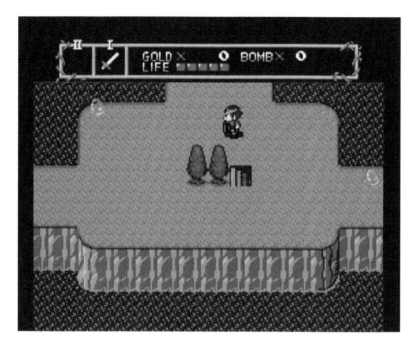

Screenshot from the *The Legend of Zelda*–inspired *Neutopia* for the NEC TurboGrafx-16.

However, the games have perhaps exerted an indirect in u-ence on RPGs for computer and console, which have moved far away from the stat-heavy, turn-based games of the 1980s. We can see this clearly in games such as Blizzard's *Diablo* (Chapter 4, "*Diablo* (1997): The Rogue Goes to Hell"), and might well have inspired the ill-fated push towards arcade action we saw in the latter *King's Quest* (Chapter 11, "*King's Quest: Quest for the Crown* (1984): Perilous Puzzles, Thorny Thrones") and *Ultima* games. We might hunt for *Zelda*'s in uence in other games classified as "action-adventures," such as *Tomb Raider* (Chapter 18, "*Super Mario 64/Tomb Raider* (1996): The Third Dimension") and even Capcom's *Resident Evil* (Chapter 1, "*Alone in the Dark* (1992): The Polygons of Fear"), though admittedly these linkages seem a tri e far-fetched.

Nevertheless, what seems to set the *Zelda* series apart is not so much its originality or innovation, which it had in spades, but its immaculate polish and sense of mysterious adventure. These are games that were built to stand the test of time. It's obvi-ous that the developers took nothing for granted, scrutinizing every detail, even when occasionally reimagining a new entry in the series. Although it's of course possible to point out the occa-sional misspelling or questionable translation, these lavish pro-ductions heightened gamers' expectations and have helped establish videogames as a respectable and even artistic form of entertainment.

22

THE SIMS (2000): WHO LET THE SIMS OUT?

Will Wright's *The Sims* (Electronic Arts, 2000; Apple Macintosh, Nintendo GameCube, PC, and others) is one of those rare games whose appeal extends to people who wouldn't normally consider themselves gamers. Plenty of people who would never dream of playing *Halo* or *John Madden Football*[1] are diehard fans of *The Sims*, and, conversely, many gamers who obsess over the latest shooter or MMORPG[2] have little knowledge of Wright's virtual playground,[3] or, as he called it, "Virtual Dollhouse."

Thus, although the game and its sequels constitute the best-selling franchise of all time for the PC, it's not hard to find seasoned gamers who've never played it. Indeed, it's estimated that a full 50% of the series' fan base is female, a key demographic that many game developers have either failed to interest or simply ignored entirely.[4] This isn't to say that *The Sims* is not accessible or intriguing to all sorts of gamers, but its focus on family and furniture is a radical alternative to almost any other game we might find on the shelf. Nevertheless, for the millions of gamers turned off by shooters, MMORPGs, sports, and strategy titles, *The Sims* is the best game in town. In this chapter, we'll explore the history

---

[1]See Chapters 5 and 10, respectively.

[2]Massively Multiplayer Online Role-Playing Game.

[3]A virtual playground's primary goal is to essentially play with or manipulate pre-made elements, with less focus on creativity and creation. Compare this to the primary goal of a "Software Toy," like *Pinball Construction Set* in bonus chapter, "*Pinball Construction Set* (1982): Launching Millions of Creative Possibilities," which is to provide either the parts or allow the creation of the parts to build a game in a typically creative manner, and "sandbox" games, like *Grand Theft Auto III* in Chapter 9, "*Grand Theft Auto III* (2001): The Consolejacking Life," in which the player is able to move about a large environment and perform a wide range of typically realistic activities, but with a primary focus on accomplishing various goals and activities over any type of creative or creation possibilities.

[4]See http://news.cnet.com/Will-Sims-Online-alter-gaming-world/2100-1040_3-977912.html.

In *The Sims*, the player's family can interact in all sorts of ways, such as dancing (shown here). These interactions have varied effects on the sims themselves; it's important to keep track of their needs (notice the panel on the bottom right of the screen). PC version shown.

of *The Sims*, analyze its unusual gameplay, and speculate on the future of the franchise.

As its title suggests, *The Sims* has much in common with Wright's earlier masterpiece *SimCity* (see Chapter 15, "*SimCity* (1989): Building Blocks for Fun and Profit"), whose invisible citizens were called "sims." However, whereas that game cast players in the role of a mayor or city planner, *The Sims* puts them in charge of a family of semi-autonomous characters (the titular "sims"). Like real people (or pets), sims require food, sleep, and the occasional trip to the bathroom. Beyond these simple physical needs, they also require entertainment and fellowship with their friends and loved ones. Another important part of the game is building an appropriate home, reveling in the possibilities of interior design. Wright has described the game as a "Virtual Dollhouse," and originally conceived of it as having more to do with building houses than the virtual people who'd live in them. However, as the concept evolved, it embraced both themes. What *SimCity* is to cities, *The Sims* is to citizens. If *SimCity* is a macrocosm, *The Sims* is a microcosm, a zoomed-in view of one of those ant-sized dots that   ow between the buildings of *SimCity*.

Although *The Sims*, like *SimCity* before it, has no definite goals for players to accomplish, most players adopt one of three styles of gameplay. The first focuses on the "virtual pet" aspects; that is, carefully managing and controlling one's family of sims. Players creating sims can adjust the levels of five different personality attributes: neat, outgoing, active, playful, and nice. The aggregate of these attributes is calculated as a sign of the zodiac.

Players can also choose their sims' skin tone, sex, and age, and customize their appearance with different heads and outfits (the latter expansions greatly expand the options). Once the sims are created, the player must strive to satisfy their many needs or "motives." These are hunger, comfort, hygiene, bladder (need to urinate), energy (sleep and caffeine levels), fun (entertainment), social (talking to other sims), and room (decor). Although some of these needs are straightforward (characters who don't get to a bathroom will soil their clothes), others are more complex and are affected by the personality traits. For instance, a very playful character will get more fun out of a game than a book.

Another important part of *The Sims* is the build and buy menus, which let players customize their sims' environment. There are countless options available, and the many expansion packs extend them further. The captions are often quite witty and wry, contributing to the game's "smart" aesthetic and tongue-in-cheek humor. PC version shown.

The sims are conspicuous consumers, deriving much more satisfaction from high-end products than cheap stuff. The manual puts it this way: "Sims get the most gain from 'high-quality' objects: that is, a small TV is less efficient at entertaining than a large TV." These are simple but compelling utilitarian principles: "good" decisions amount to what brings the greatest pleasure and least pain to the most people. What makes *The Sims* interesting to play, however, is the challenge (if not the impossibility) of pleasing people with such radically different personalities. The ensuing drama is what makes the game unpredictable and fun, but might also inspire gamers to re ect on their social life. Why, for instance, does one spend so many hours playing *The Sims* when there are so many other ways to spend one's time? It's also likely that the chance to "play God" is quite compelling for many gamers.

Another important part of a sim's life is a job, as money is required for buying things. The type of job a sim can get depends on his or her skills, which are improved in specified ways. The skills are cooking, mechanical, charisma, body, logic, and creativity. Cooking and mechanical skills are improved by reading (a bookcase is all but a requirement) charisma requires a mirror, and body requires physical exercise (swimming, working out, dancing, and so on). Logic and creativity are increased by playing chess or the piano, respectively. With the right skills, a character can land a job advertised in the newspaper or online. The jobs vary in terms of pay and satisfaction, of course, but players don't get to see or control sims that are away at work except to respond to workplace crises (how the player handles these determines whether the sim gets promoted or demoted). The original game included 10 career tracks, each with prerequisite skills. Perhaps the two most unusual career paths are crime (pickpocket) and "x-treme" (daredevil). Eventually, sims can get married (same-sex is allowed) and even have children, though anyone expecting torrid sex scenes will likely be disappointed by the comical way these activities are represented.

Back of the box for 2004's *The Sims: Bustin' Out* on the Nokia N-Gage handheld. Console and handheld versions tend to play a bit differently than their computer counterparts, often allowing for more direct control and having more predefined goals.

We should note that sims don't talk to each other using English or any other language, but rather a form of gibberish called "Simlish." Simlish is spoken but also depicted in small comic book-like bubbles, though with icons rather than words. Simlish, which had been pioneered in Maxis's earlier *SimCopter* (see Chapter 15, "*SimCity* (1989): Building Blocks for Fun and Profit"), became one of the series' most defining characteristics and was even parodied in an episode of *The Drew Carey Show*.[5] Since Simlish is essentially a made-up nonsense language, there was no need to worry about translators or hiring different groups of voice actors for non-English versions of the game.

In yet another adaptation from *SimCity*, *The Sims* threw a variety of random events at players to keep them from getting too comfortable with their routines. These included natural disasters (oods and fires) and burglars. The sims could also die in accidents or from neglect. For example, forgetting to put ladders in a pool will prevent swimming sims from escaping; they will eventually drown. If the entire family dies, the house is sold.

Although many players lavished most of their attention on their sims, others focused on building things—what we might call the "dollhouse" approach to the game. The game offered countless ways to customize and renovate homes, turning players into virtual Bob Villas or Martha Stewarts. Players could add pools, fences, columns, plants, stairs, wallpaper, and windows just to name a few—and each type of object had dozens of variations. Lighting was a key concern, because sims languished in dark rooms. Ambitious builders could even add extra stories onto their homes. Many avid fans of the game spent hours and hours decorating, landscaping, and building, creating the perfect dream home for their lucky sims.

A last approach to *The Sims* is reminiscent of one of the game's in uential predecessors: *Game of Life*,[6] a mathematical simulation created in 1970 by British mathematician John Conway. In *Game of Life*, "players" began by setting up the initial conditions, then studying how these conditions determined the evolution of living cells, which the game's algorithms were supposed to model. Although *Game of Life* was highly abstract, it's easy to see how the same principles can apply to *The Sims*, where players could set up a huge variety of conditions, then sit back to watch how their sims respond. The thrill of this "great watchmaker" approach was that the player could never predict the outcome of such grand experiments—there were just too many variables. We might call this the "ant farm" approach, as it emphasizes observation over interaction.

Obviously, a project as ambitious as *The Sims* presented a formidable challenge from a technological perspective, and publisher Electronic Arts was initially skeptical that Wright's vision was feasible. The final product offered a combination of 2D and 3D graphics to maintain smooth performance on the era's

---

[5]Episode s06e01. Drew Carey even appeared as a character in the 2001 *House Party* expansion pack. *Malcolm in the Middle* , episode 16 in season three, also featured a lengthy parody, with the titular character becoming obsessed with "The Virts."

[6]Sometimes referred to as *Conway's Game of Life*. Many clones were created for various platforms over the years.

Screenshot from the Apple II version of *Life*, part of *Golden Oldies Volume 1: Computer Software Classics* (Software Country, 1985), which also features versions of *Adventure* (Chapter 25, "*Zork* (1980): Text Imps versus Graphics Grues"), *Eliza* (a "computer shrink"/ artificial intelligence simulator), and *Pong* (bonus chapter, "*Pong* (1972): Avoid Missing Game to Start Industry").

hardware. Although the buildings and objects were rendered in 2D, the sims were 3D, consisting of what was then a high number of polygons. A later expansion allowed advanced gamers to create their own furniture, clothing, hairstyles, makeup, and more, and share them with their friends. The game and its sequels have all boasted sleek production values, with high-quality sound effects and catchy music.

To say that the *The Sims* was a commercial success is an understatement. The game and its countless offshoots have sold well over 100 million copies, making it one of the best-selling franchises in history.[7] Although originally available only for computers, well-received ports were later developed for consoles and handhelds, introducing an even larger audience to the joys of satisfying sims.

Before moving on to the many expansions, sequels, and spin-offs, it's worthwhile to re ect on the game's antecedents. Besides the aforementioned *SimCity*, what other games may have in u-enced or at least anticipated *The Sims*? Although an exhaustive list of all such games would test even the most patient reader, no responsible historian could omit such obvious examples as David Crane's *Little Computer People* (1985), Paul Reiche's *Mail Order Monsters* (1985), Peter Molyneux's *Populous* (1989), and Yasuhiro Wada's *Harvest Moon* (1996). We'll also brie y compare *The Sims* to Ubisoft's *Petz* series (1995), which also embodies many of the

---

[7]See http://thesims2.ea.com/images/100million/100mmLetter.jpg.

concepts present in Wright's masterpiece. In each case, the key similarity is the "pet raising" aspect of these games.

Screenshot from the Commodore 64 version of *Little Computer People*, illustrating the game's full-time point of view, a cross section of the little computer person's house.

Little Computer People[8] was released by Activision for most viable computer platforms of the mid-1980s, though never for the IBM PC. It has a great deal in common with *The Sims* and is a clear progenitor—Wright himself acknowledged that he had played the game and even knew several of its developers, who later provided feedback on *The Sims*.[9] Like *The Sims*, *Little Computer People* offers open-ended gameplay, with no clear way to win or lose. The gameworld is 2D, resembling a slice-away of a three-story house. A "little computer person" moves into the house and goes about his daily activities. The player can interact with him in various ways, including playing games (poker, "Card War," or anagrams) or giving him presents. Players interacted by typing commands blindly into an unseen text parser, such as "please play piano for me," sometimes eliciting no noticeable response. Strangely, although *Little Computer People* was highly original and compelling (critics tended to rave about it), it faded into obscurity.

---

[8]Also known as *The Activision Little Computer People Discovery Kit, Little Computer People Research Project*, and *House-on-a-Disk*. It was also released in a modified and less interactive form in Japan for the Nintendo Famicom as *Apple Town Story*.

[9]See "A Chat About 'The Sims' and 'Simcity'" at http://www.cnn.com/chat/transcripts/2000/1/wright/index.html.

Back of the box of the
Commodore 64 version of *Mail
Order Monsters.*

Mail Order Monsters was another original game from 1985, released by Electronic Arts for the Atari 8-bit and Commodore 64 platforms. Although *Mail Order Monsters* was primarily an action game, it did have various ways for players to improve their pet monsters with equipment or genetic enhancements. It's the player's job as a type of rancher to successfully manage his or her stable of monsters in order to do weapons-based gladiatorial combat in a variety of arenas. Up to two players could battle it out in the arenas or in a game similar to capture-the- ag. For additional motivation, the game kept track of won-lost records and other stats. The head-to-head aspects of *Mail Order Monsters* seems to have been a precursor to Satoshi Tajiri's immensely popular *Pokemon* series (starting in 1995) for Nintendo platforms. However, we should note that *Mail Order Monsters* did allow players direct control over their pet monsters during combat; later "pet" games would increase their autonomy.

Bullfrog's *Populous* is one of the first "god games," a description that characterizes the players' relationships to the game's characters and world. Simply put, players act as deities, affecting the destiny of the population by shaping the land, causing natural disasters, and raising up a hero to overthrow the people of their rival god. The player's ability to in uence the world depended

Back of the box for Tecmo's *Monster Rancher* from 1997 for the Sony PlayStation, a series that has much in common with Electronic Arts' much earlier *Mail Order Monsters*. The *Monster Rancher* series is notable for allowing unique monsters to be created by reading data from external sources, which in this case is other CDs.

on "mana," a divine substance generated by one's followers. *Populous* was immensely in uential, eventually seeing release on almost every viable platform of its time, and was highly praised by critics for its originality.

Populous is the first of the major "god games." Rather than put players directly in control of a person or group, these games give players indirect control over their lives. For instance, a player can flatten terrain to make it easier to build more complex structures.

Harvest Moon, first released on the Super Nintendo, is a "farm simulator"; that is, a game that tasks players primarily with growing fruits, owers, vegetables, and herbs. The player assumes

Lionhead Studios' *Black & White* from 2001 is a modern "god game." Players can be good or evil deities and have many ways to interact with the world and its people. The game begins with a lengthy playable tutorial that slowly introduces players to the game's many features. PC version shown.

the role of a young boy who has inherited his grandfather's old, dilapidated farm. The boy can also get married, though doing so means working hard to attract a spouse and building on to his home. Despite its seemingly banal and repetitive gameplay, *Harvest Moon* was a huge hit, and spawned many sequels and spin-offs.

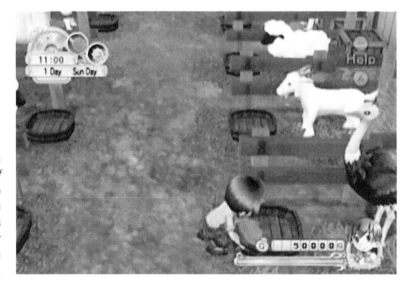

Tending to the farm animals in Natsume's *Harvest Moon: Tree of Tranquility* (2008) for the Nintendo Wii. In an increasingly common occurrence for the series, players can choose a female character instead of the standard male main character.

Although *The Sims* is ostensibly a "people simulator," the game treats the sims more like pets than persons. Why, for instance, can a sim who can successfully hold down a 9-to-5 job not visit a bathroom on his or her own initiative?

Factors such as this are reminiscent of "pet" games like Ubisoft's *Petz* series. The first of these games, *Dogz: Your Computer Pet* was developed by PF Magic and published by Virgin Interactive Entertainment in 1995 for PC. *Dogz* is essentially a virtual pet; a sort of evolving toy that required regular attention from their owners. Players (if we can indeed use that term) could pet and play with their dogs and even teach them tricks. Perhaps the most intriguing aspect of the game was that it was played right on the desktop; the dog could scamper right across a Microsoft *Excel* spreadsheet or be confined to a playpen. Players could also spray them with water if they misbehaved. *Dogz* was followed in 1996 by *Catz* and *Oddballz*, the latter of which featured bizarre alien pets. These games were an amazing success for the company, which ended up shipping more than 500,000 units by 1997.[10] Sequels and spin-offs are still being published by Ubisoft today, and feature many different kinds of pets—such as *Bunnyz*, *Hamsterz*, *Horsez*, and *Tigerz*—just to name a few. All of the games seem to focus on the "cute" aspects of the animals and seem to appeal mostly to children.

Dogz is one of the many *Petz* games that lets players control a virtual pet. The pets have enough artificial intelligence to learn tricks as well as play simple games. The pets behave better if the player treats them well, giving them treats or petting them. These games evolved from simple desktop toys to rather sophisticated simulations, and versions are available for almost every conceivable type of pet.

Some readers may wonder how Aki Maita's Tamagotchi toy compares to games like *Petz*. The Tamagotchi is essentially a

[10]See http://www.virtualpet.com/vp/farm/petz/petz.htm, which reprints an article from *Business Wire* on the topic.

handheld version of such games. It's egg-shaped (the name means "cute little egg") and meant to be carried by the user at all times. Users interact with the pet by feeding it, playing with it, cleaning it, and keeping an eye on its steadily evolving stats. The original unit was released in 1996, and sold more 40 million units worldwide and 12 million in North America.[11] There have been five versions of the toy so far, and though their popularity has waned over the years, we're likely to see many more. There are also plenty of videogame interpretations, as well as knock-off toys from other companies, like Tiger Electronics' *Giga Pets,* which debuted in 1997.[12]

What makes these games so appealing to children and even many adults? Aki Maita says that "It is dependent on you. That's one reason it became so popular. ... I think it's very important for humans to find joy caring for something."[13] Maita's insight seems to extend to games like *The Sims,* who share much of the behavior of the Tamagotchi. Neglected sims can get into all sorts of trouble, such as setting their house and themselves on fire while making dinner. Naturally some players will feel more guilt at such calamities (or elation when their sims are happy), but it seems safe to say that most players who enjoy games of this sort do form a bond with their sims or virtual pets comparable to that experienced by real pet owners. Indeed, one of the more popular expansions for *The Sims 2* allows sims to adopt and train their own virtual pets; it's an interesting case of a virtual pet with a virtual pet.

The Humane Society of the United States offers several reasons why people enjoy pets, including that "caring for a companion animal can provide a sense of purpose and fulfillment and lessen feelings of loneliness and isolation in all age groups."[14] Although it's of course arguable that no virtual pet can ever compete with "the real thing," as technology improves, we'll no doubt see closer and closer approximations—and, let's face it, a virtual device is infinitely more convenient and less messy.

On December 17, 2002, Electronic Arts published Maxis' *The Sims Online.* As the title suggests, this was an effort to adapt their best-selling franchise to the MMO[15] format. Players would

---

[11]See http://www.mimitchi.com/tamaplus/tama_history.shtml.

[12]These types of toys have aroused some controversy among parents and school administrators. Tamagotchi can compete quite maddeningly for children's attention, making regular demands on them to feed or play with their pets—who will "die" if neglected. Later Tamagotchi models offered pause options that let owners go about their day without worrying over their pet.

[13]See Murakami Mutsuko's "Just Another Day's Work: The Strange Tale of How a Craze Was Born" at http://www.mimitchi.com/html/aki.htm.

[14]See http://www.hsus.org/pets/pet_care/how_pets_help_people/.

[15]Or MMOG: Massively Multiplayer Online Game.

buy the product, then pay a monthly fee (which was later made optional) to gain access to the game's servers.

The idea seemed sound; if players were having so much fun playing with *virtual* people, wouldn't they have even more fun with *actual* people? Naturally, there were several key changes to the gameplay to accommodate online play—the most noticeable was the lack of Simlish. Now, characters spoke English to each other. Players were also limited to controlling a single sim, rather than a whole family. The graphics were kept mostly consistent with *The Sims*, which some critics felt gave the game a dated look.

Unfortunately, the online experience was sorely lacking in fun, and the game didn't last long. Most gamers didn't seem to find the social elements very compelling, and gameplay tended to boil down to repetitive actions intended to raise skill levels (and generate more income). The stand-alone game had generated tension with a series of timed activities; *The Sims Online* took a more relaxed but ultimately less exciting approach. In 2008, Electronic Arts rebranded the game as *EA Land*, added customization features and made it free—most likely as an attempt to compete with the much more popular virtual world of *Second Life*. Unfortunately, this experiment didn't pan out either, and EA took the game of ine permanently on August 1, 2008.

It's only fair to say a few words about *Second Life*,[16] an MMO developed by Linden Research and released for computers on June 23, 2003. *Second Life* has become the most successful of all social-based MMOs, receiving many awards and generating large amounts of buzz in the mass media as well as academic circles. Although *Second Life* has superficial similarities to other MMORPGs (such as *Ultima Online*), its key appeal seems to lie in the creative opportunities that it extends to users. Players are given several ways to add their own content to the game; this "user-generated content" ranges from virtual objects to new gestures and animations for their characters (or "Residents"). They can also use *Linden Scripting Language* (LSL) to program behaviors, and can of course buy and sell all manner of things from other players (users retain copyright of the objects they create for *Second Life*).

Unlike *The Sims Online*, *Second Life* was a staggering success. Although the game was free to play, Linden was able to make money with an optional subscription package. For about $10 a month, players were given some land and in-game money, as well as additional tech support. For more money, players could lease more land, and companies and institutions (as well as serious individual players) can pay fees of $1,000 or more for "private

---

[16]We also brie y touch on this title in Chapter 24, "*Ultima Online* (1997): Putting the Role-Play Back in Computer Role-Playing Games"

estates" or islands. Universities seem to be particularly keen on *Second Life*, perhaps as a way to interest their students in online educational experiences.

The media is full of reports of people earning their living simply by playing *Second Life*, exchanging their in-game money for real-life dollars. Other reports concern married players divorcing their spouses for the sake of their in-game lovers, and so on. The game is fairly well known outside the gaming community, and it's not unusual to hear it mentioned or alluded to in popular TV shows like *The Daily Show* or *The Office*. Indeed, one of the characters in *The Office* is an avid fan of the game.

Shown here is the sim body shop screen from *The Sims 2*, which went fully 3D. There are many, many ways to customize the look of each sim. Some players might prefer to make sims that resemble their own families, whereas others might opt for something more creative.

Perhaps as a response to the failure of *The Sims Online*, EA Games went back to the stand-alone model and released *The Sims 2* on September 14, 2004. The key additions were a much improved 3D engine, lifetime aspirations, and genetic inheritance. Essentially, sims could strive for fortune, romance, family, popularity, or knowledge. The sims also had memories and genes that were passed on to subsequent generations. The aspiration system seemed intended most for players who disliked the open-ended nature of the first game; now, players who so desired could spend their time fulfilling specific goals for the sims. *The Sims 2* was another success, and EA eventually issued eight expansion packs and 10 "stuff packs," which consisted of new objects (such as holiday-themed objects or IKEA furniture). The latest experiment of this sort is *The Sims 2 Store*, which sells furniture, clothing, hair, and other objects in exchange for "SimPoints," the game's virtual currency. Of course, players can also exchange real money for SimPoints, and the store happily accepts all major real world credit cards.

There have been several spin-offs from *The Sims* franchise. Perhaps the most notable are *MySims*, which brought the series to the Nintendo Wii and DS platforms in 2007, and *The Sims Stories*, a series of Sims games for laptops that debuted in 2007. *The Sims Stories* tend to be more linear than other games in the franchise, and feature a "story mode" that follows a preset (and hopefully dramatic) script. There is also a "classic mode" available for those who prefer the more   exible gameplay of the main series.

The future of *The Sims* seems quite bright, with additional sequels, ports, and expansions forthcoming. Any game that has sold as many copies as *The Sims* deserves a place in any legitimate compilation of history's best games, and its in uence on both other casual games and the casual gamer market in general is undeniable. In addition, its eccentric gameplay and nontraditional fan base make it a worthwhile object of study for anyone serious about game development. Although its fans enjoy *The Sims* for different reasons, the main appeals seem to be its emphasis on nurturing (e.g., the "virtual pet" aspects), building (the "dollhouse" aspects), and experimenting (the "ant farm" aspects). Chances are good that almost any serious gamer can find satisfaction in at least one of these styles of gameplay in the virtual playground, and many will find pleasure in all of them.

23

ULTIMA (1980): THE IMMACULATE CONCEPTION OF THE COMPUTER ROLE-PLAYING GAME

The unprecedented success of *Ultima* surprised no one more than its creator, Richard Garriott, known by his friends and fans as "Lord British." Released in 1980 for the Apple II, *Ultima* wasn't the first computer role-playing game (CPRG), but it soon became the one that all others would be judged by—the one that *really* mattered. The game and its sequels would become so popular and in uential that it's hard to imagine the industry without them. The *Ultima* series would last for nearly two decades, and its pioneering online incarnation, *Ultima Online* (see Chapter 24, "*Ultima Online* (1997): Putting the Role-Play Back in Computer Role-Playing Games") is still active today. The story of *Ultima* is primarily about one man's drive for ultimate perfection—or at least his determination to make the perfect videogame. Not all the changes that Garriott would introduce to his famous series over the years would meet with universal praise, of course, and many fans consider 1992's *Ultima VII: The Black Gate* as its finest moment. In this chapter, we'll discuss *Ultima* and the vital role it played in shaping the industry—so, in the words of *Akalabeth's* famous card insert, "Beware, foolish mortal!"

Ultima was not Garriott's first attempt at a CRPG. His earlier game *Akalabeth* (circa 1979) was also released commercially, but he'd been quietly developing less-ambitious CRPGs years before. At this time, personal computers and commercial software were so scarce that it would certainly be a stretch to call it an "industry." Software was typically sold mail order and in local, privately owned computer hobbyist shops, copied by the developers themselves, and packaged in plastic baggies with amateurish inserts. Such was the case for *Akalabeth*, a very early CRPG for the Apple II that featured first-person perspective and wireframe graphics, rendered

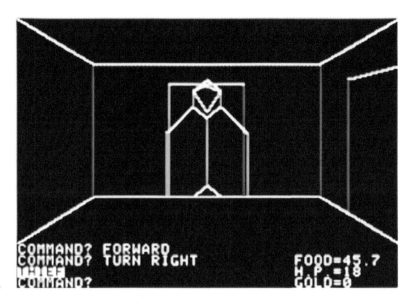

Screenshot from *Akalabeth*.

on the y. Garriott claims to have spent $200 on the plastic zipper storage bags and cover sheets, undoubtedly one of the most seren-dipitous investments in all of game history.[1]

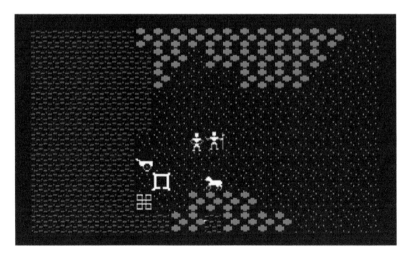

Screenshot of the self-running demo from *Ultima*.

According to Garriott, one of the eight copies he sold of the game ended up on the desk of California Pacific Computer Company. The publisher ew Garriott from Texas to California, where they worked out a deal for wider distribution. The game proved a success for Garriott and the publisher, but Lord British was just getting

---

[1]See David Taylor's 1992 interview with Garriott at http://www.uo.com/archive/ftp/text/intrview/richgar.txt.

started. He felt that *Akalabeth* had been a hobby project, an amateurish production whose unexpected success owed more to luck than his own skill and talents. Nevertheless, *Akalabeth* provided him with the capital and confidence to pursue a more ambitious goal—a game targeted squarely at the edgling computer games market. That project was *Ultima*, which—together with its sequels—not only set sales records but helped expand the market from a tiny niche to the multibillion dollar juggernaut it is today. Garriott's determination to up the ante with each new *Ultima* earned him a reputation as one of the world's best game developers, and his eagerness to take full advantage of the latest hardware and programming routines kept him (and fans) on the cutting edge of technology. In time, gamers and critics would look to the latest *Ultima* as a paradigm shift—not just a new installment in the series, but the next stage of gaming itself. Garriott's ambition and perfectionism often caused clashes with his publishers, who felt that his more radical ideas were unsound. Indeed, after Sierra On-Line failed to see things his way, he founded his own company, Origin Systems, in 1983, to publish *Ultima III*. Garriott proved himself an able publisher, selecting and releasing projects that were nearly as popular and in uential as his own games.[2]

What was it, though, about the *Ultima* series that can explain its broad appeal? How did it rise to dominance over its contemporaries, which include Sir-Tech's *Wizardry* (starting in 1981; Apple II and others) and Epyx's *Apshai* series (starting 1979; TRS-80 and others)?[3] Perhaps the best way to begin answering these questions is with a closer look at Lord British, whose amboyant public persona and concern with such "trivial" issues as packages and pack-ins helped make the series stand out against the competition.

Garriott's nickname was bestowed on him by some of his older schoolmates at Clear Creek High School in League City, Texas, ostensibly because they thought he spoke with a British accent. Although Garriott claims he never affected such an accent (at least not intentionally), it's easy to imagine that even at this early stage, he found many creative ways to express his keen interest in medieval life and fantasy fiction. Always a fan of role-playing, the Society of Creative Anachronisms (SCA), and renaissance fairs (one such festival even makes an appearance in *Ultima IV*), Garriott enjoyed re-creating the medieval life. He dressed up in medieval costumes for game conventions, and later bought a medieval-style castle, appropriately named Britannia Manor. During an interview with a public television station, Garriott remarked that "my gaming life and

---

[2]Origin would still rely on the distribution networks of other companies, such as Broderbund.

[3]For more about these and other CRPG series, see author Barton's book *Dungeons and Desktops* (A K Peters, Ltd, 2008).

my real life are very related to each other," an insight that goes a long way toward explaining the series' unique appeal.[4] It's hard to imagine a developer who could immerse himself as deeply in his subject matter as Lord British. The son of a noted astronaut, Garriott never lacked for encouragement or example, and could inspire other

Temple of Apshai TRILOGY™

A Classic Computer Age Adventure

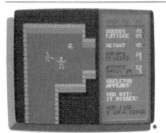

The Temple of Apshai: A Zombie attacks—you have the strength to cleave it in one blow...

The Upper Reaches of Apshai: Later, after hundreds of rooms, will you have the strength to even carry your sword?

The Curse of Ra: Will you ever know the secret of the Sphinx?

The Gates of Apshai loom before you. Many adventurers have stood here and pondered their fate. Will you plunder the grand treasures of the Apshai priests? And live to learn the secret of the Sphinx? Did the wily Innkeeper wheedle his profit from your meager purse? Or do you go forth equipped with the finest swords and armor leaving him muttering oaths and swearing you stole the food from the mouths of his babies?

Once inside the Temple you know why the Legends of Apshai speak of Magic. You will need more than a character of strength and intelligence and the keen nose of intuition to overcome the evil and power of the Curse of Ra. The monsters roam about—Zombies, Ghouls and the terrifying minions of Apshai the Insect God. Giant mosquitos, wasps, ants and beetles suddenly attack, biting and clawing. This my friend is adventure—classic adventure from the DunjonMasters at Epyx. Welcome to the Temple of Apshai Trilogy...you're just in time for lunch!

▸ **The Complete Temple of Apshai Trilogy: Temple of Apshai,* The Upper Reaches of Apshai* and The Curse of Ra.***

▸ **12 Levels, 568 Rooms With 37 Terrifying Monsters!**

▸ **New Graphics, Enhanced Sounds, Faster Play!**

▸ **Classic Cast of Characters—The Innkeeper, The Dwarf, The Magic User and The Cleric and more!**

▸ **One Player**

* Screens from Commodore 64 version of game

EPYX CODING To help you choose the game that's right for you. EPYX games are coded to indicate the degree of emphasis on "Action," "Strategy" or "Learning." These symbols will appear on the front of all EPYX packages.		
Action	Strategy	Learning

EPYX™
COMPUTER SOFTWARE

Temple of Apshai TRILOGY is a Trademark of EPYX, Inc., Sunnyvale, CA.
© 1985 EPYX, Inc.

Back of the box for Epyx's updated *Temple of Apshai Trilogy.*

---

[4]See http://www.klru.org/austinnow/archives/garriott/richard_garriott.php.

people as well. It's rare today for a developer to attain the personal fame and celebrity of Lord British—perhaps only Roberta Williams of Sierra On-Line loomed as large during the 1980s (see Chapter 11, "*King's Quest: Quest for the Crown* (1984): Perilous Puzzles, Thorny Thrones").

Garriott's perfectionism extended beyond the game to the packaging and extras. He was convinced that the buying public would take games more seriously if they came in well-designed boxes and included memorable souvenirs or trinkets (called "feelies"). These included full-color cloth maps of Britannia and small metal ankhs. Most publishers were skeptical, because the quality box and extensive printed documentation would contribute to higher costs (which would ultimately be passed on to consumers, of course). However, few if any gamers objected to these materials. Indeed, it's important to realize that many of the joys associated with *Ultima* came from reading the well-written manuals, admiring the box and map art, and cherishing the feelies. Those who acquired the game illegally (or modern users playing them in an emulator) have missed out.[5]

Let's turn our attention, though, to the game itself. Though of course primitive by today's standards, *Ultima* helped lay the groundwork for most later CRPGs. Of particular note here is the top-down, tile-based graphics. This key innovation enabled Garriott to build what felt like a large, expansive gameworld, all represented onscreen. What's even more impressive is that Garriott and his friend Ken "Sir Kenneth" Arnold were able to achieve this using only *Apple BASIC*, a simple but effective programming language for the Apple II computer. The overhead view was used whenever the main character (known after the fourth game as "The Avatar") roams outside or in towns or villages. However, when the character descends into a dungeon, the perspective shifts to the same first-person, wire-frame mode seen in *Akalabeth*; Garriott had recycled these routines from his earlier endeavor. Garriott also added plenty of new features, including quests and a definite ending. There was also a clearly defined mission: destroy the evil wizard Mondain, hated ruler of Sosaria. Achieving this goal required traveling back in time to destroy a gem that granted the wizard immortality. Naturally, traveling back in time wasn't easy—in fact, the player had to travel to outer space! The fact that the game included both fantasy and sci-fi elements generated a great deal of buzz; it was one of the most ambitious games players had ever seen.

The underlying role-playing mechanics were fairly simple. Players are given 90 points to distribute among six stats (strength,

[5]See author Loguidice's "Game Packaging: A Look to the Past when Treasures Beyond the Game Were in the Box" at http://www.armchairarcade.com/neo/node/225.

agility, stamina, charisma, wisdom, and intelligence), and can play as a fighter, cleric, wizard, or thief. There are also four races to choose from, one of which was hobbits—an obvious allusion to J. R. R. Tolkien's famous fantasy works.[6] What is perhaps most unusual is that players had to either "buy" hit (health) points for the character, which were available from kings, or receive them automatically upon leaving a dungeon. The character was also in constant need of food and water; running out of these precious items would result in instant death. Thankfully, an option existed to resurrect the character, though he ran the risk of materializing on a water tile and being unable to move.

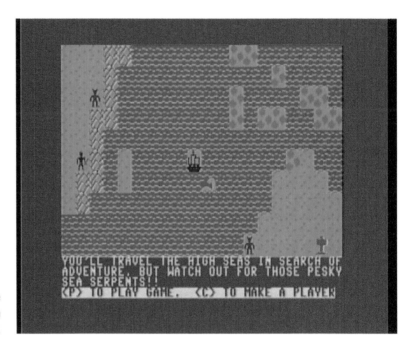

Screenshot from the Commodore 64 version of *Ultima II*.

Garriott turned to Sierra On-Line in 1982 to publish the sequel, *Ultima II: The Revenge of the Enchantress*. California Pacific had gone bankrupt, and Garriott may have been intrigued by the possibilities of working with such a noted and innovative publisher. Although the relationship was short-lived and soon went sour, Sierra agreed to let Garriott include a cloth map within each box.

The new game offered several key improvements, most notably the option to talk to other characters. It was, like the earlier

---

[6]*Akalabeth* is also a Tolkien reference, albeit a far more obscure one from Tolkien's *Silmarillion*. These allusions aren't surprising, given that Garriott refers to himself as a "big believer in what I call Tolkien game design. I believe we—as developers— must know much more about the science, philosophy, language, and history than ever comes out in the game." For the source of this quotation, see http://www .computerandvideogames.com/article.php?id=167484.

game, an immense undertaking that included both fantasy and sci-fi elements. It also marked a major leap for Garriott as a programmer, since he was now programming in assembly language rather than BASIC. The more advanced language allowed for far more efficient routines and much smoother gameplay. In any case, it says something about Garriott's personality that he would have risked creating a new game with a difficult language he hadn't mastered; indeed, he was learning as he went. As we might expect, the finished product had its share of bugs.

The game was successful, but Garriott had become disillusioned with Sierra. One problem concerned the IBM PC port of *Ultima II*, which hadn't been discussed in his contract, since that platform didn't exist (or at least wasn't viable) when it was drafted. Garriott thought Sierra was bilking him on royalties. Another problem was that Sierra felt its licensing agreement extended to making new *Ultima* games, even if Garriott wasn't involved in their production. This is the origin of the infamous *Ultima: Escape from Mt. Drash*, a 1983 game for the Commodore VIC-20. This wretched game added insult to injury with its storyline. The character had to escape from a prison, where he was being held by evil "garrintrots," a word that bears a suspicious likeness to "Garriott." However, Garriott apparently didn't hear about the game until after he'd broken ties with the company, and it sold very few copies.[7] After breaking with Sierra, Garriott decided to form his own software publisher, Origin Systems, with his father, his brother, and a friend named Chuck "Chuckles" Bueche.

The first *Ultima* game to debut under the new label was *Ultima III: Exodus*. By this time, Garriott felt that he had at last mastered assembly language and was ready to put his freshly honed skills to the test. The third game, which became the company's flagship product, introduced a number of bold changes, including the ability to create and control a party of adventurers rather than the lone Avatar. In an interview with Shay Addams, Garriott acknowledged that he was inspired by *Wizardry*, the series that represented *Ultima*'s key rival of the early 1980s.[8] Whether a player should create and/or control a single character or a whole party has long been an issue with the genre, though most modern games have opted for the former. The common belief is that the party-based games are better for sophisticated tactical combat, whereas single-character games give developers tighter control over the story, characters, and structure.

Combat was also altered, now adopting a turn-based system with time limits; if players didn't move fast enough, the mon-

---

[7]In fact, it's clear that the game received only a limited production run and distribution, making it a much sought-after and very pricey collectible today.

[8]See Shay Addams's *The Official Book of Ultima* (Compute! Books, 1990).

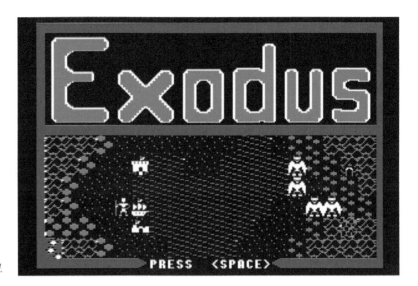

Title screen from *Ultima III*.

sters got a free swing at the characters. This model may have served as the inspiration for the Active Time Battle system of the *Final Fantasy* series (see Chapter 7, "*Final Fantasy VII* (1997): It's Never Final in the World of Fantasy"). There were also loads of new magical spells and weapons, including ranged weapons like bows. The dungeons, which were now central to the mission, had been upgraded from the monochromatic wireframe to solid color (perhaps the only similarity between this game and *Escape from Mt. Drash*). The story has the party chasing after Exodus, the child of Mondain and Minax (the villains of the previous games). It also omits the sci-fi elements that characterized the earlier games. Finally, Garriott incorporated a dynamic musical score that took advantage of Sweet Micro Systems's new Mockingboard card for the Apple II. The Mockingboard compensated greatly for the Apple's limited sound capabilities and is a good early example of how Garriott pushed the industry forward by catering to high-end gamers, rather than the far more numerous low-end gamers.

Exodus was a triumph for the series and a best-seller for Origin. It established the company as a world-famous developer and Lord British as a master craftsman of CRPGs. The game was ported to most of the popular platforms of the era, including the Nintendo Entertainment System, and is certainly the best of the early series. GameSpot selected it as one of its "15 Most In uential Games of All Time," citing it as the inspiration for later hits such as BioWare's *Baldur's Gate* (1998; Apple Macintosh, PC).

The immense popularity of *Exodus* had made Garriott a powerful and in uential figure in the industry, but he didn't necessarily feel giddy—indeed, he began to feel guilty about his previous work.

To put it comically—in the Stan Lee sense—he felt that "with great power comes great responsibility." He believed that most games, including his own, did little to promote good, ethical conduct in players, instead rewarding them for pillaging and plundering.

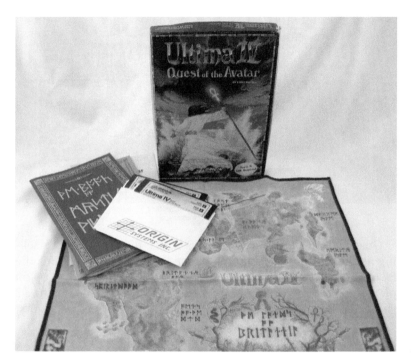

Box and contents from the Apple II version of *Ultima IV*.

The result of Garriott's soul-searching was *Ultima IV: Quest of the Avatar*, a 1985 release that debuted the "Age of Enlightenment," a trilogy of games exploring morality and society. The gameplay was reworked substantially from the previous game, and the difference was visible immediately. Rather than create a character or party based on stats, players were asked a series of questions pertaining to moral dilemmas. The system was based on eight virtues: humility, sacrifice, compassion, justice, valor, spirituality, honor, and honesty, each of which was linked to a particular character class. The goal was to let the player make a character that would truly conform to his or her own outlook and moral values, as well as take the game well away from its roots in "hack and slash."

Garriott took the real-life social aspect of the game quite seriously, and seems to have genuinely desired to use his position to improve society. The manual speaks of the game as a "search for a new standard, a new vision of life for which our people may strive," in short, a game that would make players into better people. This spiritual aspect of the game was reinforced with another feelie, this time a small metal ankh.

Title screen from *Ultima IV.*

Quest of the Avatar was another massive hit for Origin, outselling its predecessor and reaping praise from critics. It remains the favorite of many long-time fans of the series, and has shown up on plenty of "all time" lists; *Computer Gaming World* voted it the #2 game of all time in 1996, and 1UP.com named it as the twenty-first

Box and contents from the Apple II version of *Ultima V.*

Title screen from *Ultima V.*

of its "Essential 50" list. After *Quest of the Avatar,* Garriott set himself to converting the earlier games into full assembly language, updating the audiovisuals and releasing the set as *Ultima Trilogy* in 1987. The timing was perfect for such a compilation, as the countless thousands who had been introduced to the series with *Quest of the Avatar* now had a convenient way to familiarize themselves with its backstory. The trilogy sold exceptionally well, and it's likely these versions that most people have in mind when they discuss the first three *Ultima* games.

The next game in the series, *Ultima V: Warriors of Destiny* (1988), was the last to be developed on the venerable old Apple II platform—it was also the last time Garriott would take an active hand in the coding. Whereas the first game had been about the Avatar's own quest for virtue, this game put players in a more ambiguous position—what happens when the state tries to force its own interpretations of moral virtues on its people? As players explored the world, they found that some bad people prospered and some good people were condemned; the lines between good and evil were often quite blurry. *Ultima VI: The False Prophet* brought the series up to the new VGA standard on the PC.[9] It was the best-looking game of the series so far, with 2,048 different tiles in 256 colors. It also had support for the Roland and AdLib sound cards, expensive but gamer-friendly alternatives to the IBM PC's single-channel internal speaker. As with his support of the Mockingboard earlier, here Garriott was a driving force behind the wider adoption of these graphic and audio standards. The moral theme this time was racism and

---

[9]Like the earlier games, *The False Prophet* received multiple ports.

xenophobia, and again players were faced with tough decisions with disturbing consequences.

Box back from *Ultima VI*.

Ultima VII: The Black Gate, released in 1992 for the PC, was again a paradigm shift from earlier games and is often regarded as the best in the series. The game's primary feature is a huge and robust interactive world, which was far more detailed than anything gamers had experienced. Players could, for instance, plant seeds, grow wheat, bake it into bread, and sell it at the market. It also took advantage of the mouse, which had by that time begun to take root among PC users. Mouse control was perhaps a necessity given the alterations to the gameplay, which was now in real time; fast, precise control was essential. Garriott claims to have been inspired by *Times of Lore* (Apple II, Atari ST, Commodore 64, and others), a game by Chris Roberts that Origin published in 1988, and FTL's *Dungeon Master* (1987; Apple IIgs, Atari ST, Commodore Amiga, and others), a pioneering real-time game with first-person perspective and full-color 3D graphics. Though Origin spent a million dollars

Box back from *Dungeon Master II: Skullkeep.*

developing the game, they were back in black the day after it was released.[10]

Although the game had a definite storyline and mission, it was quite flexible. Players could spend countless hours in a type of sandbox mode, simply exploring and interacting without worrying about what a developer had intended them to do. Several other games used *Ultima VII*'s engine to good effect, including *Ultima VII, Part Two: The Silver Seed* (1993). The reason for the odd name is that Lord British felt it wasn't a proper sequel, because the engine hadn't changed; only major innovations deserved a new iteration. Besides expansions, we also find a short-lived spin-off series called *Worlds of Ultima: The Savage Empire* (1990) and *Martian Dreams* (1991). These games were more story-focused than *The Black Gate*, based on the works of Arthur Conan Doyle and Jules Verne, respectively. It was also during this time that Origin published Blue Sky's *Ultima Underworld: The Stygian Abyss*, a real-time, first-person 3D game that inspired id's *Wolfenstein 3D* (see Chapter 5, "*Doom* (1993): The First-Person Shooter Takes Control").

Screenshot from *Ultima VII.*

Looking back across such a succession of increasingly great games, we might expect the final two entries in the series to be even better. However, most critics see a steep decline beginning with *Ultima VIII: Pagan*, a 1994 game for PC. Garriott had signed on with Electronic Arts to publish the game, a deal that he regretted after they harried him to rush the game through production. The gameplay is a sharply different affair than previous games, involving a great deal of running, jumping, and fast-paced combat. Although these sorts of games were becoming

---

[10]See Taylor, ibid.

very popular on consoles, many found them out of place in the *Ultima* series. What's interesting here is that Roberta Williams had tried something similar with her final *King's Quest* game, *Mask of Eternity*, and in both cases the efforts to graft on elements popular in other genres did not succeed.

Screenshot from *Ultima VIII*.

The last *Ultima* game, 1999's *Ultima IX: Ascension* for PC, promptly descended from the shelf to the bargain bin. Although Garriott had been touting the game and building up buzz for months, a long and soap-opera-like production had done its damage. Perhaps still smarting from the sharp criticism he received after *Pagan*, Lord British seems to have become quite shaken and indecisive, forcing the code through four different versions. We should also keep in mind that *Ultima Online* was in production at this time, and Garriott may have struggled to stay on top of the two vastly different projects. Much like the aforementioned *Mask of Eternity*, this game was also fully 3D rendered in third-person perspective and involved quite a few action/re ex sequences. Greg Kasavin's review for GameSpot called it "both an epic and a farce," admiring its ambition but lamenting the poor implementation, which was fraught with bugs.[11] Trent C. Ward of IGN, a longtime fan of the series, faced the unpleasant task of reviewing a game he felt was "nearly unplayable," describing himself as "nearly paralyzed with disappointment over the way the last chapter turned out."[12] The criticisms were many, but

---

[11]See http://www.gamespot.com/pc/rpg/ultima9ascension/review.html.

[12]http://pc.ign.com/articles/161/161753p1.html.

the consensus seems to be simply that Lord British had lost his way. Although some fans claim (perhaps out of loyalty) to love the game,[13] most thought it was a sad ending for this magnificent and in uential series.

Screenshot from *Ultima IX.*

Ultima's in uence on the games industry is difficult to exaggerate. The games were discussed at great length in almost every gaming magazine of the day, and ports found their way onto virtually every viable platform. Countless people active in the gaming industry today were inspired by these games and their developers to pursue their careers, and plenty of talented coders and artists contribute their energies to making unauthorized remakes of their favorite games. One of the more popular of these is *xu4*, a project to update the fourth *Ultima* for use on modern PCs (including those with Linux kernels). The website *Ultima: The Reconstruction*, tracks several efforts to remake the original games with 2D or 3D engines and is certainly worth checking out if you're a new or long-time fan of the series.[14]

Compiling a list of commercial games that have been inspired by *Ultima* would be a formidable task indeed. Some, such as DieCom Production's *Gates of Delirium* (1987) for the Radio Shack Color Computer, are shameless and insipid clones. Others, such as SSI's *Questron* (1984) were authorized games based on

---

[13]In fact, there has been a long-time fan-led effort to fix the game's problems.

[14]See http://reconstruction.voyd.net/index.php?event=news.

Garriott's engine. *Questron* was admired for its smooth gameplay and accessibility to novices. This series led to SSI's later and more inspired *Phantasie* (starting in 1985), *Wizard's Crown* (starting in 1985), and the "Gold Box" (*Advanced Dungeons & Dragons;* starting 1988) series of RPGs. The *Ultima* series also had its impact on Japan, where it inspired the countless games featuring top-down perspective, randomized combat, and roaming NPCs who must be found and interrogated.

Box back from SSI's classic *Pool of Radiance* "Gold Box" game.

In general, we can describe the early history of CRPGs as falling into two camps: *Ultima* and *Wizardry*. Whereas *Ultima* and its sequels featured top-down perspective, immense gameworlds, and eventually an emphasis on character development; *Wizardry* offered first-person perspective and kept the focus on hack-and-slash combat in dungeons. Both models were essential components of later games, which often combined the two. A good example of this is Enix's *Dragon Warrior* (*Dragon Quest* in Japan) games (see Chapter 7), which offered a top-down perspective for exploration, but a first-person mode for combat.

The future of *Ultima* is bleak. A game called *Ultima X: Odyssey* was planned for release in 2004, but Electronic Arts canceled the project. Garriott had left Origin, and the project seemed doomed from the start. It would have been a multiplayer online game based on the Unreal Engine.[15] As Garriott no longer owns the rights to his *Ultima* series, the chances of his being involved in another sequel are small, and his latest project, *Richard Garriott's Tabula Rasa* (published by NCSoft in 2007), is a massively multiplayer game with a sci-fi theme. It cost over a hundred million dollars to make, but dismal sales led to NCSoft's hemorrhaging employees and frightening away investors shortly after its debut, with the game's servers shutting down for good in February 2009. In short, beyond his much publicized trip into space aboard a Russian rocket in October 2008, Garriott's finest achievements seem to be behind him, but with such an incredible legacy, pity seems misplaced. For countless gamers and developers worldwide, the name "Lord British" is synonymous with quality, sincerity, and the endless drive toward perfection.

---

[15]See http://en.wikipedia.org/wiki/Unreal_engine for more on the engine.

24

ULTIMA ONLINE (1997): PUTTING THE ROLE-PLAY BACK IN COMPUTER ROLE-PLAYING GAMES

Origin's *Ultima Online*, first released on September 25, 1997, is one of the most important games of the modern era. It marks a critical turning point from stand-alone single-player products to massively multiplayer online games, or MMOs, a genre that seems destined for dominance. Although *Ultima Online* was knocked from its throne by Sony's *EverQuest* in 1999, which was itself conquered by Blizzard's *World of Warcraft* (also known as WoW) in 2004, these and all later massively multiplayer online role-playing games, or MMORPGs, owe a massive debt to Origin's

Promotional screenshot showing the key elements of a recent version of *Ultima Online*.

pioneering game. It was *Ultima Online* that established the model and proved the viability of the MMORPG. Origin certainly didn't do everything right, but the painful lessons they learned proved invaluable for all subsequent MMORPG developers.

In this chapter, we'll discuss the often tumultuous history of *Ultima Online*, but also explain why the genre is so appealing to so many modern gamers and developers. As we'll see, perhaps its key feature is not technological but social, bringing together gamers from all over the world to share and experience a persistent virtual world.

Ultima Online was not the first MMORPG and certainly not the first online role-playing game that enabled multiple players to simultaneously enjoy the same persistent world. Predecessors include multi-user dungeons (MUDs), as well as the original *Neverwinter Nights*, *The Shadow of Yserbius*, and *Meridian 59*. Before delving into the intricacies of *Ultima Online*, let's take a moment to examine these earlier networked games.

The logical starting place for any investigation into MMORPGs is MUDs, an early genre of computer game popular among college students and others with convenient access to mainframes. They were quite limited graphically; like *Rogue* (see bonus chapter, "*Rogue* (1980): Have @ You, You Deadly Zs"), MUDs were usually housed on UNIX machines that could only output graphics in the form of character sets. Unlike *Rogue*, which used these character sets to depict crude graphics, MUDs were usually prose-based; players read textual descriptions of rooms, monsters, and so on, just like in text adventure games.

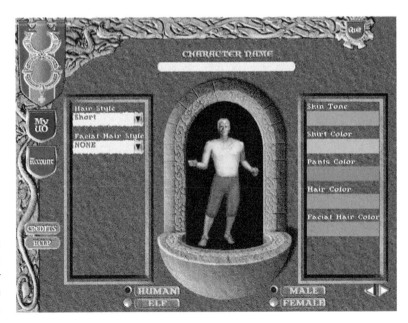

A sample character creation screen from *Ultima Online*. Although not as robust as later versions and other games, all the essentials were there.

The original MUD (simply called *MUD)* was created by Roy Trubshaw and Richard Bartle, students at the University of Essex in Britain. It was essentially an effort to combine the gameplay of *Dungeons & Dragons (D&D)*, the popular tabletop role playing system, with the computer game *ADVENT* (Adventure), also known as *Colossal Cave Adventure* (1976). The two were fans of text adventures like *ADVENT* and *Zork* (see Chapter 25, "*Zork* (1980): Text Imps versus Graphics Grues"), but felt they suffered from low replay value. Once you've solved all the puzzles, what's to keep you playing? Trubshaw and Bartle felt that perhaps the key was integrating gameplay from *D&D*. Their finished product was essentially a text adventure game with a *D&D*-style character creation and combat system. Players could also chat with one another and share in the adventure, a critical feature that would distinguish MUDs from most other types of computer games.

MUD quickly became immensely popular, even when the administrators of the university's DEC PDP-10 mainframe limited its use to off-peak hours. Bartle eventually made a commercial version of the game for the pioneering proprietary online service, CompuServe, called *British Legends*, though not before placing the name "MUD" into the public domain and allowing it to become the generic name by which such games would be known. MUDs offered countless opportunities for fantasy fans to explore rich worlds and test their mettle against the fiercest monsters, but the real appeal was connecting to like-minded people and forming or joining online communities. In many cases, by the time players were burned out on the game itself, they had built close friendships and would log in to the game simply to chat. Others became self-appointed or official mentors, helping novices learn the interface and improve their characters.

MUDs continued to gain popularity throughout the 1980s and into the 1990s, especially when the rise of the Internet made it easier to connect home computers to mainframes; prior to the Internet, most home users who wanted to go online had to connect to private networks like CompuServe or America Online (AOL). In addition to countless other features, these networks offered many online games for their customers. Simutronics's *Gemstone* series, for instance, debuted on GEnie in 1988 and attracted quite a large following. Although certainly lucrative, the private and costly nature of these services limited their appeal, especially when people discovered they could connect to a much larger public network for a much lower rate. One by one the private networks shut down, but MUD fans found that they had many more alternatives on the Internet than they ever had before. Indeed, the demand for MUDs was great enough that they split into different types for diverse applications. Perhaps the most popular type of these were MOOs (MUD Object-Oriented), which abstracts the chat and social functions from MUDs and are still used in various academic settings. Professors at St. Cloud State University in Minnesota, for instance, use them to teach English to students from other countries.

Even in the late 1990s, the majority of MUDs were still entirely text- or ASCII-based; transmitting graphics would have taken too long given the slow dial-up modems of the era, and games programmed for UNIX, while accessible via terminal programs, were typically limited to character-set graphics. However, a logical work-around to this problem was to put a game's audiovisuals on a disk and then use the bandwidth merely to update object locations, send messages, and handle the players' input. This could all be done "behind the scenes," with the installed software serving as an intermediary between the host (the mainframe running the gameworld) and the client (i.e., the user's personal computer). The host tracked the locations and activities taking place in the gameworld, whereas the client provided the user with a handy graphical interface.

One of the earliest examples of such a game is *Habitat*, a Lucasfilm Games product that debuted in 1987 exclusively for the Commodore 64. It ran for a brief period on Quantum Link, the service that would later become AOL, and was only available during nonpeak hours. It offered a third-person perspective in a 2D world, and the players' characters could communicate with each other as well as interact with the world itself. The focus was on social activities, and there were many fun things for players to do—write books, visit theaters, or even get married. The developers watched how the players performed and expanded the game accordingly, grafting on new features as they saw fit. The game didn't offer RPG elements such as leveling or skills, but did pioneer many of the technologies that would show up in later games. The license changed hands a few times after the project shut down in 1988, reappearing on Japanese and American networks in various incarnations.

A more successful early MMORPG was Beyond Software's *Neverwinter Nights*, a game hosted on AOL between 1991 and 1997. This popular online role-playing game was based on SSI's Gold Box engine, the code behind such successful multiplatform games as *Pool of Radiance* (1988) and *Curse of the Azure Bonds* (1989). For many years, the game earned high profits for AOL and Beyond Software; the addictive gameplay kept paying customers online for hours, racking up hundreds of dollars worth of fees. However, in 1996 AOL switched to a flat-fee rate, and games like *Neverwinter Nights* posed serious problems. AOL's ideal customer was now someone who made only minimal use of the service, logging on once in a while to check email, not playing

Neverwinter Nights from dusk to dawn. AOL finally pulled the plug despite opposition (and no doubt some canceled subscriptions) from fans.

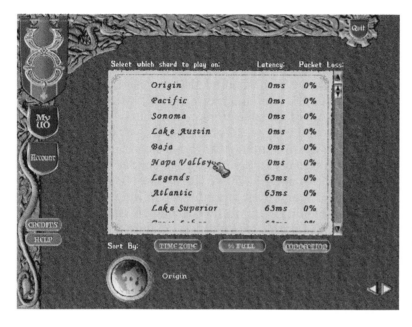

Sample screen showing *Ultima Online*'s "shards" or servers that a player can log onto. "Latency" and "Packet Loss" indicate relative performance on each shard for this particular user, which is a key issue for any online game.

Other efforts at graphical online games failed as well. One of the most spectacular failures was Sierra On-Line's ImagiNation Network (INN), also known as The Sierra Network (TSN), which operated from 1991 to 1996. The service focused mostly on boardgames, but did offer a role-playing game called *The Shadow of Yserbius* (1992) and two sequels. The game was shut down in 1996 when AOL took over Sierra's network. Like *Neverwinter Nights*, it was seen as financially incompatible with a flat-fee structure. *The Shadow of Yserbius* offered four-member parties, turn-based combat, and colorful graphics—it was certainly ahead of its time.

Ken Williams, the CEO of Sierra, blames the fall of the network on a series of bad corporate decisions. In a 2006 interview with Philip Jong of *Adventure Classic Gaming*, he confessed that "I now know that we should have continued alone. ... We sold half of TSN to AT&T, and quickly mired the project in big-company bureaucracy. As all development ground to a halt, I tried to unbreak the logjam by selling *all* of the network to AT&T with the condition that Sierra could have a proprietary position to build the games that would run on the TSN. ... This was also a disaster. ... There became an 'us versus them' mentality between Sierra and

ImagiNation."[1] Still, it's unclear how any private network could have survived the rise of the Internet.[2]

By the late 1990s, it was obvious (at least to sensible developers and publishers) that the Internet was the future of online gaming. One of the best advantages the Internet offered game developers and publishers was independence—there was no need to negotiate and share profits with a giant corporate entity such as AOL or CompuServe.

It's here that Archetype Interactive's *Meridian 59* enters the picture, an MMORPG published by 3DO in 1996 for the PC. It was billed as the "first-ever Internet-based 3D MUD," and indeed seems to live up to the hype. Here we have all the features that are now a staple of the genre: 3D graphics, RPG-style combat, player guilds, mail systems, and regular "expansions," or updates to the content or interface. The graphics were similar to those seen in id's *Doom* (see Chapter 5, "*Doom* (1993): The First-Person Shooter Takes Control"), and even offered some of the same limitations, such as the inability to jump. After buying the game, players were assessed a $10 monthly fee for access, a figure that has remained stable (give or take a few dollars) for MMORPGs ever since. 3DO pulled the plug in 2000, but some of the developers cofounded Near Death Studios and keep the game online today.

A promotional screenshot from *Meridian 59*, showing the implementation of a newer 3D engine.

---

[1]See the interview at http://www.adventureclassicgaming.com/index.php/site/interviews/197.

[2]Sierra would launch *The Realm* in 1995, a graphical MUD officially released just months after *Meridian 59*. It was later taken over by Norseman Games and is still online today.

Despite their innovative ideas and addictive gameplay, these games existed on the margins of the gaming industry. Although all of them enjoyed a core community of intensely loyal fans, most gamers lacked the requisite knowledge, interest, or resources to play them. The situation is comparable to that faced by Origin and Sierra throughout the 1980s and 1990s, when their early adoptions of advanced graphics, sound cards, and mice risked alienating gamers with older machines. Origin's decision to bring a high-profile Internet game to market was yet another bold gamble for Lord British and seems to be the last time the famous developer would sweep the table. *Ultima Online* was the first truly "massive" online RPG, the first to reach over 100,000 subscribers, peaking in 2003 at 250,000. Although its market share has declined, it is still actively played today.

Ultima Online's development was rife with drama and frustration. Despite his name recognition and fame, Garriott had a hard time getting his publisher, Electronic Arts, to fund the project. How would gamers react to an online-only game? Many were skeptical of the pay-to-play model—why would gamers buy a game and consent to a monthly fee to play it when they could buy other games outright? Although Electronic Arts and Origin finally came to an agreement, the relationship was sorely strained. According to Garriott, "I wish that things had worked out better with Electronic Arts. ... We constantly tried to tell them that we understood the online game business and give advice, but the company had a very different agenda."[3] The constant bickering at last led Garriott to leave Origin and abandon his legendary *Ultima* franchise altogether.

Ultima Online's debut was catastrophic. Like many of the MMORPGs to follow, the first few weeks were subject to intense growing pains as some 45,000 gamers swarmed on to the "shards," or servers running the game. Gamers found crashed servers, long lag times/response delays, glitches galore, and the mobs of "pkillers," or players who roamed outside the cities wantonly killing any other players naïve enough to leave. Origin moved quickly to fix these problems, but the blare of negative publicity permanently tarnished its image. GameSpot's review of the game gave it a "poor" score of 4.9, calling it a "major disappointment." The reviewer seemed incensed at the lag times and "extremely frustrating" gameplay.[4] Other reviewers were more forgiving, including Emil Pagliarulo of The Adrenaline Vault. Although acknowledging the game's problems, he still wrote that "no

---

[3]See Scott Steinberg's "A Chat with the Lord" at http://archive.gamespy.com/interviews/february03/british/.

[4]See Desslock's review at http://www.gamespot.com/pc/rpg/ultimaonline/review.html.

game has completely and utterly immersed me in a gameworld so involving, so life-like."[5] Fortunately, most of the worst problems faded in intensity over time, and a series of regular updates, patches, and expansions helped immensely.

Many of the things players found appealing could also be found in MUDs. New players were encouraged to talk to others, make friends, and explore the immense gameworld together—all aspects that are difficult if not impossible for stand-alone games. The social nature of games like *Ultima Online* hearkens back to the tabletop game *D&D*, which is intensely social, but also larger fantasy events such as Renaissance fairs (Ren fairs) and the Society for Creative Anachronism (SCA), all of which fascinated Richard "Lord British" Garriott. For instance, many players took it upon themselves to form posses to deal with the aforementioned "pkillers," a phenomenon that the game's developers didn't anticipate. The buzzword "emergent gameplay" was coined to describe such phenomena, and the developers often added direct support for them into the code of updates and expansions. Although the manual points out that "it is possible to play *Ultima Online* on your own," "the community" is what makes the game special. The manual also encouraged the sort of role-playing one might find at an SCA event or Ren fair: "While 'Sup' may be completely appropriate among your friends in the game, when speaking to strangers a nice 'Hello' or even a 'Hail' will go a long way to improving the opinion others have of you." It also encouraged adherence to grammar rules, but one suspects that those who'd type "Plz Halp me kill the dragon" would be the least likely to encounter, much less follow, such advice in a printed manual.

Besides MUDs, *Ultima Online* was also in uenced by Origin's own *Ultima VII: The Black Gate*, often considered the finest of the single-player *Ultima* games (see Chapter 23, "*Ultima* (1980): The Immaculate Conception of the Computer Role-Playing Game"). The definitive feature of that game had been its intricately interactive gameworld; gamers could do so much more than just hack and slash monsters. *Ultima Online* extended this functionality to a persistent world, so that players could perform all sorts of tasks, develop trade skills, and even earn a virtual living making and selling things to other players. *Ultima Online* also offered a 2D, isometric perspective comparable to *Ultima VII*, albeit with improved audiovisuals.

New players could opt for two basic templates for their characters: adventurer or merchant. The former was made up of the traditional RPG classes, such as warriors and mages. The latter was more concerned with the economy and trades, such as tailors and fishermen. More advanced players could distribute their

---

[5]See http://www.avault.com/reviews/pc/ultima-online/3/.

points as they saw fit. Overall, it's an impressively ﬂexible system. The game also boasted an inﬂation system for items; the in-game merchants would adjust their prices according to how many of a certain item they had in stock. This feature necessitated traveling to other towns to find better trading conditions. Skills were enhanced by a brute force approach, improving with each successful use.

Promotional screenshot from *Ultima Online: Stygian Abyss.*

The early game relied mostly on other players to deal with pkillers. The game used a simple color scheme to differentiate innocent from neutral or guilty characters, and a "karma" system encouraged law-abiding behavior. An innocent character was blue; killing one would decrease karma as well as get the offender branded as a murderer. The murdered player could then offer a bounty on the assailant's head—the idea was that other players relentlessly seeking these bounties would discourage such deviance. Murderers were also instantly attacked by town guards, and dead murderers lost a "substantial" amount of stats and skills. However, murderers could wait it out—every eight hours lowered his or her murder count by one. However, players who couldn't get the hint would become "long term murderers," and have to wait 40 hours rather than eight per tick.

All of this talk of karma and pkilling may seem super uous, but it was actually a vital issue for Origin and all subsequent MMORPGs. The fear was that some novice players would be so turned off by the pkilling aspect that they would leave the game, taking their $10 monthly fees with them. One of the first questions MMORPG fans ask about a new game is how it handles "PVP," meaning player vs. player combat, as that factor will determine much of the gameplay.

Another key consideration is death, or what happens to players whose characters were slain. In *Ultima Online*, fallen characters would return as a ghost, with no loss to stats or skills unless they were murderers (who'd lose 20% of all stats and skills!). These ghosts could be resurrected by traveling to a healer, shrine, or mage, but would then have to trek back to their corpse to regain their material possessions. This trek could prove quite difficult, because newly resurrected characters were given only the most basic equipment.

Ultima Online offered plenty of other advanced features to keep players invested in the long term. Probably the most important feature was houses, which players could build once they had accumulated sufficient capital for a deed. Houses were primarily places to store one's accumulated possessions, but could also serve as stores for selling crafted items. Unfortunately, houses tended to get routinely deleted by the system, so it was important to log in every few days to "refresh" one's house.

Players could also join one of 13 professional guilds, arranged by profession (Thieves' Guild, Fellowship of Blacksmiths, and so on), as well as player-run guilds. Occasionally these player guilds would engage in "guild wars," which allowed members to kill certain other players without fear of losing karma.

As we've already seen, there were plenty of opportunities for players who were more interested in socializing with other players than killing monsters. One such player, "Adamantyr," speaking at Armchair Arcade, was one of only 15 beta testers to become a "Seer," a high-ranking player with special powers. Instead of roaming the countryside killing monsters, Adamantyr became a bartender and chef. The small bar where his character "Ben Kahns" set up shop became a popular hangout:

> I hosted guild dinners and had dart contests, gave out little known trinkets in the game like glass mugs and doughnuts (which were in the game art files and item lists but *not* in game), and generally had a good time playing a cheerful happy-go-lucky bartender, always ready to lend an ear.

I had a regular crowd who would always show up; I'm still good friends with several of them today. My only vice was I usually would have him make fun of players with weird or silly names, and humored players roleplaying as elves or orcs (there were no races in UO initially, a state I personally think they should have kept). It helped that I can type 85–95 words per minute, so I could quickly and easily respond to questions, without using Internet shorthand or leet speak. (Which I despise.) I even ended up doing the services for in-game weddings, both in my green robe (seer disguise) and as Ben.

Even Lord British himself showed up to the tavern to meet the colorful barman. Still, even Adamantyr eventually burned out on the game. "Working volunteer work like this is, in many ways, just another job." Constant struggles with malicious players had finally turned him off his favorite hobby.

All in all, *Ultima Online* was a staggeringly ambitious game that offered a multitude of options from the beginning, but it was only a small fraction of the game it has become today. Electronic Arts churned out several expansions between 1998 and 2007, many of which significantly altered the gameworld and the gameplay. *Ultima Online: Renaissance*, which was released on April 3, 2000, doubled the size of the gameworld by offering a "mirror image" world called Trammel, which forbade pkilling. Although some players rejoiced, others were displeased, feeling that the change threatened the economy. The problem was that now players could more easily level up and work on skills and crafts, since they didn't have to worry about pkills. With the risk factor reduced, if not eliminated, the markets were soon saturated with products and in ation soared. Other critics, such as Michael E. Ryan of GameSpot, complained that the game was "getting rather long in the tooth," with audiovisuals that looked quite dated compared to its competitors—particularly *EverQuest*, which had been released a year earlier.

EverQuest had several advantages over its rival. For one, it offered 3D-accelerated graphics, which gave it a distinctly modern look compared to *Ultima Online*. PVP combat was moved to a designated server, which made it much easier (and less frustrating) for new or less aggressive players to ourish on the main servers—the emphasis there was on cooperating rather than fighting with other players. There were several means in place to ensure cooperation, such as monsters that were difficult if not impossible to beat alone. It was also less prone to lag than *Ultima Online*, even with dial-up modems. It did, however, punish death more severely: dying cost experience points as well as a tedious run to one's corpse.

Promotional screenshot from *EverQuest: Gates of Discord.*

EverQuest surpassed *Ultima Online*'s userbase by the end of 1999, reaching more than 400,000 users in 2004.[6] *EverQuest* eventually became successful enough to capture the attention of the mass media, though—as we might expect—their coverage was often sensationalized reports of addiction. They seemed particularly puzzled by the fact that players were willing to offer real money for objects or money in the game. Much was made of a study by Edward Castronova, an economics professor at California State University, Fullerton. Castronova's study suggested that the gross domestic product, or GDP, of Norrath (the gameworld of *EverQuest*) was somewhere between Russia and Bulgaria's, and that the virtual currency was worth more than several real-life currencies. The public's fascination with the "real value" of virtual economies would crop up again and again in discussions of *Second Life* (starting in 2003) and other popular MMOs. Like *Ultima Online*, *EverQuest* was regularly expanded; there were 14 such enhancements by 2007. On November 8, 2004, Sony released an official sequel, *EverQuest II*, which upgraded the audiovisuals and incorporated digitized speech for NPCs.

It's likely that the timing of *EverQuest II* was a response to Blizzard's *World of Warcraft*, released just a few weeks later. Blizzard was already a major player in the online gaming world with its Battle.net service, first introduced in 1996 with *Diablo*

---

[6]See http://championsofnorrath.station.sony.com/headset.jsp.

A scene from virtual world, *Second Life*, which mirrors many aspects of reality.

(See Chapter 4, "*Diablo* (1997): The Rogue Goes to Hell"). Blizzard had been the first company to really profit with an online model, and their hugely successful games had made them one of the most in uential companies in the industry. Blizzard's trick was to use the free Battle.net service as an incentive to get more players to buy the game—in effect using the Internet as "added value" for their product. Naturally, this same approach wouldn't work for a full-scale MMORPG, but Blizzard seems to have had no problems making the transition to a subscription model. Much as *EverQuest* had done back in 1999, *World of Warcraft* soon became *the* MMORPG, rapidly seizing market share but also swelling that market to unprecedented numbers: on September 19, 2008, Blizzard announced that the game had reached 10 million subscribers.[7] When we consider that past developers were boasting about hitting milestones of 100,000, this figure is truly amazing.

What was it about *World of Warcraft* that generated—and generates—so many sales? Besides impressive audiovisuals and an intuitive interface, the developers also seem to have benefited from a careful study of what had come before. Although there are many aspects of the game that we could talk about, perhaps the most significant is its careful balance between PVP and PVE, or Player vs. Environment. Although, like *EverQuest*, *World of Warcraft* offers dedicated servers for PVP, the rules for PVP on regular servers are relaxed. Players who want to fight other players have several options at their disposal, from harmless duels to battlegrounds, where members of the two opposing factions (Alliance and Horde) clash in battle. However, at any time players can ag their characters for PVP, making it possible for any other

---

[7]See http://www.blizzard.com/us/press/080122.html.

Promotional screenshot from
EverQuest II: Kingdom of Sky.

agged character to attack them nearly anywhere in the game. The game encourages PVP mostly in the battlegrounds, where players can compete for special titles and equipment.

PVE is probably where *World of Warcraft* shines the most, however, ensuring that even the most antisocial player has plenty of things to do. This is most evident in the quest structure; there are hundreds of possible quests to fulfill, many of which are easy enough for a solo player to complete. There are also quests for groups, which usually involve entering an "instance." This concept of "instances" is particularly important, as the problem it solved was one of the main complaints about *EverQuest*. The problem is that the nature of MMORPGs makes it hard for one person or even one group to complete certain objectives, such as defeating a specific foe. By the time the group arrives on the scene, another group has already killed the beast. To make matters worse, some players may opt to "kill steal" or "boss camp," meaning to either swoop in at the last minute to finish off a monster (and thus gaining the treasure and experience), or simply hanging around where the monster reappears after death, selfishly killing it again and again before anyone else can respond.

The "instance" solves these problems by making certain areas of the game unique to an individual player or group. When a group enters an instance together, a special version of that area is created just for them; no other players are allowed inside. This technique makes it possible for a player or group to "run instances" without interference. Furthermore, Blizzard included a "looking for group" tool to help players find others in search of groups to run these instances (a popular activity, since the

Promotional screenshot from
*World of Warcraft: Wrath of the
Lich King.*

monsters in instances tend to drop more gold and better items).
Although even *World of Warcraft* is far from perfect, it seems to
be one of the best-balanced of MMORPGs, with just the right
level of complexity. Expansions have been much less frequent
than we've seen in past MMORPGs as well; *The Burning Crusade*
was released in 2007, and *Wrath of the Lich King* in late 2008.
However, Blizzard has regularly issued patches, which add content as well as tweaks to the gameplay.

There are of course many, many other important and innovative MMORPGs that we could discuss in this chapter, but it seems
clear that the trinity of *Ultima Online*, *EverQuest*, and *World of
Warcraft* are by far the most important, at least for the computer
games industry. Console gamers have traditionally enjoyed little
access to MMOs, though that seems to be dramatically changing.
Probably the two most talked about console-based MMORPGs
are from Japan: Sega's *Phantasy Star Online* (2001 in the United
States) and Square's *Final Fantasy XI* (2002). *Phantasy Star Online*
began as a service for the short-lived Dreamcast platform, but
was later ported to the Nintendo GameCube, PC, and Microsoft
Xbox. Unfortunately, its status as a true MMORPG is open to
question; it offered a fully playable stand-alone mode and a
game-matching system comparable to Blizzard's Battle.net service. Although scores of players could interact with each other in
lobbies, the actual gameplay areas were limited to four-person
groups. *Final Fantasy XI* debuted in the United States exclusively
for the PC, with a Sony PlayStation 2 version arriving in 2004; in
2006, a version appeared for the Microsoft Xbox 360. Sony Online
Entertainment also released *EverQuest Online Adventures* for the

PlayStation 2 in 2003, but to a decidedly muted reception. Though none of these games can rival the enviable success of computer-based MMORPGs, the future of console MMOs seems bright. All three of the current consoles have made Internet access a highly desirable—if not necessary—feature, and an increasing focus on MMOs seems all but inevitable.[8]

After the roaring success of *EverQuest* and then *World of Warcraft*, *Ultima Online* seemed to sink further and further into the background. Still, it still had a considerable base of loyal users who refused to emigrate. Electronic Arts continued to support this community, steadily releasing expansions and various compilations. *Third Dawn*, which debuted on March 7, 2001, offered a 3D client and a new area available exclusively in 3D (it was later available in 2D as well). However, the results of this facelift were uneven, and critics like Michael E. Ryan of GameSpot warned that "compared with the competition ... *Third Dawn* doesn't have all that much to offer."[9] Many *Ultima Online* fans continued to use the 2D client, which they found easier to navigate.

Promotional screenshot from *Ultima Online: Kingdom Reborn*, showcasing the improved visuals.

On June 27, 2007, Electronic Arts unveiled Mythic Entertainment's *Ultima Online: Kingdom Reborn*, yet another attempt to revitalize the aging MMORPG. The goal was not just to update the audiovisuals but to make the game more inviting to novices. Unfortunately,

---

[8]Interestingly, as both the Nintendo Wii and Sony PlayStation offer web browsers, many browser-based—and often free—massively multiplayer games have been made accessible.

[9]See http://www.gamespot.com/pc/rpg/ultimaonlinethirddawn/review.html.

even though critics seem generally pleased with the enhancements, it seems to have had a hard time attracting attention outside of the existing *Ultima Online* community. Neither GameSpot nor IGN even bothered to review it.

Garriott returned to the MMORPG scene in 2007 with *Tabula Rasa*, a shooter/MMORPG hybrid that eschewed the prevailing fantasy settings for sci-fi. Garriott had successfully generated enormous buzz around the game, consenting to dozens of interviews and taking every opportunity to plug the product. Despite some intriguing ideas such as "morality quests" and the ability to clone one's character to try out new professions, the game was no *World of Warcraft* killer, despite rumors of a $100 million development that spanned more than six years. For whatever reason, the game failed to win over many subscribers, and its user base remained paltry compared to the competition. *Tabula Rasa* went from being the gaming media's 800-pound gorilla to its elephant in the room. As discussed in the previous chapter, like so many other MMORPGs that were unable to quickly build a sizeable audience, *Tabula Rasa* eventually shut its servers down for good.

Even as *Tabula Rasa* and even *Ultima Online* eventually fade away, Richard Garriott's legacy as one of the world's most innovative developers will never diminish. Just as his *Ultima* series practically defined the CRPG for decades, the in uence of *Ultima Online* on modern MMORPGs is simply undeniable. If later developers were able to do better, it was only because they had spent so many pleasant evenings in Brittania, studying under the noble Lord British.

As the case with *Tabula Rasa* shows, the MMO model seems at once promising and threatening for game developers. On one hand, the subscription model has proven quite lucrative and sustainable for the winners. Why settle for a one-time sale when you can rake in fees month after month? However, it's proven difficult for even big-budgeted and greatly hyped new MMOs to lure gamers away from the dominant MMO. Neither the aforementioned *Tabula Rasa* nor Funcom's highly touted *Age of Conan: Hyborian Adventures* (2008) seem to have dented *World of Warcraft*'s subscriber base. The latest serious contender is Mythic Entertainment's *Warhammer Online: Age of Reckoning* (2008), a game that Steven Crews of TheMMOGamer describes as a "hell of a lot like WoW."[10] Although quite promising, this game, or any other, is unlikely to topple Blizzard's champion. Despite this issue, developers do not have to have the number one MMORPG as long as they can attract a respectably sized community of dedicated players, and it seems likely that at least some gamers will gradually become disillusioned with *World of Warcraft* and seriously start exploring the alternatives.

---

[10] See http://tinyurl.com/3h6nyn.

25

ZORK (1980): TEXT IMPS VERSUS GRAPHICS GRUES

It is only fitting that Infocom's *Zork* should be the final game discussed in this book. After all, it is the only game we've covered that relies totally on text for both input and output—it's the most *book*-like of all the games we've covered! Although modern critics might take its lack of graphics and sound as proof of its obsolescence, anyone with an appreciation for human language should consider it miraculously advanced. *Zork* represents something of a paradox: it's at the same time obsolete and cutting edge. On one hand, computers and consoles have made huge gains in audiovisual technology since text adventures like *Zork* were dominating best-seller lists. On the other hand, developers have made surprisingly little progress in the areas of natural language processing. It's easier for a game to let us realistically blow a man's brains out than engage him in conversation! Where *Zork* and its heirs triumph over modern games is precisely in presenting the illusion of consciousness. Playing *Zork* isn't about moving a disembodied shotgun through a 3D battleground in search of demons to perforate with buckshot (see Chapter 5, "*Doom* (1993): The First-Person Shooter Takes Control"). Instead, *Zork* is like reading a novel as it's being written, or starring in a play without knowing one's lines.

The goal is to improvise one's way through a labyrinth, intuiting the proper responses to a series of conundrums. It's also about getting to know the narrator, whose witty repertoire and scathing one-liners come most often at our own expense. *Zork* is funny, *Zork* is witty, and—above all—*Zork* is human. Where the game fails is precisely where we glimpse the machine posing as a person; the telltale blush response that proves our seductive companion is an automaton.

It's quite likely that no computer game in history has inspired as much prose as *Zork*, even if we omit the billions of commands inputted by legions of hunt-and-peckers. *Zork* and other text-based adventure games have long been the subjects of academics writing about games, such as Brenda Laurel, Janet Murray, and Espen Aarseth. The games were also widely discussed in popular media, where journalists were fascinated by their artificial intelligence and imaginative scenarios. Although these games lacked audiovisuals, they were still widely played and admired by pretty much anyone who played them.

No doubt, many of those early visitors to the Great Underground Empire felt like they were experiencing the future of the novel. Developers dreamed of a day when interactive fiction (IF) "novels" would stand proudly alongside Thomas Pynchon and Norman Mailer on the shelves of Borders and Barnes & Noble. Sadly, it hasn't happened—but why not?

Most gamers would respond simply that these games lost their appeal as technology progressed. Modern gamers demand sophisticated audiovisuals; text alone just won't cut it. However, although television and movies have been around for quite some time, people still buy and read books. A fan of novels might respond that the pleasure she gets from reading a good novel is simply *different* than watching a film; it's not necessarily a question of which one's *better* in some universal sense. There doesn't seem to be any practical reason why *all* games should have advanced audiovisuals; conceivably there could still be an audience for games consisting of well-written text. Nick Montfort, author of *Twisty Little Passages* (MIT Press, 2003), argues that interactive fiction will remain an "essential part of digital media and literature even if no one manages to sell it," likening the genre to poetry.[1] Indeed, there are thriving niche communities of gamers who still enjoy playing (and making) interactive fiction, but this activity has sadly remained very much on the margins of the industry.[2] We'll now table this discussion and proceed to the story of *Zork*.

Zork began life in much the same way as many of the early computer games; that is, as a fruitful, informal collaboration by starry-eyed college students.[3] Indeed, it's easy (if, perhaps, a bit misleading) to compare the development of *Zork* with that of another classic computer game, *Spacewar!* (see bonus chapter,

---

[1] Unless otherwise noted, all quotations in this chapter are from private email correspondence with the authors.

[2] Today, dedicated and talented IF authors continue to advance the art of interactive storytelling as part of a mostly noncommercial effort. Unfortunately, for all of the innovation in story constructs and styles, the technology has more or less remained the same as that originally found in *Zork*. On the plus side, the modern interactive fiction creation languages are still highly portable and appear on nearly every possible platform, including directly within Web browsers. See http://www.ifarchive.org for more on modern interactive fiction.

[3] To be specific, three of *Zork's* developers were college students at MIT (Blank, Anderson, and Daniels). The fourth, Dave Lebling, was a member of MIT's staff.

"*Spacewar!* (1962): The Best Waste of Time in the History of the Universe").

Zork was developed by four members of the MIT's Dynamic Modeling Group, whereas *Spacewar!* was developed by members of MIT's Tech Model Railroad Club. Both teams were excited about the possibility of computer games, and both were fueled by the adrenaline rush of hacking. However, the authors of *Zork* had a much different vision of the future of computer games than the hackers responsible for *Spacewar!*. For, although *Spacewar!* paved the way for graphical "twitch" games, *Zork* was a game for folks who preferred prose to pyrotechnics.

The authors of the mainframe *Zork*, Tim Anderson, Marc Blank, Bruce Daniels, and Dave Lebling, began writing the program in 1977 for the DEC PDP-10, the same computer used by Will Crowther and Don Woods to create *Colossal Cave Adventure* (*Spacewar!* was programmed on the earlier PDP-1). The PDP-10 was a mainframe computer that was much more powerful than any home computer of the time, but certainly too large and expensive for the consumer market.

```
>yes
Somewhere nearby is Colossal Cave, where others have found fortunes in
treasure and gold, though it is rumored that some who enter are never
seen again.  Magic is said to work in the cave.  I will be your eyes
and hands.  Direct me with commands of 1 or 2 words.  I should warn
you that I look at only the first four letters of each word, so you'll
have to enter "NORTHEAST" as "NE" to distinguish it from "NORTH".
(Should you get stuck, type "HELP" for some general hints.  For infor-
mation on how to end your adventure, etc., type "INFO".)
          - - -
This program was originally developed by Willie Crowther.  Most of the
features of the current program were added by Don Woods (DON @ SU-AI).
The current version was done by Kent Blackett and Bob Supnik.  It is
DECUS Program 11-340.
          - - -
The rehost to a PC, under Microsoft Fortran, was done by Ken Plotkin.
See file PCADVENT.DOC for details.
          - - -
You are standing at the end of a road before a small brick building.
Around you is a forest.  A small stream flows out of the building and
down a gully.

>
```

Colossal Cave Adventure is a groundbreaking game that pioneered the adventure game. The first version was designed by Will Crowther and later substantially expanded by Don Woods. It is the progenitor of *Zork* and all later games in the genre. Screenshot from a PC conversion shown.

The few home computers that existed were so woefully underpowered compared to mainframes like the PDP-10 that most of the early game developers had little interest in trying to restrict or sell their software; if you had access to one of these behemoths, chances are you could easily acquire games like *Colossal Cave Adventure* for free using the ARPANET,[4] the progenitor to the Internet.

---

[4]The Advanced Research Projects Agency Network of the United States Department of Defense was the world's first operational packet switching network.

The "imps,"[5] as they would later style themselves, were enchanted with *Colossal Cave Adventure*, also known as *Adventure* or simply *Advent*, whose first appearance was in 1976. *Colossal Cave* is certainly a groundbreaking game, both in the figurative and literal sense—the original author, Crowther, and his wife, were dedicated cavers and he based much of the game on an actual cave system in Kentucky. Although many critics tend to overlook this caving connection, it's important if we want to fully understand the appeal of games like *Colossal Cave* and *Zork*. It's not simply a coincidence that both games are focused on the thrilling exploration one enjoys as a caver or urban explorer. These games are less "interactive novels" than "interactive maps" (or "interactive worlds" to use language popularized by Cyan of *Myst* fame). Another intriguing coincidence is that the first jigsaw puzzle ever sold was of a map.[6] It seems that maps and puzzles have been associated from very early times!

Although exploration games can be rendered with graphics instead of text, this eliminates much of the freedom (or at least the illusion of such) allowed by text—a point we'll return to later. As for Crowther, his purported intention for creating the game was chiefly as a way to share some of his enjoyment of caving and the role-playing game *Dungeons & Dragons* (*D&D*) with his two daughters. It's easy for critics, perhaps avid *D&D* players themselves, to get so fixated on this fantasy role-playing connection that they overlook the influence of caving.

Colossal Cave established many of the conventions and principles upon which almost all subsequent text adventures are based, such as the familiar structure of rooms and objects, inventory, point system, and input structure ("OPEN DOOR," "GO NORTH," and so on). The game also introduced several elements inspired by J. R. R. Tolkien's famous works, including dwarves and magic (Tolkien was always drawing maps himself). To get through the game, players frequently sketched out their own graphical maps of the areas they explored. *Colossal Cave* also famously introduced the "non-Euclidean maze," or a series of identically described rooms.

The only way players can navigate these mazes (besides cheating) is to drop breadcrumbs, or objects whose placement in a room will alter its description (thus allowing the player to retrace steps). The game also requires players not merely to collect treasures, but to deposit them in the proper location to earn points. Although *Colossal Cave* was certainly a breakthrough, it didn't take long for hackers to master it. Some hackers went a step

---

[5]Short for "implementers."

[6]See Daniel McAdam's "History of Jigsaw Puzzles" at http://www.jigsaw-puzzle.org/jigsaw-puzzle-history.html.

beyond; they had sighted a new vista and wanted to explore its possibilities to the fullest.

Much like Crowther and Woods, the imps were initially inspired more by a desire to test their hacker skills than a singular desire for wealth. Indeed, in a famous 1979 article published in the scientific journal *IEEE Computer*, the authors promised to send anyone a copy of the game who sent them a magnetic tape and return postage.

This article, written by Dave Lebling, Marc Blank, and Tim Anderson, describes the game as a "computerized fantasy simulation," and uses terminology familiar to anyone who remembers *D&D*: "In this type of game, the player interacts conversationally with an omniscient 'Master of the Dungeon,' who rules on each proposed action and relates the consequences." However, like *Colossal Cave*, *Zork* is primarily a game about exploration, involving such activities as breaking into a supposedly abandoned house, rappelling down a steep cavern, and even floating across a river in an inflatable raft (watch your sword!). Along the way, the player is continuously confronted with puzzles and even a few fights (such as a troll to be dispatched with the sword). Most famously, though, the player must at all times be wary of the grue—a mysterious beast which lurks in total darkness, always hungry for adventurers.

On the surface, *Zork* appears to have much in common with its progenitor, *Colossal Cave*, and IF scholar Dennis Jerz has gone so far as to say that "whereas Adventure began as a simulation of a real cave, Zork began as a simulation of Adventure."[7]

Zork added several key innovations, including a much more sophisticated parser capable of handling commands like "KILL TROLL WITH SWORD" and "PUT COFFIN, SCEPTRE, AND GOLD INTO CASE," whereas *Colossal Cave* (and for several years, Infocom's commercial competition) was limited to commands of one or two words ("GET BOTTLE," "PLUGH"). *Zork* also offered a more sophisticated antagonist, the famous thief, who roams about the world independently of the character and eventually plays an important role in solving the game. Montfort described the thief as a "real character with the functions of a character as seen in literature, not the mere anthropomorphic obstacle that was seen in Adventure." *Zork II* also introduces a coherent plot to add some narrative coherence to the player's treasure hunting. Overall, though, the game was praised for its humor and excellent writing.

The mainframe *Zork* was not broken into a trilogy, but rather existed as a single massive game. After the imps founded Infocom and decided to commercially release the game for personal computers, they were faced with stiff memory limitations (and a wide variety of incompatible platforms). To get around the

---

[7]See http://jerz.setonhill.edu/if/canon/Zork.htm.

problem, they broke the game up into three parts, though not without some modifications and additions. It's also worthwhile to mention the brilliant design strategy they followed.

Rather than port the code to so many different platforms, Joel Berez and Marc Blank created a virtual platform called the "Z-Machine," which was programmed using a *LISP*-like language called *ZIL*. Afterwards, all that was required to port the entire library to a new platform was to write (or have written) a "Z-Machine Interpreter," or ZIP. Scott Cutler took on the task of creating the first commercial ZIP, which was written for Tandy's TRS-80.[8] Indeed, one of Infocom's key assets as a text adventure publisher was the ease with which they could offer their games on a tremendous number of platforms; graphical games were much harder to port.

Early on, Infocom's popular software came in packaging of all different shapes and sizes. Some of the rarer types, like *Starcross*, which came in a plastic flying saucer, and *Suspended*, which came in a plastic mask, are particularly valuable collector's items today—sometimes selling for hundreds of dollars.

---

[8]These first commercial versions of *Zork* for the TRS-80 (late 1980) and Apple II (early 1981) were published by Personal Software (known for the 1979 Apple II "killer app," *VisiCalc*, one of the first spreadsheet programs) with poorly matched cover art that featured a crazed, sword-wielding warrior standing over a cowering troll. Infocom would soon take over publishing for *Zork* themselves, complete with new cover art. See http://home.grandecom.net/~maher/if-book/if-4.htm for more on the story and to see the original Personal Software cover art. Interestingly, while the Personal Software releases are generally considered the first true commercial versions of *Zork*, an early form of the Infocom company sold a crudely packaged PDP-11 version of Zork on 8" disk that is said to predate them. See http://inventory.getlamp.com/2008/11/30/pdp-11-zork-manual-save-234831/ for more information.

Indeed, for many of the more obscure platforms, Infocom's lineup was the best (if not the only) games available. It seemed like no matter what type of computer you had, you could always buy a copy of *Zork*. This fact no doubt offered them considerable leverage in the terrifically diversified home computer market of the early 1980s, when consumers could pick from many different machines, each with its own advantages and disadvantages (cost, speed, memory, ease of use, expandability, software library, and so on). However, Lebling notes that there were some "negative impacts, especially as the newer machines began to have more memory and better graphics. We had to write to the lowest common denominator, or spend time on each game fitting it to the different platforms." As the latter approach was cost-prohibitive, Infocom's games were identical on every platform. It's notable that later adventure game publishers followed Infocom's example, including Sierra (AGI) and LucasArts (SCUMM; see Chapter 11, "*King's Quest: Quest for the Crown* (1984): Perilous Puzzles, Thorny Thrones"). In each case, the idea was to separate the creative assets (script, graphics, and so on) from the machine-level programming.

Infocom's games were known for their "feelies," or extra items inside the box. Some, like letters and maps, provided vital clues or information for the game, while others—like *Wishbringer*'s glow-in-the-dark magic stone, *The Hitchhiker's Guide to the Galaxy*'s peril-sensitive sunglasses, and *Sherlock*'s key fob—were just for fun.

Infocom also lured gamers with innovative packaging and "feelies," or small items included with the disks and manuals. Usually these items were added to complement the game's theme, such as the peril-sensitive sunglasses included with *The Hitchhiker's Guide to the Galaxy* (1984). Other feelies served to curtail illegal distribution. For instance, without the "QX-17-T Assignment Completion Form," players would not be able to input the coordinates needed to access the space station in *Stationfall*. Sadly, the ambiance achieved by the clever packaging and feelies are incapable of being "emulated," and players really wanting to get the full experience would do well to own an original boxed copy.

The three commercially released *Zork* games are *Zork I: The Underground Empire* (1980), *Zork II: The Wizard of Frobozz* (1981), and *Zork III: The Dungeon Master* (1982). Although these games are based on parts of the massive mainframe version, the imps worked hard to make each game more coherent, such as the plot structure of *The Wizard of Frobozz*. Now, players had to do more than just find all the treasures—they had to find a way to bring the story to its natural resolution.

An early scene from *Zork III: The Dungeon Master* on the Apple II.

No doubt to the angst of many parents worried about the "Satanism" of so much fantasy role-playing, this story culminates in giving ten treasures to a demon, who takes them as payment for performing one critical task. The game is also noted for two infamously difficult puzzles called the "Bank of Zork Vault" and the "Oddly-Angled Room." The final game in the trilogy, *The Dungeon Master*, takes leave of much of the humor and opts for a more solemn and gloomy tone; one reviewer calls it "brooding." Instead of merely hunting for loot, the player must find items that allow him (or her) to take on the role of Dungeon Master.

In 1983, Infocom released *Enchanter*, the first of another trilogy of games set in the *Zork* universe. These games were much more focused on magic and spellcasting than *Zork*, but retained much of the humor and excellent writing. *Sorcerer* (1984) and *Spellbreaker* (1985) round out the series. Each entry in the series is increasingly difficult, to the point that some critics complained that *Spellbreaker* was a contrived effort to boost sales of Infocom's *InvisiClues* hint books.

Infocom's *Zork* and *Enchanter* trilogies were fabulous successes, and the company followed up with several other classics. To make a long story short, Infocom's business was booming, and its superior interactive fiction titles earned them enough "zork-mids" to build their own empire, not to mention throw incredible promotional parties, including the legendary "murder mystery party" thrown at the 1985 Consumer Electronics Show (CES) for *Suspect* (1984). Infocom even hired a troupe of actors and let participants indulge in some "live-action role-playing" to solve the murder. Infocom was at their zenith.

Unfortunately, the company would soon flounder. From the beginning, Infocom was not intended solely to develop and

Box back from the Coleco Adam's *2010: The Text Adventure Game* from 1984. Although still considered a text adventure, the game was played entirely with the Adam computer's arrow keys and SmartKeys (function keys), which eliminated the need for a traditional parser. Although the only real graphics and music were at the title screen, players would hear their own breathing (which would slow and quicken depending upon the situation), as if they were playing the game in a spacesuit.

publish games (one thinks of countless rock and pop bands dreaming of producing "serious" music with the London Philharmonic Orchestra). Although their text adventure games had sold amazingly well, Infocom wasn't satisfied—they were convinced they were destined for bigger and better things. The albatross flopping around Infocom's corridors was a relational database called *Cornerstone* (1985). *Cornerstone* sounded like a brilliant idea—everyone knew that database software had revolutionary potential for business, but the current offerings were far too complex for the average user. Infocom saw an opportunity, and felt that the same virtual machine strategy they used for *Zork* would work well for *Cornerstone*. But it didn't.

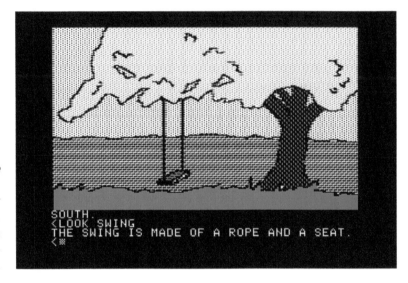

Micro-Fun's *Death in the Caribbean* from 1985, Apple II version shown, was advertised for its visuals rather than its parser, which was severely limited in comparison to Infocom's text-based games.

By the time copies of *Cornerstone* began lining up on store shelves, the IBM PC was the overwhelmingly dominant platform for business; portability was no longer an issue. Furthermore, the virtual machine setup reduced its speed, and it lacked several of the advanced features that made its rival database programs worth learning in the first place. The program was not a success, and several critics remarked that its name was apt—it sat on store shelves like a stone. Infocom had foolishly invested so heavily in the product, however, that they were unable to recover, and in 1986 the company was acquired by Activision.

What happens next is a rather dismal story indeed. Activision seemed uninterested in publishing text games, preferring instead to exploit the popularity of games like *Zork* in graphical adventure games, starting with *Beyond Zork*, in 1987, by Brian Moriarty (*Wishbringer, Trinity,* and others).

Screenshot from the Commodore 64 version of Datasoft's *The Dallas Quest* (1984). Despite having only superficial similarities to the popular television series, this text and graphics adventure was part of a unique group of surprisingly good licensed games in the format from the 1980s, which includes the text-only *Rambo: First Blood Part II* (Mindscape, 1985) and *Star Trek: The Kobayashi Alternative* (Simon & Schuster Interactive, 1985), among others.

Screenshot from the Apple IIgs version of Activision's quirky *Tass Times in Tone Town* (1986), a text and graphics adventure that can be considered a transitional type of product—the game could be played using either traditional text input or by clicking on the various icons, either in combination with or exclusive of each other.

Beyond Zork offered players a crude automap and several random and RPG elements to theoretically enhance the game's replayability. Replayability is always an issue with most adventure games: once the player figures out the puzzles and solves the game, there is little reason to play it through again—though a few years may be sufficient time to forget enough of the details to make it fun again.

Steve Meretzky (*Planetfall, A Mind Forever Voyaging,* and others) got in on the act with *Zork Zero,* another graphically enhanced game published in 1988. *Zork Zero* is a prequel to the

Screenshot from the PC version of Infocom's *Arthur: The Quest for Excalibur* (1989), one of a handful of later releases from the company that would go the text-and-graphics route.

trilogy, and offers several nice features like in-game hints, menus, and an interactive map.

The last game to be published under the Infocom label was *Return to Zork*, a 1993 game released for Apple Macintosh and PC. Developed by Activision, *Return to Zork* is quite a different animal than the previous *Zork* games, even the graphically enhanced games described previously. *Return to Zork* will no doubt remind most gamers of the far more popular *Myst* (see

Infocom's games were often more varied in theme than other companies. Take for instance, *Trinity*, pictured to the left, which blends history and fiction as part of a prose poem regarding the destructive power of the atomic bomb and the nature of war in the modern era; and *Plundered Hearts*, pictured to the right, which is the equivalent of a romance novel and casts the player as a young female in the late seventeenth century.

The Lost Treasures of Infocom, Commodore Amiga version box front and back shown, was one of several collections of Infocom's classic games released over the years.

chapter 12), which was released a few months afterwards. The parser is gone, replaced by a purely graphical interface that is surprisingly complex and multifaceted.

The game also offers live action sequences, including performances by a few recognizable but second-tier actors. Contemporary reviewers seemed to mostly enjoy the game, though *Zork* aficionados were (and are) divided over whether to include the game as part of the *Zork* canon. Very few of the original characters show up in the game, and there will always be the issue of whether *any* graphical adventure game could truly compare to the great text-based classics. Jay Kee, who reviewed the game for *Compute!* magazine, wrote that "people accustomed to the speed and flexibility of a text-only parser are going to feel handcuffed."[9]

Activision released two more *Zork*-themed graphical adventures: *Zork Nemesis: The Forbidden Lands* (1996) and *Zork: Grand Inquisitor* (1997), quietly dropping the name "Infocom." *Nemesis* offers a much simplified graphical interface and a much darker atmosphere than previous games. Like *Return to Zork*, *Nemesis* was loaded with live action sequences—to the point that the game shipped on three CD-ROMs.

Most reviewers noticed the game's intense gore, including a puzzle requiring the player to behead a corpse with a guillotine. However, *Grand Inquisitor* did try to bring back much of the humor missing in *Zork Nemesis*, and seemed to pay more homage to the series than the previous two games. Perhaps more significantly, Activision released *Zork: The Undiscovered Underground* for free, a text adventure by Marc Blank and Michael Berlyn. *The Undiscovered Underground* no doubt eased some of the bitterness that dyed-in-the-wool *Zork* fans felt toward Activision, who some viewed as merely exploiting the franchise to turn a quick buck.

Unfortunately, even a new text adventure was not enough to save *Zork*; *Grand Inquisitor* did not sell as many copies as Activision hoped. To date, there have been no more official *Zork* titles, though there have been several anthologies.

It is important to consider that even without Infocom's failure with *Cornerstone*, the desire for graphics would have likely pushed the pure text adventure to the side anyway. Many other companies had tried text and graphics adventures before, like On-Line Systems/Sierra with *Mystery House* (1980; Apple II and others), or text adventure pioneer Scott Adams's[10] Adventure International with *Return to Pirate's Isle* (1983; Texas Instruments TI-99/4a), though the parsers in such games rarely went beyond simplistic, two-word input. Even when companies like Trillium/

---

[9]See the September 1994 issue of *COMPUTE!* magazine.

[10]No relation to the author of *Dilbert*. Scott Adams began releasing often-difficult commercial text adventures with simple two-word parsers as far back as 1978.

Scott Adams and his Adventure International Company, started in 1978, preceded Infocom's philosophy of releasing games—particularly text adventures—on as many platforms as possible. The Scott Adams games had modest parsers and complexity, which—unlike Infocom's—allowed them to work on systems with limited processing power and memory, and ship on cartridge, tape, or disk. Despite moving to text and graphics adventures and having popular licenses like Marvel Comics, Adventure International went bankrupt in 1985.

Telarium with *Amazon* (1984; Apple II, Commodore 64, and others) from author Michael Crichton, or Magnetic Scrolls with *The Pawn* (1986; Atari ST, Commodore Amiga, and others), had strong combinations of graphics and parser technology, the push always seemed to be to automate the process away from natural language interaction to point-and-click simplicity. Even Legend Entertainment, founded in 1989 by Bob Bates and Mike Verdu after the official end of Infocom, eventually changed from producing text and graphics adventures with natural language input to purely mouse- and menu-driven graphics adventures,[11] until finally settling on action games before their shutdown in 2004. The market had spoken.[12]

Nevertheless, to say that *Zork* is not an influential adventure game is like saying the *Iliad* is not an influential poem. At some point, the question is not so much one of "influences" but rather

---

[11]Legend Entertainment's last game to feature a text input option was 1993's *Gateway 2: Homeworld*. Early on, the company published several titles from Steve Meretzky.

[12]In recent years, a smattering of mainstream games have tried to incorporate text input into their gameplay, but this has resulted in little to no impact on future developments. For instance, 1998's *Starship Titanic* adventure game from Douglas Adams's *The Digital Village* for Apple Macintosh and PC featured a full-sentence text parser in its conversation engine, and Konami's futuristic survival horror game *Lifeline* from 2003 for the Sony PlayStation 2 allowed the player to speak full-sentence commands to the in-game protagonist.

Box back for the PC version of text and graphics adventure, *Spellcasting 101: Sorcerers Get All the Girls*, from Steve Meretzky and Legend Entertainment Company. Note the menu-driven interface option in the screenshot on the upper right of the box.

of laying foundations. Although the game's mechanics have no doubt been surpassed by later parsers and arguably, interfaces, no one can deny the incalculable influence *Zork* has extended across a broad spectrum of games and genres. Could we have *Myst* without *Zork*? What about *Doom*? All of these games borrow and pay homage, whether directly or indirectly, acknowledged or not, from the type of gameplay found in *Zork*.

The player is still exploring spaces, uncovering possibilities, and overcoming obstacles. The only crucial differences are the ways these activities are represented on the screen, and the way they are selected by the player. In the first case, *Myst*, rooms and actions are described via graphics rather than text. In the second, *Doom*, players use arrow keys or mouse clicks rather than typing commands in the form of words and sentences. For example, if the player "goes north" in *Doom* by pressing the up arrow key, players in *Zork* type "GO NORTH" or simply "N." To say that the former method is objectively superior or more "immersive" than the latter seems foolhardy at best.

What *Zork* seemed to contribute more than anything was the idea that the computer could simulate a rich virtual environment—much, much larger and nuanced than the playing fields seen in games like *Spacewar!* or *Pac-Man* (Chapter 13, "*Pac-Man* (1980): Japanese Gumption, American Consumption"). Furthermore, the game demonstrated the literary potential of the computer. Thousands upon thousands of gamers have been charmed by the wit and elegance of *Zork*'s many descriptions. Perhaps more than anything, though, these games offered players the illusion of total freedom. Instead of merely selecting a few set commands from a menu, *Zork* encouraged players to imagine infinite possibilities.

For most players, a great deal of the fun was simply experimenting with strange commands to see whether the developers had anticipated them. For example, typing "HELLO" results in, "Nice weather we're having lately." or "Good day." Type "JUMP", and you're told, "Very good. Now you can go to the second grade." On the other hand, typing "HELP" results in "I don't know the word 'help,'" a response that seems to have unintended significance. You can try out the results of curse words and more sinister actions yourself.

There have been many claims made over the years (particularly by disgruntled fans of interactive fiction) that their games are simply more intellectually challenging, and that the reason so many modern gamers don't like them is that they simply aren't intelligent or refined enough to appreciate them. On the other hand, we might question whether a textual description really requires more imagination than an image. Perhaps a similar

Synapse's short-lived "Electronic Novel" series came packaged as hardcover books in slipcases. The parser for these products were considered comparable in most cases to the best that Infocom could offer at the time and even featured some unique capabilities. Unfortunately for Synapse, upon the games' release in 1985, the market was shifting away from pure text adventures.

sort of thing is going on in our heads whether we see the word "mailbox" or see an image of one on the screen. To make sense of either, we have to have some sort of familiarity with the concept of mailboxes, and imagine the possible reasons why the mailbox is there and what role it could play in the game. Either way, we have to use our brains to make sense of it.

What, then, is the true advantage of a text adventure over a graphical one? The answer to this question seems to be the perceived freedom and intelligence of the parser. It's nice to be able to interact with a game in such a thoroughly compelling manner, and it's here that we may see the future of *Zork*, or the future of any text-based interactive narrative. The key is an increasingly sophisticated parser, with enough artificial intelligence to make convincing responses to anything the player might type; it would be as though there was an actual person or "dungeon master" on the other side of the screen. This technology could also be useful in graphical games, where it could complement the icon-based and context-driven interfaces of modern graphical adventure games. An intriguing and important example is Procedural Arts' *Facade* (2005), an experimental videogame that had players using textual input to interact with an estranged couple. Though still clearly in its early stages, these technologies could easily lead to a true breakthrough for gaming, greatly enriching the possibilities

There have actually been three major *The Hitchhiker's Guide to the Galaxy* text-adventure adaptations of Douglas Adams legendary radio, book, and television series (among others). The first, released in the early 1980s by Supersoft for the Commodore PET and 64, was quickly pulled from the market over publishing rights. The first official translation came from Infocom in 1984 with help from Adams and proved to be one of the company's best-sellers. In 2004, the game was revived by the BBC for free play in a Web browser, shown here in its second edition. The BBC adaptation added illustrations and a visual interface to the previously text-only game.

for conversations with and between computer-controlled characters. Imagine, for instance, a role-playing game or first-person shooter in which players could talk to characters about practically anything—rather than simply clicking on a small set of options in a dialog menu. The dramatic possibilities of such a feat are practically endless.

Although such technology is far beyond what we currently have available, consider how far graphics technology has come since 1980. What if the same level of exponential growth had occurred in artificial intelligence and natural language processing? "The things that interest me," writes Montfort, "are advancing the state of the art, tackling simulation and language in new ways, and doing important work within our culture." Though we've yet to see a resurgence of text adventures in the commercial sector, there's no doubt that it's easier than ever to create them. Powerful tools like TADS[13] and Inform[14] offer would-be authors with minimal technical knowledge the chance to design their own professional-quality interactive fiction. Dennis Jerz, a scholar who frequently writes about interactive fiction, notes that these tools have contributed to the "literary feel of most of the prize-winning IF games these days." These tools and the Internet have helped foster a small but growing community of IF developers and enthusiasts, who continue to push the boundaries of the genre, and there have been recent efforts to reintroduce it commercially. Perhaps one day we will find the latest interactive fiction titles alongside other best-sellers at our local bookstore—but we may also find parsers cropping up in the latest triple-A titles, where they could greatly enrich our conversations with computer-controlled characters.

---

[13]Standing for "Text Adventure Development System." See http://tinyurl.com/4l6zxk for top titles created with the language.

[14]See http://tinyurl.com/4ceoxf for top titles created with the language.

INDEX

Printed and bound by CPI Group (UK) Ltd, Croydon, CR0 4YY

22/10/2024

01777635-0001